The Psychology of Vigilance

ORGANIZATIONAL AND OCCUPATIONAL PSYCHOLOGY

Series Editor: PETER WARR
MRC/SSRC Social and Applied Psychology Unit, Department of Psychology,
The University, Sheffield, England

The Psychology of Vigilance

D.R. Davies

Department of Applied Psychology
University of Aston in Birmingham

R. Parasuraman

Department of Psychology
University of California at Los Angeles

1982

 ACADEMIC PRESS

A Subsidiary of Harcourt Brace Jovanovich, Publishers

London   New York
Paris   San Diego   San Francisco   São Paulo
Sydney   Tokyo   Toronto

ACADEMIC PRESS INC. (LONDON) LTD.
24/28 Oval Road
London NW1

United States Edition published by
ACADEMIC PRESS INC.
111 Fifth Avenue
New York, New York 10003

British Library Cataloguing in Publication Data

Davies, D.R.
The psychology of vigilance.
1. Vigilance (Psychology)
I. Title   II. Parasuraman, R.
152   BF323.V5

ISBN 0 12 206180 2
LCCN 81-67890

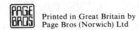 Printed in Great Britain by
Page Bros (Norwich) Ltd

Preface

The study of vigilance is concerned with the way in which human beings function as monitors, both in the somewhat artificial conditions of the psychological laboratory and in such "real world" tasks as industrial inspection, process control, the monitoring of radar, sonar and other surveillance systems and the detection of equipment failure or malfunction. This book is intended in part to update the review of the vigilance literature contained in *Human Vigilance Performance*, published more than ten years ago, and written by the first author in collaboration with Sydney Tune. Perhaps more importantly, *The Psychology of Vigilance* seeks to provide a framework within which the data from laboratory and operational studies of vigilance can be interpreted, derived first from a decision theory approach to vigilance performance, and second from a systematic analysis of vigilance tasks. The framework is presented in the first five chapters of the book and in the remaining four chapters we examine individual and group differences in vigilance, consider the effects of the environment and the observer's general state on vigilance performance, review the evidence relating to the physiology of vigilance and discuss the practical implications of vigilance research.

We are grateful to Jackson Beatty, Graham Beaumont, the late Stuart Dimond, Jim Horne, Dylan Jones and Ann Taylor Davies who made constructive criticisms of various draft chapters, and to Angus Craig who not only commented upon the whole manuscript but also provided us with extremely helpful unpublished material. Peter Warr, the editor of the series in which this book appears, read the final draft manuscript and suggested many improvements. Special thanks must go to the staff of Academic Press for their help, to Graham Smith, who drew the figures, and to Anne van der Salm, Margaret Frape, Beryl Herbert, Sue O'Connor, Debra Collie and Trish Taberner, who typed successive versions of the manuscript with speed, accuracy and, above all, tolerance and good humour.

September 1981

D.R. Davies
R. Parasuraman

Acknowledgements

We should like to thank the following authors and publishers for permission to reproduce figures and tables.

Table 1.1. The Controller of Her Majesty's Stationery Office; *Fig. 1.1.* H.J. Jerison and the United States Air Force; *Fig. 1.2.* J.A. Adams and the *Canadian Journal of Psychology;* Figs 2.1, 4.2, 4.4 and 8.3. The American Psychological Association; *Fig. 2.2.* *Science* (Copyright, 1963, by the American Association for the Advancement of Science); *Table 2.3.* R.R. Mackie and the Plenum Publishing Corporation; *Fig. 3.3.* D.R.J. Laming and Academic Press Inc. (London) Ltd. (Copyright, 1973, Academic Press); *Fig. 3.4.* D.A. Norman and *Psychonomic Science; Fig. 3.6.* J.P. Egan and the *American Institute of Physics; Fig. 4.5.* The *Human Factors Society; Tables 5.1, 6.1 and Fig. 6.1.* The Plenum Publishing Corporation. *Figs 5.1, 5.2 and Table 5.3.* Science (Copyright, 1979, by the American Association for the Advancement of Science); *Fig. 6.2.* J.L. Hastrup and *Psychophysiology. Fig. 7.1.* W.P. Colquhoun and Academic Press Inc. (London) Ltd. (Copyright, 1971, Academic Press); *Fig. 7.2.* The Professional and Industrial Publishing Co. Ltd.; *Fig. 7.3.* R.T. Wilkinson; *Fig. 7.4.* The British Psychological Society; *Fig. 8.1. The Eisevier Publishing Company; Fig. 8.2.* J. Beatty and the Plenum Publishing Corporation. *Fig. 8.4.* Science (Copyright, 1974, by the American Association for the Advancement of Science); *Table 8.1. The British Medical Association; Table 8.2.* Oxford University Press.

Contents

Chapter 1

Introduction and Background

In a famous passage, William James (1890) observed that:

Everyone knows what attention is. It is the taking possession by the mind, in clear and vivid form, of one out of what seem several simultaneously possible objects or trains of thought. Focalization, concentration, of consciousness are of its essence. It implies withdrawal from some things in order to deal effectively with others, and is a condition which has a real opposite in the confused, dazed, scatterbrained state which in French is called *distraction*, and *Zerstreutheit* in German .... It is difficult not to suppose something like this scattered condition of mind to be the usual state of brutes when not actively engaged in some pursuit. Fatigue, monotonous mechanical occupations that end by being automatically carried on, tend to produce it in men. It is not sleep; and yet when aroused from such a state, a person will often hardly be able to say what he has been thinking about .... The abolition of this condition is what we call the awakening of the attention. One principal object comes then into the focus of consciousness, others are temporarily suppressed. The awakening may come about either by reason of a stimulus from without, or in consequence of some unknown inner alteration; and the change it brings with it amounts to a concentration upon one single object with exclusion of aught besides, or to a condition anywhere between this and the completely dispersed state (James, 1890, pp. 403–405).

Thorndike, in his textbook *Elements of Psychology*, to which William James contributed a foreward, pointed out that "The words and phrases 'attend', 'attentive, 'absorbed in', 'give one's mind to', and their synonyms, like most common words, have many shades of meaning. They refer at times to what I shall call the act of attention and at other times of what I shall call the feelings of attention. In the first case they mean (1) the fact that some part of one's mind is focal, prominent, prepotent over the rest, or (2) that some one possible idea is noticed and felt to the exclusion of others .... In the second case they mean (3) the feeling of effort which so often accompanies the prevalence of one part over other parts of a feeling or of one feeling over others if the natural impulse is to attend otherwise or (4) the feeling of interest which so often accompanies such prevalence if it is in accord with natural impulse or (5) the feeling of activity,

1

– of oneself being a helper in making the part or idea prevail" (Thorndike, 1907, pp. 98–99).

It is apparent from these quotations that there are a number of ways in which the word "attention" may be understood. As Posner (1975) has noted, in a recent re-statement of many of the points made by James and Thorndike, "Attention is not a single concept, but the name of a complex field of study" (p. 441). Although Moray (1969) lists six categories of attention, including mental concentration, vigilance, selective attention, search, activation and set, Posner suggests that three senses of the term predominate. These are:

(1) Alertness, the study of an organismic state which affects general receptivity to input information.

(2) Selection "of some information from the available signals for special treatment".

(3) Effort, "a sense of attention related to the degree of conscious effort which a person invests".

Of these three aspects of attention, vigilance, which is generally regarded as being synonymous with "long-term attentive behavior" (Adams, 1963) or "sustained attention" (Stroh, 1971; Swets and Kristofferson, 1970; Warm, 1977), is most closely related to the first. Nevertheless, the selection of information may also be important in some vigilance situations, particularly those involving the monitoring of complex displays, and the concept of effort, which, as the intensive aspect of attention, is related to concentration, may play some part in the explanation of vigilance phenomena, as will be argued in Chapter 5.

Broadly speaking, "alertness" refers to the receptivity of the individual to external stimulation. Receptivity may change either because of the modification of a particular pathway in the chain linking sensory input to response (as, for example, in the case of habituation) or because the individual's *general* state has been altered, so affecting receptivity to all, or to a broad class of, incoming stimuli. An individual may be sober or intoxicated, deprived of sleep or fully refreshed, be suffering from illness or in the peak of physical condition; all these factors may be assumed to affect a general state of receptivity.

The British neurologist, Sir Henry Head, used the term "vigilance" to refer to a state of maximum physiological efficiency, not unlike the state of optimal receptivity or alertness referred to above. Subsequently "vigilance" has been used in a more restricted sense to refer to a state of the nervous system which is thought to underly performance at certain kinds of task, known as "vigilance tasks". Thus, N.H. Mackworth, who pioneered this area of research in the 1940s, and who was himself trained as a neurologist, defined vigilance as "a state of readiness to detect and respond to certain specified small changes occurring at random time intervals in the environment" (N.H. Mackworth, 1957). Vigilance tasks, then, are tasks in which attention is directed to one or more sources of information over long, unbroken, periods of time, for the purpose of detecting small changes in the information being presented. Such tasks are also known as "monitoring" or "watchkeeping" tasks.

The origins of vigilance research

Vigilance research began as an attempt to solve a serious practical problem. N.H. Mackworth (1950) noted that "towards the end of 1943, the Royal Airforce asked if laboratory experiments could be done to determine the optimum length of watch for radar operators on anti-submarine patrol, as reports had been received of overstrain among these men" (p. 12). Furthermore, "there was evidence that a number of potential U-boat contacts were being missed", and after some preliminary experiments had been carried out by Mackworth, Coastal Command began an operational study of the detection of submarines by radar operators, the results of which suggested that after about 30 minutes on watch a marked deterioration in efficiency rapidly occurred. Thus, as Mackworth later put it in a communication to Jerison, "the essential feature of the vigilance story was that its origins were without any theoretical background". (Jerison, 1970b, p. 130).

Mackworth's research programme began with an examination of the working conditions of Coastal Command airborne radar operators. These operators were mainly engaged in flying sorties over the Bay of Biscay and westward, from Cornwall, to the mid-Atlantic. As the result of a report from Middle East Command, Coastal Command had recommended that radar watches should last for no longer than one hour, although in practice the length of watch varied from 30 minutes to two hours (Craik and Mackworth, 1943). The radar operator's task was often a matter of waiting for nothing to happen, since the anti-submarine search patrols were frequently unproductive. "False alarms" were not unusual; for example, Spanish fishing vessels in the Bay of Biscay were registered on the radar screen and were indistinguishable from military vessels until visual contact was established. Mackworth observed that "the chance of an aircraft pilot agreeing to investigate a contact reported by his radar observer was only 1 in 8; there was no more than 1 chance in 30 that any such contact investigated would prove to be an enemy submarine" (1950, p. 12). The radar operator worked in isolation, except for occasional telephone calls, and no check on his efficiency was made. The target he was searching for was difficult to discriminate, being a small spot of light about 1 mm in diameter appearing on a radar screen covered in "noise". The target was present for a few seconds and if action was to be taken, it had to be taken quickly.

Mackworth designed a laboratory task which simulated the essentials of the radar operator's job. This task, known as the "Clock Test", consisted of a rotating black pointer, six inches long, whose tip described a circle ten inches in diameter against a blank white background. The pointer moved on in discrete steps once per second. Occasionally it moved through a distance of 0·6″, instead of the usual 0·3″ and this "double jump" of the pointer was the signal observers were required to detect and report by pressing a switch. Signals occurred twelve times per 30 minutes, at intervals of $\frac{3}{4}$, $\frac{3}{4}$, $1\frac{1}{2}$, 2, 2, 1, 5, 1, 1, 2 and 3 minutes in that order. This sequence was repeated three times to make a two-hour task, the normal duration of the Clock Test. Mackworth also employed two further tasks, the Synthetic Radar Test and the Main Listening Test, in both of which the temporal schedule of signal presentations was the same as in the Clock Test. In the first of these tasks, observers watched, from a distance of one foot, a five-inch diameter dark green circular screen for the appearance of a small oval patch of light covering an area of about two square millimetres, apparently "painted on" the screen by a revolving sweep line. Two versions of this task were used, one in which the "echo" was dim and one in which it was somewhat brighter. In the Main Listening Test observers listened to a series of 1000 cps tones, presented at 18 s intervals at a level of about 50 phons, and were required to discriminate the occasional tone lasting for $2\frac{1}{4}$ s from the majority of tones which had a duration of 2 s. The results from two Clock Test experiments, together with those obtained with the Synthetic Radar and Main Listening Tests are shown in Table 1.1. It can be seen from the table that in every case the percentage of signals correctly detected declines from the first half-hour of work to the second and, in most cases, continues to decline

Table 1.1. The principal results obtained by N.H. Mackworth (1950) with four different task situations.

Task	Subjects	Percentage of correct detections in half-hour periods of task			
		1	2	3	4
Clock test I	25 RAF cadets	84·3	74·2	73·2	72·0
	25 Naval ratings	82·3	72·7	72·7	72·7
Synthetic radar task					
Bright echo[a]	17 Naval ratings, 5 RAF cadets, 3 wireless operators	94·0	91·8	84·3	88·5
Dim echo	23 RAF cadets	72·0	62·2	61·2	60·1
Main listening task	22 RAF aircrews, 3 Naval ratings	80·4	71·6	70·6	64·0

[a]Average of 2 runs about 1 week apart.

slightly in the remaining two half-hour periods.

The within-session deterioration in efficiency found with the Clock Test and, as will be seen later, in a number of other tasks of a similar kind, has become known as the *vigilance decrement*. Research on vigilance has been primarily concerned with reaching an understanding of the factors which are responsible for this decrement in performance, although, as will be seen in Chapter 9, some doubts have been expressed regarding the "ecological validity" of the phenomenon. But since performance at vigilance tasks shows considerable individual variation (see Chapter 6) and also seems to be fairly sensitive to the effects of environmental stressors and a variety of pharmacological agents (see Chapter 7) some interest has also been shown in the factors which affect the absolute level of efficiency in such tasks.

Having established that a deterioration in performance took place in the task situations he employed, Mackworth attempted to discover ways of preventing the decrement from occurring. Using the Clock Test, he was able to show that the decline in performance could be abolished by providing knowledge of the results of performance, by informing observers over a loudspeaker whether they had correctly detected a signal, missed one or made a "false-alarm", that is, responded to a non-signal as if it were a signal. The decrement was also abolished by giving a 30-minute rest period after 30 minutes of work. Finally, the oral administration, one hour before testing, of 10 mg of the drug benzedrine (amphetamine sulphate) also prevented the occurrence of a deterioration in performance over time.

Mackworth's extensive researches using the Clock Test and other tasks were regarded as having important implications for real-life monitoring situations. Mackworth also put forward the first theoretical explanation of the vigilance decrement, but before providing an introductory survey of the major theories of vigilance, we first describe the principal measures of performance in vigilance and related tasks.

Measures of performance in vigilance situations

Efficiency in vigilance situations is most commonly assessed by recording the number of occasions on which a change in the state of a display, known as a "signal" is correctly reported and this measure is called the "detection rate" or sometimes the "hit rate". A second measure, which is inversely correlated with detection rate, is the detection latency, the time taken to detect a signal. In some vigilance tasks, known as "unlimited hold tasks" (Broadbent, 1958), in which non-transient signals are employed, the signal is repeatedly presented until a detection response is made, and the measure of efficiency here becomes the number of repetitions required, either at the same level or at progressively easier levels of discriminability, for the signal to be reported. In others, adaptive measures of vigilance performance have been employed (Wiener, 1973, 1974). Wiener used a computer-based vigilance task in which the discriminability of the signal was varied in accordance with the observer's detection efficiency, in order to preserve a fixed detection rate.

A final measure of efficiency in vigilance tasks is the number of occasions on which a signal is reported when none has, in fact, been presented. Such errors are variously described as "commission errors", "false alarms", "false positives" or "type 1 errors". The time the subject takes to make such errors, as well as other types of response, are also useful performance measures (Parasuraman and Davies, 1976). Thus the principal measures of performance in vigilance situations are the detection and false alarm rates and detection latencies. All three measures are necessary for the understanding of the way in which vigilance performance varies with time on task, across different experimental conditions and between different individuals. Until the late 1960s, however, most investigators of vigilance restricted themselves either to detection rate or to detection latency as a measure of vigilance performance, and false alarm rates were largely ignored, since there appeared to be no satisfactory way of combining these three performance measures into a common metric. But it became increasingly apparent that similar levels of detection rate could be associated with both high and low false alarm rates and, furthermore, that changes over time in detection rate were sometimes accompanied by concomitant changes in the false alarm rate, while sometimes they were not. As will be described in Chapters 3, 4 and 5 the application of a decision theory analysis to vigilance performance provides a resolution of these anomalies and enables the three principal measures of vigilance performance to be integrated into the same theoretical framework.

Thus there are a large number of vigilance studies using what may be described as a "traditional" approach (Broadbent, 1971) in which detection rate or detection latency is taken as the principal measure of vigilance performance, although false alarm rates may sometimes also be separately reported. There is also a smaller group of studies which have employed decision theory analyses of monitoring behaviour, in which false alarm rates are taken into account in the assessment of performance. Such analyses also provide a new perspective for viewing the vigilance decrement, suggesting that in some task situations the decrement results from a gradual change in response strategy, while in others it results from a progressive deterioration in perceptual sensitivity or the observer's ability to detect signals (see Chapters 4 and 5). However, most of the major theories of vigilance were developed on the basis of data from "traditional" studies, in which the vigilance decrement is described in terms of changes in the detection rate alone and changes in the false alarm rate are not taken into account in assessing the extent and nature of the deterioration in performance over time.

Since the signal schedule employed in each time period of a vigilance task is the same, the presence or absence of a vigilance decrement can be determined by observing whether or not correct detection scores, averaged across subjects for each time period, exhibit a statistically significant downward trend as time on task increases. The reliability of such a trend can be ascertained by parametric or non-parametric analyses which may be supplemented by an examination of the number of subjects detecting fewer signals in the final period of the task, compared to the first, or in the second half of the task compared to the first half (Bakan *et al.*, 1963). But, as Poulton (1973a) pointed out, "A failure to show a reliable decline in vigilance during the task does not prove that there is no decline. An unreliable result may be due to using too few people in the experiment, or to too much variability in performance." (p. 76). Even when a decline in detection rate fails to reach an acceptable level of statistical significance despite adequate sample sizes and a low degree of performance variability, a deterioration in efficiency with time may nevertheless be taking place if the false alarm rate either increases or shows no change over successive time periods (see Chapter 5). The presence or absence of a deterioration in efficiency cannot therefore be inferred solely from a consideration of changes in correct detection scores.

Coarse-grained analyses of the vigilance decrement, in which correct detection scores are averaged over subjects and time periods (usually ranging from 10 to 30 minutes in length) suggest that when a decline in performance does occur it becomes apparent after about half an hour of work, although it may not become statistically significant until after an hour or more. However, there are indications from fine-grained analyses of detection efficiency, in which the proportion of subjects detecting each signal is calculated, that performance may begin to decline from the presentation of the first signal (Jerison, 1959b). Figure 1.1 shows Jerison's comparison of fine and coarse-grained analyses of the performance of 36 subjects on a version of the Clock Test. It can be seen that the decline within the first

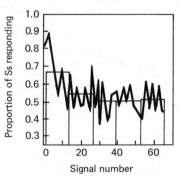

Fig. 1.1. Fine-grained analysis of the probability of making a correct detection as a function of time at work (see text). From Jerison (1959b).

period of the task (each time period was about 27 minutes long) is quite steep, whereas that between the first and subsequent time periods is much less marked. It is possible, therefore, that coarse-grained analyses of the vigilance decrement, which have been employed in the great majority of laboratory studies, may underestimate the extent of the decline in perform-ance, since, as Teichner (1974) has put it "measures based on 10–30 min intervals tend to hide that part of the curve which contains the most rapid changes" (p. 343). Coarse-grained analyses of correct detection scores thus probably provide a somewhat conservative picture of the frequency with which a deterioration in efficiency occurs during the performance of a vigilance task.

However, the vigilance decrement is not confined to correct detection responses and reliable increments in detection latency with time on task have often been obtained (Buck, 1966). Some investigators have also reported increases in the variability of detection latencies with time (Faulkner, 1962). Significant increases in mean detection latency are not only found in tasks containing faint and unpredictable signals but also in tasks in which supra-threshold stimuli and regular signal presentation schedules have been employed (Boulter and Adams, 1963; Dardano, 1962; McCormack and Prysiazniuk, 1961). Boulter and Adams compared the effects of three presentation schedules, involving respectively high, moderate and low temporal uncertainty, on performance at a three-hour vigilance task requir-ing the detection of the number 20, which was clearly visible provided that the observer was oriented to the display. Their results are shown in Fig. 1.2, from which it can be seen that detection latencies increased in all con-ditions, but that no differential effect of presentation schedule on the rate of increase was obtained. The mean detection rate in this experiment was 99·5%.

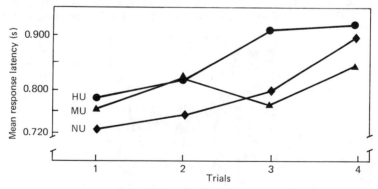

Fig. 1.2. Mean response latency as a function of time on task (blocks of trials) in a three-hour visual vigilance task under conditions of high (HU), medium (MU) and no (NU) temporal uncertainty. From Boulter and Adams (1963).

The vigilance decrement can thus be assessed both in terms of detection rate and detection latency and decision theory analyses appear to be able to encompass temporal changes in both these measures (see Chapters 4 and 5). The decrement is also found in visual, auditory and cutaneous tasks as well as in tasks employing "redundant" signal presentations in which signals are presented to two different sensory modalities. It appears to result from changes in central nervous system activity rather than from changes in the sensitivity of peripheral sense organs, since deteriorations in performance occur in the absence of any change in sensory threshold or in measures of "sensory fatigue" such as critical flicker fusion frequency (Garvey *et al.*, 1958; Whittenburg *et al.*, 1956). Thus explanations of the decrement, as will be seen below, have tended to focus on central rather than on peripheral processes, for example, inhibition, expectancy, attention, activation and motivation.

Theories of vigilance: an introduction

Theories of vigilance have addressed themselves to two main questions: what determines the decline in performance during a vigilance task? and what determines the overall level of performance? However, much greater emphasis has been placed on the development of answers to the first question than to the second and most theories of vigilance are devoted exclusively to an explanation of the vigilance decrement.

Inhibition theory

The first theory of vigilance to be put forward was N.H. Mackworth's inhibition theory (1950), which was advanced on the basis of his studies with the Clock Test, referred to above. Mackworth's theory is concerned entirely with the vigilance decrement, which he regarded as analogous to the extinction of a conditioned response when that response is no longer reinforced. In the Clock Test experiments, the depression of the response key to a "double jump" of the pointer was regarded as the conditioned voluntary response and since, as Mackworth noted, the failure to respond in experimental extinction procedures is typically negatively accelerated, experimental extinction appeared to parallel quite closely the decline in detection rate. However, the Clock Test results did not show complete extinction, instead the detection rate levelled off after about 30 minutes of work. This partial extinction was accounted for by a principle of expectancy which served to maintain performance at this level and prevented it from declining further. Crucial support for inhibition theory was considered by Mackworth to come from his experiments with knowledge of results and, to a lesser extent, with rest pauses. Knowledge of results abolished the decrement in detection rate and was regarded as a reinstatement of the reinforcing agent present during the practice period and normally absent from test sessions with the Clock Test. The alternation of 30-minute periods of work and rest also abolished the decrement and this effect was attributed to "spontaneous recovery", a phenomenon previously observed by Pavlov (1927) and explained by him in terms of the dissipation of inhibition accumulated during test trials. Inhibition, then, is a fatigue-like construct which is considered to build up with each non-reinforced occurrence of a conditioned response and, when the accumulation has become sufficiently great, the response no longer appears.

Deese (1955), in one of the first theoretical reviews of vigilance research, argued that if vigilance were to be defined as an excitatory state of response readiness, then it was unparsimonious to introduce a further opposing state of inhibition to explain the vigilance decrement. He also pointed out that detection rate does not always simply decline but may show some improvement or fluctuate "in a highly irregular manner and this creates difficulties for any simple application of the inhibitory construct" (p. 366). In one of Mackworth's experiments, a telephone message, exhorting subjects to do even better in the remainder of the task, was given at the end of the first hour of work. The telephone message produced a temporary improvement in detection efficiency, lasting for about 25 minutes, and could thus be regarded as a parallel to disinhibition. But, as Deese observed, "in strict Pavlovian usage, a disinhibitory stimulus is a neutral one" (p. 366); Mackworth's telephone message, in contrast, was certainly meaningful and probably also motivating in its effects. However the main objection to inhibition theory as an explanation of the vigilance decrement has been that increases in signal frequency do not accelerate the decrement in performance, as would be expected if inhibition were responsible for the decline, but instead reduce it.

A rather different hypothesis, although still within an inhibitory framework, as Broadbent, (1953b, 1958, 1971) has indicated, is to regard the attentional responses to the unwanted or neutral signals in the Clock Test (the single jumps of the pointer) as becoming extinguished and to consider this extinction as generalising to the wanted or critical signal. Yet although Broadbent viewed extinction and the vigilance decrement as having a common explanation, the explanation he favoured was expressed in terms of attention rather than inhibition, as will be seen below. Mackworth did entertain the possibility that secondary extinction of the occasional key-pressing response to non-signal stimuli during the practice period might be responsible for the decrement in performance in the Clock Test experiments, but rejected this explanation in the light of the effects of knowledge of results. He does not seem to have considered the possibility of other responses than key-pressing, such as attentional or observing responses, undergoing extinction.

Subsequently, Mackworth (1957) appears to have placed less emphasis on inhibition as an explanation of the vigilance decrement and greater emphasis on expectancy, largely as a result of C.H. Baker's studies of the effects of inter-signal interval regularity on vigilance (Baker, 1958, 1959a, b) conducted at the Applied Psychology Unit in Cambridge, of which Mackworth was then Director. However, Mackworth still maintained that the absence of reinforcement was "a factor of some importance" in determining the decline in performance in vigilance tasks (Mackworth, 1957, p. 393).

An inhibition-reinforcement theory of vigilance was later put forward by McCormack (1962) to explain his own findings with a task in which a 15-watt light bulb was switched on for a brief period at uncertain times and the subject was required to press a key as soon as he saw it. Since there were virtually no failures to react to the onset of the light, the measure of performance was reaction time. McCormack conducted a number of experiments with this task, exploring the effects on reaction time of the regularity and the duration of the time intervals between light onsets, of rest pauses and of complete and partial knowledge of results, in terms of whether or not a given response was faster or slower than the preceding response (McCormack, 1958, 1959, 1960; McCormack and McElheran, 1963; McCormack and Prysiazniuk, 1961; McCormack et al., 1962, 1963). As mentioned earlier, McCormack found that reaction time increased significantly with time on task even when the light was presented at completely regular intervals. This increase in reaction time could be prevented by providing rest pauses or knowledge of results. McCormack also examined the effects of inter-signal interval duration, since inhibition was assumed to increase during task performance but to be dissipated during rest pauses and during the intervals between light presentations, as well as by the provision of reinforcement in the form of knowledge of results. Thus increasing the interval between presentations of the light (in effect reducing the presentation rate) should produce faster reaction times. The evidence relating to the effects of inter-signal interval duration in McCormack's experiments is, however, inconsistent; in some studies a highly reliable inverse relationship between inter-signal interval duration and reaction time, consistent with inhibition theory, was obtained (McCormack, 1958, 1960; McCormack and Prysiazniuk, 1961), while in others no effect of inter-signal interval duration on reaction time was found (McCormack 1959; McCormack et al., 1962).

The reaction-time task used by McCormack is clearly different from the conventional vigilance task in which observers attempt to detect rare and inconspicuous signals, although McCormack (1967b) extended his theory of vigilance to encompass findings in such tasks. But this theory faces similar difficulties to those encountered by Mackworth's original inhibition theory, notably with regard to the effects of signal frequency on the vigilance decrement and, as will be seen below, the effects of knowledge of results, rest pauses and inter-signal interval duration can be at least as plausibly explained by alternative theories of vigilance, some of which can also provide a satisfactory account of the effects of signal frequency.

Expectancy theory

Expectancy theory for example, which is discussed at length in Chapter 4, hypothesizes that the observer formulates expectancies about the future probability of signal occurrence on the basis of previous experience with the task, and that detection rate is determined by expectancy level (Baker, 1959c, 1963c; Deese, 1955). Expectancy theory regards the observer as performing a continuous averaging process on the times between previous signal presentations in order to predict the occurrence of subsequent signals. If the averaging process is made easier by presenting signals at regular time intervals, detection efficiency should be greater and there should be less deterioration in efficiency with time than when the same number of signals is presented at irregular time intervals (see Baker, 1959b). On this view knowledge of results improves detection efficiency because it provides accurate information about the temporal distribution of signals and thus enables appropriate expectancies of when signals are likely to arrive to be formulated. Since the estimation of time intervals by human observers is not always very precise, however, some doubts have been expressed concerning the role of temporal expectancy in vigilance (Davies and Tune, 1970; Warm, 1977) and the ability to form accurate estimates of short time intervals has been shown to be unrelated to detection efficiency in a vigilance task (McGrath and O'Hanlon, 1967).

The observer's general level of expectancy is affected by the probability of signal occurrence. So long as the average probability of occurrence is low, the expectancy of observing a signal is low, and if the signal probability is raised, for example by altering signal frequency, the expectancy of observing a signal also increases. Expectancies concerning the probability of signal occurrence during the task begin to be formulated during the practice period and Colquhoun and Baddeley (1964, 1967) showed that a practice period in which the probability of occurrence was high produced higher detection and false alarm rates during the subsequent task than a practice period in which the signal probability was low, regardless of whether in the task itself the probability of signal occurrence was high or low. Observers appear to expect fewer signals to occur as the task progresses (McGrath and O'Hanlon, 1967) and as will be seen in Chapter 4, expectancy appears to exert a strong influence upon criterion placement.

Observing responses

The stored information from which expectancies are derived is presumably accumulated from observations of the display and, in turn, expectancies can also be regarded as controlling observing responses, directing attention to the task when the arrival of a signal is believed to be imminent. Not surprisingly, therefore, the quality and quantity of observing responses have been assumed to be highly correlated with detection efficiency, and a number of studies of the observing response have been conducted, beginning with those of Holland (1957, 1958). In these experiments observers were required to press a key which briefly illuminated a display on which a signal might or might not be present, and to press another key when they believed a signal had appeared. In this way Holland was able to distinguish between observing responses ("illumination" responses) and detection responses and he found that observers who exhibited a decrement in detection rate showed a parallel decrement in the number of observing responses emitted, while observers whose performance did not decline showed an increase in the observing rate with time on task. However, subsequent studies of observing responses have produced inconsistent results (Baker, 1960; Blair, 1958; Broadbent, 1963c; Hickey and Blair, 1958; Jerison and Wing, 1961; Schroeder and Holland, 1968) and it has been demonstrated that failures of signal detection can occur even while the display is being visually fixated (N.H. Mackworth et al., 1964), which suggests that visual fixations or key-pressing responses cannot be equated with observing responses. Nevertheless the effectiveness of procedures designed to ensure that the observer is more closely "coupled" to the display (Hatfield and Loeb, 1968; Warm et al., 1976c) implies that observing responses should not be entirely disregarded as determinants of detection efficiency and Jerison (1970b) has proposed an influential "observing response" model of vigilance behaviour, which is discussed in greater detail in Chapter 5.

Filter theory
The next theory to be discussed, filter theory, was developed by Broadbent (1957a, 1958, 1971) on the basis of experiments conducted in the areas of selective attention, vigilance, and the effects of noise on performance and is thus a more general theory than any of those considered so far. Broadbent's early work on vigilance was conducted with "unlimited hold" tasks such as the "Twenty Dials" and "Twenty Lights" tasks (Broadbent, 1950, 1951, 1953a, b); both of these are multi-source tasks in which the signal remains present until detected, the measure of performance being the number of long detection latencies or the number of signals detected within a given time. Broadbent also investigated performance at a task known as the five-choice serial reaction task. This task consisted of a board containing five brass discs, each adjacent to a bulb, arranged in the form of an equilateral pentagon. The subject was required to tap the disc adjacent to a lighted bulb with a metal stylus, whereupon the bulb was extinguished and a new one lit and

so on. Three scores were obtainable: the number of correct responses, the number of errors and the number of "gaps" or long response times, when the interval between responses was 1·5 s or greater. Broadbent compared performance at the normal unpaced version of this task, in which subjects determined their own rate of work, with that at a paced version, in which a fresh light was presented every second, regardless of how long the subject took to react. This rate of stimulus presentation was in fact equivalent to the average rate of responding in the unpaced version of the task. Under paced conditions it was found that the number of correct responses began to decline after about ten minutes of work, while in the unpaced version this measure only began to show deterioration after nearly an hour. However, an increase in the number of long response times (in this case 2 s or more) was observed after only ten minutes or so, that is, at about the same time as output began to decrease in the paced version. Broadbent concluded that the nature of the performance impairment was the same in both versions of the task but that in the unpaced version subjects could compensate for occasional very slow responses by working at a faster rate at other times. Thus a deterioration in performance would take the form of an increase in "gaps" rather than in correct responses. In the paced condition, however, such compensation had no opportunity to reveal itself and correct responses would be the measure affected by the change in performance. Broadbent argued that the occasional slow responses observed during performance of the five-choice serial reaction task were comparable to the "blocks" described by Bills (1931) as occurring in an unpaced colour-naming task and represented temporary failures of efficiency interspersed with otherwise normal performance.

Broadbent also suggested that a similar phenomenon occurred in vigilance, since the observation of the same information source for long periods was also liable to intermittent interruptions or "internal blinks" which increase with time. This is because the mechanism which selects information from the environment for further processing, known as the filter, possesses certain inherent biases, including a tendency to select information from sources which have recently been neglected. Filter theory thus attributes the vigilance decrement to periodic failures to take in task-relevant information, which become more frequent with time at work. Some vigilance tasks, namely those with transient signals (limited-hold tasks) will yield a performance decrement, while others (unlimited-hold tasks) will not, although, as with paced and unpaced versions of the five-choice serial reaction task, the nature of the performance change is held to be the same in both cases. The duration of the signal therefore becomes an important determinant of the vigilance decrement. A decline in detection rate is more likely to occur in tasks with signals of short duration, since such signals run a greater risk of being lost during brief periods of non-observation. Similarly, increasing signal intensity reduces or abolishes the performance decrement because more intense signals require less time for their significance to be appreciated. Increasing event rate enhances the decrement because more events are presented in a given time interval and hence are more likely to escape notice when attention is diverted from the task. The duplication of task information, as in "redundant" displays, will raise the probability of signal detection since there is less chance that attention will be diverted from both signal sources at the same time. Finally, monitoring tasks in which the observer works at his own pace ought to show less decrement than tasks in which he is compelled to work at a rate which is externally imposed.

However, the evidence relating to these hypotheses is at best equivocal (see also Broadbent, 1971). In respect of signal duration, signal intensity and event rate, some studies have reported reliable interactions of these variables with time at work, as filter theory would predict, while other studies have not, as is discussed further in Chapters 2 and 3. It is clear, though, that increases in signal duration and intensity and reductions in event rate improve the overall level of detection efficiency, presumably because the signal is made more discriminable by these procedures. The use of redundant displays has likewise been shown to reduce the decrement in some experiments (Buckner and McGrath, 1963b; Osborn et al., 1963) but not in others (Baker et al., 1962a; Loeb and Hawkes, 1962) and although Gruber (1964) found that alternating periods of visual monitoring with periods of auditory monitoring reduced the decrement, compared to sessions in which the task was presented to one modality throughout, this result can equally well be accommodated by alternative theories. Furthermore, the decrement in detection rate does not appear to be confined to paced vigilance tasks, as suggested by filter theory. For example, a slight but reliable decrement in performance at a 75-minute unpaced audio-visual checking task was reported by Kappauf and Payne (1959) when the first and the last quarter hours of work were compared. Wilkinson (1961a) compared paced and unpaced versions of the same vigilance task. In the unpaced condition observers pressed a key to indicate their readiness to receive a possible visual signal which could appear in any one of eight positions on a display. Whether the key was pressed or not the display was presented at an average interval of 4·5 s. Performance in this condition was compared with two paced conditions, one regular and the other irregular, in which displays were presented at the same average rate as in the unpaced condition. A decline in performance occurred in all three conditions but the decrement was greatest in the unpaced condition, although this condition also produced the largest number of correct detections for the 60-minute period of the task. Colquhoun (1962a) gave his subjects a task which consisted of a series of panels, each containing six discs, one of which would occasionally be paler than the remaining five, this being the signal subjects were required to report. Colquhoun found that similar decrements occurred not only when panels were presented for inspection at fixed rates determined by the experimenter (either 10 or 33 panels per minute) but also when subjects could determine their own inspection rate. It is apparent, therefore, that a vigilance decrement can occur both in paced and unpaced monitoring situations.

The explanation of the vigilance decrement given by Broadbent's filter theory thus appears to receive only weak empirical support and in any case it is difficult to distinguish the theory from some form of observing response theory in a clear and convincing fashion, since a failure of the filter to select information from the task would seem to be equivalent to a failure to observe the display on which the task is presented. The main differences between the two approaches are perhaps that the selection of task relevant information is presumed by filter theory to be an all-or-none process, information either being selected or ignored; whereas in Jerison's (1970b) observing response model observing behaviour consists of three classes of observing response: alerted or "optimal" observing, blurred or "sub-optimal" observing and "distracted" observing, in which the source of task information is not observed at all. The first and third classes correspond to task information selection and filter "deviations" in filter theory. Second, filter theory implies that failures to select task information are of fixed duration, an assumption not made by observing response theory.

Arousal theory

We now turn to theories which emphasize the general state of the individual at the time the task is carried out as a determinant of performance changes. Three theories of this kind have been advanced to explain the vigilance decrement: first, arousal or activation theory, which maintains that a progressive reduction in the level of arousal of the central nervous system takes place during task performance, largely brought about by the monotonous nature of the vigilance situation, and, as a result, the brain becomes less responsive to and less efficient at dealing with external stimulation; second, habituation theory, a variant of arousal theory, first proposed by J.F. Mackworth (1968b, 1969) and third, motivation theory, which maintains that the vigilance decrement is attributable to individual differences in motivational level, some subjects being more conscientious monitors than others, as well as to reductions in motivational level caused by the monotonous conditions of work and the failure to provide adequate incentives to maintain efficiency.

Arousal or activation theory has its origins in the emphasis placed upon the intensity with which behaviour occurs, and in the strength of the motives which inspire it, by various investigators in the 1930s who, influenced by Cannon's concept of "energy mobilization", attempted to relate variations in behavioural intensity and in the quality of task performance to variations in physiological activity (for example, Duffy, 1932; Freeman, 1938, 1940). This work drew attention to the idea that behaviour could be regarded as varying along a continuum of intensity, from deep sleep to extreme excitement, and attempts were made to specify the physiological changes taking place at crucial points along this continuum, which has become known as the level of activation or arousal (Duffy, 1951, 1957, 1962; Lindsley, 1951; Malmo, 1959). The development of the concept of arousal was also influenced by research on the neural systems involved in the maintenance of wakefulness, which suggested that the ascending reticular activating system and the diffuse thalamic projection system together formed a system which was highly responsive to environmental stimulation and which in turn contributed strongly to the level of activation manifested by the cerebral cortex (see Lindsley, 1960 and Magoun, 1958 for reviews). Research on the consequences of exposure to sensory deprivation demonstrated that perceptual and cognitive processes were severely impaired and led Hebb (1955) to emphasize the importance of sensory variation in preserving the efficiency of the brain. Hebb pointed out that environmental stimulation performed two functions, the first a "cue" or "steering" function and the second an "energizing" or "activating" function.

Research concerned with the effects on task performance of various stressors, such as loud noise, sleep deprivation and heat and with those of motivational factors such as the provision of incentives and knowledge of results, also lent credibility to the concept of arousal. Out of this work came the "arousal theory of stress" (Broadbent, 1963a, 1971) which assumes that there is a general state of arousal or reactivity which is increased by loud noise or by incentives and reduced by boredom or loss of sleep. The arousal theory of stress makes a further assumption, reminiscent of the Yerkes–Dodson law, that the relationship between the level of arousal and the level of performance takes the form of an inverted U. This assumption has sometimes also been made by classical activation theory (Malmo, 1959) although it is apparently not essential to it (Duffy, 1972). The inverted-U hypothesis holds that task performance is low when the level of arousal is either much above or much below an optimal point, although the nature of the performance deficit at high and low levels of arousal may well be different (see, for example, Hockey, 1970a, b, c, 1973).

Given that there is considerable evidence supporting the concept of arousal, how are the terms "aroused" and "arousal level" to be defined? Gray (1964) divided definitions of arousal into three classes. First, there are definitions which emphasize the intensity with which behaviour occurs. Duffy, for example, has stated that, "The level of activation of the organism may be defined ... as the extent of release of potential energy, stored in the tissues of the organism, as this is shown in activity or response" (Duffy, 1962, p. 17). Second, arousal can be defined in terms of the intensity of the motivational factors to which an individual is subject. Hebb, for instance, suggests that, "Activity in the arousal system has the essential characteristics of a drive; it does not literally provide the energy of response, but it determines whether the energy will be available or not, without determining how it will be directed" (Hebb, 1958, p. 158). Third, some definitions of arousal emphasize the individual's level of alertness. An example of a definition falling into this category is that given by Berlyne: arousal is "a measure of how wide awake the organism is, of how ready it is to react. The lower pole of the continuum is represented by deep sleep or coma while the upper pole would be reached in states of frantic excitement" (Berlyne, 1960, p. 48). A more laconic definition of arousal, similar to Berlyne's, has been provided by Corcoran: the degree of arousal is "the inverse probability of falling asleep" (Corcoran, 1965).

It is clear that no single view of arousal emerges from these definitions and that therefore a theory of vigilance based upon the concept of arousal faces the problem of which definition to choose. The first seems inappropriate, unless great importance is to be attached to the vigour with which the detection response is made, while the second effectively equates arousal with motivation. The third implies that detection efficiency depends upon the level of alertness, and this definition is perhaps the most useful from the point of view of the arousal theory of vigilance. But the selection of a definition of arousal does not solve all the problems faced by such a theory because of the lack of general agreement as to what constitutes an acceptable measure of the level of arousal; some investigators have preferred measures of electrocortical activity, such as the electroencephalogram or EEG, others have opted for measures of autonomic activity, such as heart rate or skin conductance. As will be seen in Chapters 6 and 8, there is little doubt that the level of arousal, as indexed by the level of electrocortical or autonomic activity, does tend to fall during the performance of a vigilance task, and that the vigilance decrement is therefore associated with a decline in arousal or alertness. However, changes in detection efficiency during a vigil do not always appear to be related to changes in psychophysiological activity and arousal level also declines in the absence of a vigilance decrement and when no task is being performed at all. Furthermore, manipulations of task factors which have been shown to result in substantial changes in performance, such as signal frequency, do not produce a corresponding change in psychophysiological measures (Eason et al., 1965; Stern, 1966).

Because of the ambiguous nature of the psychophysiological evidence, Broadbent (1971) has proposed that it is unsafe to use any physiological measure as a criterion of the level of arousal, a proposal which, if widely adopted, would relieve arousal theory of what some regard as the albatross of psychophysiology but would at the same time, deprive it of the only means of measuring its central construct. The result would be a behavioural theory of arousal, derived from the arousal theory of stress, in which, on the basis of similarities, differences and interactions between the effects of various stressors and other factors upon performance, certain variables could be presumed to induce high, and others low, levels of arousal. Loud noise and loss of sleep are obvious examples. However, as will be seen in Chapter 7, it is by no means clear that the presence of a variable presumed to induce a high level of arousal reduces, or that the presence of a variable presumed to induce a low level of arousal enhances the vigilance decrement, although it is likely that high arousal levels increase, while low arousal levels decrease, the overall level of performance. Nevertheless, the effects of some factors on vigilance performance, notably those of the time of day at which testing is conducted, do not seem to be explicable in terms of alternative theories.

Habituation theory

A physiological or behavioral response may be said to habituate if it is reduced or eliminated as a result of repeated stimulation (Groves and Thompson, 1970). The EEG desynchronization response, for example, habituates with regular presentation of the same stimulus. Sharpless and Jasper (1956) were among the first to report this phenomenon, and they also suggested that the performance decrements found in vigilance and other monotonous tasks may be due to habituation processes.

A factor that is closely related to habituation as well as influencing detection efficiency in vigilance is the rate of presentation of stimulus events, or the event rate. Generally speaking, habituation is greater at higher event rates, and it is also known that vigilance performance is lower at higher event rates (Jerison and Pickett, 1964). J.F. Mackworth (1968b) therefore suggested that the repetitious nature of the background events in a vigilance task serves to habituate the neural responses to these stimuli, as a result of which the observer's ability to detect signals in the background neural "noise" is impaired; this is a process which unfolds over time, so that there is a progressive drop in the detection rate. She argued that the habituation of the EEG arousal response (desynchronization) and of the cortical evoked response leads to the performance decrement found in a variety of prolonged tasks. Unfortunately, empirical support for this simple and elegant theory has not yet emerged (Harkins, 1974; Gale, 1977; Gale et al., 1977). At the time the theory was proposed, supporting evidence was drawn mainly from J.F. Mackworth's own studies with the Continuous Clock task, which is a modification of the Clock Test used originally by N.H. Mackworth (1944). J.F. Mackworth (1968a) reported an approximately exponential decay in detection efficiency (d') in this task (see Chapter 5); this appears to simulate a habituation process, which is usually a negatively accelerated function of the number of stimulus presentations per unit time (Thompson and Spencer, 1966). However, this result is specific to this task alone, and is probably due to the continuous visual pursuit required. In most other vigilance tasks, d' does not decay exponentially, and the time course of habituation appears too short to account for vigilance decrements which cover periods from 30 minutes to four hours (Jerison, 1977).

Habituation can be distinguished from passive processes such as fatigue or general adaptation, by the phenomenon of *dishabituation*, or the immediate restoration of response following some sudden change in the pattern of stimulation. Although the effects of factors such as rest pauses and task interruption, which, as mentioned earlier, improve vigilance (N.H. Mackworth, 1950), may be interpreted as dishabituation effects, a study which specifically examined the effects of dishabituation failed to support the habituation theory (Krulewitz et al., 1975). In this study, a shift paradigm was used in which the event rate was increased or decreased suddenly halfway through a vigilance session. Shifts from slow-to-fast and from fast-to-slow were made for separate groups of subjects and two non-shifted groups were also included in the experiment. According to J.F. Mackworth's (1968b) theory, improved performance due to the dishabituating effect of the shift should be observed for both shifted groups. Krulewitz et al. found, however, that the slow-to-fast group performed poorly compared to the non-shifted control at the fast event rate. For the fast-to-slow group, performance improved after the shift compared to the non-shifted group, but did so only after the shifted group had experienced the new event rate for about 20 minutes. These results are at odds with known facts about the time course of habituation and dishabituation (Thompson and Spencer, 1966; see also Warm, 1977), and fail to provide support for J.F. Mackworth's theory. Habituation theory is further discussed in Chapter 5 in connection with decision theory measures of vigilance performance.

Motivation theory

Although most theories of vigilance consider motivation to be an important determinant of performance, and it is frequently viewed as being of crucial importance in the debate about the practical significance of vigilance research (see Chapter 9), none of the theories discussed so far regards motivation as the most important determinant of either the vigilance decrement or the overall level of performance. However, Smith (1966) has put forward a theory of vigilance in which the interaction of monotony and motivation is held to provide an explanation of both of these phenomena. His theory emphasizes individual differences in motivation and argues that "all individuals of normal intelligence and perceptual capacities are capable of continuously attending a simple vigilance display for 1–2 hours and detecting all signals" (p. 11) but since "typical experimental subjects differ not so much in their *ability* to maintain attention as in their *willingness* to do so"

(p. 2, emphasis in original), the result is that "individuals do not attend a vigilance display to the limit of their capability" (p. 13), although some more conscientious individuals perform closer to that limit than do others. The latter are referred to as "periodic participators", who will only apply themselves fully to the task if extrinsic motivation in the form of rewards or punishments is supplied, and whose performance, without it, will invariably show a vigilance decrement. Thus the vigilance decrement results from the pooling of the performance scores of conscientious monitors with those of "periodic participators" and the overall level of performance achieved depends upon the number of subjects in the experiment who are "periodic participators". Because it is so monotonous, the typical vigilance situation provides little intrinsic motivation, although Smith suggests that the manipulation of task characteristics such as signal frequency can reduce monotony and thus increase intrinsic motivation. But the effects of increasing extrinsic motivation are more pronounced and the principal factors affecting extrinsic motivation in the vigilance situation are knowledge of results (KR), rewards and punishments and a group of factors comprising the degree and kind of supervision, "motivating" instructions and attitudes towards the experimenter.

It is clear that in some experiments the effect of KR on performance must be solely a motivational one. This is most apparent in the experiments of McCormack, referred to earlier, in which KR, in terms of whether a given response was faster or slower than the preceding response, prevented the increase in response latency with time on task observed in control conditions. In McCormack's experimental situation, the alternative explanation of the effects of knowledge of results put forward by expectancy theory (which suggests that KR improves performance by providing information about the temporal distribution of signals, and thus enables more accurate expectancies of future signal occurrences to be formulated) is inapplicable, since McCormack's task contained no signals and every light stimulus received a response. In a similar task situation even giving subjects false information concerning their speed of response has been shown to prevent an increase in response latency with time (Loeb and Schmidt, 1963). The motivational interpretation of the effects of KR is also supported by the results of studies employing false KR in vigilance tasks in which signals must be discriminated from non-signals. In such tasks, although its effects are generally not as beneficial as those of true KR, false KR has been shown to reduce or abolish the vigilance decrement and, with few exceptions, to improve the overall level of performance (Antonelli and Karas, 1967; J.F. Mackworth, 1964a; Warm et al., 1974; Weidenfeller et al., 1962). Warm et al. also found that both true and false KR produced faster and less variable detection latencies than a control condition in which no KR was given, irrespective of whether the signal presentation schedule was regular or irregular; furthermore an increase in detection latency with time was found only in the control condition. This result provides further evidence for the view that the effects of KR are primarily motivational rather than informational in character, as does the finding that subjects' own immediate evaluations of the speed of their responses, which provide much less accurate information than does true KR, maintain performance at a level which is not reliably different from that found when KR is given (Warm *et al.*, 1972).

True KR frequently either reduces or abolishes the vigilance decrement found in control conditions, although it does not always do so (Bergum and Lehr, 1963b; Coules and Avery, 1966; Montague and Webber, 1965), and usually significantly improves the overall level of performance (J.F. Mackworth, 1964a; N.H. Mackworth, 1950; Warm *et al.*, 1972; Weidenfeller *et al.*, 1962; Wiener, 1963a). The effects of a wide variety of different kinds of true KR have been investigated and studies have been conducted of the effects of the method of presentation, whether verbal or non-verbal (Hardesty *et al.*, 1963; Ware and Baker, 1964), of the modality of presentation, whether visual or auditory (Grunzke *et al.*, 1974), of the form of presentation, whether complete or partial (Chinn and Alluisi, 1964; Wiener, 1963a), of the effects of the amount of KR (Johnson and Payne, 1966), of the carryover effects of KR (Adams and Humes, 1963; Wiener, 1963a, 1968), of whether KR is given in respect of an easy or a difficult standard of performance (Warm *et al.*, 1973) and of the effects of combining KR with incentives (Grunzke *et al.*, 1974, Montague and Webber, 1965; Sipowicz *et al.*, 1962).

Summarizing the results of these studies very briefly, it appears that verbal KR produces superior performance to non-verbal KR, although the latter is still effective compared to no KR at all, and auditory KR tends to be superior to visual KR. Performance improves when KR is provided for at least 50% of the time, but any increase beyond that does not result in any further improvement, and the amount of KR given does not seem to affect the rate at which performance deteriorates. The response standard of performance in respect of which KR is given appears to be unimportant. There is some evidence of positive transfer of training following the withdrawal of KR as far as the overall level of performance is concerned, although the evidence regarding the vigilance decrement is less impressive. Generally, too, the combination of KR and financial incentives produces better overall performance than does either KR or incentives alone, although again the decrement may still occur. Finally, complete KR, in which KR is given in respect of correct detections, commission errors and missed signals, produces more correct detections and fewer false alarms than does partial KR, in which information is given only about some of these. There is also some evidence for the specificity of partial KR effects and for the interaction of the type of partial KR with the method of presentation which indicates that the effects of true KR may be more complex than motivation theory suggests. However, in general, the results of experiments with KR provide quite strong support for motivation theory, particularly with respect to the overall level of performance. It is apparent, however, that a decline in performance can still be found even when knowledge of results is provided, which suggests that, in some cases at least, motivational changes alone cannot be solely responsible for the vigilance decrement.

This conclusion is supported by the results of studies of other variables designed to increase extrinsic motivation. Wiener (1969), in a discussion of the effects of financial incentives on vigilance suggests that "the experimental results have been unimpressive" (p. 628). In some experiments the provision of incentives has been shown to exert a beneficial effect on the overall level of detection efficiency (Bevan and Turner, 1965; Sipowicz *et al.*, 1962; Smith *et al.*, 1967), while in others it has not (Levine, 1966; Wiener, 1969) and the effects of incentives seem in any case to be very short-lived (Bergum and Lehr, 1964). The effects of monetary incentives on the vigilance decrement are also far from clear, again some studies have indicated that the decrement seen under control conditions can be abolished by monetary rewards (Sipowicz *et al.*, 1962) while others have not (Bergum and Lehr, 1964; Wiener, 1969). This discrepancy cannot be attributed to the type of subject population tested or to the size of the monetary incentive. The studies by Sipowicz *et al.* and by Bergum and Lehr both employed US Army personnel as subjects and Bergum and Lehr offered slightly greater rewards for detecting a signal (20 cents) than did Sipowicz *et al.* (about 4 cents).

Other ways of increasing extrinsic motivation have also failed to produce consistent effects, particularly with respect to the vigilance decrement. Detection efficiency has been found to be enhanced and the decrement to be reduced by making the opportunity to listen to a local radio station contingent upon the detection of signals, a result shown not to be attributable to the variety of stimulation thus provided (Ware *et al.*, 1964). Similar results were obtained by Halcomb and Blackwell (1969) using course credit as an incentive with student subjects. The presence of the experimenter or some other "authority figure" in the testing room has been demonstrated to result in a significant increase in the number of correct detections (Bergum and Lehr, 1963c; Fraser, 1953; Putz, 1975) and Putz also found that detection efficiency could be reliably enhanced by other forms of supervision such as closed circuit television and a one-way vision screen. However, both Bergum and Lehr and, in two experiments, Putz, found that a decrement occurred in all their supervisory conditions. Similarly, Ware *et al.* (1964) found that subjects treated "democratically" achieved better detection scores than subjects treated "autocratically", although there was no difference in the rate at which performance deteriorated with time. Finally, subjects identifying with or admiring the experimenter are no more efficient than subjects to whom the experimenter is unknown (Halcomb *et al.*, 1970) and "motivating" instructions, while sometimes improving the overall level of performance (Lucaccini *et al.*, 1968; Nachreiner, 1977; Neal, 1967) have produced conflicting results as far as the vigilance decrement is concerned (Nachreiner, 1977; Neal, 1967).

Motivation theory, then, receives quite good support for its interpretation of differences in the overall level of performance, and there are also some indications that motivational factors reduce the variability in performance between subjects (Sipowicz *et al.*, 1962), as Smith's (1966) theory would seem to require. However, the evidence for a purely motivational interpretation of the vigilance decrement is equivocal and other factors must also be implicated. We have seen that the vigilance decrement is a widespread and persistent phenomenon for which no single theory, of those we have surveyed, can provide a completely convincing explanation. The reasons for this state of affairs are first that traditional measures of the vigilance decrement are inadequate and do not accurately reflect the changes in performance occurring during a vigilance task and second, that with few exceptions, the influence of task factors upon the decrement has been relatively neglected in theoretical accounts of vigilance performance. In the following chapters the problem of response measures will be examined and it will be seen that when more satisfactory indices of detection efficiency are employed, two kinds of performance change with time require explanation. Which kind of performance changes takes place is demonstrated to be strongly related to the information processing demands made by a particular task. However, since a great variety of tasks has been employed in the study of vigilance, some system of classifying tasks in terms of their information processing demands is clearly needed, and the development of a task classification for vigilance tasks is our primary concern in the next chapter.

Chapter 2

The Vigilance Task

The vigilance task has been regarded as providing "the fundamental paradigm for defining sustained attention as a behavioral category" (Jerison, 1977, p. 29) and various attempts have been made to specify its essential characteristics (for example, McGrath, 1963a). But such attempts run the risk of being overly restrictive in the criteria they impose and of narrowing down unduly the range of phenomena to be explained by a theory of sustained attention. It seems preferable, therefore, to adopt a fairly flexible approach to the problem of task definition and to examine instead the wide variety of tasks used by different researchers investigating vigilance and monitoring behaviour in the hope that the great majority can be encompassed within a task classification system. Different theories advocated by different experimenters appear, at least in part, to depend on the type of task they have employed. For instance, investigators who have used "stimulating" tasks have tended to favour theories concerned with the division of attention, while those who have used "unstimulating" tasks have tended to favour theories based on the concept of arousal. It is clearly important to determine at what level of generality different theories of vigilance can be applied, and this objective could be more easily achieved if a taxonomic framework were available within which the characteristics of different tasks could be listed, with particular emphasis upon those most obviously associated with changes in performance.

While there has been comparatively little progress in the development of a taxonomy of vigilance tasks, it was seen in Chapter 1 that Broadbent (1958) attempted to distinguish between tasks which did and did not yield a decrement in terms of the type of task employed. Moreover, a taxonomy of continuous work tasks has been proposed by Bergum (1966). His taxonomy was based on arousal theory and differentiated tasks in terms of their "total stimulation value". Bergum applied his classification scheme to a wide range of continuous performance tasks, including those involved in production-line, assembly and other monotonous work. As such, it is of limited value for the purposes of a taxonomic analysis of monitoring situations, since the task dimensions are too broad. Furthermore, no independent measure of the rather imprecisely defined "stimulation value" dimension was provided. Nevertheless, Bergum's analysis is important for providing one of the first attempts at task classification for monitoring and other prolonged tasks, and his analysis does allow some measure of predictive capacity across classification categories. The concept of "stimulation value", and the proposal of an optimal level for efficient performance, is related to similar conceptualizations such as the inverted-U relation (Corcoran, 1965), the Yerkes–Dodson Law (Broadbent, 1965) and Poulton's (1960) concept of "optimum perceptual load". However, Bergum's taxonomy raises the question of theoretical bias in the construction of task taxonomies. If a task classification system is to be used to evaluate different theoretical approaches to the explanation of performance changes, theoretical neutrality in the formulation of such a system must be a cardinal requirement. Thus the task characteristics included in the task classification system proposed here are those which seem to be the most crucial in producing performance changes, irrespective of their relative importance for particular theories of vigilance.

Task classification and vigilance: the major task dimensions

The task dimensions that seem to be of primary importance for monitoring behaviour include the sense modality to which events are presented for inspection, the number of stimulus sources to be monitored, the attention requirements of the task, the type of response required and the kind of discrimination involved in the detection of signals. We shall consider each of these in turn, placing particular emphasis on the last dimension. The main criterion for the inclusion of a particular dimension in the classification system is whether or not there is reliable evidence in the research literature, either that different patterns of performance can be associated with tasks placed at different points along the dimension, or that performance in such tasks is poorly correlated, suggesting that as the position of a task on the dimension is altered, different processes may come to determine either performance trends or performance levels.

Sense modality

Strictly speaking, of course, sense modality is not a dimension along which tasks can vary, although tasks presented to different modalities can be regarded as varying in the degree to which sensory information provided by the task is "coupled" to the perceptual apparatus of the subject. Thus auditory tasks can generally be considered to be more closely coupled than visual tasks (Elliott, 1960). Modality specific effects have been reported for a number of different kinds of behaviour, including vigilance. Although differences in the overall level of performance have sometimes been observed between auditory, visual and vibrotactile or cutaneous vigilance tasks, with performance at auditory vigilance tasks frequently being superior, decrements in performance have been found with all three kinds of task (for example, Davenport, 1969; Gruber, 1964; N.H. Mackworth, 1950). Since the overall level and the rate of decline of performance are fairly similar across different modalities, it appears that there is little reason to include sense modality in a task classification system. Moreover, as there is no way of equalizing inputs to different sensory modalities (Elliott, 1960), the possibility remains that any differences observed in performance across modalities are attributable to characteristics of the events being monitored, such as the signal to noise ratio, which are unrelated, or at least only partially related, to the modality in which the task is presented.

However, a comparison of performance across sense modalities has been considered to provide a test of the hypothesis that vigilance performance in different modalities is mediated by a "common central process" (see Davies and Tune, 1970). It has generally been assumed that this hypothesis does not hold, since it has been shown that monitoring performance is not correlated across sensory modalities and thus tends to be modality specific (Buckner and McGrath, 1963b; Pope and McKechnie, 1963). Although this conclusion is questionable, in view of more recent research (see Chapter 6), it justifies the inclusion of sense modality in a task classification system, since the possibility remains that different processes may underlie visual, auditory and cutaneous vigilance performance.

Source complexity

The number of stimulus sources to be monitored can be regarded as varying along a dimension of stimulus source complexity. Although the evidence relating to patterns of performance in single-and multi-source tasks is conflicting, and remains to be fully explored, a number of investigators have emphasized that this dimension effectively dichotomizes the range of monitoring tasks (Howell *et al.*, 1966; Jerison and Wallis, 1957a; Johnston *et al.*, 1969) and that monitoring performance at "simple" and "complex" tasks should be considered separately.

The attention requirements of the task

Quite apart from the demands imposed on the flexibility of attention by an increase in stimulus-source complexity, in single-source vigilance tasks the attentional requirements of a task alter with time course of events, which can vary along a continuum from slow, to fast, to continuous presentation. We have already seen in Chapter 1 that the rate at which events are presented for inspection exercises a powerful influence on detection efficiency and Simpson (1967) proposed that a performance decrement is observed only for tasks requiring "continuous" attention, that is, tasks in which the rate of event presentation is high, or in which presentation is continuous, such as the Continuous Clock Test (see Chapter 5). The regularity of event occurrence may also have an important influence on vigilance performance, as originally suggested by N.H. Mackworth (1957), although apart from a few studies of "free-response" tasks in which signals appear at random intervals in time (Egan et al., 1961; Watson and Nichols, 1976), the effects of this factor have yet to be properly examined. However, the event rate at least, is such a potent variable that it is necessary to include the time course of events as a further task dimension in a task classification system.

The type of response required

The response requirement in vigilance can also be considered to vary along a dimension of complexity, from the usual requirement of a simple detection response to more elaborate response requirements involving judgement and decision-making. Although increasing post-detection response complexity has been shown to exert a beneficial effect on the vigilance decrement (Adams and Boulter, 1960; Adams et al., 1961; Monty, 1962), the effect is slight and is not always obtained (T.S. Luce, 1964). Moreover, procedures which require different kinds of detection response, for example to respond appropriately to every event presented, whether signals or non-signals, affect vigilance performance very little, if at all (Davies et al., 1973; Guralnick and Harvey, 1970; Parasuraman and Davies, 1975, 1976; Whittenburg et al., 1956). The rating method, in which observers rate how confident they were that a signal was presented, has been used in vigilance studies (Broadbent and Gregory, 1963b; Loeb and Binford, 1964; Milosevic, 1975; Parasuraman, 1979), and produces results which correspond fairly well to those obtained with more conventional procedures, as is further discussed in Chapter 3. Thus unless the response requirement is more complex, as in certain radar tasks which entail target analysis and evaluation as well as simple target detection, the type of response required can probably be excluded from a task classification system.

The nature of the discrimination required for the detection of signals

This dimension, which appears to be one of the most important dimension of monitoring tasks, is derived from the abilities classification system developed by Fleishman (1972). The abilities classification approach is one of an interrelated set of taxonomic approaches to the evaluation of human performance and has been described in detail by Fleishman and his associates (Fleishman, 1972, 1975a, b; Theologus and Fleishman, 1971). Briefly, this system proposes that certain basic abilities can be identified as the major determinants of performance in a variety of tasks. The abilities are inferred from factor analyses of performance consistencies in different tasks. Theologus and

Fleishman (1971) identified four main ability "domains": cognitive, perceptual-sensory, physical proficiency, and psychomotor. Within each of these domains, several ability categories were identified, this procedure forms the major point of departure from other taxonomies, which have often only specified a few broad categories. In the 1971 version of the abilities taxonomy, 37 basic abilities were postulated. Each was derived from factor loadings on tasks sampling the ability, and refined rating scales were developed so that the "ability requirements" of different tasks could be quantitatively expressed. Each of these scales were "anchored" with empirically determined scale values corresponding to the ability requirements of different tasks.

In their application of the abilities classification to the organization of a portion of the literature on monitoring performance, Levine *et al.* (1971, 1973) considered two ability domains, the "perceptual-sensory" and "cognitive" domains, to be of relevance to monitoring tasks. The former domain was accorded greater importance, and two "primary abilities" were selected from this domain: *perceptual speed* and *flexibility of closure*. Perceptual speed refers to the ability to compare successively presented patterns or stimulus configurations for identity or degree of similarity. The sensory patterns to be compared occur within the same sense modalities. Flexibility of closure refers to the ability to detect or identify a previously specified stimulus configuration which is part of a more complex sensory field. Both the relevant stimulus configuration and the "noise field" occur within the same sense modality (Levine *et al.*, 1971, p. 9). Levine *et al.* also considered two "secondary abilities", *selective attention* ("the ability to perform a task in the presence of distracting stimulation or under monotonous conditions without loss of efficiency") and *time sharing* ("the ability to utilize information obtained by shifting between two or more channels of information").

Levine *et al.* classified 53 monitoring tasks used in the literature in terms of each of these four abilities, each task being categorized by the predominant ability required for efficient performance. Most of the tasks (50 out of 53) fell into either the perceptual speed or flexibility of closure ability categories. Very few tasks could be assumed to require the selective attention or time sharing abilities predominantly (hence their designation as "secondary"). It would therefore appear that these two abilities do not entirely satisfy Fleishman's (1967) criteria for a reliable classification system, namely that the classification categories should be neither too general nor too specific. The selective attention category appears to fail to satisfy the first of these requirements, in that demands on selective processing may be imposed not only in monitoring tasks, but also in many other tasks; and one would expect to find performance specificity *within* each of these categories, as for the vigilance and memory categories identified in a taxonomy suggested by Alluisi (1967). However, the two primary abilities, perceptual speed and flexibility of closure, appear to be representative of important task features in terms of which monitoring tasks may be dichotomously classified. Levine *et al.* (1973) found that there were some differences between tasks requiring these abilities, both in the average performance trends exhibited over time and in the effects of certain independent variables. For instance in tasks requiring flexibility of closure, the percentage of correct detections declined with time on task until a certain point (about 45 minutes into the vigil), and then increased, while for tasks requiring perceptual speed performance did not reverse, but levelled off. This is illustrated in Fig. 2.1, which suggests that tasks requiring perceptual speed may be more susceptible to performance decrement than tasks requiring flexibility of closure.

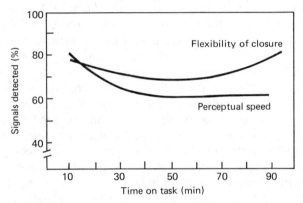

Fig. 2.1. Median percent correct detections as a function of time on task for tasks requiring the abilities of "perceptual speed" or "flexibility of closure". From Levine *et al.* (1973).

As an example of a task requiring perceptual speed, Levine *et al.* (1973) outlined the task used by Eason *et al.* (1965). In this task subjects were required to press a switch when they detected a flash of light appearing in a one-inch circular hole for 0·8 s. The light was normally flashed for 0·5 s, the interval between flashes being 3 s. As an example of a task requiring flexibility of closure the task used by Adams (1956) was described. In this task subjects were required to detect a 2 mm blip of light appearing in the centre of a circular white screen which was 5 inches in diameter. Examination of these tasks reveals that the major feature of the task requiring perceptual speed is that the detection of a change in the duration of a stimulus with respect to preceding stimuli is demanded, while for the task used by Adams (1956), involving flexibility of closure, the detection of a previously specified stimulus configuration is necessary. The abilities predominantly involved in each task category may thus be readily inferred from the signal characteristics of each monitoring task, by considering the type of signal which has to be discriminated. Monitoring tasks involving the abilities of perceptual speed and flexibility of closure may therefore be classified in terms of the type of discrimination involved, whether *successive* (perceptual speed) or *simultaneous* (flexibility of closure). Table 2.1 lists a sample of monitoring tasks, both visual and auditory, which have been classified in this manner.

Table 2.1. Examples of visual and auditory monitoring tasks classified on the successive discrimination and simultaneous discrimination task categories.

	Successive discrimination	Simultaneous discrimination
Visual tasks	1. Detect a change in the intensity of intermittent light flashes (Broadbent and Gregory, 1963b; Hatfield and Loeb, 1968). 2. Detect increase in deflection of meter needle (Baker, 1963a). 3. Detect increase in duration of intermittent light flashes (Williges, 1973).	1. Detect specified configuration in complex pattern of letters (Adams et al., 1962). 2. Detect a disc of specified hue in display of six discs (Colquhoun, 1961). 3. Detect a blip of light appearing occasionally on a screen (Adams, 1956).
Auditory tasks	1. Detect a change in the intensity of intermittent noise bursts (Hatfield and Soderquist, 1970). 2. Detect a sequence of digits in a series of auditorily presented numbers (Bakan, 1959). 3. Detect decrease in duration of intermittent tone (Deaton et al., 1971).	1. Detect a tone embedded in noise bursts (Hartley et al., 1973). 2. Detect a brief interruption in continuous white noise (Ware et al., 1961). 3. Detect occasional tone in a background of continuous white noise (Colquhoun et al., 1968a).

The task dimension relating to the nature of the discrimination necessary for the detection of signals, whether successive or simultaneous, should thus be included in a task classification system. Earlier in this chapter we have seen that other task dimensions which seem relevant to a taxonomy of vigilance tasks are the modality of presentation, source complexity and the time course of events. In considering other abilities that may be required by monitoring tasks the "selective attention" category was rejected because of its generality and imprecise definition. The "time sharing" category is also fairly broad; and it may include time sharing both within a task (for example between the different sources of a multi-source task), and between a primary (monitoring) task and a secondary task, such as tracking (Wiener, 1975), or memory and encoding (Tyler and Halcomb, 1974). To limit our classification to more specific features of the monitoring situation, we need only consider, as noted earlier, a task dimension based on source complexity: that is, whether the task contains one or more stimulus sources. Thus source complexity becomes a further dimension to be included in the task taxonomy.

The task classification proposed here, then, is based on task characteristics, and is outlined in Table 2.2. This table contains the four task characteristics regarded as being the most important of those we have considered. One

Table 2.2. The components of a proposed task classification system for monitoring tasks.

Dimension	Examples
Type of signal discrimination	Simultaneous/Successive
Sense modality	Visual/Auditory
Source complexity	Single/Multi—source
Time course of events	Discrete—slow/Discrete—fast/ Continuous

dimension which has been excluded, although it is of some importance, is visual search. This dimension obviously represents a strong candidate for future research into task classification systems, since it is an important feature of many inspection and other industrial monitoring tasks. The exclusion of visual search, in order to limit the scope of the present enquiry, indicates the preliminary and exploratory nature of this task classification system; in later chapters we shall consider how successfully the system is able to organize the existing literature on vigilance and to reconcile conflicting findings.

The psychophysics of vigilance

The psychophysics of vigilance is concerned with the characteristics of signals in vigilance tasks, such as their intensity, duration, probability and location. Most vigilance tasks employ sensory stimuli such as lights or tones and can thus be classed as "sensory" vigilance tasks, but some use letters or digits as stimuli and can be described as "cognitive" vigilance tasks. The best known cognitive vigilance task is the Bakan task (Bakan, 1959), derived from Wittenborn's (1943) factor analysis of attention tests, in which it was found that the detection of certain kinds of number sequences was most heavily loaded on what Wittenborn called an "attention factor". In the Bakan task, accordingly, a series of digits is presented in apparently random fashion and the subject is instructed to report each occurrence of three successive odd digits which are all different, or sometimes three successive digits in the order odd—even—odd. Another well-known "cognitive" task which has frequently been used in studies of vigilance is the Continuous Performance Test or CPT (Rosvold *et al.*, 1956) which was originally developed as an aid to the diagnosis of brain damage (see Chapter 8). The CPT consists of a series of letters in which each occurrence either of one letter (for example, A) or of a sequence of two letters (for example, AX) has to be detected. The CPT is usually a short-duration task, which lasts for about ten minutes, and analyses of CPT performance over time have seldom been reported. However, in similar short-duration tasks, for instance the Odd–Even Task, reliable decrements in detection and false alarm rates and significant increases in detection latency with time have been obtained (Harkins *et al.*, 1974). Decrements in detection efficiency are also found with more extended cognitive tasks such as the Bakan task, although there are exceptions to this general finding (Sipos, 1970) which are probably peculiar to the kind of tasks employed. When sensory and cognitive tasks are compared, there appears to be little difference in the trends in performance over time that are observed (Neal and Pearson, 1966), although in cognitive vigilance tasks it is more likely that false alarms will be more evenly distributed across subjects than is usually the case with sensory vigilance tasks (Davies and Tune, 1970).

A major difference between sensory and cognitive vigilance tasks is that in sensory tasks signals are presented at near-threshold levels, whereas in cognitive vigilance tasks all events are presented for inspection at levels well above threshold. In sensory tasks, the mere presence of an event can constitute the signal, as in procedures used to measure absolute thresholds, or the detection of a signal may require the discrimination of a near-threshold difference between successively presented events, as in procedures designed to measure difference thresholds. These different discrimination requirements, simultaneous and successive, were earlier put forward as a major dimension in a task classification system for vigilance, and performance in sensory tasks requiring simultaneous discriminations seems somewhat less susceptible to deterioration with time (Elliott, 1957; Hawkes and Loeb, 1961; Loeb and Hawkes, 1962; Martz and Harris, 1961) although whether a decrement is obtained may also depend on the sense modality to which signals are presented (Hawkes and Loeb, 1961). Threshold measurements have been obtained in sensory tasks requiring both simultaneous and successive discriminations but the results of different studies conflict. In some experiments both absolute and differential thresholds increase with time (Bakan, 1955; Berger and Mahneke, 1954; Gettys, 1964; Zwislocki *et al.*, 1958); in others considerable fluctuations in absolute thresholds, with no discernible trend, have been reported (Elliott, 1957; Wertheimer, 1955). However, although the results are not unanimous, such studies do provide some support for the suggestion that simultaneous discriminations show less deterioration with time.

Manipulation of what Dember and Warm (1979) describe as first order psychophysical factors, in which some physical parameter of the signal is

altered, clearly affects vigilance performance. If the signal is made more
conspicuous by increasing its intensity or duration then detection efficiency
improves. A number of studies have demonstrated that increasing signal
intensity significantly enhances detection rate or reduces detection latency
(Adams, 1956; Lisper *et al.*, 1972; Loeb and Binford, 1963; Metzger,
Warm and Senter, 1974; Wiener, 1964). Similar findings have been reported
for increases in signal duration (Adams, 1956; Baker, 1963a; Fraser,
1957; Warm *et al.*,1970).It is less certain whether increases in signal intensity
reduce the vigilance decrement, although increases in signal duration
appear to do so, as Fig. 2.2 shows. Figure 2.2 portrays the results of Baker
(1963a) who used a type of Clock Test lasting for two hours in which
the cessation of the clock hand movement was the signal to be reported.
Signal duration varied from 0·2 s to 0·8 s and, as can be seen from Fig. 2.2,
the briefer signal produced a more rapid decline in the percentage of signals
correctly detected as well as resulting in a much lower overall level of
efficiency.

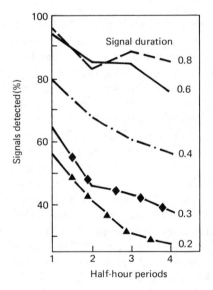

Fig. 2.2. The effect of different values of signal duration on percent correct
detections in a two-hour visual vigilance task. From Baker (1963a).

As will be seen in Chapter 5, factors which increase signal conspicuity
primarily affect the observer's perceptual sensitivity, as do other variables,
such as event rate, which we have previously considered as affecting the
attention requirements of the task. Such factors are to be distinguished
from what Dember and Warm (1979) call second order psychophysical
factors, which are characteristics of the signal which must be inferred by the

observer on the basis of his experience with the task. The most important of these second order factors is the frequency or probability of signal occurrence and, as will be seen in Chapter 4, increases in signal probability improve detection efficiency through their effects upon the response criterion rather than by affecting perceptual sensitivity.

Classification of operational vigilance tasks

As is further discussed in Chapter 9, it has frequently been pointed out that military and industrial monitoring tasks, and other tasks such as vehicle operation, which involve a vigilance component, may differ from laboratory vigilance tasks in several respects (Craig and Colquhoun, 1977; Drury and Fox, 1975b; Mackie, 1977; Smith and Lucaccini, 1969; Swets, 1976). Mackie (1977) put forward a classificatory scheme which enables comparisons to be made between different task situations in terms of the experimental variables manipulated by different investigators. In this scheme, which is depicted in Table 2.3, the task itself, the environment in which it is performed and the work schedule imposed can each be regarded as approximating more or less closely to an actual operational setting. Tasks can thus range from 3–3–3 to 1–1–1 on a dimension of "operational relevance".

The major differences between laboratory vigilance and operational monitoring tasks are in the characteristics of the target to be detected, in the number of sources to be monitored and in the post-detection response requirements.

First, targets in operational monitoring tasks tend to be more discriminable, more complex and probably occur less frequently than in laboratory vigilance tasks. Second, both in military and industrial monitoring tasks (and monitoring tasks comprise only a relatively small proportion of industrial inspection tasks; see Harris, 1969) the operator is usually required to keep watch over several potential signal sources, rather than the single display typically employed in laboratory vigilance tasks. Third, in laboratory tasks, reporting that a signal has been detected generally involves no more than the depression of a response key, while in operational tasks, the determination of the appropriate response to a defective item or a critical target is much more complex.

There are also differences between the typical environments in which laboratory and operational monitoring tasks are performed. First, subjects in laboratory vigilance tasks usually work in social isolation which, as Elliott (1960) remarks, "may be an interesting psychological phenomenon, but is not relevant to most military monitoring tasks" (p. 358). Second, operational monitoring tasks are less likely to require the long unbroken periods of watchkeeping found in laboratory situations. Third, a variety

Table 2.3. Relationships among type of experimental variable and apparent operational relevance in studies of monitoring behaviour. From Mackie (1977).

Experimental variables	Operational relevance		
	High	Moderate	Low
Task	1. Actual operational task; motivation intrinsic	2. Simulated operational task; motivation intrinsic or extrinsic	3. Abstract task; motivation extrinsic
Environment	1. Actual operational setting; naturally occurring stressors	2. Simulated operational setting; selected, controlled stressors	3. Conventional laboratory setting; operational stressors may or may not be included
Temporal characteristics	1. Actual operational schedules	2. Realistic approximations of watch durations; work/rest cycles; task repetitiveness	3. Usually short-term, non-repeated sessions; dictated by experimental convenience
	Low ⟵ Degree of Experimental Control ⟶ High		

of stressors, such as heat, noise and vibration, may constitute, either singly or in combination, a relatively permanent feature of the operational monitoring environment but such stressors are rarely present in laboratory studies.

Finally, the temporal characteristics of laboratory and operational situations tend to be quite different. Whereas military and industrial personnel frequently perform the same monitoring task repeatedly, day after day, laboratory subjects generally encounter the experimental task on one occasion only. Thus for laboratory subjects the task is novel, while for operators in military and industrial settings it has probably become overfamiliar. Nevertheless military and industrial operators have often been regarded as more highly motivated than laboratory subjects because they are working on real tasks in which errors can have serious consequences.

For a *task* classification system however, only the first of Mackie's categories, the task itself, is relevant, and the importance of the remaining two categories for the operational significance of vigilance research will be further discussed in Chapter 9. The types of operational vigilance tasks found in industrial and military environments are diverse and often quite job-specific, and we shall not attempt to provide a comprehensive classification system which would cover all such tasks. Nevertheless, in principle such a system could be formulated, and need not incorporate task dimensions that are fundamentally different from those that we have identified in our taxonomy for laboratory tasks. The task differences between operational and laboratory tasks outlined above involve for the most part differences in first or second order psychophysical factors, and not in basic task dimensions. In so far as any real-life job incorporates a "vigilance function", this aspect of the job can be analysed and classified in essentially the same way as an artificial laboratory task.

In this chapter, we have briefly surveyed a number of task dimensions which affect the information processing demands that different vigilance tasks may impose, and selected what seem to be the most important of these for inclusion in a preliminary classification of vigilance tasks. We have also considered two classes of psychophysical factors which appear to influence different measures of vigilance performance. The classification system for vigilance tasks can be used to answer questions about the task dimensions influencing criterion or sensitivity shifts; for example, it is employed in Chapter 5 in an attempt to specify the conditions under which a sensitivity decrement occurs. First, however, measures of criterion and sensitivity changes, and their relevance to vigilance performance need to be analysed in more detail; this is our purpose in Chapter 3.

Chapter 3

Decision Theory and the Analysis of Vigilance Performance

Performance in vigilance tasks is commonly assessed on the basis of the number of correct detections of signals made by the observer in a given period of time. Several other performance measures, such as the false alarm rate and reaction time, have also been employed, but the detection rate has generally been considered to provide an index of the level of vigilance or sensitivity of the observer. From the perspective of decision theory, however, the detection rate alone does not provide a pure measure of sensitivity, because it reflects both the detectability of the signal and the bias of the observer in responding positively to stimulus events. For example, an observer who is unable to detect signals can nevertheless achieve an extremely high detection rate if he always responds positively; of course he will then also make a number of false alarms. On the other hand, a competent but cautious observer may have a much lower detection rate while at the same time making fewer false alarms. Which observer is the better performer? Clearly, in assessing these performances, both the detection and the false alarm rate need to be taken into account using measures which separate detectability and bias. The provision of such measures, and the separation and analysis of detection and decision processes in the performance of psychophysical tasks, was made possible by the development of Signal Detection Theory (Green and Swets, 1966). The original application of the theory to vigilance (Broadbent and Gregory, 1963b) enabled a similar distinction to be made in the analysis of vigilance.

This chapter outlines a number of aspects of Signal Detection Theory (SDT), as viewed in the context of statistical decision theory. Such an approach involves more than just the routine calculation of SDT parameters such as d' and β. ROC curves and parametric and nonparametric indices of detectability and bias are examined and an account is given of a method for analysing response latency data within a decision theory framework. Finally, the advantages and limitations of SDT for the description of vigilance phenomena are considered.

The representation of detection performance

Signal detection theory has provided a number of techniques for the analysis of detection behaviour in psychophysical tasks (Green and Swets, 1966). Detection performance in vigilance tasks may be analysed in a similar way, given certain qualifications, as discussed later in this chapter. In the usual detection task, the observer is presented with one out of a set of n_s stimuli, and is required to make one of n_r responses. Generally, $n_s = n_r = 2$, and the observer is exposed to either signal (s) or noise (n), and required to respond appropriately (for example Yes or No, or S or N). A general proposition of decision theory is that the observer chooses between the alternative responses on the basis of some *decision rule*.

Various decision rules can be identified, but generally rules which minimize error are considered. In a two-choice detection task, two sorts of errors can be made, a false alarm or Type I error, and an omission or Type II error. The trade-off between reducing one type of error at the cost of increasing the other can be examined in a plot of $p(S/s)$ against $p(S/n)$, where $p(S/n)$ is the probability of a false alarm (Type I error) and $p(S/s)$ is the probability of a correct detection (probability of not making a Type II error). Laming (1973) has shown that all such pairs of points form a convex set within the unit square (1, 1), and that they represent the totality of decision rules for choosing between two alternatives (see Fig. 3.1). The upper bound of the

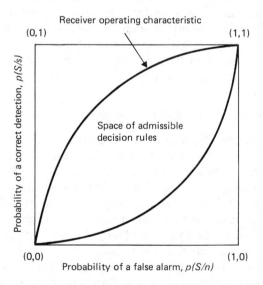

Fig. 3.1. Representation of the totality of decision rules for the making of statistical decisions. The only rules which cannot be improved upon are those lying on the upper bound of the convex set, or Receiver Operating Characteristic. After Laming (1973, p. 70).

convex set is called the Receiver Operating Characteristic (ROC; also called the Relative Operating Characteristic, after Swets, 1973).

Laming (1973) and Egan (1975) have described several properties of the ROC, given various theoretical distributions of the representation of signal and noise events. One important property is that the ROC is generally *monotonic* for certain broad classes of distribution (see Thomas, 1973); that is, for any ROC curve, any value of $p(S/s)$ can be associated with only one value of $p(S/n)$, and vice versa. A second property of the ROC is its invariance under any monotonic transformation of the "evidence" axis, which represents the continuum along which signal and noise events are represented probabilistically. Signal detection theory, for example, assumes that the "evidence", given signal or noise events, can be represented by normal (Gaussian) probability distributions; this latter property of the ROC implies that any monotonic transformation of the evidence axis for these distributions will have no effect on the ROC. (Thus the same ROC can be associated with a number of "underlying" distributions if these are related to each other monotonically.) It follows therefore that it is not necessary to assume, *a priori*, a specific form for the distributions in order to carry out a decision theory analysis. It is possible, for example, to use measures of performance based on the ROC which do not depend on the form of the "underlying" distributions; these "nonparametric" measures are described later. On the other hand, it is possible, as with signal detection theory, to make certain assumptions about the underlying decision process to enable the derivation of certain "parametric" performance indices such as d′ and β. Each of these types of approach are consistent with a decision theory analysis. The analysis of detection behaviour and its representation in the ROC thus provides a general means of evaluating performance in vigilance tasks.

Elements of signal detection theory

Theoretical approaches to the analysis of detection performance commonly assume the existence of "internal states" in the observer which serve a mediating function between stimulus and response. Differences between various detection models arise principally from considerations of the nature and representation of these states. In SDT the internal states are assumed to form a unidimensional continuum, represented probabilistically by a normally distributed random variable. Normal probability density functions of the "evidence" given either signal or noise events are shown in Fig. 3.2.

Signal detection theory provides a technique for obtaining separate measures of detectability, and of the decision criterion, which indexes response bias (the terms detectability, discriminability and sensitivity are used interchangeably throughout, although strictly one should refer to the detectability of the signal, the discriminability of a pair of stimuli, and the sensitivity of the observer). Both measures are based on the conditional probabilities of correct detections, ($p(S/s)$, and false detections, ($p(S/n)$. The ROC, which is a plot of pairs of these probabilities, indicates a given level of detectability and the balance achieved between correct and false responses with different degrees of bias. The detectability index d' is the difference between the means of the signal and noise distributions, scaled in units of the standard deviation of the noise distribution. When the two distributions have equal variance, it can be shown that:

$$d' = z(S/n) - z(S/s)$$

where $z(S/n)$ and $z(S/s)$ are the normal deviates corresponding to $p(S/n)$ and $p(S/s)$, respectively.

For example, suppose an observer has an 80% hit rate and a 5% false alarm rate for a given vigilance task. Thus $p(S/s) = 0\cdot80$ and $p(S/n) = 0\cdot05$. The normal deviates corresponding to these values are $-0\cdot842$ and $1\cdot645$, giving $d' = 1\cdot645 + 0\cdot842 = 2\cdot487$. Alternatively, d' can be obtained directly from tables provided by Freeman (1973).

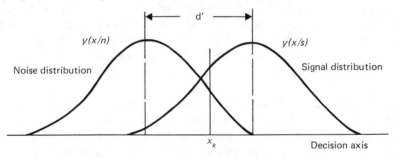

Fig. 3.2. Probability density functions of the evidence given stimulus events classified either as "signal" or "noise". In the simplest form of Signal Detection Theory, the signal and noise distributions are assumed to be of equal variance. The choice of the criterion at X_k determines the correct detection $p(S/s)$ and false alarm $p(S/n)$ probabilities.

The decision criterion may be placed anywhere along the evidence or decision axis x, and any one value, say x_k, is associated with a likelihood ratio $(y(x/s)/y(x/n))_k$ where y represents the ordinate (probability density) of the distributions. The likelihood ratio represents the odds favouring the presence of a signal. The observer is assumed to respond positively whenever the likelihood ratio exceeds some criterion value (β) and to respond negatively otherwise. The criterion thus defines the degree of bias towards responding positively to signals. β can be calculated by obtaining the ratio of the ordinates corresponding to the normal deviates of the hit and false alarm probabilities; the ordinate values for the response probabilities in the preceding example are $0\cdot280$ and $0\cdot103$ respectively. Hence $\beta = 0\cdot280/0\cdot103$

$= 2\cdot718$. Like d', β can also be obtained more directly by entering the hit and false alarm probabilities in tables such as those provided by Freeman (1973).

The decision criterion may be chosen so as to optimize different decision goals, and in practice it will be determined by the *a priori* probability of the signal and the trade-off between correct and false responses that the observer chooses. Green and Swets (1966) have shown that a number of such goals, such as maximizing expected value, minimizing the probability of a false detection, and so on, can each be expressed in terms of likelihood ratio. The decision goal most commonly considered is the maximization of expected value; it can be shown that in this case the optimum decision criterion is:

$$\beta_{opt} = \frac{1-p}{p} \cdot \frac{V_{N/n} - V_{S/n}}{V_{S/s} - V_{N/s}},$$

where p is the signal probability and V represents the costs attached to the different stimulus-response outcomes. For a symmetrical payoff, that is, $V_{S/s} = V_{N/n}$, and $V_{S/n} = V_{N/s}$, β_{opt} reduces to $(1-p)/p$. A consistent result from empirical studies of detection and vigilance performance is that the decision criterion used by the observer (β) is correlated with the optimal β specified by the above equations, although observers usually behave conservatively and use criteria that are less extreme than the optimal values (see Swets, 1977).

Some investigators have interpreted this finding as suggesting that detection behaviour is not compatible with a likelihood ratio rule but reflects instead a probability matching strategy in which the frequency of positive (Yes) responses is matched to the *a priori* signal probability (p) when the payoff matrix is symmetrical (Parks, 1966; Thomas and Legge, 1970), that is,

$$p(\text{Yes}) = p(S/s) \cdot p + p(S/n) \cdot (1 - p) = p$$

The non-optimality of decision criteria (that is, $\beta < \beta_{opt}$ when $\beta > 1$, and $\beta > \beta_{opt}$ when $\beta < 1$ is a specific prediction of the probability matching hypothesis. Partial support for the hypothesis has been provided by data from recognition studies (Craig, 1976; Tanner *et al.*, 1967). However, Dusoir (1974) found that there are large deviations from the hypothesis in the data of individual subjects performing detection tasks, and that response frequency is not constant over different detectability levels, as implied by the hypothesis. Thomas (1975) has proposed some modifications of the original model of Thomas and Legge (1970) which can account for deviations from probability matching, but the elegance and simplicity of the original hypothesis is then lost.

Systematic variations in the decision criterion generate different pairs of the "operating" probabilities $p(S/s)$ and $p(S/n)$ and map out the ROC curve. In SDT, if equal variance distributions for signal and noise are assumed, the form of the ROC is as displayed in Fig. 3.3 (a, b). When plotted in the unit square, the ROC is a bow-shaped function which is symmetrically placed about the negative diagonal (Fig. 3.3 (a)), and a straight line when plotted on double probability axes, or in z space (Figure 3.3 (b)). Each point on the ROC is associated with a particular degree of bias. If the observer is cautious about reporting the presence of a signal his behaviour is represented by points in the lower left part of the ROC. If he is less cautious, $p(S/s)$ and $p(S/n)$ increase and the observer "operates" at higher points along the ROC. Each ROC however represents a single level of detectability over a range of decision criteria. Different values of d' are associated with a family of ROC curves radiating outward from the positive diagonal (which corresponds to $d' = 0$).

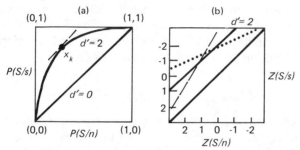

Fig. 3.3. (a) Receiver Operating Characteristic (ROC) for the case where signal and noise distributions have equal variance. The slope of the ROC at X_k is equal to the likelihood ratio at the criterion; (b) the same ROC (solid line) is shown replotted in z space, or double probability (normal deviate) axes. The dotted line shows an ROC for the case where signal variance is greater than noise variance (ROC slope less than 1). The dashed line shows an ROC for the case where signal variance is less than noise variance (ROC slope greater than 1). The convention adopted for the P to Z transformation is: $0 \geqslant Z \geqslant 0$ for $0 \cdot 5 \leqslant P \leqslant 0 \cdot 5$. This convention is followed throughout the book.

The situation is somewhat different if the underlying distributions do not have the same variance. Detectability and bias measures cannot now be estimated from a single pair of operating probabilities, since there are four free parameters (the two means and the two variances) compared to only two in the equal variance case. The ROC with unequal signal and noise variances is skewed, that is, it is asymmetrical about the negative diagonal. On double probability plots (or plots in z space), the ROC is a straight line with a slope equal to the ratio of the standard deviation of the noise distribution to the standard deviation of the signal distribution (σ_n/σ_s). Two corollaries follow from this: if signal variance (σ_s^2) is greater than noise variance (σ_n^2) the ROC slope is less than 1, while if noise variance is greater than signal variance the ROC slope is greater than 1. Double probability plots of asymmetrical ROCs ($\sigma_s \neq \sigma_n$) are shown in Fig. 3.3(b). Thus the slope of an *empirical* ROC provides an indicator of any deviance from the equal variance assumption.

The measurement of detectability and bias in the unequal variance case is less straightforward than in the equal variance case. Taylor (1967) has shown how ROCs in vigilance often conform to the unequal-variance SDT model, so that there may be distortions in the absolute values of d' and β calculated on the assumption of equal variance. However maximum likelihood techniques can be used to derive estimates of the separation of the distributions and the variance ratio (for example, Abrahamson and Levitt, 1969; Grey and Morgan, 1972). It is then possible to derive detection parameters such as d_e and d_a, which are less sensitive to deviations from the equal-variance assumption. Nonparametric indices, in which no particular form for the detection model is assumed, provide a further alternative. But the provision of a reliable index of bias is difficult, and no completely satisfactory measure is currently available, as discussed further below.

Empirical receiver operating characteristics

Empirical ROCs may be derived using two general procedures, the binary or Yes/No task, and the rating task, in which observers are required to register their confidence using one of a number of categories comprising the rating scale. A third general procedure, the forced choice task, is used to provide a relatively pure measure of detectability only, there being little concern with the observer's decision criterion (at least, for psychophysical tasks). It is generally of interest in vigilance studies only when appropriate detectability levels have to be accurately established between different conditions (for example, in the "calibration" of task difficulty).

The Yes/No procedure is the one most similar to that traditionally used in vigilance experiments. It provides data from which a single pair of operating probabilities may be estimated from the relative frequencies of correct and incorrect detections over a block of trials. The ROC then may be mapped out by inducing observers to adopt different degrees of response strictness ("lax", "moderate", "strict", etc.) in different blocks or sessions. It may also be derived by asking the observer to maximise expected value and by varying either the *a priori* signal probability or the costs and values attached to response outcomes.

The rating task is more efficient at deriving ROCs in the sense that for a q-point ROC only T trials are needed with a rating scale having q or $q + 1$ categories, while qT trials are needed with the Yes/No method. For example, 100 trials of signal and noise events with subjects having to respond to each event using a 4-category rating scale will enable a 3-point ROC to be plotted. With the Yes/No method, the same 3-point ROC will require that 100 trials be run in each of 3 conditions (300 trials in all) varying in the degree of response bias which the subject is induced to adopt (for example, by instructions, or by varying signal probability). With the rating method, ROC points are obtained by cumulating the hit and false alarm probabilities over successive categories of the rating scale, beginning with the highest category of confidence towards signal presence. For instance, with a 4-category rating scale (for example, "sure signal", "fairly sure signal", "fairly sure nonsignal" and "sure nonsignal"), successive ROC points are obtained from the cumulative hit and false alarm probabilities corresponding to (1) "sure signal", (2) "sure signal" + "fairly sure signal", and (3) "sure signal" + "fairly sure signal" + "fairly sure nonsignal". Cumulating over all four categories provides no extra information, since these probabilities will sum to the *a priori* probabilities of signal and noise events. Thus, if both signals and non-signals have to be responded to, a q-point ROC requires a $q + 1 -$ category rating scale. Alternatively, as in many vigilance tasks, subjects may be required to respond to signals only, in which case the number of ROC points equals the number of rating categories (for example, the categories "sure", "fairly sure" and "unsure" may be used).

While the rating method is more efficient than the Yes/No method from the point of view of the number of trials required to derive the ROC, it is unclear whether it yields equivalent ROCs and values of detectability. Some studies report no differences between Yes/No and rating ROCs (Emmerich, 1968; Nachmias, 1968; Swets, 1959) but others do (Clarke and Mehl, 1973; Markowitz and Swets, 1967; Weitzel and Dobson, 1974). Markowitz and Swets (1967) found ROC slope differences between normalized Yes/No and rating ROCs which they attributed to contamination from the variation of signal probability in the Yes/No method. Since ROC slope has been reported to vary with changes in signal probability (Schulman and Greenberg, 1970), a result inconsistent with the equal-variance assumption, Craig and Colquhoun (1975) therefore advised against the uncritical use of d' in the analysis of vigilance performance. This result is not generally obtained with vigilance tasks however (see Chapters 4 and 5). Moreover, the sensitivity index d_e, which is described below, was found to be invariant with changes in slope and signal probability in both the Schulman and Greenberg (1970) and Markowitz and Swets (1967) studies. Thus the rating method may be regarded as robust so long as detectability measures other than d' are considered as alternatives.

These results indicate the need for a disciplined use and interpretation of measures of detectability, irrespective of whether the Yes/No or the rating task is employed. The available evidence indicates that the two methods provide similar values of detectability in vigilance situations.

Guralnick and Harvey (1970) obtained similar Yes/No and rating d' values for a vigilance task. Parasuraman (1976a) compared rating, binary (Yes/No), and single (Yes) response modes and obtained similar detectability values, with performance being almost identical for the binary and single response modes (the mode of response "traditionally" employed in vigilance tasks). The Yes/No task is superior to the single response requirement task in that it enables the measurement of latencies associated with all four stimulus response outcomes. This provides important additional data relevant to the evaluation of decision theory and other theoretical approaches to vigilance. However, a choice between the Yes/No and rating methods depends on the relative weighting of their merits in a particular experimental situation, and, to a certain extent, on personal preference.

The measurement of detectability and bias

In the equal variance version of SDT, a reliable measure of detectability is readily available in d'. A number of other indices may be used, however, when the assumptions regarding the probabilistic representation of stimuli are not met in a given situation, or when any assumptions about the underlying detection process are to be avoided because they cannot be adequately tested. In the latter case, the best so-called nonparametric index is the area under the empirical ROC, $p(A)$. Table 3.1 lists a number of parametric and nonparametric indices of detectability.

Of the parametric alternatives to d', the index d_e is often used; it is defined as twice the ordinate of the ROC at the point where it intersects the negative diagonal. The justification for the index derives from the association of the negative diagonal with unbiased (chance) performance (Egan and Clarke, 1966), and, as noted previously, its virtue lies in its invariance with changes in ROC slope. Simpson and Fitter (1973) have proposed that their index d_a, which is proportional to the orthonormal distance of the ROC from the origin, is the best parametric alternative to d'. Simpson and Fitter appear to have considered three criteria for the "best" detectability index:

(1) it should be equivalent to the best nonparametric index, $P(A)$;

(2) it should be related monotonically to $P(C)$, the bias-free index available from the forced choice procedure;

(3) it should reduce to d' when signal and noise variances are equal.

d_a is proportional to the index D_{YN} of Schulman and Mitchell (1966). By restating Green's (1964) theorem, which proves the equality of $P(A)$ and $P(C)$ and drawing on Schulman and Mitchell's finding that D_{YN} differs from its forced choice equivalent by the constant $\sqrt{2}$, Simpson and Fitter proved the equality of D_{YN} and the normal deviate of $P(A)$, thus arguing that D_{YN} was the only index meeting all three criteria. To maintain comparisons with the two-alternative forced-choice task, they suggested the

Table 3.1. Parametric and nonparametric indices of detectability. σ_s^2 and σ_n^2 are the variances of the signal and noise distributions, respectively. $p(S/s)$ and $p(S/n)$ are the probabilities of hits and false alarms, respectively, and $z(S/s)$ and $z(S/n)$ are the associated normal deviates.

Index	Source	Formulae and Notes
A. Parametric indices assuming normal distributions		
d'	Green and Swets (1966)	$z(S/n) - z(S/s)$; assumes $\sigma_s = \sigma_n$.
$D(d, \sigma_n/\sigma_s)$	Green and Swets (1966)	d is the horizontal intercept and σ_n/σ_s the slope of the ROC (plotted in z space), respectively.
d_e, d_s	Egan and Clarke (1966)	$2d/(\sigma_s + \sigma_n)$; d_e is twice the ordinate of the ROC at the equal bias point (negative diagonal).
D_{YN}	Schulman and Mitchell (1966)	$d/(\sigma_s^2 + \sigma_n^2)^{1/2}$; D_{YN} is the orthonormal distance of the ROC (in z space).
d_a	Simpson and Fitter (1973)	$\sqrt{2}d(\sigma_s^2 + \sigma_n^2)^{1/2}$; d_a is $\sqrt{2}D_{YN}$ (see text).
B. Nonparametric (*distribution free*) indices		
$P(A)$	Green and Swets (1966)	Area under the ROC.
$z(A)$	Simpson and Fitter (1973)	Normal deviate of $P(A)$.
$P(C)$	Green (1964)	Probability correct in two-alternative forced choice task (see text).
$P(\bar{A})$	Pollack and Norman (1964)	Estimate of $P(A)$ from single ROC point (see text). Can be computed from formulae given by Grier (1971): $$P(\bar{A}) = \frac{1}{2} + \frac{(y - x)(1 + y - x)}{4y(1 - x)}$$ where $x = p(S/n)$, $y = p(S/s)$.
$C, d(A, B)$	Hammerton and Altham (1971)	$C = (n - N)/(r - 1)$, where N and n are the number of ratings given to signal and noise events, respectively, and r is the total number of ratings. $d(A, B)$ reduces to $p(S/s) - p(S/n)$ when $r = 2$.
D_{AB}	Sakitt (1973)	$(i_n - i_s)/(\sigma_s\sigma_n)^{1/2}$; i_s and i_n are the mean ratings given to signal and noise events respectively.
E	Simpson and Fitter	$\sqrt{2}(i_n - i_s)/(\sigma_s + \sigma_n)^{1/2}$; equivalent to $z(A)$ and $P(A)$.

use of $\sqrt{2}D_{YN}$ or d_a. Although the stability of d_a has not been empirically tested (as for instance has d_e), its use is recommended, and recent vigilance studies have employed the index (Murrell, 1975; Parasuraman, 1976a, 1979). This index is derived from the ROC, and it may be calculated using the formula given in Table 3.1, once an estimate of signal variance has been obtained (for example, Grey and Morgan, 1972).

To calculate parametric detectability indices such as d_a therefore, an ROC curve has to be fitted to the available data points. This may be done by eye, but for greater accuracy, estimation procedures should be used. Since there are errors in the estimation of two variables (correct detection and false alarm probabilities), the usual curve fitting procedures (which consider errors in one variable only) cannot be used. However, a number of maximum likelihood estimation procedures for ROC curve fitting are available (Abrahamson and Levitt, 1969; Dorfman and Alf, 1968; Grey and Morgan, 1972). To be capable of solution such procedures must specify a form for the underlying distributions; usually normal or logistic distributions are assumed. Grey and Morgan (1972) reported detectability estimates from data taken from performance on a vigilance task using such a procedure The estimates had large variances due largely to the low relative frequency of false alarms in the data. For this reason, it may not be necessary to use these relatively sophisticated procedures for the "noisy" data typically obtained in vigilance studies, when, for example, false detection probabilities may be estimated from a frequency of 2 or 3 in 200 or 300 trials. The reliable estimation of false alarm probability in vigilance is a particularly difficult problem for a decision theory analysis, as discussed later. When relatively more reliable data are available, however, the maximum likelihood techniques are useful for deriving bias-free parametric detectability indices, and Grey and Morgan's (1972) program is probably the easiest to use as well as being the most widely available.

Table 3.1 lists a number of nonparametric detectability indices. As already noted, the area under the ROC, $P(A)$, is the best available index. However its computation may be difficult in practice, particularly in vigilance, where the ROC is usually restricted to a small portion of the unit square, or only one point in the ROC is available. Pollack and Norman (1964) outlined a method for estimating $P(A)$ from a single pair of operating probabilities. The ROC passing through a single operating point is constrained to pass through certain regions (U1 and U2 in Fig. 3.4) since it is an iso-sensitivity curve. A rough estimate of $P(A)$ can then be taken as the mean area below U1 and U2, or $P(\bar{A})$. While this analysis is approximate, and assumes that ROCs may not cross ("skewed" ROCs may in fact do so), it does illustrate that information regarding sensitivity can be gained from even a single operating point, more so than by considering detection probability alone, which is the "traditional" way of measuring sensitivity in vigilance. Grier (1971) has given computing formulae for $P(\bar{A})$, and recent vigilance studies have utilized both $P(\bar{A})$ and $P(A)$, the latter index being used to verify results obtained with d' (Harkins and Geen, 1975; Sostek, 1976, 1978).

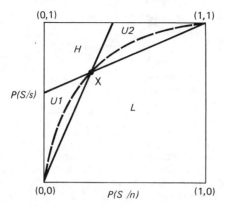

Fig. 3.4. The regions (U1 and U2) within which a symmetric ROC passing through a single operating point *X* must lie. The regions *H* and *L* represent the space of ROCs associated with higher or lower levels of detectability, respectively. The dashed curve indicates the possible shape of the ROC passing through *X*, assuming equal signal and noise variance. After Pollack and Norman (1964).

Other nonparametric indices include C and $d(A, B)$, which are based on the average ratings given over a block of trials to signal and noise events (Altham, 1973; Hammerton and Altham, 1971). The indices D_{AB} (Sakitt, 1973) and E (Simpson and Fitter, 1973) are similarly defined, except that they are scaled to the geometric mean and root mean square of the signal and noise standard deviations, respectively. Both D_{AB} and E are superior to C and $d(A, B)$, with E being the better index since it is directly related to both $P(A)$ and d_a. The problem with C and $d(A, B)$ is that each index reduced to the difference between correct and false detection probability when the number of ratings is two (that is, Yes/No). The ROC thus describes a quite specific form in the unit square, $C = p(S/s) - p(S/n)$, which is a straight line. Altham (1973) presented vigilance data showing that C was monotonically related to d'. However, C does not measure the same thing as d'. There will be conditions when C will vary and d' is constant; this is usually the case across time blocks in vigilance. The use of C will almost always indicate a decline in sensitivity whereas d' and other measures generally will not do so. Figure 3.5 shows vigilance data for two subjects and indicates that d' and d_a index no loss in sensitivity over time, while there is a steady decline in C.

Table 3.2 lists some indices of response bias which have been used in the literature. Compared to indices of detectability, considerably less effort has been invested in the development of a reliable index of response bias.

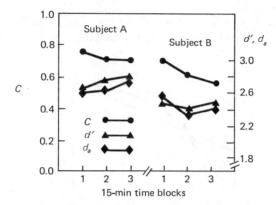

Fig. 3.5. Performance as assessed by three measures of detectability (C, d' and d_a) in consecutive 15-minute time blocks of a 45-minute auditory vigilance task. Data for two subjects are shown. In both subjects C declines steadily with time on task while there is little decrement for d' or d_a. From Parasuraman (1976a).

Table 3.2. Some indices of response bias. $p(S/s)$ and $p(S/n)$ are the probabilities of hits and false alarms, respectively, $z(S/s)$ and $z(S/n)$ are the associated normal deviates, and $y(S/s)$ and $y(S/n)$ are the corresponding ordinates. σ_s is the standard deviation of the signal distribution.

Index	Source	Computing formulae	Notes
β	Green and Swets (1966)	$y(S/s)/y(S/n)$	y is the ordinate of the normal distribution.
c	Green and Swets (1966)	$z(S/n)$	Criterion cut-off.
β'	McNichol (1972)	β/σ_s	σ_s is taken as the inverse ROC slope.
B	McNichol (1972)	Rating point at which $p(S/s) + p(S/n) = 1$	
B_I	Ingham (1970)	$z(S/s) + z(S/n)$	
B_H	Hodos (1970)	$1 - x(1 - x)/y(1 - y)$ for $B_H < 1$ $y(1 - y)/x(1 - x) - 1$ for $B_H > 1$ $x = p(S/n)$, $y = p(S/s)$	Computing formulae from Grier (1971).

This is probably due to the fact that the ROC is an iso-sensitivity curve, from which a sensitivity index can be readily derived. Less straightforward, however, is the derivation of iso-bias curves from which bias indices may be derived. Dusoir (1975) has recently reviewed this area and concluded that none of the existing indices are entirely satisfactory, either for the case where equal variances are not obtained, or where a nonparametric index is desired.

The limitations of two of these indices are considered here by way of illustration.

McNicol's (1972) index B is defined as the mean rating category for which the observer is equally disposed towards responding positively or negatively, that is, the category for which $p(S/s) + p(S/n) = 1$. B suffers from the disadvantage that it provides only one measure of bias in the rating task, whereas one at each criterion (confidence) level is desirable. Further, the value of B depends on the number of rating categories, so that comparisons across different rating tasks are difficult; there will also be a tendency for the estimate of B to improve as the number of categories increases. A final drawback is that it is difficult to compute B when bias is such that the median value of B lies outside the rating range (that is, when $p(S/s) + p(S/n) > 1$ at category 1, or < 1 at category n).

Hodos (1970) reported an index purporting to be a nonparametric measure of bias. Taking the negative diagonal as the line of zero bias, the index B_H is based on the relative displacement of a single operating point from this line. The index cannot be recommended since:

(1) it makes no reference to a sensitivity index to which it is orthogonal;

(2) it is not nonparametric because it yields iso-bias contours specific to the type of detection model assumed (the most obvious divergence is between SDT and simple threshold theory);

(3) for operating points below the leading diagonal, B_H cannot be used, although such points are compatible with the unequal-variance SDT model.

The relative neglect of iso-bias functions probably accounts for the current lack of a reliable bias index. It may be also the case that with a change in detectability, a given bias index may be affected in different ways depending upon the variable which shifts detectability. This suggests three partial solutions, none entirely satisfactory, which may be employed. First, a set of bias parameters may be used instead of a single index (Dusoir, 1975). Second, it may be useful to examine both the criterial likelihood ratio β and the criterial cut-off c, or $z(S/n)$, in analysing bias changes. Finally, if response latencies are available, they may also provide covariates of decision criteria, as discussed below.

Response latencies

The time an observer takes to respond to a signal provides an additional index of performance which is sometimes used in studies of vigilance. Usually response times are measured only when correct detections are made. Davies and Tune (1970) have described the role of correct detection latency in vigilance tasks:

> In vestigators who have collected data on detection rate and reaction time in tasks with transient signals have generally been interested in within-session

changes in reaction time. If some central process called vigilance can be considered to be mediating performance at vigilance tasks, and if changes both in the level of signal detection and in reaction time can be thought of as reflecting changes in the level of vigilance, then there should be some correspondence between the two measures". (Davies and Tune, 1970, p. 15).

Buck (1966) reviewed a number of studies reporting both detection rate and detection latency, and found some evidence for an association between the two measures. He made a distinction between tasks with "transient" signals ("limited hold" tasks) and those where the signal remains present until detected ("unlimited hold" tasks), in which reaction time provides the only measure of performance. Tasks with weak, transient signals may be characterized as "data-limited" tasks (Norman and Bobrow, 1975), or tasks where the quality of the evidence received by the observer is relatively imperfect or unreliable. Signal detection theory has generally been most successfully applied to the analysis of response probabilities in such tasks (Guralnick, 1972; Swets; 1977; Williges, 1971). Parasuraman and Davies (1976) have outlined a method whereby SDT can be extended to the analysis of response latencies, thus enabling an interpretation of both detection and latency data in vigilance within the same framework.

In SDT, the observer is assumed to take a sample (an "observation") of the "evidence" presented by signal and noise events (Green and Swets, 1966). A decision is then made between response alternatives (for example, Yes or No) on the basis of a comparison of the likelihood ratio at the observation point (or some monotonic function of likelihood ratio) and a decision criterion. The closer the likelihood ratio is to the criterion, the less "evidence" the observer has on which to base his response. This suggests that response latency may be related to the relative strength of the evidence, or the relative distance of the observation point from the criterion. Thus, the shorter the distance between observation point and criterion, the weaker the evidence, and hence, the longer the response time.

The above arguments suggest that response latency is an inverse function of the distance of the observation point from the current decision criterion, assuming that the time taken to sample the evidence is small and invariant with changes in criterion. Such *fixed-sample* models have been considered in relation to latency data obtained in psychophysical tasks (Audley and Pike, 1965; Carterette *et al.*, 1965; Emmerich *et al.*, 1972; Kopell, 1976; Pike, 1973; Thomas and Myers, 1972), but they have generally been rejected in favour of alternative models. However, there are some reasons why a fixed-sample model may be appropriate for analysing latency data obtained in vigilance tasks. First, fixed-sample models appear particularly relevant to the analysis of data from tasks with transient signals (Gesheider *et al.*, 1968), while sequential decision models appear well able to handle data from tasks where performance can be improved by successive sampling of the input (Laming, 1968). Second, slower error responses are predicted by fixed sample models, whereas sequential decision models generally predict that errors have shorter latencies than correct responses (although, with some modifications, slower errors can also be explained in some cases; see Laming, 1968, 1973). Recent studies have indicated that errors, especially false detections, have consistently longer latencies than correct responses in vigilance tasks (Colquhoun and Goldman, 1972; Davies and Parasuraman, 1976; Davies and Tune, 1970, p. 17; Parasuraman and Davies, 1975, 1976). Third, fixed-sample models may account more successfully for latency data obtained in task situations where the discrimination required is a difficult one (Audley, 1973). As noted previously, this same requirement applies to the SDT analysis of response probabilities in vigilance.

A number of straightforward predictions can be made given the proposition that response latency is an inverse function of the "distance from criterion". (Parasuraman and Davies, 1976):

(1) With a shift to the right along the decision axis in the criterion (increase in strictness), mean Yes response latencies (correct detections and false alarms) increase, since, on average, Yes responses will be distributed nearer the criterion than before.

(2) At the same time, mean No response latencies (correct rejections and omission errors) decrease, since No responses will, on average, be distributed further away from the criterion than before.

(3) Both the above predictions hold only if the distance between the two underlying distributions remains constant with the criterion change (for example, if d' remains constant, in the equal-variance case).

(4) If detectability shifts, the predictions are dependent on whether the criterion shifts as well or not. With a loss in detectability, only the latencies associated with responses to signals will change, assuming that criterion position remains unchanged with respect to the mean of the noise distribution. For Yes responses (correct detections) the mean latency will increase, since correct detection responses will be distributed nearer the criterion as the signal distribution shifts left. For No responses (omission errors), the mean latency will decrease, as these responses will be distributed further from the criterion than before.

(5) If the criterion shifts with the change in detectability, the predictions for latency will depend on the direction of the shift, as in (1) and (2) above. If the criterion shifts to the right (for example, so as to keep criterial likelihood ratio constant), correct rejection latencies will decrease because the responses will be distributed further from the criterion, while false alarm latencies will increase. The predictions for latencies associated with responses to signals (correct detections and omission errors) are the same as in (4).

(6) A final prediction is that correct and incorrect responses have unequal mean latencies. If criterion placement is such that the probability of a

correct response is greater than that of an incorrect response, error responses will be distributed nearer the criterion and will have longer latencies than correct detections. For No responses, omission errors will have longer latencies than correct responses.

Parasuraman and Davies (1976) reported two experiments in which latency data from two visual vigilance tasks were analysed. In general, the above predictions were upheld, with minor deviations. The results of this study are examined in greater detail in Chapter 4.

Response time is the only directly available performance measure not only in the "unlimited-hold tasks" mentioned previously, but also in what are known as "free-response" tasks (Egan *et al.*, 1961). These are tasks in which signals appear randomly and not in well-defined observation intervals, the observer being free to respond at any point in time. Egan *et al.* (1961) outlined a method whereby probabilities of "hits" and "false alarms" could be estimated by examining the distribution of the latencies and rate of responses following a signal. They suggested that responses which immediately followed a signal were probably made to that signal, whereas responses which occurred several seconds after the signal were probably responses to "noise", that is, false alarms. Egan *et al.* found that the distribution of the response rate as a function of time after signal onset had the form shown in Fig. 3.6, and proposed that the area under the peak of this distribution was proportional to the hit probability, $p(S/s)$, and the area under the flat tail of the distribution was proportional to the false alarm probability, $p(S/n)$. By considering different response criteria, Egan *et al.* were able to generate ROC curves based on these detection probabilities and to obtain estimates of sensitivity. Watson and Nichols (1976) have extended this approach,

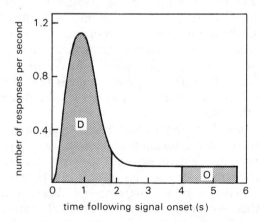

Fig. 3.6. Distribution of responses as a function of time following signal onset in a free-response task. Areas marked *D* and *O* are proposed as estimates of the "hit" and "false alarm" probabilities respectively. After Egan *et al.* (1961).

omitting the assumption made by Egan *et al.* that false alarms occur after a fixed (and arbitrary) delay following signal presentation (see the area marked O in Fig. 3.6). The method employed by Watson and Nichols assumes first that the total observation period can be divided up into imaginary *measurement* intervals containing either signal or noise and second that only the *first* response following a signal is in fact a response to that signal. The response rate to signals was estimated from the distribution of the reaction times of first responses, while the response rate to "noise" was estimated from the identically sampled distribution of latencies following measurement intervals containing only noise. Watson and Nichols applied their method to the estimation of d' and β values in a 30-min. free-response vigilance task. Their analysis indicated that d' remained relatively stable, but the β increased with time on task, a general result that will be encountered again in succeeding chapters.

Signal detection theory and vigilance: an appraisal

Signal detection theory has not undergone major revision since its original formulation in the context of the detection of weak auditory signals in noise (Peterson *et al.*, 1954; Tanner and Swets, 1954) although efforts have been made to emphasize the generality of the theory and the breadth of its application to various psychological phenomena (Swets, 1973). Vigilance provided one of the first areas of application outside psychophysics for the theory (Broadbent and Gregory, 1963b) but a number of authors have criticized the application of SDT to the analysis of vigilance behaviour (for example, Jerison, 1967a, 1977; Wiener, 1975). Their objections have been directed, in the main, at the appropriateness of particular SDT parameters such as d' and β for describing vigilance performance. However there still remains the primary issue of whether decision theory provides an adequate basis for studying discrimination and decision processes in vigilance. A separate issue is the question of whether certain assumptions needed to derive SDT parameters are violated in specific experimental situations. Both issues need to be examined in the context of vigilance. As Swets (1977) has pointed out, a distinction must be made between the postulates of a normative theory and the assumptions made in using that theory to study a real process—a distinction not often made by critics of the use of SDT in vigilance.

The role of "assumptions" in SDT is frequently misunderstood in discussions of the utility of SDT. For example, it has been incorrectly stated that the assumption of equal variance is "necessary" for the application of SDT (for example, Drury and Fox, 1975a). But the equal variance assumption is only necessary for the calculation of d' and not for the general application of the theory. Another misunderstanding of the role of SDT is implicit in the view of Hatfield and Soderquist (1970) that the assumptions of SDT are violated because d' is sometimes found to decline with time on a vigilance task. The logic of this erroneous view presumably stems from the fact that the first studies to use SDT found that the decrement was not associated with a decline in detectability but with an increase in the criterion (Egan *et al.*, 1961; Broadbent and Gregory, 1963b). However, SDT does not *require d'* to be invariant over time. As Swets (1977) has noted, SDT does not prescribe the observer's alertness, search patterns and memory processes, any of which could alter sensitivity over time.

While the above criticisms of SDT are inappropriate, the critique of SDT by Craig (1977) merits serious consideration. In an excellent and painstaking analysis of individual ROCs obtained in four vigilance studies, Craig attempted to evaluate the validity of the SDT model for vigilance. He examined the slopes of adjacent ROC segments in the unit square. Now the equal variance SDT model predicts bow-shaped ROC curves of monotonically decreasing slope as the criterion becomes less stringent. Thus the lower half of two adjacent segments of the ROC should have a greater slope than the upper half. Craig found that over 50% of the ROCs had monotonically decreasing slopes, while about 80% of the data was consistent with an unequal variance SDT model (in which slope need not be monotonically decreasing). Craig's paper highlights the importance of examining individual performance data before routinely calculating group d' values. Paradoxically, though, his analysis suggests that it may be hazardous to attempt to infer the nature of the underlying detection model on the basis of the ROC when it is restricted to such a small segment of the unit square. In the studies he analysed, false alarm probability ranged only up to about 0·05 or 0·10. The ROCs associated with different underlying detection models often do not differ so greatly in shape that they can be reliably distinguished given the typical resolution of data points obtained in psychophysical tasks. For example, it is often not possible to reject two-state low-threshold theory (R.D. Luce, 1963) in favour of SDT by examining an empirical ROC. Luce and Green (1974) have also shown how "mixed" strategies, and the influence of "non-sensory" internal states, can produce a curved SDT-like ROC even if the detection model is discrete and dichotomised rather than continuous. In vigilance, with a much lower reliability in the ROC points, distinguishing between models is even more difficult. Craig (1977) acknowledges this problem and the related one of non-occurring false alarms. Elsewhere he has also warned against the uncritical use of d' when there are many instances of zero false alarms, and more generally when ROCs have not been examined (Craig and Colquhoun, 1975).

The problem of zero false alarm rates has been dealt with in a number of ways. One solution is to estimate the maximum probability of a false alarm giving the likelihood of no such responses being observed in a given number (t) of non-signal trials. False alarm probability can then be estimated as $\text{Max}(p(S/n)) = 1 - 2^{-1/t}$ (Parasuraman, 1976a). Estimates of false alarm probability for different values of t are given in Table 3.3. If there are several such "blank" blocks, however, the derived detectability and bias indices will have large confidence limits, and any interpretations must be made cautiously (see also Macdonald, 1976). The related problem of assigning false alarms in the so-called free-response tasks (in which signal and noise events are not discretely defined) has been met by assuming an arbitrary decision interval (for example, Harkins and Geen, 1975). J.F. Mackworth (1965a) showed that while an assumed decision interval affected the absolute values of d', it had no significant influence on the trends in d' over a vigilance session (decision intervals ranging from $0 \cdot 17$–5 s were assumed). However, this procedure is still arbitrary, and does not permit a comparison across studies. Furthermore, its generality has not been demonstrated. A better approach is contained in the studies by Egan $et\ al.$ (1961) and by Watson and Nichols (1976), referred to above, in which it was shown that SDT indices could be calculated from response latency data alone.

$Table\ 3.3.$ Estimates of false alarm probability $(1 - 2^{-1/t})$ for different values of t, the number of "blank" non-signal trials during which no false alarms occur. Values of $1/t$ are also tabulated; this is the false alarm probability if one false alarm occurs in t trials.

Number of trials (t)	Estimate of false alarm probability $(1 - 2^{-1/t})$	Probability of one false alarm ($1/t$)
10	0·0670	0·1
50	0·0139	0·02
100	0·0069	0·01
200	0·0035	0·005
300	0·0023	0·0033
400	0·0017	0·0025
500	0·0014	0·0020

The problem of data reliability is one which has been least examined in vigilance, and no completely satisfactory solution is available. It does mean, however, that a degree of caution is called for in interpreting parameters derived in instances where error probability is very low. Nevertheless, it is our view that these problems do not bring into question the general usefulness of SDT, and that a closer examination of specific assumptions and limitations can enable a positive assessment of its merits to be made. These assumptions will include those inherent to statistical decision theory, as well as those needed for the application of SDT in psychophysics and vigilance.

Statistical decision theory presumes that a rational observer uses decision rules to achieve decision goals in specific contexts. Some assumptions regarding these rules and goals may be listed as follows:

(1) The observer partitions the elements of the set of "evidence" into response classes on the basis of a decision rule.

(2) The decision rule is used to satisfy some goal, such as the minimization of error.

(3) If the subject has at his disposal two decision rules P and Q such that P better satisfies a goal than Q, he consistently chooses P unless otherwise instructed.

(4) The decision rules and goals inferred from actual behavioural data bear a relation to those used by the subject.

(5) Decision goals do not fluctuate from trial to trial.

Assumptions specific to the application of SDT:

(1) The "evidence" received by the observer can be represented unidimensionally.

(2) The probability density distributions of signal and noise are Gaussian.

(3) The criterion used by the subject does not vary from trial to trial in a given block of trials.

(4) The subject has a clearly marked decision interval in which signal or noise may occur.

(5) The amount of sensory information received by the subject is limited.

Having simply stated these assumptions, their implications for the role of SDT in vigilance can be examined. It is evident that in certain experimental contexts, some of these assumptions will be met, while others may be questioned, and the rest will be of no consequence. As far as statistical decision theory is concerned, probably the only ones that may be seriously questioned are assumptions (4) and (5), regarding the equivalence of inferred decision rules to those actually used, and the invariance of decision goals. It will be recalled that it has been suggested that subjects do not use the likelihood ratio decision rule but behave instead in accordance with a probability matching rule (Thomas and Legge, 1970); but, as noted earlier, there are difficulties for this model in detection tasks.

The assumption of limited sensory information implies a fixed-sample model of decision making, as in SDT. If the available information is not limited, then performance need not lie within the convex set shown in Fig. 3.1. This assumption is almost certainly not valid for the so-called unlimited-hold tasks, where the signal remains present until detected (Broadbent, 1958), but may be considered to hold for "data-limited" vigilance tasks with weak, transient signals.

Apart from being a fixed sample model, SDT is also a fixed criterion model. Variations in the criterion are only considered across conditions where there are grounds to assume a change in response bias, such as across different signal probability levels. Recently, however, some investigators have considered the effects of trial-to-trial variability in the criterion in an SDT context (Ingleby, 1968; Thomas, 1973; Thomas and Myers, 1972). Ingleby (1968) showed that the effect of criterion variance is to increase signal and noise variability, so that apparent decreases in sensitivity may be obtained. Broadbent and Gregory (1967) put forward such an interpretation for their findings that subjects have decreased sensitivity to emotionally toned words. Thomas and Myers (1972) have also discussed the influence of criterion variance on the ROC, but on the whole this has received little attention in the literature. Estimating criterion variance in an SDT model is difficult since another free parameter is introduced. Future theoretical work in this area may benefit from an examination of criterion shifts over time in vigilance tasks in relation to detection models which allow the criterion to vary from trial to trial.

The role of assumptions in the application of SDT to vigilance is one which needs to be continually evaluated. It is evident that the marriage of SDT and vigilance is not a perfect one, and that in certain situations some assumptions will not be met. Nevertheless, there do not appear to be too many fundamental inconsistencies. Perhaps too much is expected of the theory; as Swets has argued, "there is more to vigilance than discrimination and decision, so that SDT cannot offer a total explanation of vigilance effects" (Swets, 1977, p. 715). It does however, in our view, provide the basis for a more complete understanding of the processes underlying vigilance behaviour, and a better technique for analysis of performance than the "traditional" vigilance procedures.

Chapter 4

Criterion Shifts

The criterial level of response of an observer, that is, the value at which he does or does not report the presence of some signal in the environment, is an important determinant of detection performance in vigilance tasks. Usually it is found that the criterion increases with time spent at a task, and the association between the *criterion increment* and the *vigilance decrement* is now well established (Broadbent, 1971; Broadbent and Gregory, 1963b; J.F. Mackworth, 1970). Sometimes, however, the criterion may *decrease* with time, and a *vigilance increment* may result (Williges, 1973, 1976). The special conditions in which these different trends are observed are described later in this chapter. Both sets of results may be incorporated in the general statement that *temporal shifts* in the decision criterion influence changes in the detection level in vigilance tasks. This chapter is concerned with the description and interpretation of these criterion shifts, and their relevance to theories of vigilance.

The criterion increment

The observation that the vigilance decrement in correct detections over a session is usually also accompanied by a decrement in false detections suggests the possibility that a criterion shift, specifically a criterion increment, controls the trends in both these variables. This was first suggested by Howland (1958) and by Egan *et al.* (1961), and has been confirmed empirically in several studies since the original demonstration by Broadbent and Gregory (1963b).

They used two vigilance tasks, a visual task in which a brighter flash appearing on one of three flashing lights had to be detected, and an auditory were of a form predicted by signal detection theory, and that there was an increase in the decision criterion with time on task, with no change in sensitivity.

At about the same time as this study was published, however, J.F. Mackworth and Taylor (1963) reported finding a significant decrement in sensitivity (d') over an hour-long vigilance session. They used the Continuous Clock Task, a task in which brief cessations in the continuous movement of a pointer traversing a clock face have to be detected. Thus two interpretations of the vigilance decrement are possible. The first, which has been the more widely held view, is that sensitivity is invariant over a session and that the decrement is associated with a criterion increment. The second view proposes that the decrement in detections is due to a genuine decrement in sensitivity over time. For some time these apparently conflicting views have posed a difficulty for a decision theory analysis of vigilance. Early studies by J.F. Mackworth (1965a, b) found that the sensitivity decrement was restricted to the particular visual task she used, but later other tasks, including auditory tasks, were found to be associated with this performance trend (Swets, 1976, 1977). An important requirement for the applicability of a decision theory analysis to vigilance therefore, was the specification of the types of task in which sensitivity decrements are obtained (Swets and Kristofferson, 1970). Using the taxonomic classification of vigilance tasks outlined in Chapter 2 Parasuraman and Davies (1977) have shown that it is possible to identify consistent types of task for which sensitivity decrements are obtained. Thus the vigilance decrement can be attributed to one of two underlying influences—criterion increment or sensitivity decrement—on the basis of the type of vigilance task involved, an approach which accommodates previous apparently conflicting results within a consistent decision theory model. The details of this analysis and a further discussion of sensitivity decrements are provided in Chapter 5.

Determinants of the decision criterion

In Chapter 3, a number of variables which influence the decision criterion in psychophysical tasks were mentioned. Among these are the *a priori* signal probability and the payoff matrix (that is, the costs attached to the different stimulus response outcomes). The decision criterion is also influenced by other experimental variables such as the instructions given to the subject. Furthermore, criteria of varying strictness can be associated with the different response categories when a confidence rating scale is used. Each of these determinants of the decision criterion has also been investigated experimentally in vigilance situations.

Time on task
This is a "variable" whose influence on the criterion in vigilance tasks has already been mentioned. The increment in the decision criterion with time on task is a well established finding (Binford and Loeb, 1966; Broadbent and

Gregory, 1963b; Loeb and Binford, 1964, 1968; Jerison *et al.*, 1965; Milosevic, 1969, 1975; Murrell, 1975; Taylor, 1965; Williges, 1969). Less well established, however, is the finding that the decision criteria corresponding to different categories of response (for example, as revealed by confidence ratings) show an unequal change over the monitoring period. This finding was first reported by Broadbent and Gregory (1963b, 1965), who found that while "strict" criteria (associated with confident responses) increased over the run, "risky" criteria (associated with less confident responses) remained unchanged, the implication being that there is an expansion in the scale of the "evidence" used by the observer with time at work (Broadbent, 1971). On the other hand, Milosevic (1974) reported time-related increases in both strict and risky criteria, for both visual and auditory vigilance tasks. In a second experiment, however, Milosevic (1975) found that while log β increased with time on task for both risky and strict criteria, only the change at the risky criterion proved to be significant, the opposite result to that obtained by Broadbent and Gregory. In the middle ground are the results of Levine (1966), Loeb and Binford (1964) and Parasuraman (1976a), who found increases in criteria associated with each confidence level with time at work, but with risky criteria showing less change than strict criteria.

Criterion shifts may vary according to the particular values employed at the beginning of the vigilance session, and these are usually different in different studies; what are termed "lax" criteria in one study may correspond to "strict" or "medium" criteria in another, where the overall β values are lower. The lack of a sufficient number of studies reporting rating data, and the inherent unreliability of absolute values of β in vigilance tasks, prevent a formal analysis of the data to test this hypothesis. There is a general indication, however, that Broadbent and Gregory's (1963b) study, which is the only one reporting no increase in lax criteria, had generally lower β values than the other studies cited above. Thus the criterion increment may be observed only if the initial criterion values are high, or relatively "strict" to begin with.

Signal probability

Variations in the *a priori* signal probability lead to changes in the criterion, and the ROC may then be derived as outlined in Chapter 3. In vigilance, although the complete range of the ROC has not been spanned, it has generally been found that increases in signal probability lead to a relaxation of the decision criterion, while sensitivity is not significantly affected (Baddeley and Colquhoun, 1969; Broadbent and Gregory, 1965; Murrell, 1975; Parasuraman and Davies, 1976; Williges, 1971, 1973; see also Swets, 1977). In most of these studies criterion changes were evaluated using the index β, without reference to ROCs. Figure 4.1 shows ROC data from an auditory vigilance task used by Parasuraman (1976a). The group ROCs associated with different signal probability values define similar values of sensitivity; only the range of decision criteria is affected, criteria becoming less stringent with an increase in signal probability. Supporting evidence is provided by Parasuraman and Davies (1976), who found that with an increase in signal probability, the latencies of positive responses (correct and false detections) decreased, while those of negative responses (correct rejections and omissions) increased, indicating that the decision criterion became less stringent.

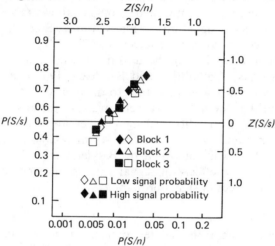

Fig. 4.1. Normalized group ROCs for each 15-min. time block of a 45-min. auditory vigilance task under conditions of high and low signal probability. From Parasuraman (1976a).

Generally any change in β with signal probability will be less than that normatively expected, given the basic SDT model. That is, if the payoff matrix is symmetrical, and the optimal β is taken as $(1 - p)/p$, where p is the signal probability, the change in β when signal probability changes from p_a to p_b may be found to be less than the optimal $(p_a - p_b)/(p_a p_b)$. Baddeley and Colquhoun (1969), for example, varied signal probability at five levels between 0·02 and 0·36, and found that although the empirical β values were not as extreme as the optimal β values, there was a perfect rank ordering between the two sets of values. This is a common finding in psychophysical studies (Green and Swets, 1966). It has also been obtained in several studies of industrial inspection. Drury and Addison (1973), for example, found that as the naturally occurring defect rate in an actual industrial inspection task changed, the inspector's response criteria changed appropriately, the correlation between the obtained and optimal values of β being 0·87. Similar findings for both simulated and real inspection tasks were reported by Smith and Barany (1970) and by Zunzanyika and Drury (1975).

Much evidence has been gathered to indicate that signal probability is an important determinant of the criterion level in vigilance tasks. The importance of this variable can be traced to the effects of *signal rate*, which is one of the earliest independent variables studied in relation to vigilance (see Davies and Tune, 1970). As noted in Chapters 1 and 2, several studies reported in the 1950s found that detection performance in vigilance tasks could be improved by increasing the signal rate. Baddeley and Colquhoun (1969) reviewed these studies and found them unsatisfactory for two main reasons. First, the rate of "unwanted" non-signal events was often varied at the same time as the signal rate in many studies. Second, pre-test expectancy was not controlled, since subjects received a low signal rate in the vigilance session after having been trained with inappropriately high signal rates (see also Colquhoun and Baddeley, 1964, 1967). Colquhoun (1961) suggested that it was important to distinguish between signals and non-signals and that the important factor was not the absolute signal rate, but the conditional probability of a signal given an event, which is related to both the signal and non-signal rates (see also Colquhoun, 1966a, and Jerison, 1966). This was confirmed by Baddeley and Colquhoun (1969), who showed that the effects of signal rate result from criterion shifts associated with changes in signal probability.

The payoff matrix

Central to decision theory is the view that decisions are influenced by the relative costs associated with different responses. In vigilance, there is some evidence that response probabilities are affected by costs and values, although as noted in Chapter 1, the results of experiments examining the effects of financial incentives on traditional measures of vigilance performance are not entirely consistent. Lack of consistency is also apparent in the results of studies which have investigated the effects of manipulation of the payoff matrix upon decision criteria in vigilance. Guralnick (1972), for example, found no differences in β between a symmetric and an asymmetric payoff condition and both Williges (1971) and Levine (1966) obtained weak or unexpected effects upon the decision criterion as a result of varying the payoff matrix. Williges factorially combined three payoff matrices, designed to encourage the adoption of "risky", "strict" or intermediate decision criteria, with two levels of signal probability and found that signal probability significantly influenced β while the payoff matrix did not. He also observed that the obtained β values corresponded more closely to the optimal β values based on signal probability alone than to those based on a combination of signal probability and the payoff matrix. Levine (1966) varied the costs attached to false alarms and omission errors and found, in contrast to Williges, that β increased as the costs attached to both kinds of error were increased. The finding that β increases even when the cost of missing a signal is raised is somewhat surprising from a decision theory point of view, since ideally a more risky criterion should be adopted.

However, Davenport (1968, 1969), employing first an auditory and subsequently a vibrotactile vigilance task (see Chapter 2) found that increasing the cost associated with false alarms exerted a significant effect on the false alarm rate, while increasing the cost associated with omissions did not, although it approached significance. Neither increasing the cost of errors nor the value associated with hits reliably affected detection rate. Davenport also reported d' and β values and although no tests of significance seem to have been conducted on these data it does appear from inspection of tabular values that β was higher when the cost of making a false alarm was greater than when the cost of an omission was greater, as would be expected on the basis of decision theory. Furthermore, when the costs attached to false alarms and misses were equated, β was higher when these costs were high than when they were low. In contrast d' appeared to be unaffected by any manipulation of the payoff matrix.

Sostek (1978), in an extremely well-conducted experiment, kept the value associated with hits constant and varied the cost attached to false alarms and omissions. He used an auditory version of the Bakan task (see Chapter 2) and examined the performance of three groups, the first two of which were encouraged to adopt either "risky" or "cautious" criteria as a result of manipulations of the payoff matrix, while the third acted as a control group and did not participate in the payoff system. Sostek's study is complicated by the fact that each group consisted of "labiles and stabiles", so classified in terms of various psychophysiological criteria (see Chapter 6). He found that log β was significantly lower for the "risky" group than for either of the other two groups but that while "labiles" modified their criterion, under different payoff conditions, "stabiles" did not. There was thus a reliable difference between the log β values of the "risky" and "cautious" groups for "labiles" but not for "stabiles". Sostek also found that for both parametric (d') and for nonparametric ($P(A)$) measures of sensitivity, sensitivity was significantly higher for the two payoff groups than for the control group. These results appear to be attributable to differential rates of decrement in sensitivity measures as a function of time on task. The control group exhibited a reliable decline with time in both sensitivity measures while the two payoff groups did not.

As is further discussed in Chapter 5, there is evidence that certain vigilance tasks, notably those with a high event rate which require successive discriminations, are uniquely associated with a reliable sensitivity decrement. The Bakan task used by Sostek is such a task and would thus be expected to show a sensitivity decrement under normal conditions, an expectation confirmed by his results for the control group. The significant effect of the payoff matrix on sensitivity can therefore be interpreted in terms of a reduction or abolition of the sensitivity decrement by the introduction of costs and values, rather than in terms of an overall effect upon the absolute level of sensitivity. Sostek's study seems to be the only one in which this type of task has been employed in conjunction with a payoff matrix; in other studies concerned with payoff either simultaneous discrimination or low event rate tasks have been used and a criterion increment with time at work has typically been reported, a result which Sostek did not obtain. Some of the cases where a reliable effect of payoff on the criterion has been obtained may also be due to an effect of the payoff matrix on the rate of criterion increment with time at work.

In summary, there is little doubt that payoff manipulations can produce effects on the criterion which are consistent with decision theory, even though they do not invariably do so. Failures to influence the observer's criterion by payoff manipulation have been noted both in laboratory studies, and, more importantly, in studies of industrial inspection (Smith and Barany, 1970). The results of such manipulations seem to be affected by task type and by individual and group differences. Payoff manipulations also appear to exert a weaker effect on criterion placement than does signal probability when both influences on the criterion are examined in the same experiment. It is not clear whether "stabiles", who seem to be relatively insensitive to manipulations of the payoff matrix in terms of criterion variation, are equally insensitive to changes in signal probability and this question merits further investigation. Swets (1977) observed that "we should expect more variability in the effects of values and costs on the decision criterion than in the effects of signal probabilities", since varying the payoff matrix "simply may not mean much in an idealized experiment in which points are later converted to fractions of cents, particularly if the prior probability is extreme" (p. 712). It would be useful, though, to see more experiments in which different potential influences on the decision criterion were combined and systematically manipulated.

Instructions and feedback

The ROC may be generated by asking observers to adopt different degrees of "strictness" in responding (bias) in different sessions. Colquhoun (1967) employed this method with a simulated sonar task. He instructed his subjects to report the occurrence of signals either (1) only when they were absolutely sure they had detected a signal, or (2) when they heard anything which might be a signal, however doubtful they were. Separate sessions were employed and, as predicted, the criterion was significantly lower in the "doubtful" condition, in which subjects made more responses (both detections and false alarms) than in the "absolutely sure" condition. Williges (1973) also found that if subjects were asked to be more or less "cautious" in different sessions, β shifted in the appropriate direction.

Knowledge of results (KR) is a form of feedback which has been found to improve detection rate in vigilance tasks (see Chapter 1), and much research has been carried out on the motivational and informational aspects of KR in vigilance (Annett and Paterson, 1967; Smith, 1966; Warm *et al.*, 1972). However, information on the influence of KR on decision processes in vigilance is meagre, and the effects reported are not very clear. Presumably effects on decision criteria alone should be obtained, but there are insufficient data to clarify this issue (Drury and Addison, 1973; Embrey, 1975; J.F. Mackworth, 1964a, 1970; Williges and North, 1972). J.F. Mackworth (1964a) also claimed that KR affects detectability, but this result has not been replicated with tasks other than the one she used.

Feedback in the form of artificial signals may also affect an observer's decision criterion. Although the evidence is equivocal, artificial signals have generally been found to improve detection performance (Davies and Tune, 1970). Since they serve to increase the apparent signal rate, it can be predicted that the introduction of artificial signals will serve to shift the decision criterion in a more "risky" direction. This was confirmed by Murrell (1975), the effect being a strong one, with the decrease in β being more extreme than that normatively expected on the basis of the SDT model. This result is one of the few obtained in vigilance running counter to the general view that the observer is "conservative" relative to an ideal observer (Green and Swets, 1966).

Response latencies and the decision criterion

Parasuraman and Davies (1976) have recently shown how a decision theory analysis can be used to interpret response latency data in vigilance. They reported two experiments which provide additional evidence for the view that criterion shifts play an important role in many aspects of detection behaviour in vigilance tasks. Before considering this evidence, however, an earlier and alternative model for response latencies in vigilance will be discussed (Buck, 1966). The model proposed by Buck sought to relate detection latency to detection rate in vigilance. In this model, the onset of the decrement in detection rate is determined by the relationship of the initial "vigilance level" to some critical level below which performance degradation occurs. The critical level is set by parameters such as signal intensity and duration. If the critical level is low, as in the so-called "unlimited hold" tasks, the decline in "perceptual vigilance" results in an increment in detection latency, but so long as the vigilance level exceeds the (low) critical level there is no decrement in detection rate. A decline in detection rate and an increment in latency only occur when the critical level is high, that is, when the signal duration is short or the signal is otherwise weak (as with transient signals).

Buck's model provides a reasonable conceptual framework for the interpretation of detection latency in "limited hold" monitoring tasks; and the significant negative correlation between detection rate and latency which is usually obtained lends some support to the notion of a common central process of "perceptual vigilance". However, the model does not make any provision for false detections, nor does it consider the latencies associated with other response categories (Davies and Tune, 1970, pp. 15–18). If, as in Buck's model, temporal changes in performance are assumed to be directly influenced by a decline in "perceptual vigilance", the latencies of all response categories should increase with time at work. That this is not the case was shown by Parasuraman and Davies (1976). Specifically, the latencies of both correct and incorrect rejections ("No" responses) either decrease or remain stable over the work period (see Fig. 4.2). At the same time, latencies of both correct and incorrect "Yes" responses increase with time on task. These results thus provide additional evidence for the view that the decision criterion increases with time at work, and that response latency is inversely related to the strength of the evidence received by the observer relative to the criterion level of evidence differentiating "Yes" from "No" responses. The relationship between response latency and the decision criterion was further examined by computing rank correlations between log β and the response latencies associated with all four categories of response. As expected, the correlations between log β and response latency were positive for "Yes"

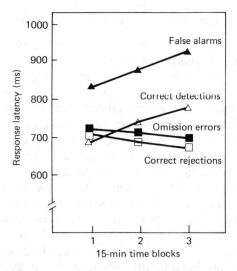

Fig. 4.2. Mean latencies of positive (correct detections and false alarms) and negative (correct rejections and omission errors) responses in consecutive 15-minute time blocks of a 45-minute visual vigilance task. After Parasuraman and Davies (1976).

responses and negative for "No" responses, the majority being statistically significant. Furthermore, with an increase in signal probability, which significantly reduced log β, "Yes" response latencies declined, while "No" response latencies increased. Both these sets of results are consistent with the decision theory model outlined above.

Further evidence for a relationship between response latency and decision criteria is provided by an experiment reported by Parasuraman (1976a) in which confidence ratings were used. As would be expected from a decision theory model, response latencies associated with intermediate confidence levels were higher than those associated with high confidence levels. Figure 4.3 shows that this pattern is maintained throughout a 45-minute vigilance task, for the four confidence ratings used (1, 2, 3 and 4 corresponding to "Sure Yes", "Not so sure Yes", "Not so sure No" and "Sure No"). Comparisons were also made between the mean latencies associated with the four stimulus response categories: detection latency (DL), false alarm latency (FAL), correct rejection latency (CRL) and omission latency (ML). These response latencies were related in the manner:

$$FAL > ML > DL \simeq CRL$$

where $>$ represents "significantly greater than" and $\simeq$ represents "not significantly different from". This relation is to be expected from a fixed-sample model (see Chapter 3), which predicts that if the placement of the decision criterion is such that the probability of a correct response is greater than that of an incorrect response the correct response latency will be shorter than the incorrect response latency.

A fixed-sample model does not consider variations in the time taken to gather the evidence with which a decision is made and changes in response

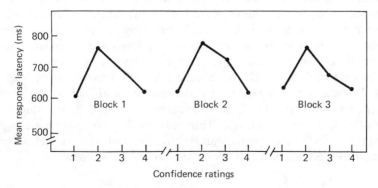

Fig. 4.3. Mean response latencies associated with different confidence ratings in consecutive 15-minute time blocks of a 45-minute auditory vigilance task. The ratings 1, 2, 3 and 4 correspond to "Sure—Yes", "Not so sure—Yes", "Not so sure—No" and "Sure—No" respectively. From Parasuraman (1976a).

time are assumed to be chiefly influenced by the time taken to decide between response alternatives. Broadbent (1973) on the other hand, has suggested that, as in a random walk model, the response latency may be related to the time taken to gather the evidence, which itself depends on the probability of the signal and the criterion level. This type of model may be fitted to some of the data obtained by Parasuraman (1976a), but, in its simplest form, the model faces the problem that it predicts equal latencies for correct and incorrect responses (see Laming, 1973, and Link and Heath, 1975, for exceptions), and the results outlined above clearly falsify this prediction (see also Colquhoun and Goldman, 1972).

Latency data obtained from confidence ratings (see Fig. 4.5) are also consistent with a fixed-sample model. The use of confidence ratings indicates that there is less movement over a session in risky criteria than in strict criteria. Broadbent (1975) therefore suggested that there should be similarly less change in latencies associated with less confident responses, if a fixed-sample model is valid; if a change in latency were obtained, then it has to be assumed that variations in input sampling rate do significantly affect the overall response latency. Although this test rests on the assumption that risky criteria do not change with time (which may be questioned), in any case Parasuraman (1976a) found no such changes in latency; he used a method of analysis similar to that used to construct latency operating characteristics (Norman and Wickelgren, 1969). Such an analysis showed that time on task had no effect on the latencies of responses "just clearing" the criterion (that is, less confident responses).

Although it does not appear necessary to consider an input sampling stage in the analysis of response latency for many types of vigilance task, it is fairly clear that such a stage has to be considered in tasks where signals are neither "weak" nor limited in duration. Here a two-process theory, combining a sequential sample stage with a subsequent decision stage, as suggested by Broadbent (1973, pp. 27–30), may be appropriate. Similar models have been examined in relation to latency data in recognition memory tasks, where attempts to interpret latencies in terms of strength theories extended from SDT have been relatively unsuccessful (Corballis, 1975). For data-limited vigilance tasks, however, and at a first level of analysis, a decision theory model of the type outlined by Parasuraman and Davies (1976) appears adequate. Thus it is possible to provide a complete description of vigilance performance, covering both speed and accuracy aspects of performance, within a common analytical framework.

The interpretation of criterion shifts

Evidence for the importance of criterion shifts has now been considered from various sources. Several variables which influence criterion placement in vigilance can be identified, such as signal probability, instructions, and costs and values. The most consistent results have been obtained with signal probability and time at work, both variables having significant but opposing effects on decision criteria (Baddeley and Colquhoun, 1969; Broadbent and Gregory, 1963b, 1965; Williges, 1973). Furthermore, signal probability is the only variable found to influence criterion *shifts* over a session; that is, for any measure of the criterion, signal probability interacts with time on task (Williges, 1971, 1973). Not surprisingly therefore, signal probability occupies a central role in interpretations of the criterion increment in vigilance. Several such interpretations have been proposed, and they are considered here in turn.

Expectancy and subjective probability

The role of expectancy was examined in one of the first theoretical papers on vigilance (Deese, 1955), and a number of other investigators have considered expectancy mechanisms in theoretical discussions of the vigilance decrement (Baker, 1959c; Broadbent, 1971; Davies and Tune, 1970; J.F. Mackworth, 1970; Warm, 1977). As noted in Chapter 1, Deese (1955) proposed that the course of events experienced by the observer during a vigilance task establishes a level of expectancy which in turn influences subsequent detection performance. Feedback from the task determines what the observer expects from further participation in the task in a simple proportional relationship, and vigilance performance varies accordingly. Deese's hypothesis implies that so long as the average frequency of signal occurrence remains low, expectancy for a signal remains low, but that as signal frequency is raised, expectancy also increases.

This suggests a role for expectancy in the interpretation of criterion shifts, if expectancy is related to apparent shifts in signal probability. Furthermore, evidence for an expectancy hypothesis, within a decision theory framework, has come from a number of experiments demonstrating the critical importance of the expectancies established during training sessions for vigilance tasks (Colquhoun and Baddeley, 1964, 1967; Williges, 1969). These experiments showed that, for both visual and auditory tasks, a greater within-session decrement in correct and false detections is observed if a training session using a high signal rate is given, than if a training session using a low signal rate appropriate to that used in the vigilance session is provided. The frequency of signals expected by subjects, which is established during training, exerts an important influence on within-session trends in performance. However, the relation between pre-task signal probability and performance may break down at extremely low event rates. Krulewitz and Warm (1977) employed an event rate of six per minute and found no effect of pre-task signal probability on detection rate, although decision theory measures were not used. But, in general, it appears that if subjects are trained with an inappropriately high signal rate, they find that signals occur much less frequently than they expected, and consequently revise their criteria towards greater strictness; this might therefore result in a sharp decline in both hits and false alarms and a rise in the criterion, as has been reported by a number of investigators. Colquhoun and his colleagues (Colquhoun and Baddeley, 1964, 1967; Craig and Colquhoun, 1975) suggest that a major part of the decrement observed in many vigilance studies is due to inappropriate expectancies developed in the pre-task period (see also McFarland and Halcomb, 1970).

It might therefore be supposed that if subjects were given appropriate training, and allowed to have practice sessions to stabilize their criterion, then there should be no increase in the criterion with time on task and no vigilance decrement. In fact, however, an increase in β is still found, even though subjects have been "expectancy matched" (Baddeley and Colquhoun, 1969; Broadbent, 1971; Milosevic, 1975; Parasuraman, 1976b, 1979; Parasuraman and Davies, 1976; Williges, 1973).

A "strong" form of expectancy theory can be postulated to account for these results. The essence of the argument is as follows. Signal probability is usually less than 0·5 in vigilance situations, and thus it may be assumed that a subject will respond positively less frequently than signals are in fact presented. This is because an observer behaving in accordance with an SDT model will set β near the value $(1 - p)/p$, where p is the signal probability, and will therefore have a response rate lower than the signal rate whenever p is less than 0·5. The subject who monitors his responses in a self-feedback loop will therefore underestimate the signal probability. Following Deese (1955), it can be proposed that this feedback will influence subsequent performance. The observer will revise his criterion to one of greater strictness appropriate to his (lower) estimate of signal probability. Revision of the criterion towards greater strictness will result in a lower hit and false alarm rate, leading to further upward revision of the criterion, and so on in a "vicious circle" (Baker, 1959c; Broadbent, 1971). Thus lowered expectancy related to lower subjective signal probability can be postulated to account for the rise in the criterion during a vigilance session. This explanation can also be applied to the finding that there is a greater increase in strict criteria over time than in risky criteria, if it is assumed that in a rating task the subject would be more likely to base his estimate of signal probability only on his confident (strict criterion) reports. The response rate for confident reports is usually less than the signal rate and thus an increase in the associated criterion is observed; less confident reports, however, may occur more frequently than signals are presented, which accounts for the fact that the associated (risky) criteria show less or no movement over the session (see Broadbent, 1971, p. 102).

One implication of the "vicious circle" expectancy approach is that an opposite trend in β over time should be observed if the *a priori* signal probability is greater than 0·5 (assuming that subjects over-respond initially). Broadbent (1971) considered this a crucial test of the expectancy approach, and, on the basis of an unpublished study by Simpson (1967), who obtained a within-session β increment even when signal probability exceeded 0·5, concluded that the expectancy explanation was not acceptable. However, Williges (1969, 1971, 1973) has shown in a series of experiments that the criterion either decreases or remains stable with time at work if signal probability is increased beyond 0·5; these studies therefore support a strong version of expectancy theory, and they are now examined in detail.

Williges (1969) used a task in which subjects were required to detect a periodic transient increase in the duration of intermittent visual stimuli. Critical signals were either presented with a low probability (0·16), or a high probability (0·84). These conditions were combined factorially with two conditions of pre-training in which subjects were either provided with accurate or inaccurate expectancies regarding mean signal frequency. In the "accurate" condition, an appropriate signal probability was used to provide a "set" for the subject (either 0·16 or 0·84), while in the "inaccurate" condition subjects received signals with a probability of 0·5. The results for β conformed to that predicted by the expectancy model, and are illustrated in Fig. 4.4. When subjects monitored under accurate instruction, β increased in the low signal probability condition and decreased (non-significantly)

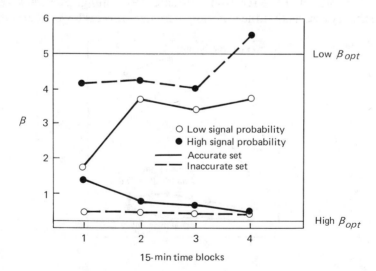

Fig. 4.4. Changes in criterion (β) over time on task as a function of pre-session expectancy (accurate or inaccurate set) and signal probability. The optimal values of β for the low (low β_{opt}.) and high (High β_{opt}.) signal probability conditions are indicated by the horizontal lines. From Williges (1969).

in the high signal probability condition. Furthermore β was higher in the former condition. Both these results are as predicted by SDT and expectancy theory. When subjects received an inaccurate "set", β did not vary over time (the trend apparent in Fig. 4.4 for the highest β values (High–Inaccurate) was not statistically significant), and β was *higher* in the high signal probability condition. These results are consistent with the assumption that subjects self-feedback to adjust their criteria during a watch.

The evidence in favour of a strong form of expectancy theory is thus greater than that available at the time of Broadbent's (1971) review. Furthermore, in another study, Williges (1973) confirmed his findings for both low and high signal probability conditions and for a condition in which signal probability changed halfway through a session (see Fig. 4.5). The unexpected result by Simpson (1967) from which Broadbent (1971) concluded that the expectancy interpretation is untenable, cannot be easily explained, except by suggesting that individual differences may be a neglected factor in this area. Some subjects show an increase in β, but since there may be a "cellar" effect for decreases in β as Figs 4.4 and 4.5 appear to show, the larger increases in β might outweigh the decreases, and a group increment in β might be observed. In these latter cases, however, both the β increment and the decrement in detection rate may be less marked.

The distinction between "weak" and "strong" forms of expectancy theory makes possible the interpretation of criterion shifts which are obtained even when subjects have received adequate pre-training. The weak version of the theory asserts that the criterion increment reflects lowered expectancy

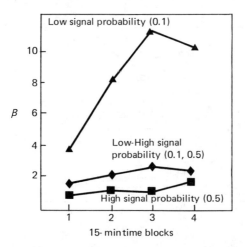

Fig. 4.5. Changes in criterion (β) over time on task under low (0·1) and high (0·5) signal probability conditions, and under a condition in which signal probability changed from low to high (0·1–0·5) during the task. From Williges (1973).

due to inappropriate training procedures, although it can be extended to cover cases where appropriate pre-task training has been given. The strong form of the theory proposes that the criterion increment (which may still be obtained with appropriate training) reflects cumulative changes in subjective expectancies of signal probability. This version of the theory depends on the assumption that the subject's behaviour approaches that of the "ideal" SDT observer. There are indications, however, that this may not be the case. The often noted finding that subjects are conservative, in that they do not employ response criteria as high or as low as that used by the ideal observer, may imply the use of a probability matching hypothesis (Thomas and Legge, 1970). Craig (1978; Craig and Colquhoun, 1977) has recently also suggested that a major part of the vigilance decrement is due to a decrement in the *response* rate, and reflects a tendency toward probability matching. Craig's study has important implications for expectancy theory and for the interpretation of the decrement, and his results are therefore examined in some detail.

Craig re-analysed data reported in 30 studies of vigilance in the literature. He computed the mean ratio of the frequency of responses (R) emitted (correct detections and false alarms) to the frequency of signals (S) presented in each study. He found a general tendency for the R : S ratio to be greater than 1·0, especially at the beginning of a session, in 14 out of 20 studies reporting within-session data. The R : S ratio showed a significant decline between the beginning and end of a session in these cases, the mean ratio at the end of a session approaching the probability matching level of 1·0. In those cases where the ratio was initially less than 1·0, there was a non-significant decline in the R : S ratio (and hence also in the response rate).

These results have an important bearing on two issues raised in earlier chapters:

(1) how genuine is the phenomenon of the vigilance decrement? and

(2) how is the decrement to be interpreted? Craig suggested that the probability matching hypothesis can answer both these questions but, as the following points indicate, there are difficulties in accepting this conclusion.

(1) First, Craig based his analysis on group data, and it is by no means certain that the same pattern of results would obtain if he had based his measures of central tendency on individual response rates (cf. ROC curves obtained from group and individual response probabilities; see Craig, 1977). It has previously been mentioned that while group data are often indicative of the use of probability matching strategies in detection tasks, individual subject data show large deviations from probability matching (Dusoir, 1974; Thomas, 1975). This would not be a serious objection of course if it could be shown that in vigilance tasks the *majority* of subjects employ a probability matching strategy (and show an associated decrement).

(2) The decrement in the response rate (and the hypothesized shift towards probability matching), although found in 14 out of 20 studies, was obtained in only 56% of the 96 experimental conditions examined. In these 54 cases the R : S ratio declined significantly from a mean of 1·7 to a mean of 1·0. In the other 42 cases the ratio was less than 1·0 initially and declined non-significantly from 0·8 to 0·7 (mean values). It is not clear whether all instances of significant *vigilance decrements* (detection rate) were restricted to the 54 cases for which R : S > 1·0.

(3) However, Craig's finding that the R : S ratio is greater than 1·0 roughly half the time does pose a difficulty for the "vicious-circle" expectancy interpretation of the decrement, since this assumes that the response rate is less than the signal rate at the beginning of the vigilance session (for signal probabilities less than 0·5). To account for this, the vicious circle interpretation must propose that subjects form expectancies of signal frequency only on the basis of responses of which they are confident; the frequency of these responses will be less than the overall response rate, and thus it is likely that the R : S ratio will be less than 1·0 (see also Broadbent, 1971, p. 102).

(4) If a probability matching strategy is employed, then presumably subjects should adjust their response rates either downwards (when R : S > 1·0), or upwards (when R : S < 1·0). However, Craig found that in the 42 cases where R : S was initially less than 1·0, the ratio did not approach unity at the end of the session, but declined further (non-significantly).

Craig's study has provided an interesting and provocative set of results, but, as the above points indicate, they are not open to a simple interpretation. The conclusion that a "major portion" of the decrement is attributable to the use of probability matching strategies appears unwarranted without the examination of individual response data. On the other hand, Craig's results do indicate that the strong form of expectancy theory, the vicious-circle interpretation, may not be tenable without modification. His results are consistent with a weak form of expectancy theory, however, since they indicate that the vigilance decrement, when it is associated with a β increment, may often be due only to the use of inappropriate training methods. But it remains unclear whether his conclusions apply to vigilance situations in which the decrement in detection rate can be reliably associated with a reduction in sensitivity (see Chapter 5), although in a recent study Craig obtained a reliable sensitivity decrement coupled with probability matching in 36 out of 48 subjects (Craig, 1978, 1979a).

Before concluding this section a distinction between the expectancy hypothesis outlined here and "traditional" expectancy theory (Deese, 1955; Baker, 1959c, 1963c) should be noted. The interpretation outlined here implies only that expectancies about the frequency of signal occurrence are developed. "Traditional" expectancy theory, on the other hand, also takes into account inter-signal intervals, and the formulation of temporal expectancies of the time of signal occurrence. Support for this aspect of expectancy theory, however, is not strong. McGrath and O'Hanlon (1967), for example, found that while subjective expectancies of signal occurrence declined during a vigilance task, subjective estimates of time intervals were unrelated to vigilance performance (see also Warm *et al.*, 1966). Davies and Tune (1970) and Warm (1977) conclude that temporal expectancy does not play a major role in vigilance behaviour.

The ideal observer

The studies of Williges (1969, 1971, 1973) provide evidence for the role of expectancy when interpreted within the general framework of decision theory. Williges (1973, 1976), however, has gone further in postulating that the observer's behaviour in vigilance tasks approaches that of the ideal observer at the end of a session. Such an interpretation assumes a strong form of SDT in which decision rules are considered to be compatible with the maximization of expected value. Williges suggested that since the mean β values obtained in vigilance approach the optimal β value toward the end of a session (see Figs 4.4 and 4.5), the observer's performance actually represents an attempt to reach optimal behaviour; this he terms the "vigilance increment" (Williges, 1976).

This novel interpretation must be tempered by three considerations. First, in Williges' experiments as they are reported, no validation of the equal variance SDT model on which absolute values of β depend is presented. It has been mentioned previously that the confidence limits on β values in low signal probability tasks may be very large, so that while the *trends* in the decision criterion may be usefully assessed using this index, attaching a meaning to absolute β values is rather tenuous. J.F. Mackworth and Taylor (1963) and Taylor (1967) therefore do not recommend the use of β at all, and it is unfortunate that no completely satisfactory index of bias is presently available (see Chapter 3). Secondly, it is almost a truism that observers do not usually make decisions based on criteria as extreme as those used by the ideal observer. Hence, for $P < 0.5$, the increase in β with time will always make it approach β_{opt}, since $\beta < \beta_{opt}$; and the reverse will be true for $P > 0.5$ when $\beta > \beta_{opt}$. Thirdly, the ideal observer takes into account both the *a priori* signal probability and the payoff matrix in the calculation of the optimal β, but a number of studies, including one carried out by Williges (1971), indicate that the magnitude and direction of the change in β need not follow that predicted by an ideal observer optimizing the payoff (Levine, 1966; Swets, 1977).

The ideal observer hypothesis has been recently criticized by Vickers *et al.* (1977). They found that if signal probability was progressively decreased from an initial value of 0.5 during the session, β did not increase, as predicted by the ideal observer hypothesis, but decreased, although not significantly.

They suggested that changes in β represent an adaptive response used by the observer to minimize any discrepancy between the *local* (present) probability of making a response and cumulative signal probability (calculated from the beginning of the test, including the training session, to the end of the current block of trials into which the vigilance task is subdivided). Increases or decreases in β during the session are accounted for in terms of the direction of the discrepancy between local and cumulative probability. In one sense this model is an extension of the adaptive expectancy hypothesis outlined previously, but it does put a greater burden on the subject's ability to estimate and store response probabilities than expectancy theory. Furthermore, the model has to resort to proposing an effect of the signal probability prior to the training session to explain the finding, common to many studies (Baddeley and Colquhoun, 1969; Broadbent, 1971, Parasuraman and Davies, 1976; Williges, 1973), that β increases even though training and main session signal probabilities are matched (in which case there is no difference between local and cumulative probability).

Subjective costs and gains

Smith (1968) has considered the influence of "cost" in relation to detection and discrimination performance. Incorporating the concept of cost into a model extended from SDT, Smith proposed that the average cost of psychophysical decisions is a linear function of the sum of the signal and noise probability densities. A "cost function" which describes a through-shaped curve with its maxima at the means of the two distributions is thus obtained. Hence for criteria placed within the area of the trough (relatively lax criteria), a change in criterion can only be achieved with an increase in cost, while cautious criteria (outside the trough area) can be increased with a concomitant loss in cost. Thus if it is assumed that the observer tries to reduce cost over a vigilance session, it can be predicted that cautious criteria will increase, while lax criteria will remain stable; this is the result obtained by Broadbent and Gregory (1963b).

This interpretation only covers this specific result, which has been previously examined from the point of view of expectancy theory. It does not handle well other more general results, for example, the decrease in the criterion when signal probability is greater than 0·5. Broadbent (1971), on the other hand, argued that changes in subjective gains might explain why the criterion increases with time. Specifically, he proposed that there is a loss in the subjective gain associated with a correct detection as the session progresses, resulting in an increment in β. This might be so since the optimal value of β is inversely proportional to the gain associated with a correct detection. However, there is no direct evidence that changes in either subjective or objective costs and gains (the payoff matrix) significantly affect trends in β over the work period; and there is only limited evidence that the overall β values are affected by the value of a correct detection in the direction predicted by SDT (Davenport, 1968, 1969; Levine, 1966). As noted above. Williges (1971) suggested that signal probability has a greater influence on the decision criterion than the payoff matrix, and the bulk of the evidence supports this view (Swets, 1977).

Conclusions

It is clear that criterion changes play an important role in variations in long term performance in vigilance tasks. The decision criterion in vigilance has been found to be significantly influenced by a number of variables such as signal probability and instructions, and the increase in the criterion with time on task is now an established and reliable feature of performance in tasks with infrequently occurring signals. Response latency data also support the view that decision criteria and confidence levels change over a session. An interpretation based on expectancy theory seems to provide the best explanation of changes in the criterion and hence of the vigilance decrement which results from a criterion increment.

Chapter 5

Sensitivity Shifts

We have seen in the two previous chapters that the application of signal detection theory to the analysis of performance in vigilance situations led to a radical re-interpretation of the vigilance decrement (Broadbent and Gregory, 1963b). A signal detection theory analysis of vigilance performance which takes into account false alarm rates, as was not done in a number of early studies of vigilance, suggests that the decline in detection rate can be viewed in terms of either an increase in the criterion or as a reduction in sensitivity.

As we have seen in Chapter 4, during most vigilance tasks, observers usually become less confident or more cautious in responding with time and make fewer positive responses as the task progresses; this increase in the response criterion is associated with a decrement in both correct and false target detections, but there is no loss in perceptual sensitivity. It has been found, however, that perceptual sensitivity may decline in some vigilance tasks. In a series of early studies by J.F. Mackworth, sensitivity decrements were reported for the Continuous Clock Task (J.F. Mackworth, 1965a, b, 1968b; J.F. Mackworth and Taylor, 1963), and subsequently declines in sensitivity have been found with other vigilance tasks, both visual and auditory (see Parasuraman and Davies, 1977; Swets, 1977).

In this chapter we will examine first those variables which are likely to produce within-session decrements in sensitivity or changes in the absolute level of perceptual sensitivity. Using the taxonomic classification of vigilance tasks introduced in Chapter 2, we will then identify the characteristics of tasks for which decrements in sensitivity are likely to be found. We conclude with a discussion of the various possible interpretations of sensitivity shifts during vigilance.

Event rate and sensitivity shifts

The first study to report a sensitivity decrement over a vigilance session was that by J.F. Mackworth and Taylor (1963). The task used in this study and in others by J.F. Mackworth (1965a, b, 1968b) was the Continuous

Clock Task (Baker, 1963b) which is similar to the Clock Test developed by
N.H. Mackworth (1950), except that the clock hand moves continuously
rather than in discrete jumps. The critical signal which has to be detected
is a brief cessation of the moving hand. The need for continuous observation
and visual pursuit is probably what distinguishes this task from others which
do not show a sensitivity decrement. This was confirmed in a study by J.F.
Mackworth (1968b) in which the task was compared to the original Mackworth Clock Test at two levels of signal rate. A decrement in sensitivity was
found only for the Continuous Clock Task. The result seemed to indicate
that, if a task requires continuous observation of the display, there is a
drop in perceptual efficiency with time, or an effect of "filtering", to use
Broadbent's (1958) term. The effects of continuous visual observation are
also apparent, albeit indirectly, in a study reported by Stern (1966), in
which subjects were required to monitor continuously a steady point
of light and detect its occasional movements. Stern did not compute detectability indices, but it is clear from his data that there was an effective drop in
sensitivity for the group of subjects as a whole, since while the number of
hits declined over the session, the number of false alarms increased.

Another prominent feature of the tasks used by Mackworth and Stern,
apart from continuous observation, is the high degree of time uncertainty
regarding the occurrence of signals. The influence of time uncertainty on
detectability was originally examined by Egan et al. (1961). They trained
subjects to detect tones in background noise in two-minute listening periods,
separated by brief rest pauses. The subjects were required to respond with
varying degrees of confidence in different listening periods. Egan et al.
found that sensitivity, as measured by d', was invariant over conditions,
and that the ROC described a downward concave curve of a form consistent
with SDT. They concluded that time uncertainty exerts a major influence
on detection strategies in the so-called "free-response" tasks, since it was
observed that there was a progressive fall in d' as the interval of time uncertainty (during which signals may occur) was increased (Egan et al., 1961).
This finding was replicated in a vigilance situation by J.F. Mackworth and
Taylor (1963). Such studies suggest the importance of the event interval
or *event rate* in determining sensitivity shifts in vigilance performance.
More generally, they indicate that "continuous" or "free-response" tasks
which do not have discrete signal and noise events may show a sensitivity
decrement, although Watson and Nichols (1976) found that it was not
marked.

This view has been recently challenged by Laming (1973) who suggested
that the reported decrement in sensitivity in certain monitoring tasks may
be an artifact of the method used to measure sensitivity. He proposed that
time uncertainty may be "resolved", to a degree, by using *continuously*

sampled data and that subjects will therefore employ a sequential sampling strategy rather than the fixed-sample strategy implicitly assumed by SDT. This may certainly be true of continuous monitoring tasks, although it remains to be empirically demonstrated. The analysis of performance with such tasks might thus benefit from a "sequential-decision" analysis, since these tasks have to be arbitrarily partitioned into "observation intervals" in order to undertake a conventional SDT analysis. Watson and Nichols' (1976) analysis of latency data enables detectability parameters to be derived in free-response tasks without the necessity of assigning an arbitrary value to the observation interval (see also Chapter 3). However, attributing the sensitivity decrement to an artifact resulting from inappropriate data analysis can only provide a partial explanation, since sensitivity decrements have also been observed for discrete tasks with well-defined observation intervals and weak signals (Benedetti and Loeb, 1972; Hatfield and Loeb, 1969; Loeb and Binford, 1968; Parasuraman and Davies, 1976; Williges, 1971).

The first experiment to examine directly the effects of event rate (that is, the rate of presentation of signal and non-signal events) was carried out by Jerison and Pickett (1964). They showed that increasing the event rate in a visual vigilance task led to a significant decrease in the overall detection rate and to a significantly steeper decrement (see also Chapter 2). This result has been replicated in a number of studies (Krulewitz *et al.*, 1975; Loeb and Binford, 1968; J.F. Mackworth, 1965a; Metzger *et al.*, 1974; Parasuraman and Davies, 1976; Taub and Osborne, 1968; Warm *et al.*, 1976).

The effects of event rate on vigilance performance have been interpreted in two main ways: first, as a direct effect of the rate of presentation of stimulus events (Jerison, 1970b), and second as an effect due to a change in the conditional probability of signal occurrence (Colquhoun, 1969). Since conditional signal probability can be expressed as the ratio of the signal rate to the event rate, it is possible, if the signal rate is held constant, to treat an increase in event rate as a decrease in signal probability, and vice versa.

Colquhoun (1961) reported one of the first experiments in which the effects of signal probability and of event rate were independently studied. He used a task in which the event was a strip bearing six green discs, the critical signal being a display which contained a paler disc. Two event rates were combined with two signal rates in three conditions such that signal probability was either 0·50 or 0·08. The results indicated that the percentage of correctly detected signals was related to signal probability and unrelated to event rate; when event rate was held constant and signal probability decreased there was a significant reduction in the percentage of signals detected, while when signal probability was held constant and event rate increased there was no change in detection rate. False alarm data were not reported, but in a later study, using the same task, these findings were confirmed and shown to result from criterion changes (Baddeley and Colquhoun, 1969).

Jerison and Pickett (1964) varied the event rate in a visual vigilance task, while keeping signal rate constant. The events consisted of a series of double movements of a bar of light on an oscilloscope screen, the signal being a larger movement of one member of the pair. With an increase in event rate from 5 to 30 events per minute, detection rate fell from 90% to 30%, and a decrement was obtained only for the high event rate condition. Since signal rate was held constant in this study, the results may be interpreted as being due to a change in signal probability rather than in event rate. However, the decrease in detection rate found by Jerison and Pickett is much larger than that generally reported for a reduction in signal rate, which leads to a comparable change in signal probability (Baddeley and Colquhoun, 1969). This would seem to suggest that the two effects are independent and that event rate does exert a direct effect upon detection efficiency.

Colquhoun (1969), using a task in which a brighter flash had to be detected in a series of circular light flashes, also found a decrease in detection rate with an increase in the event rate. Signal probability was held constant in this study, since comparisons were made across conditions in which both the signal rate and the event rate were increased proportionally. Event rate had no significant effect on d', a result also obtained by Jerison and Pickett in a re-analysis of their 1964 data (Jerison et al., 1965). However, as discussed later, a number of more recent studies have found significant effects of event rate on d' (Guralnick, 1973; Loeb and Binford, 1968; Parasuraman and Davies, 1976).

Jerison (1965, 1967b) repeated his original experiment (Jerison and Pickett, 1964) using several conditions where event rate was varied for a fixed value of signal probability. His results indicated that the event rate effect was independent of signal probability. Signal probability was found to have a much smaller effect on detection rate than event rate, but the effect was significant only at high event rates. Taub and Osborne (1968) reported two experiments which essentially replicated these results for the Mackworth Clock Test. Unfortunately neither Jerison nor Taub and Osborne reported data using sensitivity or bias measures, but this was done in another smiliar experiment by Loeb and Binford (1968). Two tasks were used in this study; the visual task was an analogue of the Mackworth Clock Test, using lamps arranged in a circle, while the auditory task consisted of a series of white noise pulses in which subjects were required to detect slightly louder pulses. Signal probability and event rate were varied independently over three levels. Both variables were found to affect the detection rate, although the effects for event rate were larger. However, the use of SDT measures revealed that while event rate significantly reduced d', signal probability did not affect detectability, but affected the criterion (β), a finding consistent with the results of a number of other studies in vigilance (see Chapter 4). These results were confirmed in two experiments reported by Parasuraman and Davies (1976). Using a vigilance task in which a transient decrease in the intensity of an intermittently flashing light had to be detected, they found that increasing the event rate significantly reduced d' and also produced a decline in d' over time. In addition signal probability and event rate affected the latencies associated with different categories of response differentially (see Table 5.1). Event rate had no effect on latencies of responses made to non-signals, whilst these latencies were significantly affected by signal probability (Davies and Parasuraman, 1977). Both these effects are consistent with the predictions of the decision theory model for response latencies in vigilance outlined previously (see Chapter 3).

Table 5.1. A comparison of the effects of an increase in event rate (ER) and a decrease in signal probability (SP) on mean latencies associated with different categories of response: Detection latency (DL), False Alarm Latency (FAL), Correct Rejection Latency (CRL) and Miss Latency (ML). From Davies and Parasuraman (1977).

Latency measure	SP	ER
DL	Increase	Increase
FAL	Increase	No change
CRL	Decrease	No change
ML	Decrease[a]	Decrease

[a]Not significant ($P > 0.10$). All other effects were significant at the 0.05 level or beyond.

The results of the studies employing SDT measures provide strong evidence for the independence of signal probability and event rate effects on vigilance performance. Nevertheless, the discrepancy between the results of Colquhoun (1961) and Jerison (1967b) needs to be explained. Jerison (1966) suggested that the visual search requirement of Colquhoun's task might be a possible intervening factor, but Colquhoun (1966a) repeated his 1961 experiment using the same task with only two sources instead of six and found essentially the same result as he had before. However, two other aspects of Colquhoun's (1961) study may be relevant. First, very low event rates in the range of 0·6–3·6 per minute were used, while Jerison (1967b) and Loeb and Binford (1968) only observed an effect of event rate for rates greater than about 20 per minute. Second, Colquhoun's task (both the 1961 and the 1966 versions) involved the discrimination of a stimulus quality (hue or increased size) in two or more stimulus sources presented simultaneously, that is, a discrimination within the same stimulus event. As mentioned previously in Chapter 2, such a task can be classified as a "closure" or simultaneous discrimination task rather than a "speed" or successive discrimination task. All the studies reporting effects of event rate have used speed-type tasks. This suggests two possibilities which may account for the discrepancy between Colquhoun's and Jerison's studies:

(1) event rate interacts with task factors;

(2) different mechanisms are operative in the two studies (criterion shifts and sensitivity shifts), and these are obscured by the examination of detection scores only.

The interaction between event rate and other task factors has been examined in a number of studies (Krulewitz et al., 1975; Metzger et al., 1974; Warm et al., 1976a). Two factors appear to be important, the discriminability of the signal, and the type of task employed. Event rate seems to affect detection rate only when "weak" signals which are difficult to discriminate are used; Guralnick (1973) has reported similar effects for sensitivity (d'). Warm et al. (1976a) have suggested that the effect of event rate may be found only with "sensory" tasks (Davies and Tune, 1970) and not with "cognitive" tasks involving the discrimination of verbal and symbolic patterns. Although no study has directly compared these two types of task with respect to the effects of event rate, it does appear that event rate interacts with other task dimensions to produce sensitivity decrements (Parasuraman and Davies, 1977). Parasuraman and Davies carried out a taxonomic study of factors responsible for sensitivity decrements, but before discussing the results of their analysis, we shall briefly consider the effects of other task variables on sensitivity.

Other variables affecting sensitivity

Apart from event rate, one of the most important variables influencing sensitivity is *signal strength*, which can be varied either by manipulating signal intensity or signal duration (see, for example, Beatty et al., 1977; Broadbent and Gregory, 1963b; Williges, 1973). J.F. Mackworth and Taylor (1963) found that the degree of decrement in sensitivity was dependent on the initial detectability of the signal. This result appears to relate to Teichner's (1974) finding that the rate of decrement (in detections, not sensitivity) in simple visual monitoring tasks is related to the initial detectability of the signal, or the initial "subjective signal strength".

Signal detectability in a monitoring situation has been shown to be adversely affected if another task has to be performed at the same time (Taylor, 1965; Williges, 1969). Time sharing between different sources of the same task would also appear to lower detectability, but there is very little evidence relating to this point. Milosevic (1974) has, however, compared one-source monitoring with five-source monitoring for a visual task in which the occasional brighter flash in a series of flashes had to be detected.

Sensitivity was significantly lower in the multi-source task than in the single-source task, but there was no change in the trend in d' over the run (d' being invariant over time in both conditions).

While time sharing between two or more sources of signals may reduce monitoring efficiency, performance is improved if signals are presented simultaneously (redundantly) over two sense modalities (Buckner and McGrath, 1963b; Loveless et al., 1970; Osborn et al., 1963). Studies which have examined differences in d' between single-mode (auditory or visual) and dual-mode (audio-visual) presentation in vigilance tasks have generally confirmed the superiority of audio-visual information presentation (Colquhoun, 1975; Craig et al., 1976; Tyler et al., 1972).

Small but reliable practice effects on d' have been shown by Binford and Loeb (1966) and Colquhoun and Edwards (1970). This might be interpreted as an effect of learning, and such effects might be especially evident in more complex tasks. Practice effects need to be evaluated since they may have a bearing on the stability of the sensitivity decrement phenomenon. For example, if the sensitivity decrement is due to inadequate learning of the signal characteristics, practice may abolish the decrement in later sessions. In point of fact, the data of Binford and Loeb (1966) and Parasuraman (1976a) show just the opposite; nevertheless the effects of repeated sessions on vigilance behaviour warrant interest and attention from both a theoretical and practical viewpoint.

Several studies have also shown that detection efficiency in various discrimination and monitoring tasks is impaired under stress or in adverse environmental conditions (Poulton, 1970). For example, detectability is reliably reduced under conditions of sleep deprivation (Beatty et al., 1977; Deaton et al., 1971; Wilkinson, 1968). These studies are examined further in Chapter 7.

Sensitivity decrements: a taxonomic analysis

As we have seen, there are a number of variables which affect the absolute level of sensitivity or detectability in vigilance tasks. However, two factors seem particularly important in producing *within-session decrements* in perceptual sensitivity: the stimulus event rate, and task classification on the "speed-closure" dimension. The influence of these two factors on sensitivity shifts in vigilance was originally identified in a taxonomic analysis of vigilance tasks reported by Parasuraman and Davies (1977; Parasuraman, 1979).

Although sensitivity decrements have been reported for certain vigilance tasks since Mackworth and Taylor's study in 1963, the distinguishing features of these tasks were until recently unclear. It was originally thought that sensitivity decrements occur only for visual displays, especially those demanding a high rate of observation (J.F. Mackworth, 1970; Broadbent, 1971).

However, as noted previously, there are examples of auditory tasks showing sensitivity decrements, and, conversely, high event rate tasks which do not show such reductions in perceptual efficiency (Swets, 1977).

A closer examination of the discrimination tasks used in studies of vigilance suggests a division of these tasks into two general categories: *successive*-discrimination or "perceptual-speed" tasks, and *simultaneous*-discrimination or "closure" tasks. Successive-discrimination tasks use targets involving a change in some feature of a repetitive stimulus (such as intensity or duration) or of a display state, such that a successive comparison or discrimination of a change in a standard value held in memory has to be made. In simultaneous-discrimination tasks, the target is specified fully *within* a stimulus event, target and non-target features being presented simultaneously, as in the detection of a disc of different hue in a display of discs, or of a tone in a noise burst. Parasuraman and Davies (1977) observed that, among the vigilance studies using measures of perceptual sensitivity, those reporting sensitivity decrements tended to have used successive discrimination tasks.

In order to test these impressions more thoroughly, a list of all vigilance studies (up to 1975) reporting sensitivity data was compiled. Thirty-three studies in which a relatively "pure", bias-free index of detectability was used (d' or a similar index) were identified. Five studies were excluded from further analysis for the following reasons:

(1) failure to analyse sensitivity data over time;

(2) inadequacy of task description;

(3) use of an atypical or special testing paradigm sharply distinguishing the study from the others in the set (for example, requiring the subject to press an "observing response" button to display signals, as in the study by Guralnick, 1972). Another study was rejected because the sensitivity data reported were computed only from group detection scores. Twenty-seven studies were included in the final set for analysis (see Table 5.2).

The tasks used in each of these studies were classified according to the target discrimination type (successive- or simultaneous-discrimination) and whether a low or high event rate was employed. The cut-off between low and high event rates was set so that tasks with an event rate of less than 24 per minute were classified as "low event rate" tasks. Tasks with an event rate of 24 per minute or greater, or those having "continuous" signals (for example, Levine, 1966) were classified as "high event rate" tasks.

In addition to the event rate and signal discrimination type, the task modality (visual or auditory) and source complexity (single source or multiple source of signals) were also noted. Thus tasks were classified along four dichotomous dimensions: target discrimination type, event rate, modality and source complexity. Brief descriptions of each task were also recorded, as were the following task variables:

Table 5.2. Reference sample used in the taxonomic study of Parasuraman and Davies (1977).

Baddeley and Colquhoun (1969)
Benedetti and Loeb (1972)
Binford and Loeb (1966)
Broadbent and Gregory (1963)
Broadbent and Gregory (1965)
Colquhoun (1967)
Colquhoun (1969)
Colquhoun and Edwards (1970)
Davies *et al.* (1973)
Deaton *et al.* (1971)
Guralnick and Harvey (1970)
Hatfield and Loeb (1968)
Hatfield and Soderquist (1969)
Hatfield and Soderquist (1970)
Jerison *et al.* (1965)
Levine (1966)
Loeb and Binford (1964)
Loeb and Binford (1968)
Loeb and Binford (1971)
J.F. Mackworth (1968a)
J.F. Mackworth and Taylor (1963)
Milosevic (1974)
Milosevic (1975)
Parasuraman (1976a)
Parasuraman and Davies (1976)
Siddle (1972)
Williges (1973)

(1) signal duration;
(2) signal rate;
(3) task duration.

Finally, the presence or absence of a significant decrement in sensitivity over the duration of the task was noted for each study.

Figure 5.1 gives the principal outcome of the taxonomic analysis. Each of the four task dimensions are represented in this figure, and in each cell of the figure a filled circle is shown if the associated task showed a sensitivity decrement, and an open circle if it did not. It is clear that all instances of a sensitivity decrement occur when the task used is a successive-discrimination task, and when a high event rate is employed, *and not otherwise.*

Thus a distinction between successive- and simultaneous-discrimination tasks, and between low and high event rates, provides a sufficient index with which to divide all vigilance studies into those which show a decrement in perceptual efficiency over time, and those which do not. This result has important implications not only for an understanding of sensitivity decrements but also for theories of vigilance behaviour. Before considering these implications, however, a number of other results from the study are discussed.

It was found that in 13 of the 27 studies examined, a reliable decrement in sensitivity was reported in at least one experimental condition, thus indicating the decrement to be a much wider and relatively more frequent phenomenon than generally realized. Furthermore, sensitivity decrements were reported for auditory tasks in seven studies, thus showing that the decrement in perceptual efficiency is not restricted to visual tasks, a view often put forward in surveys of this area (for example, J.F. Mackworth, 1970). A further finding was that signal duration, signal rate and task duration were not related in any systematic way to the presence or absence of a sensitivity decrement.

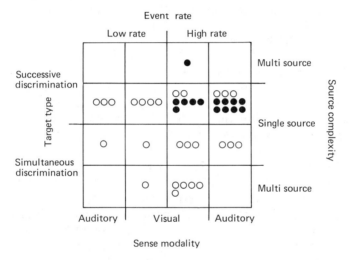

Fig. 5.1. A classification of vigilance tasks according to the presence (filled circles) or absence (open circles) of a reliable decrement in perceptual sensitivity over time. Each circle represents a task used in a study of sustained attention reporting data in terms of d' or a related index. From Parasuraman (1979).

Some exceptions and qualifications should also be noted. The reliability of the d' measure as a bias-free index of detectability was verified in only 9 of the 27 studies examined (with the use of confidence ratings). It is possible therefore that some of the results reported are unreliable, although the systematic pattern of results shown in Fig. 5.1 suggests that this would not affect the principal outcome. Furthermore, sensitivity decrements were obtained in 4 out of the 9 studies using confidence ratings, that is, in roughly the same proportion as for all the studies (13 out of 27).

Although it was true that all cases of sensitivity decrement were obtained for successive-discrimination tasks at high event rates, the reverse was not always the case, as not all such tasks showed a reliable sensitivity decrement.

Colquhoun (1969) and J.F. Mackworth (1968a), for instance, did not obtain a decrement in sensitivity for two different visual tasks. Interestingly, the study by J.F. Mackworth (1968a) is the only one reporting sensitivity data for the Mackworth Clock Test. The lack of a sensitivity decrement with this task may reflect the influence of factors not identified in Parasuraman and Davies's (1977) taxonomy. Colquhoun (1969) employed a visual intensity discrimination task similar to those used in a number of other studies reporting a decrement (Hatfield and Loeb, 1968; Loeb and Binford, 1968) and it is therefore more difficult to account for the discrepancy. One possible explanation is that this study appears to be the only one in which subjects served under more than one event rate level. Another possibility is that the arbitrary cut-off between low and high event rates employed (24 events per minute) may well be inappropriate for different categories of task. The three cases of auditory successive-discrimination tasks with "high" event rates for which sensitivity was invariant over the session employed event rates at or near (30 per minute) this cut-off value (Hatfield and Soder-quist, 1970; Loeb and Binford, 1964, 1968).

It could be argued that these exceptions weaken the importance of the joint influence of target discrimination type and the event rate on the sensitivity decrement, but the results of a study by Parasuraman (1979) suggest otherwise. This study examined the effects of event rate on two auditory vigilance tasks, a successive discrimination task, and a simultaneous discrimination task. In the former, the target was a 2·1 dB increase in the intensity of an intermittent 1000 Hz tone. In the latter, a 1000 Hz tone had to be detected within an intermittent noise burst. Performance was compared at event rates of 15 and 30 events per minute. As Fig. 5.2 shows, a sensitivity decrement in d_a (an ROC-based measure which is more robust than d'; see Chapter 3) was obtained only for the high event rate—successive discrimination task combination, although a vigilance decrement (detection rate) was obtained in all conditions.

These results were confirmed and extended to visual stimulation in a second experiment. The first experiment suggests that the memory load imposed by the successive discrimination task is an important factor which controls changes in sensitivity in vigilance. However, the simultaneous discrimination task studied in this experiment involved the detection of a pure tone in noise, while the successive discrimination task required the discrimination of an increment in the intensity of a tone. The lack of a sensitivity decrement for the former task may thus be due either to the absence of a memory load, or to the requirement to detect a stimulus in noise. In order to clarify the nature of the factor controlling the sensitivity decrement, Parasuraman (1979) carried out a second experiment in which three visual vigilance tasks were compared at a high event rate.

Two adjacent sources of visual stimulation were used in each of these tasks, for the following reasons. Consider a single-source successive discrimination task with the target specified as a decrease in the intensity of a flashing light. If an identical second source is added, with the target defined as a decrease in the intensity of both light sources, it remains a successive discrimination task. However, if the task is modified so that the target (dimmer flash) is presented on only one source, "simultaneous" discrimination is now possible since the two sources may be compared within a stimulus event. This task is referred to as simultaneous discrimination task (a). A second simultaneous discrimination task (b) in which the target was a small circle appearing at the centre of one of the two light sources was also examined. A memory load hypothesis would predict that under a high event rate only the successive discrimination task will show a sensitivity decrement.

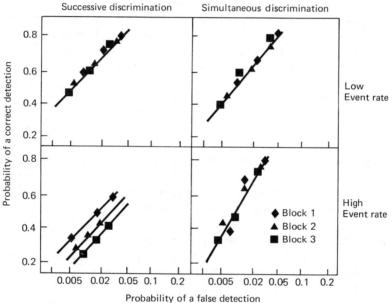

Fig. 5.2. Normalized group ROCs in consecutive 15-minute time blocks of a 45-minute vigil for successive and simultaneous discrimination tasks under conditions of low and high event rate. Each ROC point is the mean of the normalized correct detection and false detection probabilities for the ten subjects in each group. From Parasuraman (1979).

Table 5.3 summarizes the main findings of this experiment. Although the hit rate declined with time in all three tasks, sensitivity declined reliably only in the successive discrimination task, and not in the two simultaneous discrimination tasks.

These results confirm those of the first experiment, and show that memory load and event rate are the two critical factors that control temporal changes

Table 5.3. Mean values of sensitivity and hit rate (target detections) for each target type in consecutive 15-minute time blocks of each vigilance session (see text). From Parasuraman (1979).

Target type	Blocks					
	Sensitivity (d')			Hit rate		
	1	2	3	1	2	3
Successive	2·42	2·11	1·81	0·68	0·45	0·36
Simultaneous (a)	2·30	2·37	2·37	0·64	0·59	0·58
Simultaneous (b)	2·34	2·34	2·37	0·63	0·63	0·58

in sensitivity in vigilance tasks. Given the modality specific nature of many vigilance phenomena (Davies and Tune, 1970) the congruence of the findings between visual and auditory stimulation provides impressive empirical support for the distinction between successive and simultaneous discrimination in the context of vigilance (see also Chapter 6).

Stable sensitivity over the work period in a task similar to Parasuraman's (1979) simultaneous discrimination task (a) was reported by J.F. Mackworth (1965b) for an event rate of 60 events per minute. A decrement in d' was obtained, however, with a very high event rate of 200 events per minute. This indicates either that at such a high rate of stimulation a sensitivity decrement is obtained irrespective of the type of discrimination required, or that the decrement is an artifact resulting from the assumption that the decision rate is 200 per minute. For the range of high event rates encountered in most vigilance experiments however (24–60 events per minute), the results confirm those of the taxonomic analysis outlined above. It appears that it is the requirement for comparison over successive events which is the pertinent feature of "speed" or successive discrimination tasks and which, combined with a high event rate, is responsible for a decrement in perceptual efficiency over time in sustained attention.

The interpretation of sensitivity decrements

Coupling

The finding that sensitivity decrements are found with certain types of vigilance task and not with others suggests that an examination of critical task features must form a part of any interpretation of the decrement. Initially, most studies reported that sensitivity decrements were restricted to visual tasks (Loeb and Binford, 1968; J.F. Mackworth, 1970), and thus the task demands imposed by tasks employing different modalities was examined. The "coupling" hypothesis, for example, suggests that the sensitivity decrement is found only with visual tasks since they are only "loosely coupled" to the observer's perceptual system, so that perceptual efficiency is easily degraded by changes in the orientation of the peripheral receptor systems (see J.F. Mackworth, 1970).

This hypothesis fits the results of several early studies of vigilance but is contradicted by the results of later studies which indicate that sensitivity decrements may also be obtained with auditory tasks (see, for example, Corcoran et al., 1977); it should also perhaps be noted that Corcoran et al. obtained a d' increment—although based on only two data points—in one of their conditions which is somewhat difficult to explain. Furthermore, as is discussed in Chapter 6, cross-modal correlations of sensitivity measures provide uncertain support for the coupling hypothesis. For example, it is more likely for performance on an auditory task to be correlated with that on a (loosely coupled) visual task than with that on a visual task which is modified to make it more closely coupled (for example, by presenting stimuli intense enough to be perceived through closed eyes; see Loeb and Binford, 1971). The coupling hypothesis thus suffers from a certain ambiguity in that a visual task can be said to be either loosely or closely coupled. This ambiguity permits opposing sets of results pertaining to sensitivity decrements to be explained:

(1) that visual (loosely coupled) tasks show a decrement while auditory (closely coupled) tasks do not (Loeb and Binford, 1968), or

(2) that visual (loosely coupled) tasks do not show a sensitivity decrement while closely coupled (visual or auditory) tasks do (Deaton et al., 1971; Hatfield and Loeb, 1968).

The explanation for the first result is the one mentioned previously. The explanation for the second type of result, as proposed by Deaton et al., and by Hatfield and Loeb, is, that for closely coupled (usually auditory) tasks, there is less opportunity to attend to the irrelevant stimulation and thus maintain efficiency than in the case of loosely coupled (visual) tasks. The inability of this hypothesis to be falsified weakens its position and it seems clear that while coupling is a useful construct with which to view one aspect of task load in vigilance, it has not been defined in a sufficiently rigorous manner to enable it to form the basis for an interpretation of sensitivity decrements in vigilance.

Habituation

An alternative interpretation of the sensitivity decrement is provided by J.F. Mackworth's (1968b, 1969) habituation theory of vigilance (see also Chapter 1), which postulates that the habituation of the neural responses to the repetitive background events of a vigilance task underlies decreases in perceptual efficiency. Since habituation is more rapid with a high than a low event rate, this might explain why sensitivity decrements are obtained only at high event rates.

The role of habituation in the explanation of sensitivity decrements was first suggested by J.F. Mackworth's own finding that for one particular visual task, the Continuous Clock, there is an approximately exponential decay in sensitivity over time on task (J.F. Mackworth, 1970), although this result is not found with other tasks. J.F. Mackworth (1970) cited evidence that the evoked EEG response habituates in support of her theory, but there has been no study showing a direct link between evoked response decrement and performance decrement in vigilance tasks. Furthermore, while the evoked response decrement meets the criteria for the phenomenon of habituation only with some difficulty (Thompson and Spencer, 1966; see also Ritter et al., 1968; Roth and Kopell, 1969), there does not seem any justification for viewing performance decrements in vigilance within a strict habituation paradigm. Krulewitz et al. (1975), for example, used a shift-paradigm to study the possible dishabituating effect of a change in event rate within a vigilance session. According to J.F. Mackworth's theory, any change in task conditions that leads to dishabituation should lead to an improvement in performance. But, as noted in Chapter 1, the results obtained by Krulewitz et al. failed to support this hypothesis. Their main finding was that event rate was an important determinant of detection efficiency, and that a shift in event rate either decreased or increased detection rate depending on the direction of the change (low to high, or high to low).

The observing response

The event rate is accorded an important role in Jerison's (1967b, 1970a, b; Jerison et al., 1965) "observing response" model of vigilance behaviour. Jerison suggested that observing behaviour consists of three main classes of observing response; alert or "optimal" observing, blurred or "sub-optimal" observing, and "distracted" observing, which corresponds to a failure to observe the display. Jerison's hypothesis suggests that reduced efficiency in vigilance tasks is due to an increase in periods of non-optimal (blurred or distracted) observing with time at work. As far as the results obtained for detection rate are concerned, the evidence suggests that this is a plausible hypothesis (Davies and Tune, 1970; J.F. Mackworth, 1970). Some difficulties arise, however, when considering sensitivity measures of performance. The essence of the argument is as follows (see also Broadbent, 1971).

Jerison's three-way observing model implies that the relative degree of randomness in internal representation (evidence) of signals and non-signals will change with elapsed time. If this takes the form of increased variability in signal variance due to an increasing frequency of "distractions", then the ROC will be markedly skewed and become more so with time. This is illustrated in Fig. 5.3a. No vigilance study has carried out a detailed analysis of ROC skew changes with time on task (see, however, Craig, 1977) and so it is difficult to evaluate the predicted ROC shapes associated with Jerison's (1970b) and J.F. Mackworth's (1970) models. Following suggestions by Green and Swets (1966) and Taylor (1967), J.F. Mackworth proposed that ROC skew reflects the degree of uncertainty about some aspect of the signal being monitored. Theoretically, if a signal is "known exactly", while only limited information is available on some other signal, the ROC for the latter type of signal will exhibit a greater degree of variability in the signal distribution as compared to the noise distribution (Taylor, 1967). Thus if it is assumed that in a vigilance task the observer gets to know the signal characteristics better as the task proceeds, there will be a decrease in ROC skew with time on task; ROC slope should accordingly approach unity (indicating equal signal and noise variances) at the end of the session or in later sessions. This is illustrated in Fig. 5.3b.

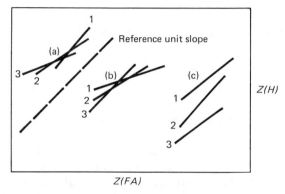

Fig. 5.3 a, b, c. ROCs consistent with the theoretical observations of H.J. Jerison (a) and J.F. Mackworth (b). ROCs associated with a typical sensitivity decrement are shown in (c). The numbers refer to successive time blocks.

Figure 5.3c shows typical ROCs obtained in a situation (a successive-discrimination task run at a high event rate) in which sensitivity declines with time on task. Neither of the predicted forms in (a) and (b) is followed, but, as mentioned previously, it is difficult to make judgements on alternative detection models on the basis of ROC curves in vigilance because of the relative unreliability of the error probabilities. The observing response model postulates that increases in event rate increase task demands on the observer in a vigilance task, since the required rate of observation rises. As a consequence, the observer may decide that the "cost of observing" is too high and performance may decline. This may be especially true of the complex visual displays found in many military "command/control/communication" systems in which a given part of the display may not be observed because the cost-benefit ratio associated with observing is high (Swets, 1976). It has been suggested that this phenomenon occurs even with simple displays

(Jerison, 1970b; Swets, 1976). Sensitivity decrements are found almost exclusively, if at all, in tasks employing simple displays for which, as we have seen, evidence supporting the observing response model is difficult to obtain. While it appears that failures of observation can account fairly successfully for the occurrence of sensitivity decrements in continuous tasks requiring visual fixation, such as the Continuous Clock Task (J.F. Mackworth, 1968a), it is less clear how the observing response model can be extended to explain sensitivity decrements in other simple display vigilance situations. In particular the model cannot explain why a sensitivity decrement is obtained only for tasks in which there is a successive-discrimination requirement. It is therefore of interest to re-examine the features of successive- and simultaneous-discrimination tasks more closely in relation to the occurrence of sensitivity decrements.

Memory load, time pressure and effort

The differences between successive and simultaneous discrimination tasks already outlined suggest that the former task places a greater load on memory, since not only has information to be integrated over successive events but the "value" of non-signal events on some stimulus dimension (for example, intensity, pitch or duration) has also to be remembered. As we have noted previously, Norman and Bobrow (1975) have pointed out that many discrimination tasks, including monitoring tasks, may be said to be data-limited tasks, in which performance is limited by the relative quality of the input data. Norman and Bobrow also distinguished between *signal data* and *memory data* limits on performance; in the former, performance is more directly dependent on the quality of the signal (as in the detection of a weak signal in noise), while in the latter, performance is affected by limitations in the stored representations of input data (as in delayed comparison tasks). A successive-discrimination task may be especially susceptible to performance degradation, therefore, because in addition to limitations on performance due to the quality of the input data, there may be additional demands placed on memory storage. It is thus conceivable that the greater dependence on memory, coupled with the demands of a high rate of stimulation, might underlie the observed decrement in sensitivity in such tasks, whether "sensory" (Loeb and Binford, 1968) or "cognitive" (Sostek, 1978).

This interpretation places a greater emphasis on memory mechanisms than is usual in monitoring research. As Davies and Tune (1970) have observed, most investigators have not given much consideration to memory in the interpretation of vigilance performance. Johnston *et al.* (1969) and Williges (1971), however, have suggested that in addition to the two general mechanisms which have been considered in relation to monitoring behaviour, namely attention and decision-making, a factor related to memory also needs to be taken into account. They did not specify the nature of this factor in detail, but proposed that tasks with a high "memory load" would be especially susceptible to performance deterioration. To demonstrate this, Johnston *et al.* tested subjects on two monitoring tasks involving the discrimination of alphanumeric stimuli presented in cells of an 8×8 matrix. In one task, signals were defined as deletions of some stimuli with respect to the previous display, while in the other task signals were added to the display. It was the former display which was hypothesized to impose the greater load on memory, and perceptual efficiency (d') was found to be reliably lower for this task. Hence the interpretation of the sensitivity decrement in terms of a memory load hypothesis appears to be a plausible explanation for the available results, despite the lack of other supporting data from studies investigating memory factors in vigilance. The hypothesis may, however, face some difficulty arising out of a consideration of the effects of signal and event rate on the sensitivity decrement. If the sensitivity decrement is assumed to be related to reductions in the output of a memory store, then an increase in the signal rate should serve to arrest this process, and hence the decrement.

In a related context, Dornic (1967) has suggested that the "memory trace" for signals is built up and consolidated by the occurrence of signals, while non-signals act as a source of interference which disrupts the memory trace; the degree of consolidation and disruption is proportional to the frequency of intervening signal and non-signal stimuli. Given this assumption, an increase in event rate, which increases the number of intervening non-signals, would lead to a reduction in efficiency over the monitoring period. This is what has been observed for successive discrimination tasks with high event rates. However, this interpretation also suggests that an increase in the signal rate should lead to a reduction or removal of the sensitivity decrement, since there will be less disruption of the memory trace. Furthermore, if there is an equal increase in both the signal and event rates, Dornic's theory predicts that there will be no change in performance since the number of intervening non-signals will remain the same (this is equivalent to the decision theory view that if conditional signal probability is held constant, there is no change in performance). However, the sensitivity decrement is not significantly affected by changes in signal probability (Loeb and Binford, 1968; Parasuraman and Davies, 1976). It is not evident whether this poses a difficulty for the theory, since Dornic's proposals do not make clear whether it is the number of intervening stimuli or the length of the intervening time interval which is the important factor in determining the effects of memory on performance. Presumably, both factors are important, but there is little evidence relating to their independent effects on monitoring performance. It is therefore difficult to evaluate the implications of Dornic's trace-interference theory for the interpretation of sensitivity decrement in terms of memory data-limitations on performance.

Another apparent difficulty with a memory data-limits theory may be considered by briefly examining the features of successive-discrimination tasks and comparing them with those of the *delayed-comparison* tasks which are often used in recognition memory research. These tasks share certain features, since in both cases a "signal" has to be discriminated by comparing it to a previously presented standard; although unlike most monitoring tasks, more than two standard and comparison stimuli are used in delayed-comparison tasks. In such tasks it is usually found that d' decreases as the delay interval between the standard and comparison stimulus increases; and a number of models of the decay in the memory trace for the standard stimulus may be proposed to account for this result (see, for example, Kinchla and Smyzer, 1967).

At first glance, this finding appears to contradict the findings obtained from the experiments reviewed earlier in this chapter which have examined the effects of event rate (which is inversely related to the inter-stimulus or delay interval) upon sensitivity in vigilance. However, the effects of event rate on sensitivity only appear after some time has been spent at the task. Parasuraman and Davies (1976), for example, did not obtain significant effects of event rate upon d' for the first 15 min. of work although thereafter large differences in d' between high and low event rate conditions were apparent, due mainly to the pronounced d' decrement found with a high event rate. There is thus no discrepancy between the effects of event rate in vigilance and delayed comparison tasks, although it is clear that in many ways the two tasks are quite dissimilar. It may be noted, finally, that in delayed comparison tasks the decrease in d' observed with an increase in the delay interval is much less marked when there is only one standard stimulus (Aiken and Lau, 1966).

The memory data-limits interpretation of sensitivity decrements in vigilance may also be related to Kahneman's (1973) conceptions of *effort* and time pressure. Kahneman proposed that effort is "mobilized" in response to task demands, and that there is a fixed allocation of effort for each task; time pressure, which is inherent in the structure of the task, therefore increases the effort demands of the task. Kahneman also suggested that "the investment of less than this standard effort causes a deterioration in performance, but in most tasks it is impossible to completely eliminate errors by a voluntary increase in effort .... Time pressure is a particularly important determinant of momentary effort. Tasks that impose a heavy load on short-term memory necessarily impose severe time pressure" (Kahneman, 1973, p. 27). If increased event rate is identified with increased time pressure, then a relationship between Kahneman's theory of effort and the memory load theory may be forged. It remains a loose relationship, but a consideration of sensitivity decrements from the point of view of the effort theory might help to resolve some of the difficulties faced by the memory load theory.

Beatty (1977b) has suggested that the information-processing load imposed by different tasks can be assessed from moment-to-moment fluctuations in the level of "task-induced activation". Several studies have indicated that changes in pupil size may reflect variations in activation and hence, presumably, in processing load, in a wide variety of different task situations (see Chapter 8). These include short-term memory (Beatty and Kahneman, 1966; Kahneman and Beatty, 1966), perceptual discrimination (Kahneman and Beatty, 1967), signal detection (Beatty and Wagoner, 1975), letter-matching (Beatty and Wagoner, 1978), as well as vigilance (Beatty and Wilson, 1977). It is possible that a comparison of successive- and simultaneous-discrimination tasks might reveal differences in pupillary movements which could be related to differences in the processing load which these tasks impose, as is further discussed in Chapter 8.

The foregoing considerations have made clear that "unitary" theories of vigilance cannot adequately deal with a majority of the available data on performance decrements. Neither the observing response and coupling models nor the neural habituation theory of J.F. Mackworth (1969) is able to provide a consistent interpretation of the data relating to the sensitivity decrement. On the other hand, a theoretical approach based on an identification of the memory demands of different monitoring tasks appears to be more promising, despite some difficulties with the approach as it stands. Further work needs to be done on the effects of practice and other variables on the sensitivity decrement within a task classification framework, in order to see whether the difficulties are major ones, in which case the approach may have to be abandoned, or are more minor problems which may be resolved as fresh experimental evidence is gathered. At present, however, an interpretation of the sensitivity decrement in terms of the information processing demands placed on the observer by different kinds of vigilance tasks appears able to account for a large proportion of the available experimental evidence.

Chapter 6

Individual and Group Differences

One of the more common findings of research on vigilance is that considerable variation exists among the performance scores achieved by different individuals working at the same task at more or less the same time and, to a lesser extent, among those achieved by any one individual working at the same or a closely similar task at different times. Thus the detection efficiency of different individuals within the same experimental condition may span a very wide range: some observers may detect scarcely any signals while others detect the majority of those presented; some observers may make no false alarms at all while others make a large number, and some may exhibit a marked decrement in detection rate while others exhibit none. In any event, the distribution of scores for any measure of vigilance performance is rarely Gaussian. Since substantial individual differences in vigilance performance are routinely obtained, it is perhaps not surprising that attempts have been made to relate scores on a variety of psychological tests to detection efficiency, frequently as a preliminary step to devising a selection battery which would discriminate between "good" and "bad" monitors. On the whole, however, such attempts have not been very successful (see Wiener, 1975 for a recent review of this area) and at present it would be extremely difficult to devise a global selection test which would prove effective in different sustained attention situations.

In this chapter we consider two questions concerned with individual and group differences in vigilance performance. First, we examine the degree to which the performance of the same individuals is consistent within the same testing session, across different sessions and across different tasks. Our main purpose here is to determine (a) whether individual differences in vigilance are highly task specific, the somewhat pessimistic conclusion of an extensive investigation conducted by Buckner and his associates (Buckner, 1963; Buckner and McGrath, 1963b, Buckner et al., 1960, 1966), or (b) whether such differences are task-type specific, in the sense that they are closely dependent on the ability requirements and demands imposed by different vigilance tasks, as more recent research appears to indicate.

Second, we review a large number of studies in which the vigilance performance of groups of individuals differing in some characteristic such as intelligence, personality, age, sex or diagnostic category has been investigated. Here we explore the question of whether membership of a particular group can account for a significant proportion of the variation in performance between individuals and, more generally, whether consistent differences in detection efficiency between, for example, introverts and extroverts, stabiles and labiles or older and younger individuals have in fact been reported.

Inter-task consistency of individual differences

Although it is a general finding that performance on vigilance tasks varies widely between subjects, it is usually observed that this variability in performance is consistent; that is, differences in performance between individuals are consistently maintained across successive time periods of the monitoring session. N.H. Mackworth (1950), who initially reported the existence of large individual differences in vigilance performance, found that the percentage of signals detected by subjects in the first half hour of work on the Clock Test was highly correlated with performance in all subsequent half-hour periods of the two-hour test. This finding has been confirmed by the results of subsequent studies (Buckner, 1963; Buckner et al., 1966). Teichner (1974) collated detection data from a number of studies using simple visual signals and also obtained a similar relationship between initial and subsequent detection rates within the vigilance session.

Task reliability

Individual differences in vigilance performance have been found to be reliable not only within a vigilance session, but also between sessions (Buckner et al., 1960; Jenkins, 1958) and between "alerted", short-duration, "pre-tests" and the main vigilance session (Benedetti and Loeb, 1972; Buckner et al., 1966; Loeb and Binford, 1971). Reliability coefficients in the range 0·72–0·91 were reported by Buckner et al. (1960) for monitoring sessions separated by up to six intervening sessions, and this result has since been confirmed by other investigators using different vigilance tasks and supplementary performance measures (Kennedy, 1971; Parasuraman, 1976a; Sverko, 1968). The available evidence therefore indicates that individual differences in vigilance performance are reliable within a session, between a pre-test and a session, and across several vigilance sessions.

Inter-task correlations in vigilance

A number of early studies in vigilance literature found that, despite the reliability of individual differences in performance within and across sessions, the correlations in individual performances between different tasks, especially those involving different sensory modalities, were very low (Baker, 1963b; Buckner et al., 1966; Pope and McKechnie, 1963). Until quite recently, this result was taken to be characteristic of monitoring behaviour in general, the inference being that individual differences in vigilance are highly task specific (Buckner and McGrath, 1963b; J.F. Mackworth, 1969). However, the generality of this conclusion may be challenged on the basis of the results of several more recent studies, which have indicated, albeit indirectly, that if certain task factors are brought under control, significant inter-modal and intra-modal correlations in vigilance performance may be obtained (Colquhoun, 1975; Gunn and Loeb, 1967; Hatfield and Loeb, 1968; Hatfield and Soderquist, 1970; Kennedy, 1971; Loeb and Binford, 1971; Sverko, 1968; Tyler et al., 1972).

The principal results obtained in these early (Type A) and more recent (Type B) studies are given in Table 6.1. None of the Type A studies obtained significant inter-modal task correlations, while a majority of the Type B studies did. In most of these later studies task factors were more closely controlled than in the earlier experiments, by matching tasks across modalities for the difficulty and type of signal discrimination. Two studies obtaining high inter-modal correlations, even though performance was not matched across modalities, nevertheless used tasks in which the signals appearing on different displays were highly compatible (Kennedy, 1971; Sverko, 1968). In the study by Sverko (1968), the dominant feature of the signal discrimination, "numerosity" or the detection of a specified number of temporally spaced stimuli was different from that normally encountered in laboratory vigilance tasks, but was common to all three of the visual, auditory and electrocutaneous tasks employed.

A further distinction between Type A and Type B studies arises from the greater number of performance measures utilized in the latter. Gunn and Loeb (1967) suggested that this might be a crucial factor in explaining why the early (Type A) studies could find no evidence for inter-modal consistency in individual differences, since in their study it was found that d' was positively and significantly correlated across modalities while a percentage detections measure was not. However a further series of experiments by Loeb and his associates, using the same tasks as Gunn and Loeb (visual and auditory tasks involving the detection of a transient increase in intensity of an intermittent stimulus), does not provide consistent support for this result. In all three experiments (Hatfield and Loeb, 1968; Hatfield and Soderquist, 1970; Loeb and Binford, 1971) a "closely coupled" (see Chapter 5) visual task in which subjects had their eyes taped (to reduce the possible contribution of "observing responses") was used. Significant correlations between tasks were obtained for subsets of the performance measures taken, but the pattern of results was not consistent between studies (see Table 6.1).

Table 6.1. Inter-task correlations in vigilance performance reported in the literature. *P < 0·05 or better; A = auditory; V = visual; E = electrocutaneous; Hits = correct detections; FAs = false alarms; DL = detection latency; [1] correlations for two orders of task performance; [2] rank order correlations computed by Davies and Tune (1970); [3] partial correlations.

		Performance measures				
	Tasks	Hits	FAs	d'	Log β	DL
Type A studies						
Buckner et al. (1960)	A-V	0·24				
C.H. Baker (1963b)	V-V	0·17, 0·64[1]				
Buckner and McGrath (1963b)	A-V	0·20				
	A-AV	0·23				
	V-AV	0·44				
Gruber (1964)[2]	A-V	0·18	0·15			0·42
Pope and McKechnie (1963)	A-V	−0·11				
Type B studies						
Colquhoun (1975)	A-V	0·71*	0·94*			
	A-AV	0·89*	0·99*			
	V-AV	0·54*	0·90*			
Gunn and Loeb (1967)						
Experiment 1	A-V	0·11	0·57*	0·48*	0·52*	
Experiment 21	A-V	0·21	0·79*	0·68*	0·78*	
Hatfield and Loeb (1968)						
Closely coupled visual task	A-V	0·65*	0·15	0·34	0·33	0·76*
Loosely coupled visual task	A-V	0·48*	0·21	0·27	0·32	0·75*
Hatfield and Soderquist (1970)						
Closely coupled visual task	A-V	−0·08	0·52*	−0·09	0·50*	0·78*
Loosely coupled visual task	A-V	0·47*	0·93*	0·14	0·96*	0·71*
Loeb and Binford (1971)						
Closely coupled visual task	A-V	0·65*	0·15	0·36	0·56*	
Loosely coupled visual task	A-V	0·67*	0·29	0·88*	0·72*	
Closely/loosely coupled visual tasks	V-V	0·69*	0·91*	0·56*	0·73*	
Sverko (1968)	A-V	0·77*	0·57*			
	A-E	0·73*	0·68*			
	V-E	0·84*	0·61*			
Tyler et al. (1972)[3]	A-V	0·80*	0·77*	0·87*	0·61*	
	A-AV	0·84*	0·85*	0·88*	0·79*	
	V-AV	0·74*	0·82*	0·87*	0·60*	

Furthermore, the results do not provide any evidence for the importance of coupling as a factor influencing performance consistency. As Table 6.1 shows, the obtained inter-modal correlations are, if anything, higher for loosely coupled visual tasks than for closely coupled visual tasks.

In Type B studies task difficulty has generally been controlled by equating group values of detectability (d') between tasks. Loeb and Binford (1971) and Tyler *et al.* (1972), however, equated task difficulty by matching individual d' values between tasks through adjustments of stimulus intensity and stimulus duration, respectively. Yet the data of Loeb and Binford (1971) do not resolve the inconsistencies in the results of Type B studies, nor do they indicate that individual matching is necessary before correlations between modalities are obtained, the view taken by Tyler *et al.* (1972), who used visual, auditory and audio-visual duration-increment vigilance tasks. Uniformly high and significant correlations (partialled to exclude order effects) were obtained between all pairs of tasks and for each of four performance measures by Tyler *et al.* They concluded, in contrast to Baker (1963b) and Buckner *et al.* (1966), that individual differences were *not* task specific and that a common vigilance factor could account for most of the variability in the performance of the tasks they used.

A taxonomic approach to performance consistency

As we have seen, the results of experiments loosely grouped under the heading "Type B studies" are varied, and in some cases, inconsistent. However, in each of these experiments, high inter-task correlations in performance were obtained for at least one of the two detection measures d' and the percentage of correct detections. On the whole, therefore, the results of these studies differ from those of Type A studies, and there appear to be certain identifiable factors responsible for this difference. One of these factors is almost certainly the degree to which tasks are compatible, in terms of the similarity and detectability of signals appearing on different displays, and of other general characteristics of the monitoring situation. Colquhoun (1975) has also suggested that variations in factors such as signal strength, testing procedure, and subject populations may account for some of the discrepancies in the literature.

   Although such discrepancies clearly exist, it remains probable that performance scores at different monitoring tasks will be correlated if the tasks possess certain features in common. The problem is to identify those features which, apart from the "common vigilance factor", are, in Jerison's words, "added when the task is changed" (see Bucker and McGrath, 1963a, p. 69). If the common vigilance factor is predominant, then one would expect significant inter-task correlations, not only between different vigilance tasks, but also between laboratory vigilance tasks and other repetitive tasks which share with vigilance task the features of monotony and prolonged duration. Baker and Ware (1966), however, did not find any evidence for an association between performance on vigilance tasks and other repetitive work tasks. They tested the same subjects on a simple vigilance task, a bean-sorting task, an addition task and an assembly task in separate sessions each lasting for two hours. There was no significant correlation between vigilance performance and performance on any of the other tasks, which were themselves moderately intercorrelated, a result which provides support for the hypothesis that individual differences are consistent only for the "compatible" tasks.

Two recent experiments attempted to test the generality of this hypothesis within a taxonomic framework (Parasuraman, 1976a, b; Parasuraman and Davies, 1977). In these experiments inter-modal and intra-modal correlations in performance were obtained for tasks which were dichotomized on two task "dimensions", modality (visual or auditory) and signal discrimination type, defined in terms of the perceptual speed and flexibility of closure categories (see Chapter 2). A total of four visual and two auditory tasks were used.

The majority of the previously described Type B studies employed compatible "speed" tasks, in which an increment or decrement in the intensity or duration of an intermittent visual or auditory stimulus had to be detected. Similar tasks were used in the experiments reported in Parasuraman and Davies (1977) but in order to determine the influence of signal discrimination type on inter-task consistency of individual differences, three "closure" tasks using the same stimuli were also used. As described in Chapter 2, a closure task involves the detection of a specified stimulus within a stimulus event, while a speed task involves the detection of a change in a current stimulus relative to preceding stimuli. The six tasks used were: two visual speed tasks (VS1 and VS2), two visual closure tasks (VC1 and VC2), an auditory speed task (AS) and an auditory closure task (AC) (see Parasuraman and Davies, 1977, for descriptions of these tasks).

Inter-task correlations were obtained for six different pairs of these tasks. Figure 6.1 shows the major results as performance correlations between selected pairs of tasks for two performance measures and indicates that reliable positive correlations in performance were obtained only when tasks were matched on either the speed or the closure categories, irrespective of modality. For tasks not matched on the speed-closure dimension, the correlations were low and insignificant, with the lowest correlation being obtained for the tasks not matched on both the signal type and the modality dimensions (VS and AC). For the two pairs of tasks equated on both these dimensions (VS1 and VS2; VC1 and VC2), the highest correlations were obtained, these being only slightly lower than the reliability co-efficients for these tasks (the mean week-to-week reliability for these tasks was about 0·89).

It is clear from the results of Parasuraman and Davies (1977) and those of the Type B studies mentioned previously that the early view of vigilance researchers that individual differences in vigilance are completely task specific (Buckner et al., 1966) is no longer tenable. This does not necessarily imply an acceptance of the opposing view, as proposed by Tyler et al. (1972), that individual differences are non-specific and are mediated by a common vigilance factor. Craig et al. (1976) have recently compared the validity of a number of models in predicting performance in bimodal vigilance tasks, given unimodal performance levels. They found that the best predictions are provided by models which do not assume that the auditory and visual systems operate completely independently. The bulk of the evidence thus points to the conclusion that individual differences are consistent to a degree; and that a number of factors influence the degree of performance consistency. One of the principal factors is whether the type of signal discrimination is the same in the different tasks. The results of Parasuraman and Davies (1977) also suggest that the different task demands of the perceptual speed and flexibility of closure categories of vigilance task are important determinants of the degree of consistency of individual differences in performance, but whether these categories define primary abilities necessary for efficient vigilance performance, as suggested by Fleishman (1972, 1975a), remains speculative in the absence of a large-scale factor analytic study of monitoring behaviour.

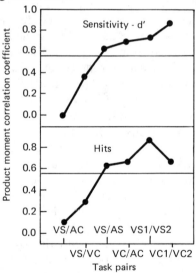

Fig. 6.1. Product moment correlation coefficents between different task pairs for two measures of detection efficency (*d'* and Hits). VS = visual speed task, VC = visual closure task, AS = auditory speed task, AC = auditory closure task; correlations above the horizontal mid-lines are significantly greater than zero ($P < 0.05$). From Parasuraman and Davies (1977).

In general, however, the results of the studies reviewed in this section indicate that for vigilance tasks as a whole, individual differences are consistent only for "compatible" tasks. This suggests that it is unlikely that one could develop a global selection test for vigilant behaviour that would predict performance on a range of tasks. The view that individual differences are *task-type specific* does not therefore lend itself well to practical application. Nevertheless it appears preferable to the rather pessimistic conclusion of some earlier studies that the best selection procedure for a vigilance-type task is the administration of a short form of the task itself (Baker, 1963b; Buckner and McGrath, 1963b; J.F. Mackworth, 1969).

Personality and vigilance

In the development of possible selection tests for vigilance and monitoring tasks, researchers have used a variety of tests aimed at providing information about different psychological functions, in the hope that one of these would prove useful as a predictor of vigilance performance. In general, however, standard psychological tests of reasoning, memory span and of various aptitudes, both general and specific, have not been very successful in providing consistent and valid correlates of vigilance performance (Buckner et al., 1966), although in the most comprehensive study yet conducted there was some indication that tests measuring clerical abilities might be useful predictors of within-session decrement scores (McGrath et al., 1960). However, this finding was not upheld in a subsequent cross-validation study (McGrath, 1963b). Similarly, attempts to establish a relationship between monitoring performance and general intelligence have not been particularly fruitful and a number of studies have failed to find differences between the vigilance performance of adults achieving relatively high and relatively low scores on standard intelligence tests (Halcomb and Kirk, 1965a; McGrath et al., 1960; Sipowicz and Baker, 1961; Ware, 1961). Incidental findings from several other experiments provide support for this result (Bakan, 1959; Colquhoun, 1959, 1962a; Jenkins, 1958; N.H. Mackworth, 1950; Wilkinson, 1961a), although one or two studies have found indications of a positive relationship between intelligence and vigilance (Cahoon, 1970a; Kappauf and Powe, 1959). But, in general, the contribution of intelligence to monitoring performance seems to be slight, and in this respect sustained attention appears to differ from selective attention (Jerison, 1977). Indeed, one study has reported no differences between the detection scores of young mental deficients, with a mean IQ of 58·1, and those of normal intelligence groups (Ware et al., 1962). In contrast to tests of abilities and aptitudes, personality tests, in particular tests of extroversion and introversion and of "cognitive style", have been shown in a number of studies to differentiate between certain aspects of performance in vigilance tasks. This section is accordingly devoted to a discussion of the findings of such studies.

Temperament and vigilance performance

The conceptual basis for investigations of the relation between the extroversion-introversion dimension of personality and vigilance derives from a number of theoretical speculations in the 1950s suggesting that introverts were better equipped for work on prolonged and monotonous tasks than extroverts because of their higher cortical arousal and their greater resistance to the setting up of inhibitory processes (Broadbent, 1958, Claridge, 1960; H.J. Eysenck, 1957). Despite some differences of emphasis between these theoretical positions, they are in agreement in predicting that extroverts should exhibit a greater decrement in performance over time on vigilance tasks.

Bakan (1959) reported one of the first experiments which aimed to investigate this prediction for a laboratory vigilance task. He used an auditory digit task, which has come to be known after him (the Bakan task, see Chapter 2), in which subjects had to detect a specified sequence (three successive odd digits which were all different) of digits in a series presented at a rate of one digit per second. Bakan found that the performance of extroverts benefitted to a greater extent from having a "secondary" task to perform (to report each occurrence of the digit "6" in addition to the "primary" signals) than did that of introverts; and that in this "dual-task" situation extroverts also manifested a greater decrement, although this result was not obtained in the single-task condition. In a second study (Bakan et al., 1963), a slightly different version of the same primary task was used (detect the sequence odd–even–odd), and the performances of introverts, extroverts, and "normals" (ambiverts) were compared. It was found that the latter two groups showed a reliable decrement in detection rate, while introverts did not, and indeed showed a slight improvement in performance during the first half of the task.

Bakan's findings therefore provided support for the suggestions of Broadbent (1958) and H.J. Eysenck (1957) that extroverts and introverts differ in the amount of decrement exhibited in sustained attention situations. A number of other investigators have subsequently attempted to replicate Bakan's results, using both the Bakan task and other laboratory vigilance tasks. The majority of these studies have found differences between introverts and extroverts in some measure of vigilance performance (see Table 6.2).

As can be seen from Table 6.2, there is general agreement that when significant differences are reported between introverts and extroverts, the former group does better, making more correct detections and fewer false alarms and showing less decrement. The only study of the 13 summarized in Table 6.2 to report no significant differences of any kind in the vigilance performances of introverts and extroverts is that of Gale et al. (1972a); this study is also among the most comprehensive, employing 60 subjects in each temperament group and testing at four different times of day.

An examination of Table 6.2 reveals that ten studies have provided data concerning a differential decrement between temperament groups. Four studies have found that introverts exhibited a significantly smaller decrement than did extroverts. These four studies can be distinguished from the rest in two main ways. First, subjects were selected from the two extremes of the distribution of temperament scores and second, "speed" tasks rather than "closure" tasks were employed. It seems, therefore, that the conjunction of the selection of extreme temperament groups and the use of "speed" tasks is likely to produce reliable differences in decrement between introverts and extroverts.

No such consistent pattern emerges from the results of studies concerned with overall differences in detection rate between temperament groups, although of the twelve studies providing relevant data the five which find significant effects at least agree on the direction of the difference (Carr, 1969; Gange et al., 1979; Harkins and Geen, 1975; Hogan, 1966; Purohit, 1972). In each of these studies introverts detected more signals than did extraverts. In addition, Bakan (1959) found introverts to detect significantly more signals during the first 32 minutes of an 80-minute task and Davies and Hockey (1966) found a difference (significant at the 10% level) in the same direction for a 32-minute task. Two studies used tasks which were too easy (over 90% of signals being correctly detected) and hence would be unlikely to find differences between temperament groups because of "ceiling" effects (Davies et al., 1969; Tune, 1966a). However, the studies of Bakan et al. (1963) and Keister and McLaughlin (1972) remain to be accounted for since there appear to be no consistent differences between these studies and those which find the performance of introverts to be reliably superior.

There are, however, a number of general factors which may account for the inconsistencies in the results of studies concerned with temperament and vigilance. These include: (a) differences in the criterion scores used to establish extrovert and introvert groups; (b) differences in neuroticism scores between temperament groups; (c) sampling bias in the selection of extroverts due to differences in sociability and impulsivity sub-scores and (d) the nature of the task employed. Certainly large differences exist in the criterion scores used to establish extrovert and introvert groups. For example, in the study of Bakan et al. (1963) the criterion score for the extraverted group was an MPI score of 40 and above, while in the study of Gale et al. (1972) the criterion score was an EPI score of 14 and above. In Hogan's (1966) study the mean MPI score for the introverted group was 19·94 whereas in Keister and McLaughlin's (1972) study the mean EPI score for the introverted groups was less than 8. The effect of neuroticism upon temperament differences in vigilance would appear to be minimal (Bakan, 1959; Colquhoun, 1959; Gale et al., 1972; Krupski et al., 1971; Wilkinson, 1961a), unless it is assumed that differences in neuroticism scores result in subjects also differing in extroversion subscores (see, for example, Thackray et al., 1974). In connection with impulsivity and sociability subscores, Krupski et al.,

Reference	Task	Duration	Measure	Questionnaire	Personality differences	Index	Result	Arousal
Davies et al. (1969)	Visual Bakan	40'	Speed (V)	Maudsley[N] and Heron (Part 2)	No (M + F)	Hits	Nsd	No
						FAs	Nsd	No
Krupski et al. (1971)	Bakan	48'	Speed (A)	Eysenck	— (M)	FAs	Extroversion significantly ($P < 0.10$) and positively correlated with FAs	NR
Gale et al. (1972d)	Bakan G	60'	Speed (A)	Eysenck[N]	No (M + F)	Hits	Nsd	No
Keister and McLaughlin (1972)	Bakan	48'	Speed (A)	Eysenck[N]	Yes (M + F)	Hits	Nsd	Yes (I < E)
Purohit (1972)	Detection of increase in intensity of light.	40'	Speed (V)	Neymann–Kohlstad	Yes (M + F)	Hits	Yes (I > E)	NR
						FAs	I < E (significance level not reported)	NR
Harkins and Geen (1975)	Detection of unmodulated line on noisy CRT.	42'	Closure (V)	Eysenck	Yes (F)	Hits	Yes (I > E)	No
						FAs	Yes (I > E)	No
						d'	Yes (I > E)	No
						$\log \beta$	Yes (I > E)	No
Gange et al. (1979)	Detection of unmodulated line on noisy CRT.	42'	Closure (V)	Eysenck	Yes (M)	Hits	Yes (I > E)	No
						FAs	Nsd	No

Table 6.2. A summary of the principal features of 13 studies of temperament and vigilance. G indicates that subjects were group-tested; A = Auditory, V = Visual; N indicates studies matched extroverts and introverts for Neuroticism scores or reported no correlation between Neuroticism and performance; M = Male, F = Female; Nsc = No significant correlation, Nsd = No significant difference; NR = Not reported.

Source	Task	Task duration	Task type	Personality test	Extreme groups	Performance measure	Mean difference	Differential decrement
Bakan (1959)	Bakan	80'	Speed (A)	Heron (Part 2)	No (M)	Hits	I > E (first two subperiods only)	No
Bakan et al. (1963)	BakanG (half the Ss only)	48'	Speed (A)	MaudsleyN	Yes (M + F)	Hits	Nsd	Yes (I < E)
Davies and Hockey (1966)	Visual checkingG	32'	Speed (V)	MaudsleyN	Yes (F)	Hits	Nsd	Yes (I < E)
						FAs	Nsd	No
Hogan (1966)	CPT	10'	Speed (V)	MaudsleyN	No (F)	Hits	Nsd	No
						FAs	Nsc	No
Tune (1966a)	Detection of 3 consecutive and different odd digits from 10 digit sequence. Sequences presented at 10" intervals.	40'	Speed (A)	Heron (Part 2)	— (M + F)	d'	Nsc, Unsociability (introversion) significantly and negatively correlated with FAs	NR
						β	Nsc, Unsociability (introversion) significantly and positively correlated with β	NR
Carr (1969)	Detection of increase in duration of tone burst.	40'	Speed (A)	Eysenck	Yes (F)	Hits	Yes (I > E)	Yes (I < E)
						FAs	Yes (I < E)	Yes (I < E)
						d'	Yes (I > E)	No
						β	Yes (I > E)	No
						DLs	Yes (I < E)	No

(1971) and Thackray *et al.* (1973, 1974) have suggested that it is the impulsivity component of extroversion that is primarily responsible for the poorer performance of extroverts in sustained attention tasks. Krupski *et al.* found that there was a higher correlation between impulsivity and false alarms than between sociability and false alarms, although neither correlation was significant. Evidence from studies of sustained attention in children also suggests that impulsivity is related to the frequency of false alarms (Doyle *et al.*, 1976; Sykes *et al.*, 1973).

Differences between studies in terms of the type of task employed may also account for some of the inconsistencies arising from studies of temperament and vigilance. However, differences in overall detection rate are found both with "speed" and "closure" tasks and with auditory and visual tasks. Failures to obtain overall differences in the performance of different temperament groups seem most likely to occur with auditory speed tasks, although no study has yet made use of an auditory closure task, and the number of studies in each modality/task-type category is not large. Since interpretations of differences in monitoring performance between introverts and extroverts have frequently been put forward in terms of the inverted-U model hypothesized to relate arousal and performance (for example, Corcoran, 1965), a distinction is sometimes made between stimulating and unstimulating tasks. For example, the auditory task used by Bakan *et al.* (1963) may be assumed to be highly stimulating on the grounds that it is both a "cognitive" and a "closely coupled" task, so that on being given the task the arousal level of introverts becomes supra-optimal, while that of extroverts reaches the optimum level for that task. It would then be hypothesized that as arousal declines with time on task introverts will improve initially and extroverts will suffer a continuous decrement; these results were obtained by Bakan *et al.* (1963). If the task were unstimulating it could be assumed that the arousal level of introverts would be optimal while that of extroverts would be sub-optimal; then any time-related decrease in arousal would mean that both extroverts and introverts would show a decrement. This model is so flexible, however, that a differential decrement even in an unstimulating task could still be accommodated, since it can be assumed that there is a slower rate of change in performance with arousal near the optimal arousal level than at other levels (see Colquhoun, 1971; Corcoran, 1972). This type of interpretation would be attractive if there were a simple means of assessing the stimulation value of different vigilance tasks. As noted in Chapter 2, Bergum (1966) attempted to provide the basis of a taxonomy of all continuous performance tasks in terms of their stimulation value. Unfortunately this taxonomic approach does not provide much predictive capacity as far as vigilance tasks are concerned, with the result that judgements about what constitutes an "arousing" task are largely intuitive. Thus an auditory task, with its inherent "coupling", might be supposed to be more stimulating than a simple visual task, as suggested by Harkins and Geen (1975); an interaction between temperament and time on task might therefore be expected only for auditory tasks. Unfortunately there are instances of visual tasks providing evidence for differential decrement between extroverts and introverts (Davies and Hockey, 1966) and instances of auditory tasks not reporting this result (Gale *et al.*, 1972d). It does not at present seem possible, therefore, to explain the lack of consistency between studies in terms of differences in stimulation value between tasks. There appears to be no very compelling single explanation of why the vigilance performance of introverts sometimes is, and at other times is not, reliably superior to that of extroverts except that the effect of temperament on overall detection efficiency is not, perhaps, particularly strong.

However, when superior performance by introverts is found, does it result from a difference in sensitivity or in criterion placement? Data on false alarm rates would enable a decision to be made between these alternatives. As can be seen from Table 6.2, the majority finding from studies that have provided such data is that introverts make fewer false alarms than do extroverts (Carr, 1969; Harkins and Geen, 1975; Krupski *et al.*, 1971; Purohit, 1972; Tune, 1966a), although the studies by Davies and Hockey (1966) and Davies *et al.* (1969) found no reliable difference between temperament groups on this measure. The implication of the majority finding, when considered with the significantly superior detection performance of introverts found by Carr, Harkins and Geen and Purohit, is that the sensitivity of introverts is superior to that of extroverts. Both Carr (1969) and Harkins and Geen (1975) conducted decision theory analyses of their data which support this conclusion. In each case extroverts were found to be less sensitive than introverts and to adopt more risky response criteria; these differences in sensitivity and criterion placement were maintained throughout the vigil.

There are thus two main findings that emerge from the studies of temperament and vigilance that we have surveyed. First, extroverts show a greater decrement than introverts when a "speed" task is employed and when extreme groups of subjects are selected. All the tasks in which a differential decrement was found are also speed tasks with a high event rate (above 24 events per minute) which, as noted in Chapter 5, are tasks associated with a sensitivity decrement. It would be expected, therefore, that a sensitivity decrement would be found in the four studies finding a differential decrement in detection rate, and that the decline in sensitivity would be greater for extroverts than for introverts. Unfortunately, in two of the studies (Bakan *et al.*, 1963; Keister and McLaughlin, 1972) no false alarm data were provided and it is thus impossible to determine whether a sensitivity decrement was obtained, although Sostek (1976) has observed a sensitivity decrement with the same task that these two studies employed. Davies and Hockey (1966) did find a sensitivity decrement for extroverts but not for introverts in their experiment (see J.F. Mackworth, 1969, p. 117) but their decision theory analysis was based on group means, hence this finding needs to be treated with some caution. Carr (1969), as can be seen from Table 6.2, did not find a sensitivity decrement with his task, although the event rate (30 per minute) was only slightly in excess of the criterion point of 24 events per minute dividing high-rate from low-rate tasks and, as mentioned in Chapter 5, one or two other studies with event rates around this level have also failed to obtain sensitivity decrements. As noted above, however, Carr did find a temperament difference in sensitivity across the whole vigil, with the sensitivity of extroverts being reliably lower. Hastrup (1979), who divided her subjects into introverted and extroverted groups on the basis of the median extroversion scale score, observed a greater sensitivity decrement for extroverts, which just failed to reach significance, in the "easy" version of her task (see below), although not in the "difficult" one. Although the evidence is equivocal, it seems likely that if an experiment were conducted using a high event rate (say 40 events per minute) speed task and extreme groups of extroverts and introverts, selected with a personality scale containing a measure of impulsivity, then a differential decrement in sensitivity would be obtained, provided, of course, that the task was of an appropriate duration. Extroverts should show the greater sensitivity decrement in this situation.

If such a finding were obtained then in terms of the interpretation of the sensitivity decrement put forward in Chapter 5, it could be argued that extroverts experience greater difficulty in maintaining the level of effort required to deal with the memory and time pressure demands of high event rate speed tasks. The level of effort maintained by extroverts in such tasks would thus show greater moment to moment fluctuation and would be reflected in a greater performance variability. Some support for this view comes from a study by Thackray *et al.* (1974) who found that the variability of response times increased for extroverts but not for introverts over a 40-minute serial reaction task. Thackray *et al.* also found that of the two components of extroversion (sociability and impulsivity) the latter was primarily responsible for the observed decrement in performance. The finding of a connection between impulsivity and performance decrement has two implications for the selection of temperament groups for vigilance experiments. First, in order to demonstrate differential decrement between temperament groups, it seems probable that a scale containing a measure of impulsivity should be used, rather than one which is solely a measure of sociability, such as Part II of the Heron Scale, which has been used as a measure of extroversion in a number of studies. Second, extreme groups should be selected, in order that differences in impulsivity between groups are maximized.

The second main finding to be accounted for is that of an overall difference in sensitivity between temperament groups. One possible interpretation of this result can be made in terms of arousal, for which there is some supporting evidence from studies of temperament and time of day. Colquhoun (1960, 1962a), using a closure task, has found that detection rate is reliably correlated with introversion if testing is conducted in the morning and with extroversion if testing is conducted in the afternoon. The personality test used by Colquhoun was Part II of the Heron scale which, as has been mentioned, provides a measure of sociability. Nearly all the studies summarized in Table 6.2 appear to have controlled for possible time-of-day effects and there is thus no conflict between the results of these studies and those of Colquhoun. However, the one study in Table 6.2 which specifically tested for the presence of time-of-day effects failed to find a significant interaction between temperament and time of testing (Gale et al., 1972d).

Other evidence for temperament differences in the effects of time of day on performance has been provided by Blake (1965, 1967b, 1971) who showed that performance at a cancellation task varied with body temperature at five different times of day, being lowest at 08.00 hours and highest at 21.00 hours. Blake also observed a positive correlation across subjects between performance and body temperature at each time of day. Blake (1967b) went on to demonstrate that as the day progressed, the correlation between introversion (as measured by Part II of the Heron Scale) and body temperature (measured orally), which was significantly positive at 08.00 hours, gradually became negative, reaching significance at 21.00 hours. Significant negative correlations were also obtained at 23.00 and 01.00 hours. Blake's results, largely confirmed by Horne and Ostberg (1977), indicate that the body temperature of introverts is higher than that of extroverts from around 06.00 to around 14.00 hours, that there is little difference between the curves of the two groups from around 14.00 to around 18.00 hours and that the body temperature of extroverts is higher thereafter, until around 05.00 when the curves again briefly merge. However, these differences in body temperature only become reliable, in terms of a significant interaction between sociability score and time of day, when relatively extreme groups of introverts and extroverts are considered and no significant differences between less extreme groups appear to have been obtained. Horne and Ostberg (1977), using the EPI as a measure of temperament differences, also found no reliable differences between introverts, extroverts and ambiverts over the period 09.00 to 23.00 hours. Furthermore, Blake (1971), using an auditory vigilance task, did not find a significant correlation between introversion and either correct detection or false alarm rates or, with one exception, between body temperature and the same two measures at five different times of day ranging from 08.00–21.00 hours. It thus seems unlikely that differences in detection efficiency between introverts and extroverts at any one time of day can be attributed to differences in body temperature. But Carr (1969) did find that extroverts showed reliably lower levels of electrodermal arousal during monitoring performance (see also p. 129). Differences in arousal level may thus provide a possible explanation for temperament differences in sensitivity during vigilance, although the evidence bearing on the question of whether introverts and extroverts differ in arousal level is far from being conclusive (see, for example, M.W. Eysenck, 1977, pp. 195–201).

Eysenck observed that the behavioural evidence suggesting that introverts are more aroused than extroverts is much stronger than the psychophysiological evidence. For example, Farley and Farley (1967) and Sostek (1976) obtained a significant positive correlation between extroversion and "sensation-seeking", as measured by the Sensation Seeking Scale (Zuckerman et al., 1964) and certainly extroverts seem to behave in monotonous situations as if they were "stimulus hungry" (Davies et al., 1969; Gale, 1969; Hill, 1975). Furthermore, introducing varied auditory stimulation (VAS) into a vigilance situation improves the performance of extroverts but not that of introverts (Davies et al., 1969). In this study VAS significantly reduced the number of false alarms made by extroverts and slightly but not significantly improved their correct detection rate, the implication being that the sensitivity of extroverts, but not of introverts, was increased by VAS. If, therefore, changes in the variety of stimulation differentially affect the sensitivity of introverts and extroverts in vigilance situations, it might be expected that under the monotonous conditions of the typical vigilance experiment the sensitivity of extroverts would be lower than that of introverts, as the results of Carr (1969) and Harkins and Geen (1975) suggest.

The lowered sensitivity and more relaxed criterion placement of extroverts compared to introverts perhaps result from attempts made by extroverts to increase the variety of sensations available to them during vigilance performance. Gale et al. (1972b) obtained a significant positive correlation between extroversion and scores on the Betts Vividness of Imagery Scale (Betts, 1909) with extroverts reporting more vivid imagery than introverts. Morris and Gale (1974) also found vivid imagery to be more prevalent among extroverts. It is possible, therefore, that extroverts are more likely to generate mental imagery while performing a vigilance task and that this could impair their detection efficiency. Antrobus et al. (1967) divided subjects into high and low day-dreaming groups, on the basis of their responses to a day-dreaming questionnaire, and found that although there was no significant difference in the detection rates of the two groups in a fairly brief detection task with a high frequency of signals, the performance of the high day-dreaming group deteriorated at a faster rate. This group also reported significantly more "task irrelevant thoughts" during the vigil, the incidence of which tended to increase with time on task. Furthermore, since performing a vigilance task under conditions of divided attention (in this case the requirement to perform another task simultaneously) results in a decrease in sensitivity (Broadbent and Gregory, 1963a), it might be supposed that the allocation of attention to internal imagery, especially if that imagery were vivid, would produce similar effects. Hill (1975) found that extroverts introduced more variety into their patterns of responding during the performance of a monotonous task; if, during vigilance, this were to take the form of an increased rate of responding, it is likely that the false alarm rate would rise and an apparently more risky criterion would result. This change in criterion placement would probably be accompanied by a reduction in sensitivity.

These explanations of differences between extroverts and introverts in sensitivity and bias during vigilance are speculative, and clearly require empirical support; moreover, they do not appear to be favoured by the results of what seems to be the only study of sensation seeking and vigilance (Cahoon, 1970b). Cahoon's experiment was primarily concerned with the effects of hypoxia on vigilance (see Chapter 7) but he reported the incidental finding that no correlation was obtained between scores on the Sensation Seeking Scale of Zuckerman *et al.* (1964) and a variety of measures of vigilance performance, either at sea level or at the equivalent of an altitude of 17 000 feet. It would obviously be useful to have more data on the relation between sensation seeking and vigilance.

Finally, it is probably advisable to control for smoking behaviour, which may relate to sensation seeking, in experiments concerned with temperament differences in vigilance. Although the effects of smoking on vigilance performance are discussed in Chapter 7, it is worth noting here that the detection efficiency of non-smokers has been reported to be superior to that of smokers whether or not the latter are permitted to smoke during the experiment (Tong *et al.*, 1974) and that there may be an interaction between temperament and smoking behaviour in their effects upon performance (Tarrière *et al.*, 1966; Tong *et al.*, 1974).

Field dependence and vigilance performance
It has been suggested that the field dependence–independence dimension of Witkin (Witkin *et al.*, 1962) may be related to vigilance performance (see, for example, J.F. Mackworth, 1969), and in view of the nature of the tests used to discriminate relatively field independent from relatively field dependent individuals, it might be expected that the former would perform particularly well on closure-type tasks. Indeed, Thornton *et al.* (1968) found that scores on the Embedded Figures Test, a high score indicating relative field independence, were significantly positively correlated with the ability to identify targets correctly in aerial photographs, a good example of a closure task. There are also some indications that extroverts are more likely to be field dependent (Evans, 1967; Kennedy, 1977).

It would thus be reasonable to expect relatively field independent individuals to perform somewhat better in vigilance situations than individuals who are relatively field dependent. This expectation is confirmed by the very few relevant studies. Cahoon (1970a) found that at sea level scores on the Embedded Figures Test were significantly negatively correlated with the number of false alarms and significantly positively correlated with hit and false alarm latencies and with d'; that is, field independent subjects tended to make fewer false alarms, to have higher sensitivity and to respond more slowly when making correct detection or false alarm responses. These relationships held for the most part under a further three hypoxia conditions. Broadly similar results were obtained by Moore and Gross (1973) using the Mackworth Clock Test. Both of these studies employed speed tasks. Kennedy (1977), however, using a complex vigilance task which is more difficult to classify, found no relation between field dependence and performance. In general, then, field-independent subjects appear to be rather more efficient at detecting signals in vigilance situations, although it is possible that performance differences between field-independent and field-dependent groups may be affected by task type.

Subjective reactions in vigilance and monotonous work situations
Individuals also differ considerably in their subjective reactions to vigilance situations and the attitudes they develop towards the task may exert some effect upon their performance. It is possible too that personality influences the kind of attitudes that are developed towards the task, but this question has received little consideration. There is a general belief, however, stemming originally from the industrial studies of Wyatt and his co-workers in the 1920s and 1930s (Wyatt and Fraser, 1929; Wyatt and Langdon, 1932, 1937; see also Wyatt, 1950), that extroverts are more easily bored by monotonous work situations, and are more distractible.

Whether or not this belief is correct, groups of individuals differing in boredom and distractibility have been shown to differ also in the performance levels they achieve in monotonous work situations. Thackray *et al.* (1977) examined the relations between ratings of boredom and monotony and a variety of physiological measures taken during the performance of a 60-minute simulated air traffic control task. At the beginning and end of the experimental session 45 subjects were given nine-point scales on which they rated their levels of boredom, monotony, irritation, attentiveness, fatigue and strain. The boredom and monotony scale scores obtained at the end of the experiment were summed for each subject and two sub-groups, each of eight subjects, were selected, one a High Boredom and the other a Low Boredom group. There were no differences between the groups in the boredom/monotony scores obtained at the beginning of the task. The two groups were then compared with respect to performance, assessed by response latencies, and to physiological changes during the task. The High Boredom group produced significantly longer response times than the Low group and the proportion of long response times increased from the first half of the task to the second for the High group while decreasing for the Low group. The High group also showed a greater increase in strain and a greater decrease in attentiveness. The only physiological measure which differentiated the two groups was heart rate variability, which decreased with time at work for the Low Boredom group while increasing for the High group. This study provides some evidence suggesting that there may be a constellation of factors distinguishing those subjects who become bored during the performance of a monotonous task from those who do not. Davies *et al.* (1972) reported significant positive correlations between self reports of boredom and of daydreaming and between boredom and perceived task difficulty during the performance of a self-paced problem-solving task lasting for about half an hour. Significant negative correlations were obtained between boredom and concentration and between boredom and the perceived expenditure of effort in the same situation.

Thackray *et al.* (1973) gave their subjects a 23-item distractability questionnaire and divided the scores at the median to obtain a high distractibility and a low distractibility group. The two groups of subjects then performed a 25-minute self-paced serial response task. The high-distractability group responded significantly more slowly throughout the task and their response times also became much more variable with time on task. Various psychophysiological measures were also recorded, including heart rate variability, but no significant differences between the groups on any of the measures were obtained. Corcoran (1965) also found that extroverts produced significantly fewer responses and a significantly greater number of long response times in Leonard's (1959) five-choice serial reaction task. It seems quite probable, therefore, that extroverts are more distractible and that their performance on such tasks, as well as being generally inferior to that of introverts, becomes increasingly more variable with time at work. It would be of interest to determine whether the vigilance performance of extroverts also exhibits greater variability (see Faulkner, 1962 and Chapter 1). The sharper decrement which tends to be shown by extroverts in speed vigilance tasks with a high event rate, and their more pronounced performance variability in self-paced serial reaction tasks, may well be manifestations of the same underlying performance change.

Although most people performing a vigilance task become bored at one time or another, their attitudes towards the task may nevertheless differ, and undergo some change over repeated sessions with the same task. Some people maintain a neutral attitude towards the task situation, others intensely dislike it, while others still come to regard the task as a challenge and hence to adopt a positive attitude towards it. Yet the adoption of a positive attitude does not seem to exert much influence on detection efficiency. McGrath (1960) found no significant difference between the detection rates of subjects adopting either positive or negative attitudes towards the vigilance tasks used in a study by Buckner *et al.* (1960), although subjects who adopted a neutral attitude performed significantly worse than either of the other two groups. Some subjects preferred the visual task to the auditory while others preferred the auditory to the visual, and subjects tended to detect more signals in the task which they preferred. McGrath also obtained subjective estimates of tiredness and found that feeling of tiredness increased throughout the day while feelings of restlessness reached a peak in the mid-morning and mid-afternoon. Not surprisingly, 'perhaps, subjects performed worse when they felt tired than when they felt rested, but no relation was found between feelings of restlessness and detection efficiency, a finding also obtained by Baker (1958) who measured restlessness directly, by recording bodily movements via microswitches placed beneath the subject's chair.

Psychophysiological studies of individual differences in vigilance

In this section we are concerned with the contribution psychophysiological studies have made to the understanding of individual differences in vigilance performance. Since the majority of such studies have employed measures of autonomic nervous system (ANS) activity, rather than measures of the electrical activity of the brain (see Chapter 8), the present discussion considers only studies using electrodermal measures (skin conductance, skin potential or skin resistance), measures of cardiovascular activity (mean heart rate or heart rate variability), and adrenalin and noradrenalin levels, although a brief reference is also made to studies employing respiration rate and muscle tension. We begin with an examination of the relation between ANS measures and detection efficiency before describing in some detail the psychophysiology of individual differences in vigilance.

The ANS and vigilance performance

Much effort has been devoted to attempts to find reliable physiological correlates of the vigilance decrement and, to a lesser extent, of omission and commission errors. Two requirements seem mandatory in this regard: first, that the decrement is accompanied by a reliable change in a physiological index; and second, that performance is correlated with the index. Skin conductance, for example, decreases during a vigilance task, but its correlation with performance is either weak or unstable (Davies and Krkovic, 1965; Eason *et al.*, 1965; O'Hanlon, 1970). The mean heart rate also either declines or remains stable with time, but is uncorrelated with performance (Griew *et al.*, 1963; O'Hanlon, 1970; Thackray *et al.*, 1974). Essentially negative findings have been obtained for other variables such as respiration rate and muscle tension (Eason et al., 1965: Groll, 1966; Lucaccini, 1968; O'Hanlon, 1970; Stern, 1966).

More promising results have been obtained with heart rate variability and with adrenalin and noradrenalin levels. Heart rate variability has been found to increase during a vigilance task (Kibler, 1968; O'Hanlon, 1970), during a control condition in which subjects viewed a series of slide projections of travelogue scenes (O'Hanlon, 1970), during a 40-minute serial reaction task (Thackray et al., 1974), and during continuous driving over a prescribed circuit on the California highway (O'Hanlon, 1971; O'Hanlon and Mackie, 1977). Furthermore, O'Hanlon (1970) reported significant negative correlations (both inter- and intra-subject) between heart rate variability and detection rate. Griew et al. (1963) obtained a significant positive correlation between heart rate variability and total error score (omissions + false alarms) and Thackray et al. (1974) reported a series of increasingly positive correlations between heart rate variability and response-time variability as their serial reaction task progressed. These were significant for all but the first 12 minutes of a 40-minute task.

In several experiments O'Hanlon and his associates (O'Hanlon, 1964, 1965, 1970; O'Hanlon and Beatty, 1976; O'Hanlon and Horvath, 1973b) have demonstrated a strong association between adrenalin levels, assessed both from blood and urine samples, and monitoring performance. In some of these studies an association between noradrenalin levels and detection efficiency has also been observed, but this appears to depend upon task duration (see O'Hanlon and Beatty, 1976). O'Hanlon (1970) compared adrenalin and noradrenalin levels obtained from blood samples during the performance of two one-hour visual vigilance tasks differing in signal discriminability and during a control condition in which subjects watched a series of slides depicting travel scenes. In both tasks performance declined significantly with time on task, as did adrenalin level, although there were differences in the amount of change with time between the three conditions. Significant positive inter- and intra-subject correlations between adrenalin level and both correct detections and false alarms were observed. No reliable change in noradrenalin level during any condition was apparent however, and there was no relation between noradrenalin level and performance.

Similarly, O'Hanlon and Beatty (1976), using a simulated radar monitoring task, found that performance (measured in terms of the number of sweeps required to detect a target) reliably deteriorated in both a two-hour and a one-hour version of the task. Adrenalin and noradrenalin levels were assessed in this experiment from urine samples. In both versions of the task, adrenalin levels were significantly and negatively related to performance, while a significant negative correlation with noradrenalin level was only found in the longer task. In this task the correlations remained significant after corrections were made for body weight.

It appears, then, that both heart rate variability and adrenalin level are strongly associated with detection efficiency in monitoring situations and also with performance in other tasks requiring sustained attention. But overall, as we have seen, the results obtained from psychophysiological studies of vigilance are not particularly encouraging. This is perhaps not too surprising since a number of general criticisms can be made of such studies. First, and perhaps most importantly, control data are often lacking so that while changes over time in some psychophysiological measure are well documented, it remains unclear what changes would have taken place had a different task been performed, or had the subjects simply done nothing at all for the duration of the task. In other words, evidence for task or for situational specificity of the observed psychophysiological changes is frequently not provided. It also seems that a number of studies have failed to take appropriate measures of resting psychophysiological activity, or under "alerted" conditions, so that any changes in such activity during the vigil must be interpreted cautiously (O'Hanlon, 1970). Second, the task employed is frequently modified, in order to meet the requirements of a satisfactory psychophysiological experiment often in such a way that it is at least questionable whether the task remains a vigilance task. Third, from the perspective of decision theory, performance assessment has been generally inadequate in such studies, in that measures of sensitivity and bias have been largely neglected.

Welford (1962, 1978) has argued that changes in activation or arousal, which are presumed to be reflected by changes in physiological activity (see Chapter 1), influence criterion placement (β) rather than sensitivity (d'). Welford's hypothesis is supported by the results of Milosevic (1975) who obtained a reliable increase in skin resistance (corresponding to a decrease in skin conductance) for a low event rate speed task. There was also a significant increase in β with time on task while d' remained constant. Subjects were divided also into two groups, fast and slow, on the basis of the rate at which skin resistance changed during the vigil. No change in detection measures with time on task was found for the slow change group but significant declines in detection and false alarm rates and a significant rise in log. β occurred for the fast change group. The amount of change in skin resistance was also significantly and negatively related to pre-test values; that is, subjects showing slower changes in skin resistance during the task had higher initial levels. Milosevic also computed rank correlations between the amount of change in detection measures and in skin resistance from the first 20 minutes of the task to the last but only the relation between skin resistance and detection rate proved to be significant: the greater the increase in skin resistance, the greater the decline in the number of signals correctly detected.

The only other ANS study relevant to Welford's hypothesis seems to be that of Carr (1969), although in this experiment no reliable changes in sensitivity or in criterion measures with time at work were obtained and while detection rate declined, the decline was not significant. Carr found that skin resistance increased from pre-test levels for the first 20 minutes of a 40-minute task but had returned to these levels by the end of the task. Correlations between the slopes of skin resistance values and those of behavioural measures were calculated but only one, that between skin resistance and the total number of responses (correct detections + false alarms) which was positive, proved to be significant. Additional data from psychophysiological studies employing tasks in which reliable sensitivity decrements are obtained would appear to be needed. In our view, a likely outcome would be that similar physiological changes occur when either a sensitivity decrement, with a constant or near constant criterion, or a criterion increment, with constant sensitivity, as was found by Milosevic, is obtained. However, it is possible that physiological measures can distinguish between good and bad detectors, a question which is now explored.

Psychophysiological studies of vigilant observers

O'Hanlon (1964, 1965) demonstrated that the concentration of adrenalin in the blood reliably diminished during the performance of a three-hour vigilance task, requiring the detection of changes in a small spot of light, in subjects whose detection efficiency declined with time at work (described as "decrementers") but not in subjects whose performance remained stable (known as "non-decrementers"). A highly significant positive correlation between adrenalin level and detection rate was observed for decrementers. The adrenalin levels of this group showed no change in a control condition in which a three-hour series of silent motion pictures, including westerns, sports, travel and comedies, was presented. O'Hanlon also took measures of the amount of noradrenalin in the bloodstream but no difference between decrementers and non-decrementers on this measure was found. There was a significant negative relationship between the performance of decrementers and noradrenalin level, although O'Hanlon regarded this finding with some caution because of the extreme variability of the noradrenalin measure.

In a broadly similar study, Verschoor and Van Wieringen (1970) employed two 90-minute auditory vigilance tasks in which subjects were required to detect changes in the intensity of a tone. The first task was a standard vigilance task in which the signal consisted of a small increase in intensity, the second was described by Verschoor and Van Wieringen as a "choice reaction" task. Half the signals in this second task consisted of increases, and half of decreases in intensity, and subjects were provided with two keys in order to report separately the occurrence of each signal type. Skin conductance measures were taken during the performance of each task. After each task had been completed, the median detection score was calculated and subjects were divided into two groups, one of "good detectors" whose scores were above the median, and one of "bad detectors", whose scores fell below it. In both tasks it was found that good detectors showed no change over time in either detection rate, skin conductance or detection latency. Bad detectors, on the other hand, showed reliable declines in the first two measures and a significant increase in the third. No significant differences between good and bad detectors in pre-task skin conductance levels were observed.

For each task separately, Verschoor and Van Wieringen also determined the percentage of subjects detecting each signal, the average detection latency, and the average skin conductance level at the time the signal was presented. They then computed rank correlations between these measures based on the 18 signals in each task. When good and bad detectors were combined a significant positive correlation was found between the average skin conductance level and the percentage detection measure for each task, together with significant negative correlations between detection latency and skin conductance and between detection latency and the percentage detection measure. When correlations were computed separately for good and bad detectors, however, no correlation proved to be significant for the good detectors, while five out of six were significant for the bad. This result suggests that detection efficiency and skin conductance are related for "decrementers", who also detect fewer signals overall, but not for "non-decrementers", and thus provides a possible explanation both for the low inter-subject correlations and for the small proportion of reliable intra-subject correlations mentioned above.

Subjects who make many false alarms are frequently regarded as "poor" vigilance performers and one study has examined possible psychophysiological characteristics differentiating these subjects from those who make few false alarms (Krupski et al., 1971). These investigators recorded skin conductance during a 48-minute auditory vigilance task, the Bakan task. In a post-hoc analysis Krupski et al. divided subjects into three groups of ten on the basis of the number of false alarms made during the task. They found, first, that the high false alarm group showed a pronounced decrement in detection rate with time on task and the moderate false alarm group a less marked decrement, while the detection rate of the low false alarm group improved with time, although the performance of this group was much lower initially. Second, a GSR amplitude score was computed for each subject, based on the average amplitude for detected signals, and a significant negative correlation between the number of false alarms and the mean GSR amplitude score was obtained. Third, an "orienting response" measure, the initial GSR amplitude measured at task onset, was taken and again a significant negative correlation between the amplitude of the orienting response and the number of false alarms made by each subject was found. A marginally significant negative correlation between basal skin conductance to presented signals and the number of false alarms was also observed. Finally, a marginally significant positive correlation was obtained between extroversion scores on the EPI and false alarm scores, implying that extroverts are likely to make more false alarms. The conclusions drawn from this experiment were that individuals who make relatively more false alarms "may be characterised as lower in electrodermal arousal and subject to vigilance decrement over time." (p. 310). These results broadly agree with those of the temperament studies discussed earlier.

Individual differences in psychophysiological activity and vigilance performance

The greater part of this section is devoted to a discussion of the relation between autonomic, or more specifically electrodermal, lability and vigilance performance, although psychophysiological studies of the detection efficiency of groups differing in age, sex and personality are also briefly mentioned.

Lacey and Lacey (1958) distinguished between electrodermal "stabiles" and "labiles" in terms of the frequency of spontaneous electrodermal responses (EDRs) emitted during rest or during stimulation. This measure has subsequently been shown to be inversely related to the speed with which the electrodermal orienting response habituates to a series of neutral, above-threshold stimuli, such as tones (Corah and Stern, 1963; Katkin and McCubbin, 1969; Koepke and Pribram, 1966). Thus "labiles", who produce a greater number of spontaneous EDRs, tend to show a slower rate of EDR habituation than do stabiles, and there is a positive correlation between the number of spontaneous EDRs and the number of trials required to reach a criterion of habituation. Such correlations range between $+0.48$ and $+0.75$ (Coles *et al.*, 1971; Crider and Lunn, 1971; Sostek, 1976). The test–retest reliability of electrodermal lability over days varies between $+0.54$ and $+0.89$ (Corah and Stern, 1963; Docter and Friedman, 1966; Johnson, 1963). Over longer time intervals, the reliability falls slightly but is generally in the region of $+0.50$ (Bull and Gale, 1973; Dykman *et al.*, 1963). Lability does not, however, seem to be highly correlated with other electrodermal measures, such as basal skin resistance or conductance or GSR amplitude (Galbrecht *et al.*, 1965; Koepke and Pribram, 1966; Lader and Wing, 1966) or with other psychophysiological measures such as heart rate or EEG amplitude (Johnson, 1963).

Crider and Lunn (1971) reviewed a number of studies of electrodermal lability and suggested that lability should be regarded as a dimension of personality, measurable in terms of either the number of spontaneous EDRs or by the rate of habituation of the orienting response. Sostek (1976) has labelled these two measures spontaneous lability and trial lability respectively. Lability does not seem to be strongly related to questionnaire measures of manifest anxiety or of neuroticism (Burdick, 1966; Katkin and McCubbin, 1969; Koepke and Pribram, 1966; Koriat *et al.*, 1973; Sostek, 1976), although Coles *et al.* (1971) reported reliable differences in trial lability, but not in spontaneous lability, between groups differing in neuroticism scores and Lader and Wing (1964) found differences between anxiety patients and normals on both spontaneous and trial lability measures. The relation of lability to extroversion is confused, some studies reporting significant correlations, or reliable differences between criterion groups (Coles *et al.*, 1971; Crider and Lunn, 1971; H.J. Eysenck, 1967; Lader and Wing, 1966; Mangan and O'Gorman, 1969) while others do not (Burdick, 1966; Hastrup and Katkin, 1976; Koriat *et al.*, 1973; Sostek, 1976). When a significant relation between extroversion and lability has been reported, there is a tendency for extroverts to produce fewer spontaneous EDRs and to habituate more rapidly, that is, extroverts resemble "stabiles".

A number of studies have examined the relation between lability and vigilance performance either by correlating lability with detection efficiency or by pre-selecting groups of "stabiles" and "labiles" on the basis of one or more lability measures (Coles and Gale, 1971; Crider and Augenbraun, 1975; Siddle, 1972; Sostek, 1976). Coles and Gale employed a 60-minute version of the Bakan task and found a significant positive correlation between one measure of trial lability and detection rate although no correlation between detection rate and spontaneous lability was obtained. A second measure of trial lability, which Coles and Gale considered to be more closely related to changes in performance with time, also showed no correlation with the total number of correct detections and, since no decrement in detection efficiency was observed, it proved impossible to correlate this measure of trial lability with declines in detection rate. Siddle (1972) also used an auditory vigilance task, lasting for 50 minutes, in which occasional changes in the loudness of a one-second tone, presented at two-second intervals, had to be discriminated and for which it had already been established that a reliable decrement in sensitivity (d') occurred. Taking the rate of habituation of the GSR orienting responses as a measure of trial lability, Siddle compared the performance of fast and slow habituators and found that the former group (stabiles) showed a reliably greater decrement in detection rate, and hence presumably in sensitivity, than did the latter (labiles). Crider and Augenbraun (1975), like Coles and Gale, used an auditory version of the Bakan task, lasting for 64 minutes, and selected labile and stabile groups on the basis of the habituation of spontaneous skin potential responses to the presentation of a tone (trial lability). They found that stabiles detected fewer signals than did labiles but, again like Coles and Gale, failed to obtain a reliable vigilance decrement, although there was a tendency for stabiles to show a greater decline in performance. No differences between stabiles and labiles were found for false alarm rates or d' scores but labiles were found to have reliably lower response criterion levels (β), in all three periods of the task. No change in β with time at work occurred however.

Parasuraman (1975), using an auditory discrimination task which lasted for about 25 minutes, and employing a four-category confidence rating scale, obtained similar results. Labiles, selected on the basis of both spontaneous and trial lability scores, detected significantly more signals at each of three criterion placements (strict, moderate and lax), made significantly more false alarms and had reliably lower β values. A sensitivity measure (d'), did not differentiate between the labile and stabile groups. Sostek (1976, 1978), who also employed the Bakan task, in a 48-minute auditory version, selected labiles and stabiles on the basis of both spontaneous and trial lability, separately and in combination (see also Chapter 4). He found that trial labiles made more false alarms than trial stabiles and had lower response criteria (log. β). Labiles selected on the basis of the combined lability measures detected reliably more signals than did stabiles but the spontaneous lability measure alone did not relate to any measure of overall detection efficiency. However, stabiles on all three lability criteria showed a significant detection rate decrement while labiles did not. Trial stabiles and "combined" stabiles also showed reliable decrements in sensitivity as indexed by both a parametric (d') and a non-parametric measure ($P(A)$) while labiles did not; the $P(A)$ decrement was also found in spontaneous stabiles. Log β showed no significant change with time. In general trial lability showed a greater relation to detection efficiency than did spontaneous lability. In a similar study, Hastrup (1979) compared the performance of labiles and stabiles, classified on the basis of both spontaneous and trial lability, an easy and difficult versions of the same 48-minute auditory vigilance task, in which subjects were required to detect occasional louder tones from a series of 440 Hz standard tones presented at a rate of 30 per minute. In the "easy" condition the signal tone was 2dB, and in the difficult condition 1dB, louder than the standard. The results of this study are given in Fig. 6.2 and it can be seen that sensitivity ($P(A)$) declined significantly for both lability groups in the easy condition, but that only stabiles exhibited a reliable sensitivity decrement in the difficult condition. Both groups showed a significant criterion increment in the easy task and a non-significant trend in the same direction was apparent in the difficult version.

Hastrup's findings suggest that task difficulty, considered in terms of signal discriminability, influences whether or not differential sensitivity decrements are obtained for labiles and stables. It is thus possible that differential rates of decline in vigilance performance are only found in labiles and stabiles when the task exceeds a certain level of difficulty.

These six studies of the relation of electrodermal lability to vigilance

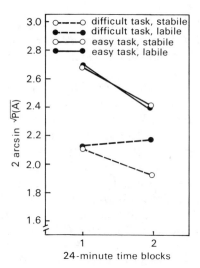

Fig. 6.2. Vigilance performance for stabile and labile subjects in two levels of task difficulty. From Hastrup (1979).

and discrimination performance provide reasonably consistent results. In every case where a vigilance decrement was reported, stabiles showed a greater decline in performance with time than did labiles and in two experiments, those of Sostek (1976, 1978) and Hastrup (1979), showed a greater sensitivity decrement, although it is likely that Siddle's (1972) data would yield a similar finding. In all five vigilance experiment high-rate auditory speed tasks were used so it is surprising that a reliable sensitivity decrement was not obtained by Crider and Augenbraun (1975) who analysed their results in terms of decision theory measures. A further general result is that stabiles adopt more cautious response criteria. In many ways then, the vigilance performance of stabiles seems to resemble quite closely that of extroverts, although extroverts tend to adopt more risky response criteria, and it is unclear why the relation between extroversion and electrodermal lability is not stronger than it appears to be, there being sometimes indeed a weak trend for extroverts to be more labile (Hastrup, 1979). One reason may be that in studies of the vigilance performance of extroverts, neuroticism has usually been controlled for, whereas in studies of the relation between extroversion and lability such a control has frequently been lacking. As Coles and Gale (1971) have demonstrated, lability measures seem, at least occasionally, to be related both to extroversion and to neuroticism. Another possibility is that:

> ... those aspects of individual behaviour which are related to individual differences in electrodermal lability and also to individual differences in such behavioural phenomena as orienting response habituation rate, vigilance

performance and response to stress, apparently elude subjects' self-descriptions and are likely to be independent of self-awareness.

(Hastrup and Katkin, 1976 p. 300)

If extroverts are to be tentatively identified with stabiles it might be expected that levels of electrodermal activity during monitoring would indicate lowered arousal on the part of extroverts. This result has been obtained for skin resistance by Carr (1969), who found that the skin resistance of extroverts was reliably higher throughout at a 40-minute visual vigilance task. Gange *et al.* (1979) found that heart rate (which declined reliably with time on task) although not skin conductance (which significantly increased during task performance) was reliably lower for extroverts than for introverts in the vigilance condition of their study (see p. 111). Introverts also emitted significantly more spontaneous skin resistance responses than did extroverts in all experimental conditions. Siddle and Smith (1974) found that EEG abundance in the 9–13 Hz range declined more rapidly in trial stabiles than in trial labiles under conditions of monotonous stimulation and there is some evidence that extroverts also show signs of lowered electrocortical arousal in similar situations (Gale, 1973; Gale *et al.*, 1969). However, arousal is by no means the complete answer to the problem of individual differences in vigilance. Gale *et al.* (1972a), for example, found that "good" vigilance performers, on a 60-minute version of the Bakan task, showed signs of lowered arousal compared to "poor" vigilance performers, both in the resting EEG record and in electrodermal activity taken while subjects were listening to tones to which no response was required. Although this result may merely indicate that "good" vigilance performers are more easily able to mobilize and demobilize their cognitive resources in accordance with task demands it remains, nevertheless, something of a puzzle for arousal theory.

Despite a number of promising results from well-conducted experiments it is difficult to arrive at firm conclusions when evaluating the results obtained from psychophysiological studies of vigilance performance. It appears highly probable that physiological activity during task performance is different for "good" vigilance performers as opposed to "bad" but the weakness of arousal theory in explaining such findings suggests that an alternative hypothesis is needed. Furthermore, the evidence is not available to determine whether a progressive reduction in ANS activity with time on task, and hence presumably a decline in arousal, is associated both with a change in criterion placement and a change in sensitivity, or with only one of these. The relation between autonomic lability and personality is not well defined and it is far from clear in what sense autonomic lability can itself be regarded as a personality dimension. The relation of trial lability to monitoring behaviour seems to be reasonably well established, although this conclusion is somewhat limited by the fact that the few studies of autonomic lability and vigilance have not always obtained a vigilance decrement.

Vigilance in specific subject populations

In this section, studies comparing the vigilance performance of groups of individuals differing in age, sex or diagnostic category are reviewed. The results of such studies have, perhaps, fewer implications for theories of vigilance than for psychological theories of ageing and development or of sex differences. When the performance of individuals in different diagnostic categories has been compared, vigilance tasks appear to have been used principally as part of a test battery intended to discriminate between the behaviour of different clinical groups and little theoretical emphasis has been placed upon the results obtained, once a difference between the performance of a control group of "normals" and that of a group diagnosed as belonging to a particular clinical category has been demonstrated. Nevertheless, it will be seen that a few general conclusions can be drawn from such studies and they are also of some practical interest.

Age

Investigators working in the field of ageing have traditionally employed one of two research designs, the *cross-sectional*, which provides information about age differences, and the *longitudinal* or follow-up design, which yields data on age changes. Most studies of age and vigilance have investigated the performance of younger and older adults, and all such studies have been cross-sectional in design. This design confounds effects due to age with effects attributable to generational differences, more often than not with a result unfavourable to the elderly (for a comprehensive discussion of the methodological issues see Bromley, 1974, pp. 330–371). Thus the nature and extent of possible adult age changes in vigilance, as distinct from age differences, remain unknown.

The results obtained from 11 studies of age and vigilance are shown in Table 6.3. from which it can be seen that when reliable age differences in performance have been reported, older individuals have consistently performed less well than younger individuals. In six of the experiments listed in Table 6.3 the detection rate of older individuals is lower, in four their false alarm rate is higher, and in four their detection efficiency declines at a faster rate with time at work. Age differences seem equally likely to occur in speed and closure tasks, although there is a tendency for such differences to be found more frequently in visual tasks than in auditory ones; age differences in at least one performance measure are found in five out of six experiments where a visual task was used but in only four out of nine cases where an auditory task was employed.

Older people are generally believed to show less confidence in their responses and to display greater caution, a belief supported by the results of a number of experimental studies (see, for example, Botwinick, 1966, 1969;

Wallach and Kogan, 1961). It appears that in task requiring difficult discriminations to be made older people require more evidence before initiating a response (Botwinick *et al.*, 1958); thus the time taken by the input-sampling stage of information processing probably increases with age. Older people are also more reluctant to produce a response under conditions of uncertainty, particularly if they are asked to guess (Silverman, 1963). In paced situations the performance of older individuals benefits more than does that of younger ones from an increase in stimulus duration, or a reduction in the rate of pacing (Eisdorfer, 1963, 1965; Eisdorfer *et al.*, 1963). In both cases the improvement in performance can be attributed to an increase in the number of responses made by older subjects.

There are good grounds, therefore, for expecting that older people would adopt more stringent response criteria, compared to younger people, in tasks requiring the detection of signals presented at near-threshold levels, and this expectation is confirmed by the available evidence. Craik (1966, 1969) for example, presented three-second bursts of white noise in which, on 50% of trials, a faint 1000 Hz tone was embedded, to 20 older (mean age 64·2 years) and 20 younger (mean age 28·1 years) subjects. The detectability of the signal was equated for all subjects before the main experiment commenced and each subject performed the task under two conditions, one involving a yes–no procedure and the other a confidence rating procedure. With the yes–no procedure Craik found that older subjects did adopt a significantly more cautious criterion, although with the confidence rating procedure no differences in criterion placement between the two age groups were found. However, there was a tendency for older subjects to restrict the range of their criteria, that is, they adopted a more risky criterion at the cautious end of the rating scale but also a more cautious criterion at the risky end of the scale. The finding of a more cautious criterion in older subjects has also been obtained in other experiments employing yes–no procedures and auditory tasks (Milner *et al.*, 1967; Rees and Botwinick, 1971). Older subjects have also been observed to adopt more conservative response criteria in pain threshold studies employing weak stimuli (Clark and Mehl, 1971; Harkins and Chapman, 1976).

It would also be expected that fast presentation rates would exert a greater adverse effect on the efficiency of older subjects compared to younger ones, and this expectation has also been confirmed (Davies, 1968b; Thompson *et al.*, 1963). Thompson *et al.* used the Odd–Even task, in which the signal consists either of two successive odd or two successive even digits. They presented two versions of the task, one visual and the other auditory, to older and younger subjects at three different event rates (15, 30 and 60 events per minute). In all conditions the task duration was five minutes. Thompson *et al.* found that in the auditory task the percentage of correct detections made by older subjects fell from around 82% at the slowest presentation rate to

Table 6.3 A summary of the principal features of 11 studies of age and vigilance. A = Auditory, V = Visual; Y = Young, MA = Middle-aged, O = Old; M = Male, F = Female; N = Number in group; CD = Correct detections, FA = False alarms, DL = Detection latencies; nsd = no significant difference.

Source	Task	Task duration	Task type	Composition of age groups Mean Age (Years)	Age Range	Mean difference	Differential decrement
Canestrari (1962)							
Experiment 1	CPT	10'	Closure (Signal: X or T) (A)			CD: Y > O FA: O > Y	
Experiment 2	CPT	10'	Speed (Signal: A followed by X) (A)			CD: Y > O FA: nsd	
Griew and Davies (1962)[a]							
Experiment 1	Bakan	40'	Speed (A)		Y (19–31), N = 20 M; O (45–60), N = 20 M;	CD: Y > O FA: nsd	
Experiment 2	Audio-visual checking	40'	Speed (A)		Y (20–33), N = 20 M; O (48–66), N = 20 M;	CD: nsd FA: nsd	
Experiment 3	Bakan	40'	Speed (A)		Y (18–31), N = 12 M; O (44–61), N = 12 M;	CD: nsd FA: nsd	No
York (1962)	Detection of double flash from background of single flashes.	?	Speed (V)	Y (c 30·0), N = 12 M; MA (c 50·0), N = 12 M; O (c 70·0), N = 12 M;		CD: nsd	
Davies and Griew (1963)	Bakan	75'	Speed (A)		Y (17–29), N = 15 M; O (41–58), N = 15 M;	CD: nsd FA: nsd	
Surwillo and Quilter (1964)	Clock Test	60'	Speed (V)	Y (43·7), N = 53 M; O (71·0), N = 53 M;		CD: Y > O DL: nsd	Yes O > Y
Neal and Pearson (1966)							
1. Bakan		64'	Speed (A)		Y (21–30), N = 16 M and F; O (39–62), N = 8 M;	CD: nsd FA: nsd	
2. Detection of increase in duration of 1000 Hz tone.		60'	Speed (A)		Y (21–30), N = 16 M and F; O (39–62), N = 8 M;	CD: nsd FA: nsd	

Study	Task	Duration	Type	Subjects	Age range	Results	Conclusion
Surwillo (1966)	Clock Test	60'	Speed (V)	Y (36·4), N = 33 M; O (74·3), N = 33 M;	Y (22–45); O (69–85);		Yes O > Y
Tune (1966b)	Detection of 3 consecutive digits from 10-digit sequence. Sequences presented at 10″ intervals.	40'	Speed (A)	Y (36·9), N = 14; O (60·6), N = 14;		CD: nsd FA: O > Y	
Bicknell (1970)	Detection of a greater downward deflection of a dot of light in the second of a pair of downward light movements presented as one event.	60'	Closure (V)	Y (21·0), N = 10 M and F; MA (40·9), N = 10 M and F; O (70·6), N = 10 M and F;	Y (17–29); MA (30–53); O (60–85);	CD: nsd FA: O > MA and Y	Yes O and MA > Y Yes O > MA and Y
Harkins et al (1974)[b]	Odd–Even Task	10·2'	Speed (V)	Y (21·3), N = 41 M and F; O (67·6), N = 105 M and F;		CD: Y > O FA: O > Y DL: O > Y	Yes O > Y
Davies and Davies (1975)[c]	CPT	20'	Closure (Signal: A or X) (V)		Y (18–31), N = 20 M; O (65–72), N = 20 M;	CD: Y > O	No

[a] In this study there was a difference in the response requirement between Experiments 1 and 3. In Experiment 1 subjects were instructed to write down the digits constituting each signal, in Experiment 3 they were asked to press a response button whenever they detected a signal.
[b] In this study a middle-aged group of subjects was also tested.
[c] This study also investigated the effects of noise and time of day. Only the results for the quiet condition, pooled over times of day, are shown here.

around 35% at the fastest; for younger subjects the corresponding percentages were around 80% and 48%. A similar reduction in detection rate with
an increase in presentation speed was found for both age groups in the visual
version of the task, but it was less marked. Davies (1968b) used an auditory
version of the Odd–Even task and obtained essentially the same results
for detection rate but he also found that at the faster presentation rate false
alarms increased to a greater extent for older subjects than for younger
ones. This result suggests that, as noted in Chapter 5, increasing presentation speed reduces sensitivity and that the reduction is greater for older
individuals.

This conclusion can also be inferred from the results of a study by Talland
(1966), who required 200 subjects aged between 20 and 69 years to detect
each occurrence of the digit four in a display which changed continuously
and showed randomly varied patterns of nine or fewer digits. The exposure
duration and presentation rate of the displays were also varied. Using task
durations of 30, 36 and 48 min. Talland found that at presentation rates of
27 or 54 displays per minute no effect of age on detection rate was found
up to the age of 60 years, whereas at a presentation rate of 109 displays per
minute, omission errors increased with age for each decade group, although
false alarm rates remained fairly constant. Again, presentation rate would
seem to be exerting a greater effect on sensitivity as age increases.

The evidence outlined above suggests that in vigilance tasks older individuals should exhibit lower sensitivity and a more cautious response criterion
and that performance differences between older and younger age groups
are more likely to be found in tasks in which the event presentation rate is
high. Since, however, there are no studies which have systematically examined
the effects of event rate on age differences in vigilance, the brief discussion
that follows is concerned only with possible age differences in sensitivity
and bias.

Although decision theory measures have seldom been employed in
studies of age and vigilance, it does appear that sensitivity does decline
with age. Tune (1966b), for example, obtained a significant negative correlation (-0.50) between age and d' and Davies and Davies (1975) found that
correct detections declined with age while the "true" false alarm rate
remained about the same, suggesting a reduction in sensitivity with increasing
age (see also Chapter 8). Similar results were obtained by Canestrari (1962;
Experiment 2) and Griew and Davies (1962; Experiment 1). However,
although in Bicknell's (1970) study d' values appear to be slightly lower
overall for older than for younger subjects, middle-aged subjects had higher
d' values than both older and younger subjects; furthermore, in a re-analysis
of the data of Griew and Davies (1962; Experiment 3) d' values were found
to be virtually identical for older and younger groups. Thus although on
balance it is probable that sensitivity declines with age it is possible either

than the reduction is fairly small and occurs quite gradually (Sheehan and Drury, 1971, for instance, estimated from their studies of industrial inspection that d' might diminish by about 0·2 each decade) or that little change in sensitivity is apparent until very late in life unless brain damage is also present (see Chapter 8). Within-session declines in high-rate speed tasks such as the Clock Test used by Surwillo (Surwillo 1966; Surwillo and Quilter, 1964) may also be more pronounced in older than in younger subjects but an adequate test of this hypothesis remains to be made.

Although older people seem to adopt more cautious criteria in signal detection tasks and perhaps also in industrial inspection tasks (see Craik, 1969) there are also some indications that they may adopt more risky criteria in some vigilance situations. Tune (1966b) found a significant negative correlation ($-0·42$) between age and β and Bicknell's (1970) data also show that β values were much lower for her older group than for her middle-aged or her younger groups, although no statistical tests were apparently conducted. The re-analysis of Experiment 3 by Griew and Davies (1962) also indicated that the older group adopted more risky criteria, the difference between younger and older groups being marginally significant. However, in Bicknell's study, in which a closure task was used, the difference in rate of decrement shown by older and younger subjects is attributable to a differential criterion increment which is much more marked for the older group. Thus although in some task situations older people may adopt somewhat more risky criteria overall, in closure and probably also low-rate speed tasks they may well display a greater increase in caution with time on task.

Although scarcely any relevant research has been conducted, personality and physiological factors may exert some influence upon age differences in vigilance. For example, Tune (1966a) found that older extroverts made over three times as many false alarms as did older introverts, although detection rates were about the same in both groups. Younger extroverts also made more false alarms than younger introverts but the difference was much less marked. There is some evidence too that older people show less spontaneous autonomic lability than do younger people (Davies and Treacher, 1966; Malmo and Shagass, 1949; Surwillo and Quilter, 1965) and, although the evidence is extremely difficult to interpret, that older people exhibit lower levels of electrocortical and autonomic arousal (see Marsh and Thompson, 1977 and Thompson and Marsh, 1974 for reviews).

There are comparatively few studies of vigilance performance in children. Gale and Lynn (1972), however, investigated developmental changes in auditory vigilance performance in young children. They administered a simple vigilance task involving the detection of a digit from a series of spoken letters to groups of children between the ages of seven and 13 years. Gale and Lynn found that the number of correctly detected signals increased with age, although a decrement in detections was observed at all ages. The greatest changes in performance occurred between the ages of eight and nine, a finding which Gale and Lynn suggested was consistent with other evidence indicating a change in sustained attention capacity between these ages. Anderson *et al.* (1974) also reported that there was an improvement in vigilance performance in children aged nine years and older as compared to children between six and eight years of age. Sykes *et al.* (1973) found a significant correlation between age and performance on the CPT for children in the age range five to 11 years. When age is held constant, middle-class children have been shown to detect significantly more signals in an extended visual vigilance task than lower-class children (Knopf and Mabel, 1975), class being determined by various indices of socio-economic status.

A number of studies of vigilance and sustained attention have also been conducted with children experiencing "learning disabilities", a loosely defined diagnostic category referring to children with a variety of psycho-logical and behavioural disorders which impair their learning ability. It overlaps considerably with two other diagnostic categories in popular usage in the United States, "minimal brain dysfunction" and "hyperactivity". Children who are clinically diagnosed within one of these categories may have disorders in a variety of psychological functions, including the ability to sustain attention (Dykman *et al.*, 1971).

Anderson *et al.* (1973) tested children clinically diagnosed as learning disabled (LD) on a simple 30-minute vigilance task in which a red–green combination of lights was the signal to be detected, the non-signal events being red–red and green–green combinations. LD children detected signifi-cantly fewer signals and made more false alarms than normal children (normal children were presumably matched on such variables as socio-economic status, age and intelligence, although this is not stated). Anderson *et al.* (1973) did not analyse performance data over time, but in another study (Doyle *et al.*, 1976) it was found that there was a tendency for LD children to exhibit a steeper decrement, although there were also differences within the LD group between hyperactive and hypoactive children. Within the group of LD children, both studies found that hyperactive children had a lower detection rate and a higher false alarm rate than either hypoactive or normoactive children. These results were confirmed in a further study using the same task (Anderson *et al.*, 1974), where another principal finding was that the administration of methylphenidate (Ritalin), a stimulant which is often given to improve the learning efficiency of LD children, significantly improved the vigilance performance of younger LD children.

The finding that LD children, especially those who are hyperactive, have lower detection and higher false alarm rates than normal children suggests that they have a lower sensitivity, which may be taken to indicate an "attention deficit", as suggested by Doyle *et al.* (1976) and Dykman *et al.*

(1971), although there are logical difficulties in attributing an "attention deficit" to poor performance on a task requiring attention (Kupietz, 1976). Hyperactive LD children also adopt a much riskier response criterion and make many more false alarms than do normoactive and hypoactive LD children and normal children. Doyle *et al.* (1976) reported, for example, that hyperactive children made an average of 19 false alarms compared to one false alarm by hypoactives and four by normoactives. The lower criterial threshold of hyperactives probably arises out of their relative inability to control impulse, and their susceptibility to interference from extraneous, task-irrelevant information. Sykes *et al.* (1973) also found that hyperactive children made fewer correct detections and more incorrect responses than normal children and arrived at a similar conclusion. These findings and their interpretation in terms of the failure of children with hyperkinetic behaviour syndromes to sustain attention and control impulse are treated in greater detail by Douglas (1972).

Children whose reading is retarded, compared to a control group matched for age, sex and general intelligence, have also been found to make reliably fewer correct detections in a 30-minute visual vigilance task (Noland and Schuldt, 1971) although no differences were found between the reading retarded and the control group in either the amount of decrement shown or the average time taken to detect a signal.

In LD children then, especially those with hyperkinesis, sustained attention capacity (as measured by the d' index of perceptual efficiency) is lower and impulsivity tends to be higher. The principal contribution of such studies to vigilance research in general is the confirmation of the positive relationship between the false alarm rate and impulsivity (Anderson *et al.*, 1973, 1974; Doyle *et al.*, 1976) and of the importance of pacing and memory demands in determining performance differences between groups, for example, hyperactive and normal children. Sykes *et al.* (1973) compared the performance of these two groups on two sustained attention tasks, a serial reaction task (SRT) and the CPT. An impairment in performance was found in both tasks but the greatest difference between groups was found for the CPT (the "speed" version of this task being used); hyperactive children detected fewer signals and made more overall incorrect responses than normal children. In addition while the performance of hyperactives declined with time on task on the 15-minute CPT, no decrement was observed for normal children. For the SRT, the only difference between groups was in the number of incorrect responses, there being no differential decrement over time between the groups.

Sex

In their review of studies of sex differences in vigilance Davies and Tune (1970) concluded that there was no reliable evidence for the existence of such differences. The majority of the studies published since this review also do not provide any evidence for performance differences between males and females, either in children (Kirchner and Knopf, 1974; Sykes *et al.*, 1973) or in adults (Gale *et al.*, 1972d; Parasuraman, 1976a; Tolin and Fisher, 1974).

The majority of these studies did not treat sex as the primary variable of interest in their investigations. However, Waag *et al.* (1973) carried out a very thorough study of the main effects of sex on monitoring performance. They used large sample sizes (220 males and 220 females) and provided data for correct and false detection scores. They used a visual monitoring task of the type used by Jerison and Pickett (1964), in which subjects had to detect the occasional increase in the second deflection of a dot which made periodic double deflections on a visual display. Although it was found that males detected 10% more signals than females and made fewer false alarms in the first 20-minute period of monitoring, the magnitude of these differences was very low, sex differences accounting for 4% of the variance in detections and less than 1% of the variance in false alarms. Waag *et al.* (1973) therefore concluded that sex differences in vigilance are likely to be small, and that to obtain them requires statistical designs of sufficient power to detect such low magnitude effects. They estimated the power of their design to be 0·19, a value which accords well with the finding that roughly 20% of the studies in the literature have reported finding significant sex differences in vigilance performance.

It can be concluded that sex differences in vigilance performance are slight and therefore of little theoretical or practical importance. Nevertheless, it is probably still wise to control for such effects in multifactor designs, since, as pointed out by Waag *et al.*, the magnitude of the effect in which the experimenter is interested may be of the same order of magnitude as the effect of sex.

Clinical disorders
A few studies have compared the vigilance performance of normal controls with that of patients diagnosed as suffering from various clinical disorders, or with that of subjects showing extreme scores on diagnostic questionnaires. In every study of this kind the performance of normal control subjects has been superior. Byrne (1976) compared the performance of 20 hospitalized depressive patients, divided into two equal groups of neurotic and psychotic depressives, with that of a group of ten normal controls on a 30-minute version of the Bakan task containing 30 signals. Normal controls detected 88% of the signals presented, while neurotic depressives detected 72% and psychotic depressive 25%; all these differences proved to be significant. Psychotic depressives also showed a significantly greater performance decrement than normal controls. Neurotic depressives, on the other hand, made significantly more false alarms than either psychotic depressives or

controls, there being no reliable difference in the false alarm rates of the latter two groups. Byrne interpreted these differences in terms of arousal. Orris (1969) found that male delinquents who scored highly on the psychopathic dimension of a questionnaire made significantly fewer correct detections and responded significantly more slowly than either "neurotic" or "subcultural" delinquents during a 100-minute dial-monitoring task. No differences in decrement between the groups on either measure were obtained, however. Finally Dardano (1969) noted differences in observing-response patterns between chronic schizophrenics and normals using a fixed-interval reinforcement schedule in a dial-monitoring task similar to that used by Holland (1957; see Chapter 2).

Vigilance in the blind

A refreshing exception to the general finding that "abnormal" groups perform worse in vigilance situations is provided by Benedetti and Loeb (1972), who compared, in two experiments, the performance of blind individuals drawn from the Louisville Metropolitan area with that of student controls. The students were divided into two groups, one working in a lighted room and the other in the dark (see Chapter 7). Measures of absolute and differential thresholds were also taken and performance was assessed in a signal detection task under "alerted" conditions. The task Benedetti and Loeb employed was an 80-minute auditory speed task in which subjects were required to detect the occurrence of slightly louder white noise pulses. The detection rate of blind subjects was found to be reliably superior to that of sighted subjects and this was found to be attributable to significant differences in sensitivity (d') rather than to any difference in criterion (β). With time on task sensitivity declined and criterion placement became more stringent for all groups. Essentially similar results were obtained in a second experiment with the same task.

Benedetti and Loeb point out that the superiority of the blind group in these experiments "cannot be attributed to 'sensory compensation' or heightened physiological sensitivity since there were no differences in absolute or differential thresholds and no comparable increase in blind Ss' capability to detect signals under the alerted conditions of the signal detection task" (p. 15). They suggest, therefore, that blind individuals are in effect more practised listeners and are thus capable of making finer discriminations among auditory stimuli.

Summary

We began this chapter by reviewing studies of the inter-task consistency of individual differences, and suggested that differences in task type make a considerable contribution to the consistency of performance in monitoring situations. The distinction between "speed" and "closure", or successive- and simultaneous-discrimination tasks, thus remains a useful one. Comparisons between the performance of different temperament groups do not provide unambiguous results, but in general introverts, younger individuals and labiles exhibit greater overall detection efficiency. The link between temperament and the lability dimension is, however, a tenuous one. Speed tasks seem somewhat more likely to yield a differential decrement between criterion groups than do closure tasks, although there is insufficient evidence to resolve this point. The performance of "disadvantaged" groups is, with the exception of the blind, always markedly worse than that of control groups who are not disadvantaged. Finally, the practical implications of research concerned with individual differences in vigilance are disappointing, and at present the prospects for the development of a selection battery for use in monitoring situations do not seem particularly bright, despite the fact that some people are clearly more efficient monitors than others.

Chapter 7

Effects of the Environment and General State on Vigilance

In this chapter we shall be concerned with the effects of various environmental variables and with factors affecting the general state of the observer upon vigilance performance. Environmental variables which affect vigilance include noise, vibration, high or low ambient temperatures, factors which increase or reduce the variety of stimulation available to the observer, such as music or sensory deprivation, and changes in atmospheric conditions resulting from the introduction of pollutants into the work environment. Many, if not all, of these factors will exert an effect on the general state of the observer; for example, the level of behavioural arousal or reactivity may alter and a qualitative change in the activation of the brain may occur. The observer's general state is also influenced by the sleep schedule on which he is working, by the time of day at which testing takes place and by whether drugs have been taken before the task begins. Environmental factors may also moderate the effects of state variables and *vice versa*; two variables may thus combine to produce effects on performance which are additive, where the effect on performance of the two variables in combination is the sum of their independent effects, greater than additive (synergistic) or less than additive (antagonistic or interactive). Most combinations of environmental factors appear to be additive in their effects on performance, a few are antagonistic and scarcely any are synergistic (Grether, 1971).

The way in which the effects of environmental factors and state variables reveal themselves depends to a great extent on the performance measure employed and on the kind of task that is selected. Thus, when an environmental factor or a state variable is observed to exert no significant influence upon performance at a particular task, it may be that performance is genuinely unaffected or that the measure of performance chosen, or the task yielding the measure, is insufficiently sensitive to the level of the variable employed. Poulton (1965) and Wilkinson (1969) discuss a number of factors that should be taken into account in order to ensure that a task is maximally sensitive to environmental and other variables. These include the duration of the task, task difficulty, the degree of familiarity with the task and acclimatization to the variable being manipulated, and the subject's motivational level.

The choice of experimental design is of some importance for experiments investigating the effects of environmental factors or state variables, and the adoption of a repeated measures design, in which the same individuals participate in all conditions, may lead an experimenter to draw inappropriate conclusions concerning the effects of a particular variable on performance (Poulton, 1970, 1973b, 1977a; Poulton and Freeman, 1966). The reason for this is that asymmetrical transfer effects between treatments may be present and the operation of such effects may reduce the probability of finding a reliable difference between experimental and control conditions. Although the presence of asymmetrical transfer effects can be detected fairly easily and conclusions concerning the effects of a particular variable suitably modified, this procedure has not always been followed in experiments investigating the effects of environmental factors and state variables (see Poulton, 1977a).

In the remaining sections of this chapter we consider evidence concerning the effects of state variables and environmental factors on vigilance performance derived from both laboratory and field investigations, and examine the ways in which such effects have been interpreted.

State variables and vigilance performance

In this section we are concerned with the effects on vigilance of variables which, while leaving the environment in which the task is performed unchanged, may be assumed to affect the general state of the observer. The major variables in this category are the time of day at which performance is assessed, the degree to which the observer is deprived of sleep, and whether or not various drugs have been ingested before or during task performance. We begin by considering the effects of time of day.

Time of day
It is well established that the time of day at which testing is conducted can reliably affect performance at a number of different tasks (Colquhoun, 1971). Performance at most tasks tends to improve from early to late in the day; examples include card sorting, choice reaction time, letter cancellation and mirror drawing (Blake, 1967a, 1971; Kleitman, 1939, 1963). The direction of the time-of-day effect upon performance seems to depend upon the degree to which the task imposes a load on memory, particularly short-term memory (Hockey and Colquhoun, 1972). In "pure" short-term memory tasks fewer items are correctly recalled as the day progresses (Bad-

deley *et al.*, 1970; Blake, 1967a; Folkard *et al.*, 1977; Hockey *et al.*, 1972) although exceptions to this general finding have also been reported (Adams, 1973; Jones *et al.*, 1978). An excellent discussion of research concerned with time of day and memory is provided by Folkard and Monk (1979a).

Since the work of Kleitman in the 1920s and 1930s (Kleitman, 1939, 1963), it has been known that oral temperature fluctuates over the 24-hour cycle (see Fig. 7.1) and it appears that the performance of many tasks co-varies with such temperature changes. Measures of autonomic nervous system and endocrine activity, in particular the blood plasma levels of adrenal cortical steroids, also follow a diurnal rhythm (Colquhoun, 1971; Perkoff *et al.*, 1959) and there is evidence suggesting that steroid activity is related to the sensory detection threshold (Henkin, 1970). Although significant changes in electrocortical arousal, inferred from EEG activity, have not always been obtained when different times of day have been compared (Gale *et al.*, 1972a), reliable increases in the dominant EEG frequency over the day have been reported when subjects are engaged on a demanding task (Jones, 1974). There are thus good grounds for hypothesizing that variations in task performance with time of day are related to variations in diurnal rhythm and that the diurnal rhythm reflects changes in a general state of arousal or reactivity, the level of arousal being presumed to increase from the morning to the afternoon and evening.

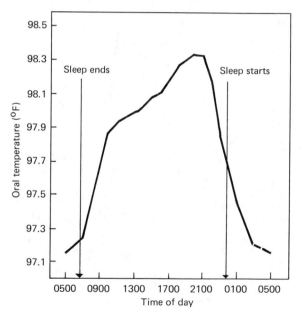

Fig. 7.1. The circadian rhythm of oral temperature in a group of 70 young men. From Colquhoun (1971).

We have already noted that task demands seem to influence the relationship between time of day and efficiency. Folkard *et al.* (1976), for instance, varied the memory load in a memory and search task and found that performance improved as the day progressed when the memory load was low, but deteriorated over the same period when the memory load was high. In tasks requiring the immediate processing of information, and hence where the memory load is low, efficiency tends to improve from the morning onwards. Immediate processing is a characteristic of most vigilance tasks and reliable improvements in detection rate from morning to afternoon or evening testing have been obtained in several studies (Adams *et al.*, 1972; Baekeland and Hoy, 1970; Blake, 1967a; Colquhoun, 1962a, 1977; Colquhoun *et al.*, 1968a, b; Davies and Davies, 1975; Mullin and Corcoran, 1977). Some results of Colquhoun (1962a), who employed both paced and unpaced versions of the same task, are shown in Fig. 7.2. Colquhoun found, for example, that at the fast presentation rate (33 slides per minute) subjects tested at 10 a.m. detected significantly fewer signals (19%) than subjects tested at 3.15 p.m. (38%), with subjects tested at 12.15 p.m. detecting 28% of the signals presented. Reducing the presentation rate to ten slides per minute improved detection efficiency, but abolished the time-of-day effect.

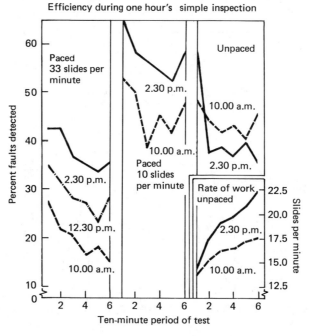

Fig. 7.2. Performance at a paced and an unpaced inspection task at different times of day. Data from Colquhoun. From Broadbent (1961).

No reliable effect of time of day on detection rate was apparent for the unpaced version of the task either, although as Fig. 7.2 shows, the average rate of inspection was somewhat higher than in the more slowly paced condition and became faster during the task, the rate of increase being significantly greater for the afternoon group. It appears from these results that the attention requirements of the task, defined by the rate at which events are presented for inspection, can determine whether or not reliable time of day effects on detection efficiency are obtained.

However, other experiments in which a high rate of event presentation has been used have either not obtained a reliable effect of time of day on detection efficiency (Gale *et al.*, 1972d) or have found that morning performance was significantly superior (Bonnet and Webb, 1978; Jenkins, 1958), the reverse of the usual effect of time of day upon vigilance. Although in both the studies reporting morning superiority the experimental design did not permit the effects of time of day to be separated from those of practice and fatigue respectively, the results indicate that the effects of time of day on efficiency may also depend on the type of discrimination the task requires. The studies of Bonnet and Webb and of Jenkins used successive discrimination tasks while Colquhoun (1962a) employed a simultaneous discrimination task, and it has earlier been noted that successive discrimination vigilance tasks impose a memory load while simultaneous discrimination tasks do not. Since, as we have seen, performance at memory-loaded tasks is generally superior early in the day, it is possible that performance at vigilance tasks involving a successive discrimination would also be better in the morning than in the afternoon or evening, and the results obtained from a preliminary study by Toh (1978) suggest that this hypothesis may be correct. In this study different groups of subjects performed either a 30-minute auditory successive discrimination task or a 30-minute auditory simultaneous discrimination task, in the morning (between 0800 and 1000) or in the afternoon (between 1600 and 1800). For each subject the discriminability of the signal was adjusted to yield a similar level of detection efficiency during a pre-task practice period. A significant interaction between task type (successive or simultaneous discrimination) and time of day (morning or afternoon) was obtained for correct detections, although not for false alarms. In the successive discrimination task more signals were correctly detected in the morning than in the afternoon, while in the simultaneous discrimination task more signals were correctly detected in the afternoon than in the morning. If this finding is confirmed, then the type of discrimination required by a vigilance task would appear to influence the direction of the time-of-day effect upon detection efficiency, a result consistent with the effects of time of day upon performance at other memory-loaded tasks, such as those referred to earlier (Folkard *et al.*, 1976).

It is tempting to conclude, therefore, that two attributes of a vigilance task principally determine the effects of time of day upon detection efficiency: the attention requirements of the task and the type of discrimination involved. A time-of-day effect will not be observed unless the attention requirements of the task are fairly demanding and the type of discrimination involved may also exert an influence upon the direction of the effect. However, the results of Gale *et al.* (1972d) and of Mullin and Corcoran (1977) cannot be encompassed by this account, since in both of these studies the attention requirements were demanding and a successive discrimination was involved. Yet Gale *et al.* found no significant effect of time of day on performance at the "Bakan" task and Mullin and Corcoran obtained a reliable improvement in detection efficiency from morning to evening testing when an auditory task, similar in many respects to the successive discrimination task used by Toh (1978), was presented at a level of 75 dB, although not when the same task was presented at a level of 90 dB. Other factors must therefore also be important in determining the extent and direction of time of day effects on vigilance and these probably include "psychophysical" aspects of the signal (see Chapter 2), such as its probability and discriminability, task duration, the amount of practice with the task and the range of testing times employed. In a cancellation task for example, Davies and Davies (1975) found that the detection of "difficult" signals reliably improved from morning to afternoon while the detection of "easy" signals did not, although signal discriminability does not appear to have been investigated in relation to time of day in a vigilance situation.

When decision theory measures have been employed to describe the effects of time of day on vigilance performance, it appears to be measures of sensitivity rather than of criterion placement that show the greater change (Colquhoun *et al.*, 1968a, b). Furthermore, in studies where such measures have not been used, correct detections tend to be reliably affected by time of day whereas false alarms tend to remain fairly constant, and significant changes are not found (Baekeland and Hoy, 1970; Blake, 1967a; Davies and Davies, 1975). It thus appears that time of day may produce a genuine change in the efficiency with which signals are detected, although the issue is far from being resolved and Craig (1979b) has reported that time-of-day effects on discrimination performance are primarily due to changes in response criteria, there being little change in perceptual sensitivity. But whether or not it is perceptual sensitivity or criterion placement that is mainly affected by the time of day at which testing takes place, it seems clear that time of day influences the overall level of vigilance performance rather than the rate at which performance deteriorates over time, since the extent of the vigilance decrement is seldom affected by the time of testing.

The results obtained from laboratory studies of circadian variations in efficiency have implications for the design of shiftwork systems, which are being increasingly employed in Europe and the United States, and probably involve, in one form or another, about 20% of the labour force (Folkard and Monk, 1979b). Folkard and Monk further observed that the jobs on which shift-workers are currently engaged predominantly involve the exercise of mental and cognitive skills, rather than perceptual-motor and manual skills. The number of studies which have investigated the efficiency of shift-workers in "real-life" settings is fairly small, but there appears to be general agreement that performance is likely to deteriorate during the night shift (see Klein *et al.*, 1977). The circadian rhythms of body temperature and performance reach a low point during the night and seem to require a lengthy period of adjustment to a regime of working at night and sleeping during the day, before stabilization of performance occurs. The circadian performance rhythm appears to vary with the nature of the task demands that are imposed so that, as mentioned earlier, performance at high memory load tasks peaks much earlier in the day than does performance at tasks in which the memory load is low or non-existent. Furthermore, there are individual differences in the rate at which circadian rhythms adjust to shiftworking, which may be predictable from questionnaire responses (Folkard *et al.*, 1979). It appears, therefore, that both task demands and individual differences should be taken into account in the selection of a shiftwork system (Folkard and Monk, 1979b).

It further appears that there are differences in the circadian performance rhythm of moderate to extreme "morning" and "evening" types (see Chapter 6), who, together, probably comprise about 45% of the adult population (Horne and Ostberg, 1976). Horne *et al.* (1980), for example, found that in a simulated inspection task morning types correctly detected reliably more faults than did evening types in the morning, but reliably fewer in the evening, and that the performance of morning types progressively deteriorated throughout the day while that of evening types improved. However, no circadian trends or differences between morning and evening types were obtained for the number of items erroneously rejected, which supports the view expressed above that time of day primarily influences perceptual efficiency, rather than merely affecting standards of reporting.

Sleep deprivation
Many investigators, beginning with Patrick and Gilbert in 1896, have been interested in the effects of loss of sleep, in the expectation that the biochemical, physiological and behavioural changes resulting from sleep deprivation might provide some information concerning the functions of sleep. Most sleep deprivation studies have examined the effects of total sleep deprivation, that is, of the number of hours of continuous wakefulness, irrespective of the timing of the normal sleep period. In such studies the length of the deprivation period has generally been less than 100 hours, about four nights without sleep, although in some studies it has been in excess of 200

hours and the longest period of sleep loss from which data are available appears to be 264 hours (Johnson et al., 1965). However, several studies have also been conducted of the effects of partial sleep deprivation, in which the amount of sleep permitted is restricted to some fraction of that taken normally, and of selective sleep deprivation, in which individuals are deprived of a particular type of sleep, either rapid eye-movement (REM) sleep, sometimes described as "dreaming sleep", which comprises between 20 and 25% of total sleep time in young adults and occurs predominantly in the last third of the nocturnal sleep period, or deep non-rapid eye-movement (NREM) sleep (sleep stages 3 and 4), often called slow wave sleep (SWS), which comprises between 20 and 30% of total sleep time in young adults and occurs predominantly in the first third of the nocturnal sleep period.

The consequences of total sleep deprivation seem to be principally psychological and there are few major biochemical or physiological changes, although body temperature declines progressively and EEG frequency slows considerably, with a corresponding increase in amplitude (see Horne, 1978, for a review). However, sleep deprivation imposes a strain on energy production and transfer systems, although it is unclear whether this is attributable solely to lack of sleep or to the increased effort expended in maintaining wakefulness. If, as often happens in sleep deprivation studies, the sleep-deprived individual is required to achieve or maintain a reasonable standard of task performance during the deprivation period, compensatory biochemical or physiological changes may occur and these will add to the biological cost of continued wakefulness. But although the biological effects of total sleep deprivation can be regarded as mildly stressful and debilitating, they are not long-lasting, and recovery takes place rapidly following a period of sleep taken *ad libitum*, which is always much less than the period of sleep deprivation and only about 50% above the normal duration of sleep. For example, the recovery sleep of the individual who remained awake for 264 hours, a 17-year old American high-school student, lasted for only 14 hours 40 min. (Gulevich et al., 1966).

Total sleep deprivation
The main psychological effects of total sleep deprivation are on task performance and on mood. The average level of performance at many tasks, particularly those which require continuous information processing with no opportunity for rest pauses, shows a progressive deterioration with the number of hours of wakefulness and the variability of performance also increases (Wilkinson, 1965, 1968). As Broadbent (1963b) has put it, in summarizing the effects of sleep deprivation on performance,

a (sleep-deprived) man is not like a child's mechanical toy which goes slower as it runs down, nor is he like a car engine which continues until its fuel is exhausted and then stops dead. He is like a motor which after much use misfires, runs normally for a while, then falters again and so on. (p. 210)

Thus the principal way in which sleep deprivation impairs performance is by imposing periodic lapses in efficiency upon an otherwise unchanged level of performance; these lapses are frequently coincident with a slowing of the EEG frequency and/or a brief period of apparent sleep (Bjerner, 1949; Williams *et al.*, 1959), and in the majority of individuals there is a high negative correlation between EEG frequency and the speed of performance, which increases as the deprivation period progresses (Williams *et al.*, 1962). All the observations of EEG changes during sleep deprivation indicate that the alpha rhythm becomes markedly depressed as the deprivation period increases (for example, Blake and Gerard, 1937; Armington and Mitnick, 1959; Naitoh *et al.*, 1969; Rodin *et al.*, 1962). Although the disappearance of the alpha rhythm may led to its replacement in the EEG record either by faster (beta) or slower (theta or delta) rhythms, there is little doubt that in virtually all cases the subject's behaviour is sufficient to indicate that the reduction of alpha activity represents a shift in the direction of sleep rather than in the direction of increased alertness or excitement.

In unpaced tasks, such as the five-choice serial reaction task (see Chapter 1), one night of total sleep deprivation, about 30 hours without sleep, produces a marked increase in the number of long response times and a reduction in the number of correct responses (Wilkinson, 1961b, 1963a; Wilkinson and Colquhoun, 1968); sometimes too the number of errors also rises significantly (Wilkinson and Colquhoun, 1968). In paced tasks, such as vigilance, the number of omission errors reliably increases (Poulton *et al.*, 1974; Wilkinson, 1958, 1960; Williams *et al.*, 1959), signals are detected significantly more slowly (Poulton *et al.*, 1974) and the decrement in detection rate is also more marked following one night of sleep deprivation than after a normal night's sleep (Wilkinson, 1958, 1960), as Fig. 7.3 shows. It also appears that the degree of impairment of vigilance performance is greater for tasks in which the temporal occurrence of signals has no identifiable pattern (Williams *et al.*, 1965).

Detection efficiency further deteriorates as the length of the sleep deprivation period increases. Bergstrom *et al.* (1973) for example, who employed a 40-minute simulated radar task, found that after six hours without sleep, all targets were correctly detected, while after 30 hours 90%, after 54 hours 80% and after 66 hours only 70% of targets were detected, the reduction in each case being significant. But performance does not decline monotonically from the control level with time spent awake, since the amount of impairment also depends upon the time of day at which testing is conducted during the deprivation period, being greater at night than during the day, and reaching a low point in the early hours of the morning. Thus performance is likely to be worse on the first night without sleep than on the second day, on the second night than on the third day and so on (Drucker *et al.*, 1969; Morgan *et al.*, 1970, 1974). Hence fluctuations in performance attributable to variations in the circadian rhythms are superimposed upon a steadily increasing degree of impairment as the deprivation period progresses. Although performance can be fairly rapidly restored to the baseline level by a period of rest and recovery, an after-effect of sleep deprivation may occur, possibly because of the time required for the circadian rhythms to re-establish themselves after a period of sleep loss followed by recovery sleep (Wilkinson, 1963b). Wilkinson found that young enlisted men deprived of sleep for 34 hours, who were then given a period of 13 hours for rest and recovery, detected about 20% fewer signals in a visual vigilance task administered on the following day, compared to control levels. This deterioration was more marked, although not significantly so, in the morning than in the afternoon. It seems, therefore, that efficiency does not return completely to pre-deprivation levels until the circadian rhythms have re-establised, which probably takes about 24 hours in young and healthy individuals.

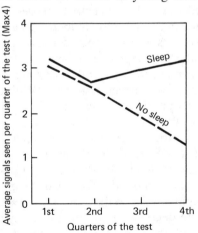

Fig. 7.3. The effects of lack of sleep on the detection rate in a visual vigilance task. From Wilkinson (1958).

Lack of sleep clearly produces feelings of increased sleepiness and fatigue, which appear to be closely, though inversely, related to circadian variations in body temperature during the deprivation period, so that subjectively experienced fatigue is greater when body temperature is falling and *vice versa* (Murray *et al.*, 1958). Furthermore, the effects of fatigue on efficiency are very similar to those of total sleep deprivation. Mast and Heimstra (1964), for instance, found that working for four hours on various tasks, including mental arithmetic and two versions of a simulated driving task, impaired detection efficiency in a subsequently performed two-hour visual vigilance task, although the only significant reduction in detection efficiency, compared to a control condition, was obtained with the mental arithmetic task, which was held to involve "mental fatigue". However, it is clear that physical fatigue can also produce impairments in vigilance and in the performance of a wide range of other tasks. In an ingenious experiment, Bonnet (1980) administered several performance and mood tests to 12 US Marine volunteers on each of three successive days. On the second day of testing, the Marines marched for $6\frac{1}{2}$ hours on a treadmill, wearing a backpack, commencing at 0745 hours and covering a distance of some 20 miles. The first and third days of the study were used as baseline and recovery days respectively. After each hour of the march a 15-minute rest break was provided, in which short performance tests and mood scales were given, and at the end of the march and during the evening a number of longer performance tests, including a 50-minute auditory vigilance task (Wilkinson, 1968), were completed. On the day of the march the energy expenditure was approximately 5000 kcal, about the same as that incurred during 40 hours of relatively inactive sleep deprivation. Bonnet compared the results of his performance and mood tests with those obtained from studies which had examined the effects of 40 hours of sleep deprivation on comparable tests, and found that they were very similar, significant decrements being observed for performance at a mental addition task, a four-choice serial reaction task, a tapping task, a short-term memory task and a symbol substitution task, as well as in vigilance. In the vigilance task sensitivity (d') was found to be reliably reduced by exercise, a similar result to that obtained by Wilkinson (1968) with the same task following sleep deprivation. On the basis of these results, Bonnet suggested that the most important factor in determining the effect of sleep deprivation on performance was the total amount of energy consumed, although such an explanation would appear to be unable to account for the reduction in the effect of sleep deprivation produced by noise, knowledge of results and other variables, referred to later in this chapter.

Partial sleep deprivation
The effects of partial sleep deprivation are likely to be of more immediate practical significance than are those of total sleep deprivation, since the demands of many occupations probably result in chronic limitations of normal sleep length (see Masterton, 1965), the sleep debt thus incurred being made up on "rest days" or weekends (see Tune, 1968). Since deep NREM or SWS occurs during the first part of the nocturnal sleep period and the majority of REM sleep later, the principal effect of partial sleep deprivation is to reduce REM sleep time. For effects of partial sleep deprivation to appear in task performance, the limitation of sleep length needs to be quite severe (see Wilkinson, 1972) so that the time spent in

SWS is likely to be affected.

Vigilance performance appears to be particularly susceptible to the effects of partial sleep deprivation. Webb and Agnew (1974), for instance, restricted the sleep of their subjects to $5\frac{1}{2}$ hours per night for 60 days. Although several performance tests and measures of mood were administered each week, the mood scales showed no effect of the regime and the only performance test to show any significant impairment compared to control levels was an auditory vigilance task. Generally, however, the effects of partial sleep deprivation on vigilance are less marked than are those of total sleep deprivation. As might be expected, the degree of performance impairment is related to the amount of sleep lost (Wilkinson, 1968; Hamilton et al., 1972). Wilkinson et al. (1966) found that reducing the amount of sleep to $5\frac{1}{2}$ hours increased the number of omissions in an auditory vigilance task and Wilkinson (1968) reported that reducing the amount of sleep to 2 hours on one night or to 5 hours on two successive nights significantly reduced efficiency on both a vigilance task and an adding task. The effects of a regime of reduced sleep are cumulative, although they are also not particularly easy to detect (Naitoh, 1975). Hamilton et al. (1972), for instance, concluded from their study of auditory vigilance performance that the principal effect of $3\frac{1}{2}$ hours of sleep deprivation over each of four successive days was to reduce the improvement in sensitivity (d') seen with practice under conditions of normal sleep. They also observed that reliable time-of-day effects on performance were not apparent under conditions of partial sleep deprivation.

Hartley (1974) compared the effects of continuous and distributed reduced sleep schedules on the performance of a successive discrimination visual task, the control condition being a regime of normal sleep. Over a period of four days the continuous schedule group obtained four hours sleep in one block and the distributed sleep group three 80 minute periods of sleep during each 24 hours. The 70-minute task was performed four times, once on each day of sleep loss. Hartley found that the continuous sleep group made fewer correct detections and fewer false alarms than the control group, with the distributed group occupying an intermediate position. The continuous sleep group thus employed a more cautious criterion, as indicated by the measures β and c (see Chapter 3), and both experimental groups showed an increasingly cautious criterion as sleep loss increased, with the continuous sleep group being reliably more cautious than either of the other two groups at the end of the work period. However, the distributed sleep group showed a reliable sensitivity decrement, which would not be expected with this type of task since the event presentation rate (five per minute) was very low. Sensitivity decrements have been observed in other sleep deprivation studies in which high event rate successive discrimination tasks have been used (Deaton et al., 1971; Wilkinson, 1969) and these studies also found that one night of total sleep deprivation reliably reduced d'. It thus appears that task type interacts with sleep deprivation to produce effects either on sensitivity or on criterion placement.

Wilkinson (1965) found that subjects' ratings of various tasks in terms of the degree of interest of the task correlated highly with the degree of impairment produced by loss of sleep. That is, tasks which were rated as uninteresting, among which were vigilance tasks, were considerably impaired by sleep deprivation whereas other tasks such as a "battle game" (Wilkinson, 1964b) which subjects found very interesting showed little or no impairment. Wilkinson argued that the interest of a task could be increased by providing knowledge of results and that the effects of sleep deprivation on performance should be reduced by this procedure. As predicted, knowledge of results was found to reduce the number of long response times in a five-choice serial reaction task to a level below that of normally rested subjects to whom knowledge of results was not given (Wilkinson, 1961b). These results suggest that sleep deprivation reduces motivation and it might therefore be expected that sleep deprivation would affect criterion placement, as in Hartley's (1974) experiment, unless the task is a very demanding one.

Impairments of efficiency have also been shown to result from *increases* in the amount of sleep taken, over that taken normally, and the influence of extended sleep on performance has been described as the "Rip Van Winkle Effect" (Taub and Berger, 1969). These investigators used a 15-minute auditory task and found that detection rate was reliably lower after 11 hours of sleep than after the usual eight hours. In a further study, Taub and Berger (1973) found that when the amount of sleep was kept at eight hours, but was shifted forward or backward from the habitual time of going to bed, either forward to 0300 hours or backward to 2100 hours then the effects on vigilance were similar to those obtained in conditions in which the amount of sleep was reduced to 5 hours or extended to 11 hours per night. Subjects were tested in the morning (0830 hours), the afternoon (1230 hours) and the evening (1730 hours), with appropriate controls being applied for the effects of time of day, and the number of signals missed was found to be reliably smaller for the control condition of normal sleep compared to all other treatments, although no differences were found between treatments for false alarms, d' or β. Detection latencies during evening testing were also found to be significantly faster in the normal sleep condition than in the experimental conditions and, surprisingly, were also faster in the afternoon following reduced sleep than following extended sleep. Clearly, then, any alteration in the normal sleep schedule can produce impairments of vigilance and the deprivation of sleep is not the only factor involved (see Taub and Berger, 1974, 1976). Such effects are probably attributable to the disruption of established circadian rhythms and further emphasize the relationship between changes in performance resulting from variations in the time of testing and those resulting from the manipulation of habitual sleep-waking schedules. Both these factors may relate to individual differences in sleep patterns (see Davies and Horne, 1975; Tune, 1969).

Drugs and vigilance performance

Under this heading stimulants such as amphetamine, nicotine and caffeine are considered first, followed by a discussion of the effects on vigilance of depressant drugs, such as alcohol and various tranquillizers. A discussion of the pharmacological effects of many of these drugs and their probable sites of action in the central nervous system can be found in Iversen and Iversen (1975).

Amphetamines

There seems little doubt that amphetamines improve vigilance performance. Solandt and Partridge (1946), N.H. Mackworth (1950), J.F. Mackworth (1965c) and Loeb et al. (1965) all found that although amphetamines had no effect on the initial level of detection, they reduced the amount of decrement during a session. In N.H. Mackworth's (1950) experiment, the administration of 10 mg of benzedrine (amphetamine sulphate) one hour before testing commenced resulted in faster responses being made to signals, while in J.F. Mackworth's (1965c) study the same dose of the same drug did not affect the commission error rate and produced the same effect on d' as on the percentage of correct detections. In neither experiment was there any "carry-over" effect of the drug to later testing sessions. Smaller doses of the drug (5 mg), however, have been found to exert no effect on the detection rate in two auditory vigilance tasks (Neal and Pearson, 1966).

The effect of amphetamines on vigilance performance appears from these experiments to be purely a pharmacological one, uncontaminated by suggestion effects. In the experiments mentioned placebos were also administered and in N.H. Mackworth's (1950) study the performance curves for placebo and control (no drug) subjects were virtually identical. Mackworth did not give his subjects any information regarding the probable effects of the two kinds of tablet, amphetamine and placebo, but in a later study (O'Hanlon et al., 1964) in which information was given to subjects who received only placebos, no effect on visual vigilance performance was found. One placebo, coloured white, was alleged to contain chemicals which affected performance in an unknown fashion, another, coloured orange, was alleged to increase alertness while a third, coloured yellow, was alleged to decrease alertness. A fourth group, the control group, received no placebo. No significant difference between the four groups was found either in terms of the mean detection rate or in terms of the amount of decrement shown over the 90-

minute task. The detection rate of all groups showed a significant decline with time at work.

Talland and Quarton (1966) showed that 15 mg (per 150 lb body weight) of methamphetamine improved efficiency on a visual vigilance task but this improvement reached statistical significance only in the second testing session. Six sessions were given in all. Pentobarbital, a depressant drug, significantly reduced the mean detection rate compared to a control group. It was argued that familiarity both with the effects of the drug and with the experimental situation in general also determined the change in performance resulting from the administration of amphetamines. However, Talland and Quarton's task was unusual in that placebo and pentobarbital subjects showed no decline in the detection rate over the hour-long vigil. Indeed, subjects under the influence of methamphetamine and pentobaribital improved as the session progressed. On this task at least there is thus evidence for an absolute improvement in vigilance performance resulting from the administration of methamphetamine rather than the relative improvement, that is, a reduction in the vigilance decrement, found in the other studies mentioned. A further examination of the effects of amphetamines on vigilance would appear to be necessary in order to determine under what conditions absolute and relative improvements occur.

Talland and Quarton (1966) made the point that "performance that depends on sustained concentration has . . . shown the most reliable response to amphetamines" (p. 266) and, as already noted, the effects of amphetamines on vigilance performance are usually, although not always, to reduce or prevent altogether the vigilance decrement observed in no-drug or placebo conditions. Barmack (1939) suggested that the effect of amphetamines on performance arose from a reduction of boredom and an enhancement of motivation which presumably result in a narrower focusing of attention (Callaway and Dembo, 1958). Both of these changes are generally held to result from the effects of the drug on the ascending reticular activating system.

Amphetamine has also been shown to prevent performance decrements in active tasks containing a large monitoring component, such as the multidimensional pursuit test employed in a series of studies by Hauty and Payne (see Hauty and Payne, 1955; Hauty et al., 1957; Payne and Hauty, 1954). In these studies amphetamine was found to be effective in maintaining performance at a high level over extended periods of work and to counteract the impairments produced by oxygen deficiency. This enhancement of efficiency was not accompanied by side-effects of the drug. It thus seems that amphetamine contributes to performance "something above and beyond what can be achieved with good human engineering and high motivation" (Weiss and Laties, 1962, p. 16). As we have seen, similar effects of amphetamine are apparent in conventional vigilance situations in which amphetamine prevents or attenuates the decrement in correct detections without increasing the false alarm rate. Amphetamine therefore appears to arrest the sensitivity decrement found in successive discrimination task with high rates of event presentation, or in tasks which demand continuous observing (J.F. Mackworth, 1965c; Neal and Pearson, 1966). However, it has also been shown to prevent a criterion increment in a successive discrimination task with a lower event rate (Loeb et al., 1965).

Caffeine

Hauty and Payne found that caffeine reduced decrements in monitoring performance on their multi-dimensional pursuit test, although the reduction was less marked than with amphetamine. Caffeine has also been reported to reduce the vigilance decrement. Keister and McLaughlin (1972), using the Bakan task, divided their subjects into introverted and extroverted groups (see Chapter 6) and found that four 50 mg capsules of caffeine, ingested about 15 minutes before testing, abolished the decrement seen in extroverts in a no-drug condition. Introverts showed no decrement in the no-drug condition and caffeine exerted no effect on their performance.

Depressant drugs

In general depressant drugs have been shown either to impair or to exert no effect upon the overall level of vigilance performance. Neal and Pearson (1966) found that 50 mg of Benadryl, an antihistaminic drug, reliably increased the false alarm rate in two auditory vigilance tasks while leaving the detection rate unchanged, indicating an effect on criterion placement. Colquhoun (1962b) observed that performance at an audio-visual checking task was significantly impaired by hyoscine, although not by meclozine; both drugs have been used to prevent motion sickness. However, when these drugs were taken in conjunction with alcohol, performance deteriorated in both cases. Detection efficiency at both the X and AX versions of the CPT have been shown to be reliably worse following the ingestion of chlorpromazine, and the amount of impairment becomes greater as the dose is increased (Mirsky and Cardon, 1962; Primac et al., 1957). Bakan (1960) found no effect of 400 mg of meprobamate, a tranquillizer, on detection rate in the Bakan task and Peck et al. (1976) observed no effects of two hypnotic drugs, butobarbitane and nitrazepam, on performance at an auditory vigilance task requiring a successive discrimination of differences in duration.

The depressant drug most frequently investigated in relation to vigilance is alcohol, although the results obtained are suggestive rather than conclusive. Small but reliable adverse effects of alcohol on performance at a prolonged and complex meter-monitoring task were reported by Pearson (1968) and Erwin et al. (1975) found that omission errors increased as a function of blood alcohol level in a 30-minute visual vigilance task in which subjects were required to detect the occasional increase in the horizontal distance between two dots of light presented on an oscilloscope. Erwin *et al.* also recorded EEG activity, skin potential levels and eye movements and were able to demonstrate that omission errors occurring when the eyes were closed increased with blood alcohol level, but omissions occurring when the eyes were open did not, a finding which suggests that alcohol increases the number of "microsleeps" and lapses of attention and reduces the number of occasions on which the display is directly observed. However, other studies of the effects of alcohol on vigilance have obtained negative results. Colquhoun (1962a) failed to obtain any effects of a dose of alcohol equivalent to three whiskies given 45 or 225 minutes before the performance of a 60-minute simultaneous discrimination task, although he did find a reliable negative correlation between blood alcohol level and detection rate in one of his subject groups. Studies by Docter *et al.* (1966) and by Talland and Quarton (1966) also failed to observe any significant impairment of vigilance performance following alcohol ingestion. Moskowitz and DePry (1967) suggested that alcohol impaired performance at divided attention but not at sustained attention tasks and their results support this suggestion. It appears that reliable effects of alcohol on vigilance have yet to be demonstrated.

Smoking and vigilance

Tong *et al.* (1974) have argued that smoking may be a much more important contaminating factor in psychological experiments than it is generally believed to be, and they reviewed a number of studies in which smoking has been shown to affect measures of task performance. Small doses of nicotine appear to function as a stimulant to the central nervous system while larger doses act as a depressant; it is thus possible that smoking has opposite effects on the level of arousal in light and heavy smokers. Smokers may, therefore, adjust their smoking behaviour in order to maintain a particular level of arousal (Fuller and Forrest, 1973) and treatments designed to alter arousal levels may have different psychophysiological and behavioural effects in smokers than in non-smokers. In the majority of experimental situations however, smoking appears to maintain the level of behavioural arousal during task performance and in vigilance and other monotonous tasks it prevents a decrement in performance from occurring.

Tarrière *et al.* (1966) found that when smokers were allowed to smoke during the performance of a 150-minute visual vigilance task their performance was significantly better than when smoking was not permitted. The principal difference was in the amount of decrement shown. When the performance of smokers was compared with that of a group of non-smokers, the latter showed a greater deterioration in performance with time at work. Of the three groups tested, smokers who were permitted to smoke produced the best performance, followed by non-smokers, and smokers unable to smoke performed worst. Heart rate records were also taken and the decline in this measure with time at work was much the same in all three groups. However, the mean heart rate levels were different in each group and corresponded to the mean levels of performance, particularly during the first 90 minutes of the task. Thus the group which detected most signals had the highest mean heart rate and the group which detected fewest, the lowest. Frankenhaeuser *et al.* (1970) also found that smokers permitted to smoke during the performance of an 80-minute visual choice-reaction time task showed no change in efficiency with time while the response times of non-smokers increased with time on task.

Tong *et al.* (1974) found non-smokers to detect reliably more signals in a 60-minute Bakan task than smokers allowed or not allowed to smoke, although the trends over time were much the same as those found by Tarrière *et al.* and Frankenhaeuser *et al.* However, their study differs from those experiments in two important respects. First, the task was divided into five 12-minute blocks separated from each other by a two-minute rest period, so that the task was not truly continuous. Second, smokers allowed to smoke were given one cigarette before the task began, while in the studies of Tarrière *et al.* and Frankenhaeuser *et al.* smokers were allowed to smoke during task performance (an average of six cigarettes and exactly three respectively). These differences in procedure probably account for the discrepancy between the results of the three studies. It can be concluded therefore that smoking arrests the vigilance decrement and tends to improve the overall level of performance.

Summary of the effects of state variables on vigilance

All the state variables considered in this section have been shown to exert reliable effects on vigilance performance, although it is clear that these effects are not always entirely consistent. Most commonly state variables affect the overall level of performance, usually altering the omission error rate. Although effects on the vigilance decrement have been less frequently examined, some studies have reported that state variables can change the rate at which performance deteriorates with time at work. Sleep deprivation, for example, probably enhances the vigilance decrement, while the administration of amphetamine or caffeine is likely to arrest it. Smokers permitted to smoke during the performance of a vigilance task also tend to exhibit little or no performance decrement. The most popular general interpretation of the effects of state variables on performance has been expressed in terms of arousal theory and this approach will be considered in the final section of this chapter.

Environmental factors and vigilance performance

In this section we consider first the effects on vigilance of environmental factors which increase or reduce the variety of stimulation in the work environment and second the effects of noise, environmental temperature and atmospheric changes.

Increases in the variety of stimulation

Music is the most frequently. used method of increasing the variety of stimulation in the work environment and Henkin, O'Neill and others have made attempts to specify musical selections in terms of stimulation value. In Henkin's case this was done by factor analysing ratings of musical selections and in O'Neill's by an analysis of the effects on mood and task performance of different musical variables, such as tempo, rhythm, instrumentation and orchestral size. O'Neill (1966) maintained that the stimulation value of a musical selection depends upon the musical variables already mentioned and probably others that are more difficult to specify. The stimulation value of a selection depends not so much upon a melody as on the way in which it is arranged and recorded. Fairly clearly, the same melody can be made more or less stimulating by changing tempo, rhythm or instrumentation and its stimulation value also depends upon the contrast with other selections heard before and after it. O'Neill (1966) laid down some general guidelines for assessing the stimulation value of a musical selection, and the conclusions he arrived at tend to be supported by rating scale data.

Wokoun (1963, 1968, 1969) has carried out experiments on vigilance using music programmes which increase, decrease or continually vary with respect to stimulation value. First, 23 musical selections (all instrumental) were ranked in terms of stimulation value, using O'Neill's guidelines, and then three programmes were made up from the rankings. The effects of the three programmes on detection latencies (response times to signals detected) at a 60-minute vigilance task (requiring the detection of brightness increments in an intermittent light source) were subsequently examined. Wokoun found that a significant performance decrement occurred with the descending programme but that this decrement was not apparent with the other two programmes. Detections were made more quickly with the ascending programme and performance was also less variable and more consistent over the work period.

In a further study, Wokoun attempted to isolate the effects of one of the musical variables thought by O'Neill to affect stimulation value, namely instrumentation. Since the effects of instrumentation can be reduced by filtering out higher frequencies, Wokoun compared vigilance performance under a music programme in which frequencies above 3600 Hz were filtered out, with performance under a programme in which the same selections were played with a wide frequency range extending beyong 8000 Hz. The two programmes were matched for subjective loudness. Wokoun found that the wide range programme produced significantly shorter detection latencies, although it had no effect on performance decrement. Since the effects of instrumentation were presumably minimized in the narrow range programme, this result was interpreted as showing that instrumentation enhances alertness, in Wokoun's situation at least. Differences in the effects of different music schedules upon vigilance performance have also been demonstrated (Davenport, 1974). Davenport found that random and variable interval temporal schedules produced faster detection latencies than either continuous music or music presented on a fixed interval temporal schedule.

Most studies of the effects of music on vigilance have found that music produces superior performance to that found with noise of the same, or of lower intensity (Davenport, 1972; Davies, 1972; Tarrière and Wisner, 1962; Ware et al., 1964), although there are occasional exceptions to this general finding (for example, Poock and Wiener, 1966). These investigators found that a tape recording of a poorly-tuned radio conversation between pilots flying in the Miami area and flight controllers at Miami International airport produced a significantly higher detection rate than either tape recordings of preferred and non-preferred music (based on a survey of musical preferences) a tape recording of white noise, or a condition in which subjects could select any one of these four backgrounds at will. No reliable differences in false alarm rates between the five conditions were obtained and decrements in detections and in false alarms with time were found with all auditory backgrounds. The results of this study suggest that other varied backgrounds can sometimes produce greater effects on detection rate than can music, but support the general finding that varied auditory stimulation enhances detection efficiency.

However, the effects of varied auditory stimulation on detection rate also appear to depend upon the attention requirements of the task and possibly also upon the discriminability of the signal. McGrath (1963c), for instance, found that continuous varied auditory stimulation, in the form of music, excerpts from radio and television programmes and traffic noise, relayed to subjects at an intensity of 72 dB, significantly improved the detection rate (by about 4%) in a 60-minute visual successive discrimination task with an event presentation rate of 20 per minute. The control condition was white noise of the same intensity and the difference between performance in the two conditions was confined to the second half of the task. But in a subsequent experiment in which the event presentation rate was increased to 60 per minute and the signal duration reduced from one second to a third of a second, detection efficiency was reliably better (by about 6%) in the noise condition. It thus appears that varied auditory stimulation may act as a distractor when the attention requirements of the task are high; when task demands are increased by raising event rate and decreasing event duration the consequent reduction in signal discriminability outweighs the beneficial effects of varied auditory stimulation upon performance.

Since McGrath did not report false alarm rates in either of these experiments it is not clear whether the effects of varied auditory stimulation were on sensitivity or criterion placement. But an experiment by Hartley and Williams (1977), in which the task used was very similar to McGrath's low event presentation rate task, found a reliable difference in sensitivity (d_e') between continuous and variable white noise conditions presented at the same level as in McGrath's experiments, sensitivity being lower in the variable noise condition. However, Hartley and Williams' results were in the opposite direction to those of McGrath's first experiment, since detection rate was higher (by about 10%) in the continuous than in the variable noise condition, although the difference did not prove to be significant. There was also a decline in d_e' during the task in the variable but not in the continuous noise condition, although variable noise prevented the rise in the cautious criterion with time on task observed with continuous noise. A similar, but less marked tendency, was observed for the risky criterion. When varied auditory stimulation impairs performance, therefore, it appears to reduce sensitivity.

Davies et al. (1973) compared the effects of music and white noise, presented at levels of 75 dBA on detection efficiency at a 40-minute visual successive discrimination task in which the discriminability of the signal was varied by altering the signal-to-noise ratio. The event presentation rate was 12 per minute. The effects of music and noise upon performance at "easy" and "difficult" versions of the same low event rate task were thus determined. Davies et al. found that in the "easy" version of the task the percentage of signals correctly detected in music and noise was about the same, whereas more signals were correctly detected in the music condition when the task was difficult. But the most marked effect of music was upon detection latencies, as Fig. 7.4 shows. For the "difficult" version of the task, the rise in detection latencies with time, seen in the noise condition, was absent in the music condition, although in the "easy" version no decrement was apparent in either condition. Sensitivity (d') was reliably lower in the difficult version of the task and the beneficial effects of music in the "difficult" condition probably resulted from a criterion shift in the risky direction, since music did not affect sensitivity but did result in a significantly higher false alarm rate. However, sometimes varied auditory stimulation has been shown to reduce the false alarm rate significantly, at least in extroverted subjects, without affecting the detection rate (Davies et al., 1969). It seems reasonable to conclude, although not all the relevant experiments have been conducted, that the effects of music and varied auditory stimulation upon the overall level of vigilance performance, whether beneficial or detrimental, result from effects on sensitivity, while beneficial effects of music on the deterioration of performance with time can result from an influence upon the criterion increment or the sensitivity decrement, depending upon the precise requirements of the task.

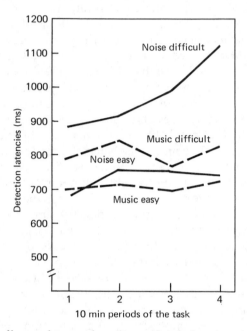

Fig. 7.4. The effects of type of auditory stimulation (music or noise) and task difficulty (easy or difficult) on mean detection latencies during a 40-minute visual vigilance task. From Davies *et al.* (1973).

According to early reviews of the effects of music in industrial situations (for example, Uhrbrock, 1961), there is not a great deal of evidence that music improves output very much and some studies suggest that the quality of output can be impaired. Where music does improve output, it appears to do so on simple and repetitive tasks, as opposed to more complex ones (Wyatt and Langdon, 1937). However, it seems clear from the results of several studies (Kerr, 1943, 1945; Kirkpatrick, 1943; McGehee and Gardiner, 1949; Newman *et al.*, 1966; Smith, 1947) that the attitude of factory employees to music tends to be extremely favourable, although it also appears that from 1 to 10% of individuals, depending on the study, are annoyed by it. But later studies of the effects of music on industrial output and productivity have reported more positive results (for example, Fox and Embrey, 1972) and music has been shown to abolish the decrement in inspector accuracy with time at work observed in a number of inspection tasks (Fox, 1975).

Reductions in the variety of stimulation

Suedfeld (1969, 1975) reviewed over 80 sensory deprivation experiments and demonstrated that exposure to sensory deprivation often facilitated the performance of simple tasks, but was much more likely to impair the performance of complex cognitive tasks. Tasks of moderate complexity, for the most part, showed no effects of exposure to sensory deprivation. Since vigilance tasks can reasonably be regarded as simple tasks, detection efficiency should be enhanced by reductions in the variety of stimulation. Although this hypothesis was confirmed by a study of the effects of prolonged immobilization (Zubek and Macneill, 1966), vigilance appears to be impaired *following* a prolonged period of sensory deprivation (Zubek *et al.*, 1961). Zubek *et al.* confined 16 subjects, who were instructed to lie quietly on an air mattress, in a dark and sound-proofed cubicle for one week. Before and after the sensory deprivation period the subjects performed a two-hour visual vigilance task, a modified version of the Mackworth Clock Test, in which 32 signals in all were presented, eight in each half-hour period. At the same time they performed an auditory discrimination task, requiring the detection of intensity and frequency changes in an 1100 Hz tone. The sensory deprivation group detected significantly fewer signals after the week's confinement than they had before it. In addition, the performance of the sensory deprivation group showed significantly greater decrement with time on task. No difference was found in performance at the auditory discrimination task before and after sensory deprivation. In the experiment of Zubek *et al.* sensory deprivation was found to produce slowing of the EEG and this may account for the performance changes observed, although subjects may also have been experiencing "potentially disruptive entry phenomena" (Smith *et al.*, 1967) brought about by the great increase in stimulation at the end of the confinement period.

In other studies (Johnson *et al.*, 1968; Myers *et al.*, 1966; Smith *et al.*, 1967), it was reported that *during* sensory deprivation vigilance performance was reliably superior to that of two non-confined control groups, who performed the task either in a dark or a lighted room. Although decrements were observed in the experimental and the control groups, the experimental group missed fewer signals overall and detected signals more quickly. Smith *et al.* (1967) suggested that subjects become more "stimulus bound" in the sensory deprivation situation, and that the vigilance task itself represented a source of stimulus enrichment for sensory deprivation subjects. Auditory vigilance performance during short-term visual deprivation, however, is sometimes improved (Bakan and Manley, 1963; Dudley, 1966) and sometimes impaired (Benedetti and Loeb, 1972; Davies, 1961).

Smith *et al.* also reported that sensory deprivation subjects become significantly more restless during the task than did subjects in the control groups, and it is possible that the increased kinesthetic feedback thereby generated enabled sensory deprivation subjects to maintain their alertness. That kinesthetic feedback can have this effect on vigilance and alertness has been demonstrated in two experiments (McFarland et al., 1942; Zuercher, 1965). Zuercher's experiment was a replication of the study of McFarland et al. and a task similar to that used by Bakan (1955) was employed. During part of a 48-minute vigil subjects were instructed to stand, stretch and breathe deeply under one experimental condition (the "movement" condition), and to converse with the experimenter under another (the "verbal" condition). Both conditions improved performance significantly with reference to a control condition, with the movement group improving to a slightly greater extent. Care was taken to ensure that the two experimental conditions were not confounded with rest, and subjects were instructed to maintain their vigil during each experimental condition. Thorsheim (1967) repeated Zuercher's experiment using a measure of integrated EEG alpha activity which was taken for six seconds before and after a signal occurred. He found that when the inter-signal interval was long EEG arousal was greater before a signal occurred in subjects who partook of mild exercise than in control subjects who did not. In the mild exercise group EEG arousal decreased slightly after signal presentation while in the controls EEG arousal increased. No effect of mild exercise upon response latency was found however. It thus seems that mild exercise is centrally arousing, as Zuercher supposed. However, although increased movement when experimentally imposed can improve vigilance performance, increased restlessness on the part of the subject during a vigil does not always have this effect. Bowen (1956) and Baker (1958) both found that there were marked individual differences in the amount of motor activity displayed by subjects performing a visual vigilance task. In both situations, motor activity increased considerably with time at work but less restless subjects tended to achieve superior performance. The association of increased restlessness with increased alertness may thus be specific to sensory deprivation situations.

Noise

Noise is usually defined as unwanted sound, and there seem to be certain stimulus characteristics of noise that contribute particularly to its unwantedness (Kryter, 1970). These include the masking of wanted sounds, especially speech, excessive loudness, a general quality of "bothersomeness", and the capacity of certain noises to produce startle responses on the one hand and auditory fatigue—together with damage to the auditory system—on the other.

Three main behavioural consequences of exposure to loud noise may be distinguished. First, a temporary or, with repeated exposures over a prolonged period, a permanent and irreversible hearing loss may result; second, noise may produce feelings of annoyance and irritation; third, noise may affect the efficiency with which a variety of different tasks are performed, usually impairing but sometimes also enhancing efficiency. These three effects are not necessarily related. Noise which produces hearing loss may not impair efficiency, noise which improves efficiency may nevertheless be annoying and noise may be found acceptable even though it produces hearing loss (Broadbent, 1970).

Much of the research to be reviewed in this section is laboratory based, since studies of noise and efficiency in industrial settings are relatively rare and in many cases suffer from methodological deficiencies which render their results virtually uninterpretable. Although industrial studies possess the undoubted advantage that they are carried out on people accustomed to working in noise, one of the major difficulties they face is the "Hawthorne effect", whereby the investigation of behaviour in an industrial setting appears itself to exert a powerful influence upon the outcome. Thus many studies of noise in industry suggest that reduction in noise levels enhance efficiency, but some investigations have also found that restoring the noise to its original level produces the same result (see the reviews by Broadbent, 1957b, 1979). As Broadbent pointed out, in many industrial studies noise levels are not the only variables to be manipulated during the course of an investigation, since changes in other features of the work situation, such as lighting conditions or temperature levels or a move to a new building, often occur at the same time. It is therefore extremely difficult, if not impossible, to distinguish the changes due to the manipulation of noise levels from those due to the manipulation of these other potential influences. Despite these difficulties, however, a few well designed studies (some of which are briefly outlined below) have succeeded in demonstrating that noise reduction can exert a beneficial effect upon efficiency in industrial situations.

In laboratory studies of the effects of noise on performance, a variety of different kinds and levels of noise has been examined, although in most recent experiments, noise of mixed frequencies, taken from a wide range of the frequency spectrum (described variously as "wide spectrum", "broad band" or, when the constituent frequencies are of the same intensity, as "white" noise) has been utilized. However, there has been a lack of consistency among investigators with respect to the noise levels selected for the experimental and control conditions of noise experiments, so that in some studies a sound pressure level (SPL) of 80 dB has been selected for the "noise condition", while in others the same level has been used for the "quiet condition". Furthermore, since two noises having similar overall SPLs can differ quite considerably in their frequency distributions, it is important to specify the frequency composition of the noise used, and this has not always been done. It seems probable that noise containing predominantly higher frequencies (that is, above 1500 Hz) produces both greater feelings of annoyance and greater impairments of task performance than does noise of predominantly lower frequencies.

Noise is usually replayed to subjects through a loudspeaker (that is, "free field") although sometimes it is presented through headphones. "Free field" noise is perceived as being louder than headphone noise of the same SPL and frequency composition (Kryter, 1970) but, presumably because of the occurrence of head movements, noise presented over headphones provides a "less variable and more coherent input" than does "free field" noise, is more likely to mask sounds generated by the experimental apparatus, and appears to impair performance of the five-choice serial reaction task (see Chapter 1) in a different way from "free field" noise (Hartley and Carpenter, 1974). Noise levels, expressed in dB, are measured by sound level meters (see Bruel, 1976), many of which incorporate weighting networks, the most commonly employed being the A- and C-weighting networks. The A-weighted network corresponds most closely to subjective loudness, since it progressively attenuates frequencies below 1000 Hz, in much the same way as the human ear does, while the C-weighted network provides a more or less flat frequency response curve, passing all frequencies nearly equally, and hence closely approximates the unweighted sound level, expressed as dB (SPL), or simply as dB, where there is an equal contribution from all frequencies. With noise containing predominantly low frequencies, sometimes described as "green noise", there will be a noticeable difference in loudness for a given SPL depending upon whether an A-weighted or a C-weighted sound level meter is used, although with "white noise" the difference in loudness will be perceived as minimal.

Performance at many tasks, for example simple and choice reaction time tasks, psychomotor tasks and "intellectual" tasks, seems to be relatively unaffected by the presence of continuous loud noise, that is, at sound levels at or above 90 dB (SPL), and may even improve slightly at more moderate levels (Broadbent, 1979; Davies and Jones, in press). However, continuous loud noise produces consistent and reliable changes in performance at certain kinds of task, such as the five-choice serial reaction task, in which errors and long response times tend to increase in noise, although the overall rate of work is unaffected. Since the average speed of performance remains unchanged, although its variability increases, subjects working at this task in loud noise have been considered to suffer from brief interruptions in the intake of task information, an hypothesis which has been interpreted in terms of "filter theory" (see Broadbent, 1957b, 1958, 1971). It appears that when a series of rapid actions has to be performed in response to an unpredictable sequence of inputs, as in the five-choice serial reaction task, efficiency deteriorates in loud noise.

Since vigilance tasks generally require subjects to make rapid observations of a constantly changing display in order to detect the presence of faint signals occurring at unpredictable times, it might be expected that detection efficiency would also be impaired by loud noise. But, in general, noise exerts a negligible effect on performance at single-source vigilance tasks. For example, Jerison (see Jerison, 1959a; Jerison and Wallis, 1957b), using a repeated measures design, found that neither detection rate nor the extent of the vigilance decrement in a 105-minute version of the Mackworth Clock Test was reliably affected by 112·5 dB broad-band noise, compared to a quiet condition of 79 dB. Davies and Hockey (1966) also observed no effect of 95 dB white noise, compared to a control condition of 70 dB, either on the mean level of performance, or on the rate of performance decline, in a 32-minute visual checking task. Other studies which did not find significant effects of noise on performance at single-source monitoring tasks include those of Blackwell and Belt (1971), Davies and Davies (1975), Poulton and Edwards (1974a), Tarrière and Wisner (1962) and Tolin and Fisher (1974).

There are, however, two exceptions to the general finding that noise exerts little or no effect on single-source vigilance performance. First, noise does appear to affect the confidence with which detection responses are made in single-source monitoring tasks, there being a fall in the proportion of doubtful responses while the proportion of confident responses rises (Broadbent and Gregory, 1963b, 1965; Poulton and Edwards, 1974a). Subjects are thus much more likely in noise to report that a signal definitely was or was not presented. If, therefore, subjects adopt a cautious criterion either as a result of the instructions they have received, or because their experience with the task has led them to believe that signals occur very rarely, and hence report signals only when they are quite sure that one has been presented, detection efficiency may show no change or even a slight improvement in noise. Thus the hit rate at the cautious criterion is likely to be as high or higher in noise than in quiet. However, if a risky criterion is adopted, either as a result of instructions or because signals occur very frequently, then detection efficiency may well deteriorate in noise. The hit rate at the risky criterion is thus likely to be lower in noise than in quiet. It would be expected, therefore, that noise would impair performance at single-source vigilance tasks in which the signal probability is high. Broadbent and Gregory (1965) compared the effects of 100 dB and 75 dB white noise on the detection efficiency of subjects working at a 70-minute visual successive discrimination task with an event rate of approximately 16 per minute and in which the probability of signal occurrence was either high or low (the probability of a signal given an event being 0·200 and 0·067 respectively). Subjects were instructed to report their degree of confidence about each event and to respond "sure yes" if they were certain they had seen a signal, "sure no" if they were sure that a signal had not been presented and "unsure" if they were at all uncertain whether a signal had been presented or not.

From an inspection of the graphical data presented by Broadbent and Gregory it seems that there is an interaction between noise level and signal probability, the probability of a detection ("sure" plus "unsure" detections) being higher in noise than in quiet at the low signal probability, although it also appears that somewhat unusually, the overall detection probability was higher in the low signal probability condition than in the high one. In the high signal probability condition the number of "unsure" responses dropped significantly during the last part of the watch in noise, but not in quiet, and the number of "sure no" responses following the presentation of a signal was reliably greater in noise than in quiet. Broadbent and Gregory concluded that the adverse effects of noise are less severe under low signal probability conditions both because the adoption of a cautious criterion is encouraged and because there is little or no reduction in the number of "unsure" responses in such a situation.

In an attempt to summarize the conditions necessary for loud noise to exert a detrimental effect on vigilance performance Broadbent (1979) suggested that, first, the noise level must be fairly high (over 95 dB SPL); second, that the signals must be of low discriminability; third, that the task situation must be one that does not encourage caution (such as a task where the probability of signal occurrence is very low) and finally, that the task should be long and uninterrupted. However, it appears that adverse effects of noise on performance at single-source vigilance tasks can also be obtained with comparatively low noise levels if "cognitive" or "verbal" vigilance tasks, such as the Bakan task (see Chapter 2) are employed (Benignus et al., 1975; Jones et al., 1979). Benignus et al. found that low frequency noise (with a frequency composition of either 91–350 Hz or 11·5–44 Hz) relayed "free field" at a level of 80 dB reliably increased omission errors, compared to a "no-noise" control condition, in a visual task requiring the detection of digit sequences which was performed for nine periods of $12\frac{1}{2}$ minutes, separated from each other by a three-minute rest period. False alarm rates were not significantly affected by noise and no differences were observed in the trend of omission errors over time. Jones et al. (1979), using a 20-minute visual version of the Bakan task, obtained a similar result. They reported that broad band noise, relayed at levels of 80 or 85 dB (C), reliably increased omission errors compared to a control level of 55 dB (C). Since Jones et al. obtained no support for the hypothesis that errors in noise are due to the masking of internal speech, a view put forward by Poulton (1976, 1977b), it is possible that the verbal nature of the task they used is less important in determining its vulnerability to low noise levels than task type, even when the task is relatively short. Both Benignus et al. and Jones et al. employed a high event rate successive-discrimination task, and it seems that the relation between task type and susceptibility to impairment by noise needs to be further explored, particularly since the effects of event rate may be more pronounced in noise (Cohen *et al.*, 1973).

Effects of loud noise are also found in multi-source monitoring tasks. Broadbent (1950, 1951, 1954) used two such tasks, the 20-dials task and the 20-lights task, and compared performance in noise (100 dB) and quiet (70 dB). In the 20-dials task he found that noise had no effect on the total number of signals detected but did reduce the number of "quick founds", that is, signals detected within nine seconds of onset. Some impairment of noise was also found with the 20-lights task, but in both cases this impairment tended to be restricted to those areas of the display which were not in the direct line of vision, the displays being arranged to form three sides of a square with the subject facing the central portion. One possible interpretation of this result is that noise produces a change in the way in which attention is allocated to the different components of a multi-component task, high priority components being given more attention and low priority components less. Support for this interpretation comes from a series of studies by Hockey (1970a, b, c, 1973). Hockey (1970a) required subjects to perform a combined tracking and multi-source monitoring task for 40 min. In the instructions given to subjects the tracking task was designated as the "high priority" task and the monitoring task, which required the detection of the onset of lights at different spatial locations, as the "low priority task".

Tracking performance was unaffected by 100 dB (A) noise, compared to a 70 dB (A) quiet condition, and signals appearing at central sources were detected more frequently in noise. However, signals appearing in peripheral locations were detected less frequently. Hockey (1970b) showed that this differential detection of signals at different spatial locations resulted from the expectation that signals were more likely to appear at central locations than at peripheral ones. In a third experiment, Hockey (1970c) found that sleep deprivation produced changes which could be interpreted as being the opposite of those obtained with noise, impairment of performance being greater on the high priority task (tracking). Hockey (1973), using a three-source monitoring task developed by Hamilton (1969), which required the subject to make a sampling response in order to obtain a brief glimpse of the present state of one of the three sources which might or might not contain a signal, found that 100 dB noise produced increased sampling of the source on which signals had a high probability of appearing, while the opposite effect was again found with sleep deprivation. Noise also reduced the frequency with which repeat observations of a source were made before a signal was reported, while sleep deprivation increased it, an effect similar to the reduction of doubtful responses noted above in connection with the performance of single-source monitoring tasks.

These results and others (for example those of Woodhead, 1964, 1966) suggest that noise produces a structured change in the way in which attention is distributed over the different components of a task, resulting in an increase in selectivity, whereby the range of cues that a subject uses in the performance of a task becomes progressively restricted (see Easterbrook, 1959), so that attention is diverted more and more away from irrelevant or subjectively unimportant aspects of the task. An alternative explanation of the effects of noise in dual task situations, expressed in terms of the reduction of spare information processing capacity (Boggs and Simon, 1968; Finkelman and Glass, 1970), is not necessarily incompatible with the selectivity hypothesis. Noise also appears to increase selectivity in memory situations, where intentional memory for words has been shown to remain unchanged or to improve slightly in 80 and 95 dB noise, while incidental memory for the locations in which the words were presented deteriorated markedly (Davies and Jones, 1975; Hockey and Hamilton, 1970). Similar effects on "selectivity" in monitoring and memory have been shown to result from smoking (Andersson and Hockey, 1977; Hartley, 1973b). It should be noted, however, that the appropriateness of Hockey's (1970b) experimental situation for demonstrating effects of noise on attentional selectivity has been questioned by Forster and Grierson (1978), who failed to replicate Hockey's results (see also Loeb and Jones, 1978). However there are some important differences between Forster and Grierson's study and Hockey's original experiment (see Hartley, 1981; Hockey, 1978) which suggest that their results should be interpreted with some caution.

Intermittent loud noise, particularly if it is aperiodic, and hence unpredictable, also produces impairments of task performance (see, for example Conrad, 1973), although its effects on monitoring performance have not been as extensively explored as those of continuous noise. Dardano (1962) found that, compared to a control condition of 68 dB, intermittent noise of variable intensity, ranging from 73–93 dB, reliably increased detection latencies when the range of intersignal intervals was narrow, so that signals occurred fairly regularly and hence detection responses were normally made quite rapidly. However, noise did not increase response speed when signals occurred very irregularly, so that detection latencies were normally extremely long. This effect of intermittent noise may be related to temporal expectancy; when the range of intersignal intervals is small, the subjective probability of signal occurrence at any particular time will be high and responses will be made, on average, fairly quickly, but when the range is greater, the subjective probability will be lower, leading to a more cautious rate of responding. The effect of noise on detection latency in Dardano's experiment thus to some extent resembles the effect on detection efficiency observed by Broadbent and Gregory (1965) referred to earlier.

Noise often exerts a different effect on performance towards the end of a long task than it does at the beginning. Jerison and Wing (1957), for example, found that detection efficiency in a multi-source monitoring task showed a decrement in 114 dB noise but not in a quiet condition of 83 dB, although initially performance was better in noise. Hartley (1973a) has described the influence of noise on performance as that of a "slowly accumulating stress, the effects of which take a similar time to dissipate" (p. 260). He found that performance at the five-choice serial reaction task was impaired to approximately the same extent either by 20 minutes of prior exposure to 100 dB noise while not performing the task or by 20 minutes of prior task performance in quiet. A prior noise exposure of 40 minutes produced much greater impairment of subsequent performances than did the 20-minute exposure. Since the effects of noise take some time to dissipate, the influence of noise may thus extend beyond the period of exposure, even when, during this period, noise does not impair task performance (Glass and Singer, 1972; Wohlwill et al., 1976). Such "after effects" of noise on performance (see S. Cohen, 1980 for a review) have been interpreted in terms of a "cognitive fatigue" hypothesis (S. Cohen, 1978), which suggests that they may result from exposure to any situations in which high attentional demands are imposed as well as to stressors such as loud noise. Supporting evidence for this hypothesis has been reported by S. Cohen and Scapacan (1978).

As noted earlier, noise reduction can also exert a beneficial effect upon efficiency in industrial situations, although satisfactory studies of the effects of noise in industry are relatively rare. Noise effects on efficiency can thus appear in individuals who are accustomed to the noise and who have had plenty of experience in the work situation (see, for example, Broadbent and Little, 1960; Weston and Adams, 1935). It was also mentioned earlier that, in laboratory studies, noise appears to affect the distribution of attention in such a way that relevant or important task components receive more attention while irrelevant or unimportant components receive less. One consequence of this may be that unexpected signals or pieces of information are inefficiently dealt with. It is possible, therefore, that accidents may be increased by noise, since they result, in part at least, from the misperception of potentially dangerous situations (Broadbent, 1970). A. Cohen (1973), in an investigation of industrial accident rates in two factories in the United States did in fact find that accident rates were very substantially higher for people working in noise at levels of 95 dB (A) or above than for people working at levels of 80 dB (A) or below. Kerr (1950) examined possible correlates of accident rates in a number of different work settings and obtained a significant correlation of 0·40 with noise level, a higher correlation than for any of the 40 variables studied except a measure of job mobility. These findings indicate that noise level may be an important determinant of accidents in industry, although clearly more evidence is needed.

Environmental temperature

Poulton (1977a) provides a useful summary of the effects of heat on vigilance

and behavioural arousal. Arousal increases when subjects are first exposed
to heat and vigilance performance improves (Poulton and Kerslake, 1965).
At moderate levels of heat with effective temperatures (ET) between 31° and
36°C, arousal level falls as the length of exposure to heat increases and both
detection rate and sensitivity (d') can be reliably reduced, compared to
ET conditions of between 19° and 28° (N.H. Mackworth, 1950; Pepler, 1953;
Poulton and Edwards, 1974a, b; Poulton et al., 1974). At very high effective
temperatures (50°C) arousal increases but detection rate falls (Benor and
Schvartz, 1971). Such conditions lead fairly rapidly to heat collapse.

In two experiments heat stress has been produced by raising body temperature rapidly (Colquhoun and Goldman, 1972; Wilkinson et al., 1964).
Colquhoun and Goldman found that performance was better at a rectal
temperature of 38·6°C than at 38·0°C, resulting from increases in the false
alarm rate. The criterion thus moved in the risky direction. Wilkinson
et al. also found that detection rate improved at the higher body temperature
but the false alarm rate showed little change, suggesting an improvement in
sensitivity. Poulton suggests that the differences between the results of these
two experiments may be due to the presentation modality employed;
Colquhoun and Goldman used an auditory task and Wilkinson et al. a
visual one. In general, then, mild heat increases detection efficiency and
the level of behavioural arousal. Cold, on the other hand, impairs performance in vigilance situations (Poulton et al., 1965).

Miscellaneous Stresses
Under this heading the effects of vibration and of various atmospheric
conditions on vigilance performance are briefly surveyed.

Vibration
Vibration is generally experienced in moving vehicles, such as cars, trains,
ships and aeroplanes, when in contact with powerful machinery, as in the
operation of hand-held power tools or pneumatic drills, or when an individual is exposed to very intense noise. The effects of vibration have been
examined in the laboratory using platforms which can move in the horizontal
or vertical planes. A chair is placed on the platform, and the subject sits
on this while performing a task. Like sound, vibration can be specified
in terms of its frequency and amplitude. But unlike sound, which is airborne,
vibration is structure-borne and is transmitted through those parts of the
body which are in contact with the source of vibration. The resonant frequency of the human body to vertical vibration is about 5Hz (Poulton,
1977a), with the shoulders being most affected. Different parts of the body
vibrate at different rates depending upon the amplitude, frequency and
direction of the vibratory stimulus, and the transmission of the amplitude
of vibration through the body can be attenuated by compensatory tension

of the muscles. If prolonged, this leads to muscular fatigue (see Poulton, 1970).

Poulton (1977a) noted that the principal effects of vibration at amplitudes within the tolerable range are to "blur vision and to reduce the accuracy of precise limb movements" (p. 448). Visual tasks should thus be affected to a greater extent by vibration than auditory tasks. In the two studies concerned with the effects of vibration on vigilance (Shoenberger, 1967; Wilkinson and Gray, 1974) it was found that vertical vibration, at a frequency of 5Hz, reliably enhanced detection efficiency. In both experiments within-subjects designs were employed. Shoenberger observed that 5Hz vertical vibration reliably reduced detection latencies in a multi-source visual monitoring task lasting for 30 minutes in which immediate knowledge of results of whether or not responses were correct was continuously provided. Wilkinson and Gray found the detection rate was significantly improved in a 60-minute successive discrimination auditory vigilance task administered after 100 min. of exposure to 5Hz vertical vibration, though no such improvement occurred in the same task administered after 30 minutes of exposure, the two tasks being performed in the same experimental session. In the control condition, without vibration, the two tasks were presented at the same times during the three-hour work period. However, when subjects were informed that they would be given knowledge of results concerning their performance at the end of the work session, the control (no vibration) group detected reliably more signals than the group exposed to vibration, and the difference between the efficiency of the two groups was much more marked in the task administered second. For the experiment as a whole, there was thus a significant interaction between the effects of vibration and the expectation of knowledge of results on detection efficiency.

Poulton (1977a) attributed the improvements in detection efficiency with vibration to an increase in arousal level; an increase in the tension of the trunk muscles, which would reduce the amplitude of vibration of the shoulders at 5Hz by about half, can be assumed to exert an alerting or arousing effect on the brain. If it is also assumed that knowledge of results is arousing or motivating (see Chapter 1), then the interaction between the effects of vibration and of knowledge of results could be explained in terms of overarousal. But it is unclear why the hypothetical arousing effect of vibration only begins to manifest itself after 100 minutes of exposure when knowledge of results is not provided.

Atmospheric conditions

Here we summarize the few studies concerned with the effects of decompression, the air pollutant, carbon monoxide, and air ionization on vigilance.

Decompression increases with altitude above sea level and at high altitudes produces hypoxia, a condition characterized by increased respiration rate and amplitude due to the reduction in the amount of oxygen in the air, and by a decrease in the supply of oxygen to the brain. For experimental purposes, hypoxia can be produced in a decompression chamber or by the administration of appropriate gas mixtures through gas masks, and appears to affect performance at a variety of tasks (see Poulton, 1970; Tune, 1964 for reviews). Cahoon (1970a) compared performance on a two-hour successive discrimination visual vigilance task at oxygen levels corresponding to those found at sea level, 13000 feet, 15000 feet and 17000 feet and found that increasing hypoxia impaired detection rate and sensitivity (d') but left the criterion (β) unchanged. Sensitivity decreased in linear fashion as a function of decreasing oxygen content. Similar effects of hypoxia on detection rate in visual vigilance were obtained by Christensen *et al.* (1977) and O'Hanlon and Horvath (1973a).

In a subsequent experiment Cahoon (1970b) compared performance on the same visual vigilance task at sea level and at an altitude of 17000 feet and replicated his earlier finding. He also demonstrated that the introduction of either one or three 10-minute rest periods did not reduce the extent to which performance was impaired, although there was some incidental evidence from the two experiments taken together that the effects of hypoxia were greater when a financial incentive was given for the highest level of performance achieved. In a third experiment, Cahoon (1973) extended his previous paradigm to auditory vigilance performance and obtained virtually identical results to those obtained with visual vigilance. It thus appears that hypoxia significantly reduces the average level of perceptual efficiency in both visual and auditory vigilance tasks, but does not affect the rate at which performance declines over time.

Hypoxia also results from exposure to an atmosphere polluted by carbon monoxide (CO) which combines with the pigment haemoglobin in the bloodstream and displaces the oxygen that haemoglobin normally transports. Prolonged exposure to high CO levels thus reduces the oxygen-carrying capacity of the circulatory system and places an increased load on the heart and respiratory system. For example, an eight-hour exposure containing 80 parts per million (ppm) of CO reduces the oxygen-carrying capacity of the circulatory system by about 15% (Ehrlich and Ehrlich, 1970). The major source of CO pollution is car exhaust systems, and Haagen-Smit (1966) reported that the average and peak levels of CO in the atmosphere to which drivers in Los Angeles were exposed were 26 and 111 ppm respectively. In addition, industrial and residential sources, as well as tobacco smoke, contribute lesser amounts of CO pollution to the atmosphere. However, these sources omit other noxious substances, for example, hydrocarbons, nitrogen and sulphur oxides and tetraethyl lead, as well as CO, and although some studies have examined the effects of traffic pollution on task performance (for instance, Lewis *et al.*, 1970), most laboratory studies have focussed on the effects of CO exposure alone. It is worth noting however, that Lewis *et al.* found that detection rate in an auditory vigilance task was reliably reduced by exposure to an atmosphere polluted by a traffic volume of 830 vehicles per hour.

The normal range of CO in the human body (see Coburn, 1970) is less than 1% of blood saturation level or 1% blood carboxyhemoglobin (COHb). There are two ways in which the magnitude of CO exposure is expressed (Laties and Merigan, 1979), the first being in terms of the COHb percentage and the second in terms of the duration of exposure to a specified CO concentration in ppm. Table 7.1 gives an indication of the relation between these two indices obtained in four experiments, all of which were concerned with the effects of CO on vigilance. In view of the differential effects of CO concentrations on the COHb levels of smokers and non-smokers shown in Table 7.1, smokers are usually excluded from such studies. The vigilance performance of smokers has also been shown to be relatively unaffected by CO concentrations of 111 ppm, an exposure which reliably decreased the detection efficiency of non-smokers (O'Hanlon, 1973).

CO effects on vigilance performance have been quite extensively investigated, although the results are not altogether consistent. Some studies have obtained significant reductions in detection rate at COHb levels of around 5% (for example, Beard and Grandstaff 1970; Horvath *et al.*, 1971) while others have not (Benignus *et al.*, 1977; Groll-Knapp *et al.*, 1978; Putz, 1979; Winneke *et al.*, 1978). However, CO does not appear to affect the vigilance decrement.

Ordinary outdoor air generally contains between 200 and 1100 ions per cubic centimetre (Chiles *et al.*, 1960), some of which are positively and some negatively charged. Both the total number of air ions and the ratio of positive to negative ions tend to increase in certain meteorological conditions and these changes have been considered to have both biological and psychological consequences. A number of experiments, using commercially available air ionizers, have examined the effects of increases in the concentration of both positive and negative air ions on task performance under laboratory conditions and the evidence, although far from being conclusive, suggests that negatively ionized air sometimes exerts a beneficial effect on efficiency (see, for example, Hawkins and Baker, 1978). Only a few such studies have been concerned with vigilance and neither Chiles *et al.* (1960) nor Chiles *et al.* (1962) found any reliable effect of ionized air on vigilance performance. However, Halcomb and Kirk (1965b) found that negatively ionized air attenuated the increment in detection latencies observed under control conditions.

Conclusions

Most, though not all, of the environmental factors and state variables whose

Table 7.1. Carboxyhemoglobin (COHb) levels (percent saturation) after exposure to various levels of carbon monoxide (CO) for varying lengths of time. Both means ($\bar{x}$) and standard deviations (SD) are given. Data from four experiments.

Source	Group	CO inhaled (ppm)	Exposure time				
			0 min	60–65 min	135–140 min	200 min	240 min
Horvath et al. (1971)	Non-smokers (N = 10)	0	$\bar{x} = 0.80$ (SD, 0.35)	$\bar{x} = 0.80$ (SD, 0.23)	$\bar{x} = 0.80$ (SD, 0.21)		
		26	$\bar{x} = 0.80$ (SD, 0.57)	$\bar{x} = 1.60$ (SD, 0.60)	$\bar{x} = 2.30$ (SD, 0.55)		
		111	$\bar{x} = 0.90$ (SD, 0.46)	$\bar{x} = 4.20$ (SD, 1.15)	$\bar{x} = 6.60$ (SD, 1.27)		
O'Hanlon (1975)	Smokers (N = 5)	0	$\bar{x} = 3.20$ (SD, 0.49)	$\bar{x} = 2.90$ (SD, 0.41)	$\bar{x} = 2.60$ (SD, 0.40)		
		26	$\bar{x} = 2.90$ (SD, 0.96)	$\bar{x} = 3.40$ (SD, 0.79)	$\bar{x} = 3.60$ (SD, 0.56)		
		111	$\bar{x} = 2.80$ (SD, 0.55)	$\bar{x} = 5.10$ (SD, 0.50)	$\bar{x} = 6.90$ (SD, 0.55)		
Benignus et al. (1977)	Non-smokers (N = 52)	0	$\bar{x} = 1.00$			$\bar{x} = 0.01$ (SD, 0.46)	
		100				$\bar{x} = 4.61$ (SD, 0.90)	
		200				$\bar{x} = 12.62$ (SD, 1.36)	
Putz (1979)	Non-smokers (N = 30)	5	$\bar{x} = 1.50$ (SD, 0.27)				$\bar{x} = 1.00$
		35	$\bar{x} = 1.30$ (SD, 0.39)				$\bar{x} = 3.03$ (SD, 0.71)
		70					$\bar{x} = 5.10$ (SD, 0.57)

effects on vigilance have been reviewed in this chapter can be regarded as "stressors" and insofar as this chapter has a theoretical perspective, rather than a purely empirical one, its starting point must be the arousal theory of stress, which was introduced in Chapter 1. The arousal theory of stress is a product of research on the effect of various combinations of stressors, from which the mode of action of an individual stressor is inferred. For example, studies using both physiological and psychological measures have provided evidence which suggests that loud noise raises the level of arousal while sleep deprivation lowers it. Noise increases skin conductance and other measures of autonomic activity (Berlyne and Lewis, 1963; Davies, 1968a, 1976; Helper, 1957), while sleep deprivation produces changes in the direction of lowered arousal in several physiological measures (Wilkinson, 1965). Wilkinson emphasized, however, that the interpretation of changes in physiological measures during sleep deprivation depends very much on the experimental situation in which the measures are taken. Thus, if a sleep-deprived subject is performing a very demanding task in which successes are rewarded and failures punished, concomitant physiological measures are more likely to be indicative of increased arousal, although it is probably more fruitful to regard them as reflecting the increased cost of maintaining efficiency under stressful conditions. Because of the difficulty of interpreting changes in physiological measures in different experimental situations it is advantageous to consider more psychological approaches to the relation between arousal and performance, that is, to consider arousal as a behavioural construct (see, for example, Broadbent, 1971).

If noise raises and sleep deprivation lowers the level of arousal it would be expected that the effects of noise would, to some extent, cancel those of sleep deprivation. This appears to be the case, on some tasks at least. On the unpaced five-choice serial reaction task (see Chapter 1), sleep-deprived subjects made fewer correct responses, more errors and a greater number of long response times in quiet than under conditions of high intensity noise, although only the difference in errors was significant (Wilkinson, 1963a). Corcoran (1962) found that the increase in the number of long response-times from the first half of the task to the second was significantly less marked in sleep-deprived subjects working in noise. Noise had no effect on the number of errors made by sleep-deprived subjects although it tended to reduce the number of long response times after loss of sleep and also to increase the number of correct responses. However, neither of these effects was statistically reliable.

Such results are typical of the kind of evidence adduced for the arousal theory of stress and a large number of studies have been conducted along these lines. There are, however, very few studies in which the effects of two environmental factors, or of an environmental factor and a state variable on vigilance have been examined. Poulton and Edwards (1974a) found that heat on its own reliably reduced d', while low frequency noise also reduced d' but not significantly. When heat and noise were combined, noise reduced the adverse effects of heat, since the reduction in d' was no longer significant. Loss of sleep also partially reduced the adverse effects of heat on vigilance (Poulton *et al.*, 1974). Increasing event rate reduces the effects of sleep loss on vigilance performance (Corcoran, 1963). This last result is surprising since both sleep loss and increased event rates appear to reduce d' when administered in isolation, yet to improve detection rate when they are combined.

The majority of environmental effects and state variables discussed in this chapter appear to exert little or no effect upon decrement but merely raise or lower the overall level of performance. However, stimulating drugs, sleep loss, music and ionised air have all been shown to exert reliable effects upon the vigilance decrement, which suggests that the level of arousal can affect the way in which performance changes with time on task. We have earlier argued that it is task factors that principally influence the nature and extent of the vigilance decrement but in order to accommodate the results mentioned above it must be assumed that the level of arousal can contribute to the effects of task factors on the decrement. That is, at low and high levels of arousal the effects of task factors on the decrement may be different from those found at intermediate levels. This possibility remains to be explored.

As noted in Chapter 6, Welford (1962) has suggested that the principal effects of increased arousal are to produce a change in the criterion setting in the direction of increased riskiness. As we have seen in this chapter there is some evidence which supports this hypothesis, particularly from studies of noise and heat, but the evidence is conflicting and there are several studies which suggest that arousal affects sensitivity (d'). There is, unfortunately, a dearth of studies relevant to Welford's hypothesis, especially studies which have taken task factors into account.

Almost certainly there is insufficient evidence concerning the effects of particular stressors, individually or in combination, to warrant the application of arousal theory to the results reviewed in this chapter. First, it needs to be demonstrated that the variables discussed earlier exert effects in common upon performance, mediated through a central state of activation or arousal, in addition to any specific peripheral effects they may exert upon task-related behaviours, for instance, upon the visual or auditory systems or upon parts of the body involved in the execution of motor responses. As noted above, attempts have been made to solve this problem by demonstrating additive and interactive effects between environmental and state variables on task performance but the range of tasks used has been narrow, and the implications for vigilance performance are not entirely clear. It appears, too, that the occurrence of additive and interactive effects is influenced not only by the variables employed but also by a variety of other factors including individual differences, time of testing, the stage of practice that has been reached with the task being performed and the degree of acclimatization to the stressor. Furthermore, assessments of arousal level based on self-reports do not always agree with physiological measures of arousal, which themselves show generally low intercorrelations, and neither of these indices may relate to performance.

Second, with some "stressors", for instance carbon monoxide, ionized air and various drugs, the subject will often be unaware that he has been subjected to stress, whereas with noise, heat and vibration the presence of the "stressor" will be readily apparent. What difference, if any, does the awareness of being stressed make to the effects observed on performance? Presumably the presence of a "stressor", whether or nor it is readily detected, makes some difference to the way in which the task situation is perceived.

Finally, how does arousal level alter performance? One possible answer to this question has been enshrined in the Yerkes–Dodson Law in which the relation between arousal level and performance is described by an inverted U, with the optimal level of arousal being inversely related to task difficulty. However, as Revelle et al. (1980) have observed, the Yerkes–Dodson Law merely describes a relationship between two variables, without providing an account of the processes producing that relationship. With respect to dual tasks and multi-source monitoring tasks it appears from Hockey's work (1970a, b, c, 1973) that manipulation of arousal level may affect the distribution of attention over task components, thus producing a change in "selectivity", as mentioned earlier in the section on noise effects. But again it is unclear how this analysis might apply to performance in single-source vigilance tasks.

Difficulties with the traditional formulation of arousal theory have led to the view that there may be "qualitatively different activation states" resulting from the combination of specific processing demands required by task situations and the presence of particular "stressors" (Hamilton et al., 1977; see also M.W. Eysenck and Folkard, 1980). As Eysenck and Folkard remark, "There is a potentially important distinction between arousal in the sense of what is done to the individual (for example, exposure to white noise or electric shock) and arousal produced as a by-product of active processing effort" (p. 39). While this hypothesis has scarcely begun to be developed, it is likely that any statement of the relation between arousal and performance will need to take such a distinction into account.

Chapter 8

Vigilance and the Brain

Speculation as to how the brain controls behaviour has a very long history, although it is only during the past two centuries that significant advances have been made in our understanding of the ways in which brain mechanisms regulate certain psychological functions.

Research on the nature of the brain mechanisms underlying attention, and sustained attention in particular, has an even shorter history. There are a number of reasons for this, perhaps the most important being that the psychological study of attention, although highly regarded by Titchener, was itself neglected during the early years of this century, largely because of the ascendance of classical behaviourism and the subsequent neo-behaviourist approaches to the conduct of experimental psychology. The concept of attention was seen as being too closely allied to that of consciousness which, as Boring (1957) observes, was regarded as an impediment to the study of behaviour in animals and man. Since the 1950s, however, with the resurgence of interest in the psychology of cognition, and against a background of rapid development in the neurosciences, research into the brain mechanisms underlying attention and related mental processes has begun to flourish.

In this chapter we focus upon four separate but related areas of research concerned with vigilance and the brain. First the relationship between measures of brain electrical activity and vigilance performance is examined. The principal questions of interest here are whether these measures are differentially related to performance changes during a vigil and whether they can reasonably be viewed as correlates of decision processes or primarily as measures of electrocortical arousal. Second, an appraisal is given of experiments concerned with biofeedback and vigilance, in an attempt to determine whether this technique is helpful in preventing a deterioration in performance. Third, there is a brief discussion of pupillometric studies in relation to task demands and task performance. As noted in Chapter 5, the emphasis here is on pupillary diameter as a measure of cognitive load and mental effort. Finally neuropsychological studies of vigilance are reviewed, the major questions here being whether damage to specific regions of the brain can be associated with impairment of vigilance and whether the capacity for sustained attention differs between the left and right cerebral hemispheres.

Vigilance and the electrical activity of the brain

The electroencephalogram (EEG)

One of the most commonly employed measures of brain electrical activity is the EEG which is recorded from small electrodes placed at various locations on the scalp, usually in accordance with an internationally agreed arrangement known as the "Ten–Twenty System" (Jasper, 1958), shown in Fig. 8.1. Provided that certain artifacts of measurement can be excluded (see, for example, Harding, 1974, and Lindsley and Wicke, 1974), the EEG record can be taken to represent brain electrical activity. In EEG studies of vigilance interest has been mainly focused on activity in the alpha (8–13 Hz), beta (14–30+ Hz) and theta (4–7 Hz) frequency bands and electrode placement has frequently, although not exclusively, been restricted to the occipital region (O_1 and O_2 in Fig. 8.1), which is the richest source of alpha activity.

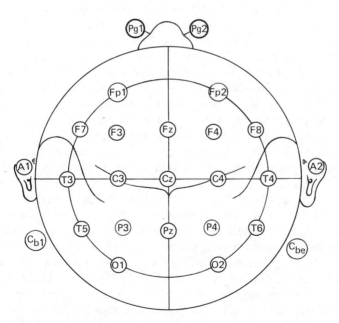

Fig. 8.1. A single plane projection of the head viewed from above, showing the standard electrode positions in the International Ten–Twenty System. After Jasper (1958).

Most, if not all, of these studies have interpreted their findings in terms of an arousal or activation framework (Carriero, 1977; Daniel, 1967; Davies and Krkovic, 1965; Gale *et al.*, 1971, 1972c, 1977; Groll, 1966; Gulian, 1970; O'Hanlon and Beatty, 1977).

Davies and Krkovic (1965), using a 90-minute version of the Bakan task, were among the first to report a direct relation between the abundance of alpha activity recorded from the occipital region and the number of correct detections. In this experiment subjects reclined on a bed with eyes closed and reported the occurrence of signals by pressing a hand-held toggle switch, a situation likely to induce drowsiness. Subjective reports of drowsiness, obtained from a questionnaire given at the end of the task, did in fact coincide with the appearance of slower EEG (theta) activity in the EEG record and performance also reached its lowest level (50%) around this time. EEG activity was recorded while the subjects relaxed for 15 minutes after the task had ended. Alpha activity declined from 99% of the pre-task resting value in the first 15-minute period of the task, to 87% of this value in the final period while detection rate declined from 88% in the first period to 58% in the last (see Davies, 1962).

Daniel (1967), however, obtained an inverse relation between the abundance of alpha activity recorded from the occipital region and performance at a 60-minute version of the Bakan task. But subjects in this experiment performed the task with eyes open and, as O'Hanlon and Beatty (1977) point out, when alert individuals perform a task with eyes closed, the EEG record shows a relatively high level of alpha activity which diminishes at the onset of drowsiness and slower EEG activity (theta) becomes more prominent. In individuals performing a task with eyes open, on the other hand, faster EEG activity (beta) predominates, being replaced by increasing alpha activity as drowsiness occurs. This explanation provides a way of reconciling the conflicting findings outlined above, and, as O'Hanlon and Beatty observe, indicates the importance of recording not merely from the alpha frequency band but from the beta and theta bands as well.

This recommendation was followed in an experiment conducted by O'Hanlon and Beatty (1977) in which subjects performed a 120-minute simulation of a visual radar monitoring task. EEG activity was recorded from the occipital and parietal regions and alpha and theta activity showed a reliable increase during task performance while beta activity showed a significant decline. Detection efficiency was assessed in terms of the number of "sweeps" of the radar sweep line occurring before a target was detected, and this measure reliably increased with time on task, indicating a deterioration in performance (see Fig. 8.2). Significant negative intra-subject correlations were observed between the percentages of theta and alpha activity and detection efficiency (-0.44 and -0.68 respectively) while a significant positive correlation ($+0.67$) was obtained for beta activity.

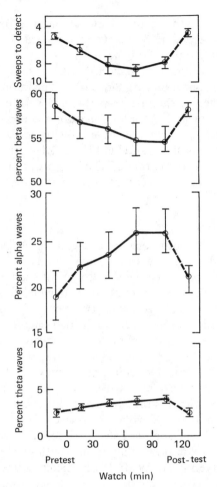

Fig. 8.2. Mean (± S.E.) sweeps to detect and percentages of spontaneous EEG activity in the beta (13–30 Hz), alpha (7–13 Hz) and theta (3–7 Hz) frequency bands in the pre- and post- tests and during the four 30-minute time blocks of a two-hour vigil in which a simulated radar task was employed. From O'Hanlon and Beatty (1977).

Groll (1966) examined EEG frequency changes below 12 Hz during the performance of a 90-minute visual vigilance task requiring the detection of brightness changes. She found that both the number of correct detections and the dominant frequency of EEG activity reliably declined during the task. Essentially similar results were obtained by Gale *et al.* (1977), using a task in which subjects were required to respond to particular digits while ignoring others, under five different conditions of signal probability (each lasting for 16 minutes), all of which were presented in the same session of attendance. Gale *et al.* found that EEG abundance for the lower frequencies within the alpha range (7·5–9·5 Hz) increased as the task progressed, while the mean dominant alpha frequency declined.

The results of these experiments suggest that EEG activity shifts to lower frequencies during the course of a vigilance task. The initial level of activity is dependent upon whether the task is performed with eyes open or eyes closed, but at the end of a vigil there is usually a predominance of theta activity in the EEG record. Since a similar slowing in EEG frequencies is also found in states of drowsiness and light sleep (Kleitman, 1963; Lindsley, 1952) it is perhaps not surprising that EEG changes during the performance of a vigilance task have generally been interpreted as an indication of lowered electrocortical arousal.

Event-related potentials

The EEG represents the continuous spontaneous electrical activity of the brain and usually little response to external stimulation can be reliably detected in the EEG record since the amplitudes of such evoked responses are smaller than that of the spontaneous activity in which they are embedded. It is only comparatively recently (since the early 1960s) that computer averaging techniques have been developed which enable the evoked EEG response to be measured. Such techniques effectively increase the signal strength of the response using various signal averaging techniques (see for example, Donchin, 1969, and Donchin and Heffley, 1975). The signal-to-noise ratio of the evoked response is usually enhanced by averaging the EEG over a number of stimulus presentations. The use of these techniques rests on the assumption that the evoked response will be "time-locked" to the stimulus event, while the spontaneous EEG activity will bear a random relationship to it, an assumption that is not without certain difficulties (see Harding, 1974; Sayers *et al.*, 1974). If a particular stimulus is repeatedly presented, and on each occasion the time-locked EEG response is stored, the common features of the response will slowly summate to produce a clearly defined evoked response (see for example Donchin, 1975). The spontaneous EEG activity, on the other hand, will tend to summate to zero, enabling the characteristics of the evoked response or *event-related potential* (ERP) to be clearly distinguished.

While the complete range of potentials subsumed within the rubric of ERPs are of relevance to the further study of brain-behaviour relationships, in general it is the longer-latency potentials, and in particular P300, a positive-going potential peaking approximately 300 ms after the delivery (or expected delivery) of a stimulus, which are of greatest psychological interest (Callaway, 1975; Donchin *et al.*, 1978; Hillyard and Picton, 1978; Tueting, 1978). The substantial literature which has been amassed indicates that P300 and other late ERP components are related to various aspects of human information processing (see Price and Smith, 1974). Sutton *et al.* (1965) were the first to report the existence of the P300 wave. In their study subjects had to guess whether the second of a pair of stimuli would be a tone or a flash which could occur with either low or high probability. ERPs averaged to low probability stimuli indicated a large positive wave at a latency of approximately 300 ms after the delivery of the stimulus. P300 amplitude was inversely related to stimulus probability, and, in a later study, it was confirmed that P300 is elicited by rare, task relevant events (Sutton *et al.*, 1967). At present, however, the specific aspects of information processing activity to which P300 is sensitive remain unclear. The better controlled studies indicate that P300 is not a unitary phenomenon, but represents a conglomerate of waves which may be differentially related to such factors as task relevance, subjective probability and criterion placement (Donchin *et al.*, 1978; Rohrbaugh *et al.*, 1974; Squires *et al.*, 1975a, b; Tueting, 1978).

Early ERP studies of vigilance, however, were conducted with the general aim of obtaining evidence for a decline in electrocortical arousal during a vigilance task. Haider *et al.* (1964), using a visual task, and Wilkinson *et al.* (1966), using an auditory task, both found parallel declines in ERP amplitude and detection rate over time. In the study by Haider *et al.* (1964) the principal ERP component analysed was a negative wave with a peak latency of about 160 ms. Wilkinson *et al.* (1966) obtained averaged ERPs to the 50 non-signal events preceding each signal and identified three main ERP components: a negative component, with a peak latency of around 95 ms (described as N_1); a positive component with a peak latency of around 170 ms (P_2) and a later negative component with a peak latency of around 265 ms (N_2). Wilkinson *et al.* found that a reduction in the amplitude of N_2, and, to a lesser extent of P_2, accompanied the decline in the detection rate. The amplitude of N_1, however, showed little change with time on task, although the latency of this component significantly increased.

In a later experiment, Wilkinson and Haines (1970) found that the amplitude of the contingent negative variation (CNV) also declines during a vigilance task. The CNV is an event-related potential which is recorded as a slow negative shift between a warning and an imperative stimulus (Walter *et al.*, 1964). It appears that the CNV, like P300, is not a unitary process but comprises at least two components (Loveless, 1976; Rohrbaugh *et al.*, 1978; Weerts and Lang, 1973).

For their experiment on vigilance and the CNV, Wilkinson and Haines (1970) developed a task consisting of pairs of clicks. The interval between the "warning" and the "inspection" clicks was fixed at 1·92 s and each pair of clicks was separated by a variable interval whose average length was 10 s. Occasionally the "inspection" click was slightly quieter than normal and this was the signal which subjects were required to report. The task lasted for 22 minutes and consisted of 128 pairs of clicks. In a high signal frequency condition there were 32 signals and in a low signal frequency condition only four. Wilkinson and Haines found that the percentage of correct detections reliably declined from the first half of the task to the second but only in the high signal frequency condition. The percentage of false alarms showed no change with time in either condition and detection latencies rose significantly in both. The amplitude of the CNV also declined with time on task in both conditions and there was a significant positive correlation between CNV amplitude and detection rate which remained when the effects of time on task were partialled out. The significant positive correlation with the reciprocal of response latency disappeared when time at work was held constant. In a subsequent experiment, Wilkinson and Seales (1978) employed an auditory vigilance task requiring the detection of a faint tone embedded in continuous white noise. On each of 240 trials a high-pitched warning click was followed by an observation period, bounded by the offset of a light-emitting diode and then by a low-pitched click cueing the subject's response. The signal probability used in this study (0·50) was much higher than in either of the conditions of the Wilkinson and Haines (1970) experiment and the positive correlation between CNV and detection rate was not replicated, although, as before, CNV amplitude significantly declined with time on task. The CNV thus appears to be yet another cortical measure which declines during the course of a vigilance task, although to some extent independently of performance, since in the low signal frequency condition of Wilkinson and Haines no decrement in detection rate occurred.

An interesting variant to the typical study examining the relationship between electrocortical arousal and the vigilance decrement was reported by Hink et al. (1978). Hink et al. required their subjects to listen to a sequence of four tones, two of which were presented to each ear, and detect a designated target tone in a specified ear; the ear to be attended was alternated over a vigil lasting about 70 minutes. Now a number of studies using short-term versions of such tasks have shown that the N100 component of the ERP is larger for stimuli presented to the attended ear than for stimuli arriving in the unattended ear (Hink et al., 1977; Hillyard et al., 1973; Parasuraman, 1978), although it has also been argued that this apparent modulation of N100 is due to an underlying slow negative wave which displaces N100 (see Näätänen and Michie, 1979). Hink et al. therefore reasoned that if the vigilance decrement is related to changes in selective attention, the difference in N100 amplitude between attended and unattended ears should change with time on task. The results showed, however, that there was a decrement in N100 amplitude which was comparable for both attended and unattended stimuli. Hink et al. interpreted this finding to mean that the vigilance decrement is primarily associated with changes in general state, although they did not in fact obtain a vigilance decrement, probably because short rest periods were interpolated at periodic intervals during the vigil. The results of this study appear to support Jerison's (1977) proposal of a fundamental distinction between selective and sustained attention, referred to in Chapter 1.

Electrocortical activity and response type

The studies reviewed thus far have demonstrated that changes in both EEG and ERP measures of brain electrical activity during the course of a vigilance task are indicative of long-term declines in electrocortical arousal. In an attempt to investigate the relationship between short-term or momentary EEG changes and vigilance performance, a number of studies have also examined differences in EEG and ERP activity associated with different categories of response. Of particular interest is the question of whether correct and incorrect responses can be distinguished on the basis of the brain electrical activity either preceding or following the response.

The idea that subjects miss signals in a vigilance situation because of brief periods of lowered arousal preceding a critical signal has intuitive appeal, and there is some evidence for this hypothesis from EEG studies. It has been reported, for example, that subjects are more likely to miss signals when theta activity is predominant in the EEG record, both when they are normally rested (Oswald, 1962) and when sleep-deprived (Mirsky and Cardon, 1962; Williams et al., 1962). Horvath et al. (1975) have also reported that omissions are preceded by higher levels of theta activity than correct detections. However, the opposite result has been reported by Daniel (1967), a finding that is anomalous and unreplicated (O'Hanlon and Beatty, 1977). Daniel (1967) based his measure of theta activity on the number of zero crossings of the EEG in a specified interval, and thus, as Horvath et al. (1975) point out, a reduced number of zero crossings is not necessarily inconsistent with slower EEG activity in the theta frequency range.

Overall, then, the evidence points to an inverse relationship between theta activity and detection performance in vigilance tasks; and recent findings on the operant control of posterior theta rhythms during vigilance tasks have provided support for this conclusion, as will be seen later. Furthermore, the finding that missed signals are associated with periods of lowered arousal may have some operational significance with respect to the design of alerting or warning devices (see Chapter 9).

EEG alpha activity has been related to changes in subjective response or "expectancy" in a series of studies reported by Gale et al. (1971, 1972c; Haslum and Gale, 1973). These investigators used a version of the Bakan task in which subjects had to detect three consecutive odd digits which were all different in a continuous quasi-random series. When this target sequence was compared to other non-target sequences, short-term fluctuations in abundance of EEG alpha activity (recorded trans-occipitally, $O_1 - O_2$)

fluctuated in parallel with the waxing and waning of subjective response or "cumulative expectancy" (Gale, 1977; Gale *et al.*, 1971) within each three digit sequence. McCallum (1976) has reported a similar result for the CNV; in this study a negative baseline EEG shift developed whenever an odd digit followed an odd digit but not otherwise. The CNV developed further if a third odd digit followed (completing the target sequence), but returned to baseline if an even digit occurred.

Differences in post-stimulus activity associated with correct and incorrect responses have also been examined in ERP studies. Haider *et al.* (1964) found that the amplitude of the N160 component of the visual ERP was reduced following missed signals as compared to detected signals. Wilkinson *et al.* (1966), on the other hand, found that the N265 component of the auditory ERP was larger for missed than for detected signals; but since this component has been noted to *increase* in amplitude with drowsiness and with the onset of sleep (Williams *et al.*, 1962; Fruhstorfer and Bergstrom, 1969), this result is consistent with the suggestion of Haider *et al.* that missed signals are associated with periods of lowered cortical arousal.

Ritter and Vaughan (1969) repeated the study of Haider *et al.* using both visual and auditory tasks, and they noted that their failure to obtain a late positive component (P300) could be accounted for by their usage of a bipolar linkage between the vertex and occipital leads, P300 being common to both leads. With monopolar recording, Ritter and Vaughan found that a late positive component (latency 300–350 ms) occurred when signals were detected, but was reduced or absent for omissions or non-signal events. Since P300 was found to be present both when subjects witheld their motor responses for one second following detection and also when they made similar motor responses to signal and non-signal events, Ritter and Vaughan argued that P300 is not related to central processes underlying motor responding. (For a discussion of the dissociation between P300 and the CNV, motor potentials and other slow waves, see Donchin *et al.*, 1975.)

Ritter and Vaughan's (1969) study suggests the possibility that P300 may be related to detection performance and decision processes in vigilance tasks. This possibility was explored in a series of experiments reported by Parasuraman and Davies (1975; Davies and Parasuraman, 1976, 1977). Davies and Parasuraman (1977) recorded ERPs from the occipital region in a visual vigilance task performed under different levels of event rate and signal regularity. Subjects were required to respond "Yes" (signal present) or "No" (signal absent) to each event, and ERPs were averaged selectively to each of the four stimulus-response categories: correct detections, correct rejections, omissions, and false alarms. However, since few false alarms were made, analyses of ERP data associated with this response were not carried out. Four ERP components were identified: N_1 (peak 157 ms, range 140–175 ms), P_2 (peak 206 ms, range 183–225 ms), N_2 (peak 257 ms, range 231–281 ms), and P_3 (peak 321 ms, range 294–371 ms). The amplitudes of these four components declined with time on task in all conditions, as did the number of signals correctly detected. Detection latencies increased significantly with time in all conditions. Spearman rank correlation coefficients were computed between the amplitudes of ERPs to detections and both correct detections and detection latencies. For both indices of detection performance significant correlations were obtained only for the late components N_2 and P_3, positive in the case of correct detections and negative in the case of detection latencies. Similar correlations were computed between the two performance indices and component amplitudes of ERPs to both omissions and correct rejections, but none of these proved to be significant. Hence the amplitudes of N_2 and P_3 were correlates of detection efficiency for ERPs averaged *to correct detections only*.

Since the ERPs associated with other responses were unrelated to detection performance, an interpretation in terms of a general state of electrocortical arousal, as suggested by Haider *et al.* and Wilkinson *et al.*, cannot accommodate these results easily. These data suggest instead that the amplitude of the late ERP components is specifically related to the information processing activity leading to the selection of a particular response in the vigilance task; changes in general state affect all ERP components, but it is only the late ERP components, which have been linked to decision processes, which are in turn related to detection efficiency.

A number of studies have also reported that the latencies of P300 and other late ERP components may be related to the timing of information processing or decision making activities (Donchin *et al.*, 1978; Tueting 1978) although the relationship is not a simple one but varies with factors such as the speed/accuracy trade–off. Parasuraman and Davies (1975) investigated the relationship between ERP latencies and response latencies in a visual vigilance task similar to that used by Davies and Parasuraman (1977), except that the signal discrimination was made more difficult in an attempt to increase the false alarm rate. Individual ERP components P_1, N_1, P_2, N_2, and P_3, (latencies defined as previously) were identified and it was found that the latencies of P_2, N_2, and P_3, increased significantly with time on task for ERPs averaged separately to both correct detections and false alarms; at the same time the latencies associated with these behavioural responses also increased. False alarm latencies were longer than correct detection latencies, and these differences were also reflected in the late component latencies of the associated ERPs. The response latency data obtained were consistent with a model of the decision process in which the timing of responses is related to the criterion level above which responses are elicited (see Chapter 3 and 4); it also appeared that the timing of the late ERP components was related to this process, slower responses being associated with ERP components which peaked later. This interpretation receives support from a further study (Davies and Parasuraman, 1977) in which ERPs were recorded selectively according to the responses made on a four-category confidence rating scale used in a visual vigilance task. ERPs were averaged to correct detection responses made at two levels of confidence, "certain" and "doubtful", and it was found that "doubtful" ERPs had smaller amplitudes and longer late component latencies than "certain" ERPs. These latency differences were accompanied by an increased mean latency for "doubtful" responses over "certain" responses.

These results suggest that the amplitude and latency of late ERP components may be related to decision processes as they are reflected in variations in decision criteria. Several studies employing signal detection tasks have examined the relationships between decision criteria and the late ERP components, in particular P300. Paul and Sutton (1972), for instance, manipulated the decision criterion (β) by varying both the *a priori* signal probability and the payoff matrix and found that the amplitude of P300 was systematically related to the strictness of the response criterion. Similar results have been reported by Hillyard, Squires and others (Hillyard *et al.*, 1971; Squires *et al.*, 1975a, b). Squires *et al.* (1975a) averaged ERPs selectively in accordance with the objective criterion cut-off on blocks of trials and found that there was a remarkably close covariation between both the amplitude and latency of P300 for correct detections and the observer's decision criterion. The same relationship between P300 amplitude and the criterion was preserved whether the criterion was derived from ratings or from variations in signal probability (see Fig. 8.3). It seems therefore that

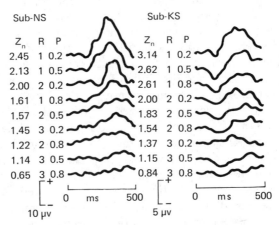

Fig. 8.3. Effects of variations in the criterion cut-off (Z_n), derived either from confidence ratings (R) or signal probability (P) changes, on the P300 component of the event-related potential. Data for two subjects. In both subjects there is a monotonic relationship between the criterion value and the amplitude of the P300 component. From Squires *et al.* (1975b).

for such tasks the amplitude of P300 is closely related to the subject's decision that a signal is present. Other experiments have reported that late component latency measures are sensitive to both between- and within-subject variations in decision time (Donchin and Lindsley, 1966; Donchin *et al.*, 1978; Squires *et al.*, 1975a, b; Tueting, 1978). In general, therefore, the evidence from ERP studies of signal detection tasks suggests that the amplitude and latency of late ERP components are related to fluctuations in criterion placement and to variations in the time course of decision processes, although these results remain to be fully confirmed for vigilance tasks, in which task duration is an important factor contributing to performance changes and where, as we have seen, a decrement in detection rate with time at work is a principal finding.

Some progress has already been made in this direction, however. For example, in their experiment concerned with CNV amplitude and auditory vigilance performance, referred to earlier, Wilkinson and Seales (1978) also examined the relationship between P300 and various indices of detection efficiency. In their task, which appears to have lasted for about 48 min., a comparatively high signal probability (0·50) was used, and the signals also varied in intensity, two-thirds of them being easy and one third being difficult to detect. Nevertheless, reliable decrements both in detection and false alarm rates from the first half of the task to the second were obtained. A significant β increment was also found, but d' showed little change with time at work. Wilkinson and Seales observed that for the task as a whole P300 amplitude was significantly positively correlated with d' and significantly negatively correlated with β, while CNV amplitude was not significantly correlated with either measure; P300 amplitude reliably declined over the task and was also significantly negatively correlated with the amount of decrement in the false alarm rate. Comparisons were also made between the amplitudes of P300 associated with different response categories, different signal intensities and different levels of response confidence, and detection responses, highly confident responses and responses to "intense" signals were all found to have reliably greater amplitudes.

Although many of these findings have been obtained with signal detection tasks of relatively brief duration, the relationship between P300 amplitude and the criterion, suggested by several such studies, is also clearly influenced by time on task. In brief signal detection tasks, as has already been noted, P300 amplitude increases as the criterion becomes more stringent, yet during vigilance performance, although P300 amplitude is similarly related to variations in response confidence from trial to trial, P300 amplitude decreases over time while criterion placement becomes more cautious. This suggests that different factors may be responsible for producing the positive correlation between the criterion and P300 amplitude in brief signal detection tasks and the negative correlation between these two variables obtained in vigilance tasks. However, it should be noted that the β increment in Wilkinson and Seales's study was very slight, the mean values in successive halves of the task being 1·5 and 2·1. This is probably because they used a signal probability of 0·5. As noted in Chapter 4, criterion *increments* are found only for signal probabilities less than 0·5; above this value, the criterion *decreases*, while it remains stable for a value of 0·5 (see Williges, 1973, 1976). It is possible that the small increase in β noted by Wilkinson and Seales represents a decrease in arousal rather than a "true" criterion increment due to changes in expectancy normally found in low signal probability tasks. Arousal or habituation processes could have contributed to the decrement in hits and false alarms and hence to the small increase in β.

Wilkinson and Seales considered three other related possibilities: first, that in vigilance tasks P300 amplitude may in part be reflecting variations in motivation, since they noted that P300 amplitude is reduced when incentives are withdrawn; second, that P300 amplitude is determined both by the prior state of negativity present in the EEG record when the stimulus arrives, which is probably influenced by motivational factors, and by the characteristics of the stimulus and the subject's response to it. This is the prior state/reactive change hypothesis developed by Karlin (1970) and modified by Wilkinson (1976). On this view, prior state, assessed in terms of the CNV, should be related to P300 and Wilkinson and Seales observed a significant positive correlation between CNV and P300 amplitude. A third possibility is that since doubtful responses in vigilance tasks appear to be associated with a reduced amplitude of P300 (Davies and Parasuraman, 1977) the decrease in P300 with time on task results from an increase in the number of doubtful responses with time at work. However, this hypothesis is not supported by the results of Wilkinson and Seales who obtained a non-significant decline in response confidence over time. This latter result further suggests that the obtained changes in β do not represent a change in response criteria.

The interpretation of electrocortical changes during vigilance

The results of studies of the electrical activity of the brain in relation to vigilance present on the whole a reasonably clear and consistent picture. It seems almost indisputable that the level of arousal declines during the course of a vigil and it appears probable too that short-term fluctuations in electrocortical activity are related to performance. This latter result can also be interpreted in terms of momentary fluctuations in arousal level. However, such results do not necessarily imply that an arousal theory of vigilance should be accepted; a number of problems with arousal theory have previously been outlined (see Chapter 1).

A major difficulty arising from the results of studies surveyed in the present chapter is that changes over time in electrocortical activity, as in many of the autonomic measures reviewed in Chapter 6, appear to be unreliably related to performance. Similar declines in electrocortical activity with time on task are found when a reliable vigilance decrement is present (Davies and Krkovic, 1965; O'Hanlon and Beatty, 1977; Wilkinson and Seales, 1978) when a decrement is not obtained (Hink *et al.*, 1978; Wilkinson and Haines, 1970) and when the decrement is attributable to either a criterion or a sensitivity shift (Davies and Parasuraman, 1977). Declines in electrocortical activity also occur if the individual relaxes and performs no task at all for a comparable period, as Fruhstorfer and Bergstrom (1969) have shown for auditory evoked responses. Indeed the only prerequisite for obtaining a decline in electrocortical activity with time seems to be that the experimental situation is monotonous and prolonged. In such conditions EEG signs of lowered arousal are observed not only in typical vigilance tasks involving discrimination or monitoring but also in long-term tracking tasks (Kornfeld and Beatty, 1977).

While the maintenance of a minimum level of electrocortical arousal is a necessary condition for efficient performance, the level of arousal seems to relate primarily to the general level of performance, trends in performance over time being more closely associated with cognitive and decision processes. In previous chapters we have considered the roles of subjective probability as well as memory load and time pressure in the determination of criterion and sensitivity shifts in vigilance, and have suggested that the interaction of task demands and cognitive processes strongly influences the kind of performance change that occurs with time at work. Although changes in the general level or arousal presumably affect all ERP components, when ERPs are separated according to the type of response, detection efficiency in vigilance is related only to the late components of target-evoked ERPs. It is these late components which have been related to the efficiency and duration of information processing and decision making activities. The finding that variations in decision criteria are reflected in the amplitudes and latencies of late ERP components may profitably be extended to studies of sustained attention although it remains the case that these components have not so far been found to distinguish between sensitivity and criterion shifts in vigilance.

Vigilance performance and operant control of electrocortical activity

Operant conditioning techniques have been utilized to regulate the abundance of EEG activity in various frequency ranges (Beatty, 1971; Black 1971). In a review of research on the learned regulation of EEG alpha and theta activity Beatty (1977a) observes that the majority of studies have addressed "questions that are primarily demonstrational (Can the alpha rhythm be operantly regulated?), technological (Which procedure yields the most effective control?), or correlational (If the alpha rhythms are operantly modified, does something else also change?) Such experimental questions can, of course, help disclose the characteristics of underlying brain mechanisms, but do not constitute a direct frontal attack on the question of mechanism" (p. 354). Studies of the operant control of electrocortical activity and vigilance are demonstrational in nature; they seek to demonstrate that the learned suppression of EEG frequencies which reflect low levels of alertness and hence are associated with inefficient monitoring performance can exert a beneficial effect on the detection of signals in vigilance situations and thus arrest any performance decrement that may be present. Sometimes, too, observers have been trained to augment activity in these frequency ranges in the expectation that vigilance performance would deteriorate. The use of a bidirectional design, in which both the suppression and the augmentation of electrocortical activity in a particular frequency range is effected, permits conclusions to be drawn regarding the specific effects of the experimental treatment upon performance.

As noted earlier, increases in theta activity seem to be quite strongly related to loss of vigilance (O'Hanlon and Beatty, 1977) and it is with the control of electrocortical activity within the theta range that EEG autoregulation studies have been chiefly concerned. In a pioneering experiment, Beatty et al. (1974), using the simulated radar monitoring task employed by O'Hanlon and Beatty (1976, 1977) described previously, showed that detection performance could be reliably improved through the learned suppression of theta activity and reliably impaired through theta augmentation. One group of university student volunteers was trained to suppress theta activity and a second group to augment it and both groups performed the radar monitoring task for two hours while regulating their EEG activity and while not doing so. The group trained to suppress theta activity showed significantly less occipital theta activity during monitoring performance when EEG activity was being regulated than when it was not and the abundance of theta activity for the theta-augment group under EEG regulation conditions was also greater, although the increase was only marginally significant. As Fig. 8.4 shows, under regulated conditions detection efficiency was highest in the group trained to suppress theta activity and lowest in the group trained to augment theta activity, and the latter group also displayed a marked vigilance decrement. Under unregulated conditions no differences in the monitoring performance of the two groups were observed.

The subjects in the experiment carried out by Beatty et al. were unused to performing prolonged monitoring tasks and, in a subsequent study, O'Hanlon et al. (1977) examined the effects of learned regulation of the EEG upon the detection efficiency of highly skilled, experienced radar operators and air traffic controllers. O'Hanlon et al. argued that operant control techniques might well be helpful in improving the performance of task-naive observers but that experienced radar operators would already have acquired

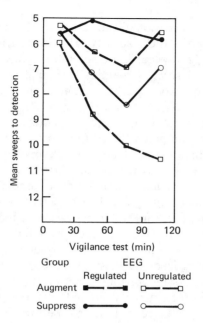

Fig. 8.4. Mean number of sweeps required to detect targets as a function of time on task in a two-hour simulated radar task under conditions of theta augmentation and suppression and when the EEG was regulated or unregulated. From Beatty *et al.* (1974).

other methods of maintaining alertness during a vigil. It was possible, therefore, that such techniques would prove ineffective when used with trained professional observers. In their first experiment O'Hanlon *et al.* trained ten experienced radar operators to suppress occipital theta activity and familiarized them with a three-hour version of the vigilance task used by Beatty *et al.* (1974). The radar operators then performed the task under EEG regulated and unregulated conditions in counterbalanced order. The incidence of theta activity in the regulated condition was reduced compared to the unregulated condition although, again, the decrease was only marginally significant. However, as in the experiment of Beatty *et al.* (1974), the radar operators detected targets significantly more rapidly under regulated than under unregulated conditions. Six of these operators were able to return to the laboratory for a second experiment in which they were given theta-augmentation training, and this procedure resulted in theta activity being reliably greater in regulated than in unregulated conditions. Detection efficiency in unregulated conditions was also reliably worse. In a third experiment, O'Hanlon *et al.* tested 14 radar operators in a three-hour monitoring task, using real radar equipment and imagery, actual air traffic in the Los Angeles area serving as a background into which synthetic targets were occasionally injected. In this experiment, subjects were trained to suppress theta activity. However, a decline in efficiency with time at work did not occur in this monitoring task under unregulated conditions, although there was a marginally significant tendency for targets to be detected more quickly in the final hour of the vigil under conditions of theta suppression.

In a further experiment Beatty and O'Hanlon (1979), again using a simulated radar task, compared the EEG records and detection efficiency of three groups of university students, two groups having been trained to suppress or augment theta activity and the third acting as a control group, over six one-hour sessions administered on the same day. During the first session, baseline levels of unregulated theta activity and of detection performance were assessed and no differences were found between the three groups. In the remaining five sessions, feedback and no-feedback conditions were alternated in an attempt to determine whether the control of theta activity achieved during feedback sessions transferred to sessions in which feedback was absent. As in previous experiments, the groups trained to augment and suppress theta activity differed reliably both in the amount of theta present in the EEG record during performance under feedback conditions and also in detection efficiency and these differences increased over successive feedback sessions. However, although similar differences between the groups in respect of theta activity were obtained in sessions where feedback was not given, thus providing evidence for transfer, the difference in detection efficiency between the groups in the absence of feedback was only marginally reliable. As in the third experiment of O'Hanlon et al. (1977), a vigilance decrement was not obtained and this seems to minimize the effects of the operant control of theta activity upon performance.

It appears that in situations in which performance exhibits a significant deterioration with time, operant control of the EEG can reliably enhance performance in monitoring tasks in which the signal remains present until detected, whether the observers are inexperienced university students or experienced radar operators. But in situations where a deterioration in efficiency is not found under unregulated conditions, learned suppression of theta activity is unlikely to result in a significant enhancement of performance over baseline levels.

Attempts to replicate and extend the results reported by Beatty, O'Hanlon and their associates have been made by Hord et al. (1975) and Morgan and Coates (1975), although there is some doubt as to whether the study of Hord et al. constitutes an appropriate replication (see O'Hanlon et al., 1977, p. 162). Hord et al. trained 19 naval subjects to suppress theta activity and compared performance in a three-hour sonar task under regulated and unregulated conditions, using a yoked control procedure. No reliable differences in performance were obtained in this study or in that of Morgan and Coates (1975), who examined the effects of the suppression of theta activity over a 48-hour period of the performance of various tasks, taken from the Multiple Task Performance Battery (see Morgan and Alluisi, 1972), coupled with loss of sleep. Although subjects in this experiment were able to regulate theta activity quite well during the early stages of the testing period, their ability to do so gradually deteriorated. Hord *et al.* have also observed that the ability to regulate EEG activity is reduced following one night of sleep deprivation (see Lawrence and Johnson, 1977). It thus seems likely that although the training procedures used by Beatty and O'Hanlon may produce reliable enhancements of efficiency in situations where declines in performance are usually obtained, such procedures may only be effective for a limited period of time and may not survive a departure from normal sleep-waking routines. In general, the results of experiments of the operant control of EEG activity in relation to vigilance performance demonstrate that when efficiency falls as a result of a reduction in alertness, reflected in an increase in theta activity, theta suppression can be a very useful way of restoring performance to a level consistent with a high level of alertness. When the observer is already fully alert, however, performance is unlikely to improve further as a result of theta suppression. Furthermore, although declines in alertness or arousal are perhaps appropriate for explaining deteriorations in efficiency in "unlimited hold" monitoring tasks, with non-transient signals, it is more questionable whether performance decrements in "limited hold" tasks can be most usefully accounted for within an arousal framework, as was noted earlier in this chapter.

Pupillometry and vigilance

The diameter of the pupil in human beings can extend from about 1·5 to more than 9 mm (Goldwater, 1972) and normally responds to stimulation within 200–400 ms following onset. The control of pupil size is effected by two smooth muscles in the iris, one of which, *the dilator pupillae*, is innervated by the sympathetic, while the other, the *sphincter pupillae*, is innervated by the parasympathetic division of the autonomic nervous system. Strictly speaking, therefore, pupil size is an autonomic measure, although the brain also plays a part in the regulation of pupillary activity. The nature of its involvement is, however, not completely understood (Hess, 1972). But pupil size is considered here, rather than in Chapter 6, in view of the evidence linking pupillary movements to variations in cognitive load and brain activation.

Lowenstein (1920) suggested that pupillary dilation accompanied increases in attention and recent pupillometric studies have tended to support the view that pupillary movements reflect the momentary level of mental effort or "intensive attention" which in turn reflects fluctuations in the activation of the brain resulting from varying task demands (Beatty, 1977b; Kahneman, 1973). As Beatty (1977b) remarks, "the idea is that cognitive functions can be characterized by their information-processing load—the demands for capacity that they impose upon the organism—and that this processing load can be measured by the momentary level of task-induced activation" (p. 68). Evidence favouring the construct of "mental effort" has come from several experiments in which task difficulty or the presumed level of cognitive functioning has been varied and changes in pupil size during task performance observed. Hess and Polt (1964), for example, examined changes in pupillary activity during the performance of four mental arithmetic tasks of varying levels of difficulty and found that pupillary dilation gradually increased following the presentation of the task, reaching a maximum immediately before the subject reported his solution. Subsequently, pupillary constriction occurred until the initial level of dilation had been achieved. Pupillary dilation was greater when the problem was more difficult.

Kahneman and Beatty obtained similar results in a series of experiments using mental tasks. The pupil dilated as information was presented for processing and then constricted once the response had been completed. The amount of pupillary dilation was shown to increase with task difficulty in both short-term and long-term memory tasks (Beatty and Kahneman, 1966; Kahneman and Beatty, 1966) and in a digit transformation task also involving recall (Kahneman and Beatty, 1966). These investigators further showed that in a dual-task situation, in which the digit transformation task was performed in conjection with a secondary visual detection task, thus increasing cognitive load, pupil size increased compared to a single-task condition.

Results from studies of signal detection and vigilance tasks indicate that pupillary dilation occurs when a signal is presented (Beatty and Wagoner, 1975; Beatty and Wilson, 1977; Hakerem and Sutton, 1966; Kahneman and Beatty, 1967). The amplitude of pupillary dilation is also inversely related to the discriminability of the signal (Kahneman and Beatty, 1967). Using an auditory signal detection task and a confidence rating procedure, Beatty and Wagoner (1975) found that the magnitude of pupillary dilation varied as a monotonic function of likelihood ratio, a result which has also been obtained for P300, as mentioned previously (Squires *et al.*, 1975b).

We indicated in Chapter 5 that a decrement in sensitivity may result when the level of mental effort required to detect targets cannot be sustained over a period of time. This suggests that the amplitude of pupillary dilation should decrease during a vigilance task if a sensitivity decrement is obtained. A study by Beatty (in preparation) provides partial confirmation for this view. Using an auditory successive discrimination task with a moderately high event rate (18·75 per minute), Beatty found a small but reliable decrement in perceptual sensitivity and a decrease in the amplitude of pupillary dilation to non-signal events over time. This result cannot be interpreted in arousal terms, since the baseline pupillary diameter, which is an index of the general level of arousal (Yoss *et al.*, 1970), did not change during the course of a task. These results provide confirmation for the view expressed in Chapter 5 that sensitivity declines during a vigilance task as a result of the combined demand on mental effort imposed by a short-term memory load (due to successive-discrimination) and a high event rate.

The neuropsychology of vigilance

Neuropsychology is principally the study of the structural and functional organization of the brain and its relation to behaviour. The systematic observation of patients who have sustained brain damage is perhaps the most commonly used method in neuropsychology, although it is beset by two major difficulties. First, the exact location and extent of the damage is frequently uncertain; second, it is usually impossible to make a comparison of performance on the same task before and after the injury occurred, except, occasionally, in cases where surgical intervention is inevitable to relieve the patient's condition. Furthermore, different individuals exhibit differential recovery of function following brain injury and this also affects the extent of any behavioural deficit observed. Notwithstanding these difficulties and others not mentioned here (see Miller, 1972; Williams, 1970), studies of brain damaged patients have provided some insights into the brain regions involved in sustained attention in normal subjects. Following a discussion of the effects of brain damage on vigilance, studies which have attempted to elucidate the involvement of the left and right hemispheres in vigilance are surveyed.

Vigilance and the effects of brain damage

As mentioned in Chapter 2, the Continuous Performance Test, or CPT, was originally developed as a diagnostic instrument for the investigation of brain damage (Rosvold *et al.*, 1956) and as discussed in Chapter 7, this test has also been used to assess the effects of sleep deprivation and of various drugs (Mirsky and Cardon, 1962). There is no doubt that brain damaged patients, both adults and children, make reliably more errors on this task than do normals, and the difference in error rates increases in the more difficult A–X version, in which a memory load is imposed. It seems too, that patients with epileptic foci in the mesodiencephalic reticular formation exhibit a much greater performance deficit than do patients with epileptic foci in the frontal or temporal lobes (Mirsky *et al.*, 1960) and patients in whom the frontal or temporal lobe has been unilaterally removed show little deterioration in performance on this task compared to normals (Mirsky and Rosvold, 1960). However, as noted in Chapter 7, 68 hours of sleep deprivation and a 200 mg dose of the drug chlorpromazine both produce considerable impairments of performance, approaching the level found in patients with epileptic foci in the mesodiencephalic reticular formation.

As mentioned in Chapter 1, there are good grounds for supposing that the reticular system is involved in the maintenance of wakefulness and alertness and the results of a number of animal studies indicate that electrical stimulation of the mid-brain reticular formation produces improved discrimination and perceptual efficiency. The results obtained by Rosvold, Mirsky and their collaborators suggest that subcortical structures, and in particular the mid-brain reticular formation, are implicated in the performance of paced versions of the CPT and that one behavioural manifestation of damage to these structures is an inability to sustain attention. This impairment is likely to reveal itself in the form of attentional lapses, however, rather than as a steady decline of detection efficiency although, as noted in Chapter 2, reliable decrements in detection rate in similar brief duration tasks have occasionally been reported (Harkins *et al.*, 1974).

Alexander (1973) used the CPT in a comparison of the performance of hospital patients with organic senile dementia, of patients in whom brain damage had not been diagnosed and of a group of non-hospitalized subjects. He found that the senile dementia group detected significantly fewer signals than did either of the control groups and that this group was also the only one to make more false alarms than omissions. It was noted in Chapter 6 that older subjects who have not sustained brain injury also perform worse at the CPT than do younger subjects (Canestrari, 1962; Davies and Davies, 1975). From a consideration of the demands imposed by brief paced inspection tasks used to assess the effects of ageing and brain damage, it seems possible that performance at the CPT and similar tasks (see for example, Thompson *et al.*, 1963) may not reflect solely a change in the capacity to sustain attention but may also be a consequence of the well-established loss of response speed that accompanies normal ageing and which also results from brain injury. In many versions of the CPT, responses made within 700 ms following a signal are scored as correct detections, while responses made after this period has elapsed are scored as "errors". Some of these "errors" are undoubtedly false alarms but others may be long-latency correct detection responses. Davies and Davies (1975) analysed their CPT data in detail and attempted to separate false alarms from other errors. They found no age differences in false alarm rates but did obtain a highly reliable effect of age for "mixed errors", a category which would include slow correct detections. Older men, aged between 63 and 72 years, made many more of these "mixed errors" than did younger men aged between 18 and 31 years. Subjects in the Davies and Davies experiment also performed an unpaced cancellation task of the same duration (20 minutes) as the CPT. The view that detection efficiency is related to response speed was supported by the finding for younger subjects of a highly significant positive correlation ($+0.66$) between the number of correct detections in the CPT and the number of lines checked in the cancellation task, a measure of the speed of performance. For older subjects, however, the correlation, although positive, was not significant.

The question of what kind of scoring procedure should be employed in attention tests such as the CPT, which are frequently used to assess clinical state, has been addressed by Pigache (1976). He proposes an error index given by the formula:

$$I_E = (O_m/V) + (2C_o/W),$$

where I_E is the error index, O_m the number of omission errors, V the number of omission error opportunities, C_o the number of commission errors and W the number of commission error opportunities. The score on the error index would thus be 0 for an observer who correctly detected all targets and made no commission errors, 0.5 if 50% of the targets were correctly detected and no commission errors made, 1.0 if all targets were missed and no commission errors made, 1.5 if performance was random and 2.0 if all task events received a response. Pigache notes that the implication of this scoring procedure is that observers who respond to every event are more severely disturbed than observers who make no response at all during the task and suggests, on the basis of clinical ratings, that this is in fact the case.

Tasks in which time pressure is less apparent, and in which performance is continued for a longer period, might be thought to provide clearer evidence of the effects of brain injury upon sustained attention than highly-paced brief-duration tasks such as the CPT. Unfortunately, scarcely any studies seem to have been conducted in which brain damaged subjects were tested on standard vigilance tasks. In one of the very few such studies, McDonald and Burns (1964) examined the performance of brain damaged subjects, hospital controls, most of whom had sustained fractures to the lower limbs, and a group of normal controls during a 45-minute visual vigilance task requiring the detection of slight deviations in the movement of a pointer on a dial. Movements of the pointer occurred about once per second. Two signal frequency conditions, high and low, were employed, in which the task contained 45 and nine signals respectively. Three groups of subjects, one in each of the above categories, performed the task at the high signal frequency condition and three different groups of subjects served in the low signal frequency condition. The results obtained by McDonald and Burns are shown in Table 8.1. Reliably more signals were detected at the high signal rate than at the low by the brain damaged and hospital control groups and detection efficiency significantly declined with time on task for the hospital control group in the low signal rate condition, the normal control group in the high signal rate condition and for the brain damaged group in

Table 8.1. Mean percentage of signals correctly detected in each of the three 15-minute periods of the task by brain damaged, hospital control and normal control subjects under high and low signal probability conditions. After McDonald and Burns (1964).

Group (N = 10 in each group)	15-minute periods of task		
	1	2	3
Low signal probability condition			
Brain damaged	57%	27%	26·8%
Hospital control	73·5%	53·8%	43·7%
Normal control	80·2%	76·8%	60·1%
High signal probability condition			
Brain damaged	60·1%	54·8%	46%
Hospital control	84·9%	76·8%	68·1%
Normal control	94%	77·3%	70·1%

both conditions. At both high and low signal frequencies the brain damaged group detected significantly fewer signals than the other two groups and in the low signal rate condition the hospital control group also detected significantly fewer signals than did the normal control group. False alarms were not analysed in detail but were "slightly more frequent" in the high signal rate condition than in the low. However, false alarm rates were much the same for all subject groups within a signal frequency condition, implying that the difference in performance between the brain damaged group and the other two lies in sensitivity rather than in criterion placement. A similar conclusion appears warranted for age differences on the basis of the results of Davies and Davies (1975), referred to above.

There is some indication from the results of McDonald and Burns that patients in whom damage to the basal ganglia was suspected made many more errors of omission than did patients with injuries to other areas of the brain. The basal ganglia consist of three large nuclear masses (the caudate nucleus, the lentiform nucleus, comprising the putamen, the globus pallidus and the claustrum, and the amygdaloid nucleus) which lie within the cerebral hemispheres, extending through the telencephalon into the diencephalon, and which together form part of the extrapyramidal motor system. Sometimes parts of the midbrain reticular formation and of the hypothalamus are also included in the delineation of the basal ganglia.

Many investigators have regarded the basal ganglia as playing an important role in "events basic to psychomotor performance" (Hicks and Birren, 1970) and structures of the extrapyramidal motor system were believed by Jung and Hassler (1960) to function as the motor mechanisms underlying attentive behaviour, with the reticular system of the brainstem acting chiefly as a centre for motor co-ordination. In this account, as Hicks and Birren (1970) observe, "the psychological aspects of attention are seen as secondary derivatives of this motor regulation" (pp. 390–391). Hicks and Birren offer the suggestion that the brain mechanism principally implicated in the psychomotor slowing and the increased variability of response speed exhibited by both older individuals and brain damaged patients in a variety of task situations is "a system consisting of extrapyramidal centers of the basal ganglia, midbrain, and thalamic reticular formation, and their rostral and caudal connections" (p. 389). It is possible that one of the general behavioural consequences of the effects of ageing and brain injury on this system is an increase in "neurological noise" (Gregory, 1959) or "stimulus persistence" (Axelrod, 1963). Layton (1975) reviews evidence relating to the neurological noise and stimulus persistence hypotheses, as well as that concerned with his own hypothesis of "perceptual noise". A probable result of any increase in neural noise would be a reduction in sensitivity which, as indicated above, appears to take place with age and with brain damage.

Hemisphere differences in vigilance

Vigilance may be impaired following damage to either half of the brain. The same is not true of many other functions. Broca (1865) first observed a tendency of disorders of language to follow damage to the left cerebral hemisphere, and since that time a considerable body of evidence has accumulated which confirms Broca's observation and which also indicates "a right hemisphere specialization for a variety of non-verbal visuo-spatial cognitive processes" (G. Cohen, 1977). This evidence comes from four sources:

(1) studies of patients who have sustained brain damage of comparable extent and location to either the left or right hemisphere;

(2) studies of patients in whom the cerebral commissures have been cut, with the result that the two hemispheres are effectively disconnected;

(3) studies of normal subjects employing various techniques to direct input to one hemisphere or the other; and

(4) studies which have monitored the electrocortical activity of one or both hemispheres during the presentation of verbal and non-verbal materials.

Here we shall review studies of vigilance concerned primarily with the first three of these general procedures. There are various methodological problems which limit the usefulness of electrocortical measures in the assessment of hemisphere differences (Donchin et al., 1977) and a study by Gevins et al. (1979) suggests that electrocortical evidence for hemisphere differences in verbal/spatial tasks may not be forthcoming when factors such as the responding limb and the task situation are carefully controlled.

Several experiments have been concerned with hemisphere differences in vigilance, although the results that have been obtained are somewhat inconsistent. Patients who have undergone total commissurotomy have been reported to detect many fewer signals than partially commissurotomized patients or normals (Dimond, 1976; see also Dimond, 1977). The task used in this experiment consisted of four lights placed in a horizontal plane at 11° and 22° on each side of a central fixation point, so that signals occurring on the left of the midline were transmitted to the right hemisphere while those occurring on the right of the midline were transmitted to the left hemisphere. The signal was the extinction of one of the lights for a period of about 350 ms. A response button was placed in front of each light and subjects reported the occurrence of signals by pressing the appropriate button, using the left hand for left-sided (right hemisphere) signals and the right hand for right-sided (left hemisphere) signals. The task lasted for 30 minutes and 60 signals were presented during this time, 20 in each ten-minute period. The task was given to six total commissurotomy patients, two partial commissurotomy patients and three non-patient control subjects. The results are shown in Table 8.2 and it is clear that, compared to the other two groups, not only did total commissurotomy patients detect fewer signals overall but they also displayed a substantial decrement in performance with time at work. The total commissurotomy group also made significantly more false alarms than the partial commissurotomy group who in turn made more than the non-patient controls. However, the false alarm rate remained stable over time, suggesting a progressive reduction in sensitivity.

Table 8.2. Percentage of signals detected by total commissurotomy patients, partial commissurotomy patients and normal subjects with time at work. After Dimond (1976).

	Ten minute periods of task		
	1	2	3
Total commissurotomy patients (N = 6)	54%	46%	30%
Partial commissurotomy patients (N = 2)	100%	96%	96%
Normals (N = 3)	100%	100%	100%

Dimond also compared the detection rates of the left and right cerebral hemispheres and found that although an equal number of signals were presented to each hemisphere, in the total commissurotomy group significantly more of those directed to the right hemisphere were detected. Stimuli presented to the right hemisphere were also significantly more likely to produce false alarms. It thus appears, that in total commissurotomy patients at least, a less stringent criterion is adopted for events presented for inspection to the right hemisphere. The task also permitted successive presentations of the signal to be given (up to a maximum of ten) until a detection response was made. Reliably fewer additional signal presentations were required to secure a right hemisphere as opposed to a left hemisphere detection response and significantly more signal presentations were required as the task progressed, particularly for left hemisphere presentations. It appears from this study, then, that a right hemisphere superiority exists for split-brain patients in the performance of a visual vigilance task based on the discrimination of the presence or absence of a light and that this superiority may be attributable to a relaxation of criterion placement.

Similar results were obtained with the same subjects for vibrotactile and auditory vigilance performance (Dimond, 1979), although the decrement in detection rate was less marked. In both cases detection efficiency was superior for the right hemisphere although, in contrast to the results obtained with the visual task, the false alarm rate in the auditory task was higher for the left hemisphere than the right. Virtually no false alarms were made during the performance of the vibrotactile task and so no comparison between hemispheres was possible. It appears then, that the right hemisphere superiority in both these tasks is due to an enhancement of sensitivity rather than to any criterion change.

Experiments concerned with hemisphere differences in vigilance have also been conducted with subjects in whom the cerebral commissures are intact (Dimond and Beaumont, 1971, 1973; Warm et al., 1976b). Dimond and Beaumont (1971), using an 87-minute visual vigilance task, presented an equal number of signals (26), consisting of a brief increment in the brightness of an otherwise constant illumination source, to the left and right hemispheres and compared their detection efficiency. Both detection and false alarm rates reliably declined with time and no difference in detection rate between the hemispheres was found. The left hemisphere, however, produced reliably more false alarms, indicating presumably a riskier criterion placement, exactly the opposite result to that obtained by Dimond (1976) with total commissurotomy patients. In a second experiment (Dimond and Beaumont, 1973) a similar task was employed, although the task duration and the number of signals were both slightly reduced. In this experiment, however, signals were presented either to the left hemisphere or to the right hemisphere only, two groups of subjects being used. Here the left hemisphere produced reliably more correct detections and reliably fewer false positives indicating, presumably, a sensitivity difference. Neither hemisphere exhibited a significant decrement in detection efficiency. These results are also at variance with those obtained by Dimond (1976) and with those of the more comparable study of Dimond and Beaumont (1971). The results of these three experiments, together with those of Warm et al. (1976b) are summarized in Table 8.3 for comparison purposes. The experiment of Warm et al. showed that signal probability interacted with ear of presentation in a 60-minute auditory vigilance task requiring the detection of an increment in the duration of recurrent white noise pulses presented at an intensity of 78 dB. The task was presented to one ear or the other

Table 8.3. The results of six experiments on hemisphere differences in vigilance (see text). L = Left, R = Right, H = Hemisphere, A = Auditory, V = Visual, T = Tactual; [a]P < 0.001, [b]P < 0.001, [c]P < 0.05.

Experiment	Subjects	Signal Frequency (signals per minute), Signal Duration and Presentation Modality	Response	Performance Hits	FAs	RT	Decrement
Dimond (1976)	Total commissurotomy patients (N = 6)	2.00 350 ms (V)	RH signals Left hand LH signals Right hand	R > L[a]	R > L[a]	—	Yes: L > R[a]
Dimond (1979)	Total commissurotomy patients (N = 6)	2.00 350 ms (T)	RH signals Left hand LH signals Right hand	R > L[a]	—	—	—
	Total commissurotomy patients (N = 6)	2.00 100 ms (A)	RH signals Left hand LH signals Right hand	R > L L > R		—	—
Dimond and Beaumont (1971)	University students (N = 12)	0.59 200 ms (V)	?	R = L	L > R[c]	—	Yes: L and R[c]
Dimond and Beaumont (1973)	University students (N = 22) Two groups: LH = 11, RH = 11	0.60 200 ms (V)	?	L > R[a]	R > L[b]	—	No
Warm et al. (1976b)	University students (N = 48) Three groups of 16, one at each signal probability	1. 0.40 2. 0.80 3. 1.60 500 ms duration increment (A)	Right hand	—	—	R = L	Yes: L and R[a]

for five minutes at a time and subjects responded to signals with the index finger of the right hand. At a high signal probability (96 signals per hour) left ear (right hemisphere) performance was superior in terms of detection latencies, while at a low signal probability (24 signals per hour) right ear (left hemisphere) performance was superior. At an intermediate signal probability (48 signals per hour) no difference between the hemispheres in terms of detection latencies was found, as indeed was the case for the experiment as a whole (see Table 8.3).

From Table 8.3 it can be seen that none of the results obtained with normal subjects is comparable to that found with total commissurotomy patients, supporting the view that the functional organization of the cerebral hemispheres in split-brain patients is different from that in subjects in whom the cerebral commissures are intact (Moscovitch, 1976; Searleman, 1977). However, the results obtained with normal subjects also lack consistency, although no hemisphere differences were found in the two experiments in which signals were alternated between the hemispheres (Dimond and Beaumont, 1971; Warm et al., 1976b). Since it is less likely in these experiments that subjects would be able to anticipate to which hemisphere signals would be directed, as is possible in the experiment by Dimond and Beaumont (1973), this result seems somewhat more plausible. Some general methodological criticisms of the Dimond and Beaumont experiments can however be made. Even though eye movements were monitored in these experiments, the signal duration used (200 ms) approached the lower boundary of eye movement latencies, allowing the possibility that signal presentations were not confined to the contralateral hemisphere. Furthermore, the illumination sources in these experiments were not so placed at either side of the central fixation point as to ensure adequate parafoveal visual acuity (G. Cohen, 1977) although since a simple, unpatterned stimulus was used, this is, perhaps, of minor importance. Perhaps, therefore, the most appropriate conclusion to be drawn from experiments on hemisphere differences in vigilance is that although the right hemisphere may exhibit superior detection efficiency in split-brain patients, possibly because the left hemisphere is unable to exert an inhibitory effect upon criterion placement or possibly as a consequence of genuine differences in sensitivity between the hemispheres, in normal subjects differences between the hemispheres in the capacity for sustained attention remain to be reliably demonstrated.

Chapter 9

The Practical Significance of
Vigilance Research

The practical significance of vigilance research has been questioned by several investigators (for example, Chapanis, 1967; Elliott, 1960; Kibler, 1965; Nachreiner, 1977; Smith and Lucaccini, 1969), one of the chief criticisms being that performance decrements are seldom if ever found in "real life" monitoring situations. The vigilance decrement frequently observed under experimental conditions has thus been attributed to an amalgamation of factors found only in the laboratory. It has been suggested that neither the subjects, nor the tasks they carry out, nor the environment in which the tasks are performed are representative of real world situations demanding sustained attention, such as sonar and radar monitoring, process control, industrial inspection or vehicle operation. Before considering the question of whether performance decrements do in fact occur in real world situations, we examine more closely some of the principal differences between laboratory and operational procedures.

Differences between laboratory and operational monitoring tasks

In most vigilance experiments the subjects, who are usually students or military personnel, are generally untrained and unpractised when they encounter the task for the first and often the only time. The conditions under which the task is carried out are often deliberately designed to be as monotonous as possible. The task is performed in isolation, smoking is not permitted, and frequently watches are removed in order that subjects will not be sure when the task is about to end, to prevent "end spurt" effects (Bergum and Lehr, 1963a; Dannhaus et al., 1976). If subjects are paid at all, it is for participation rather than as an incentive for good performance. Laboratory subjects are thus scarcely representative of the often highly trained and motivated operators engaged in military monitoring and watchkeeping tasks, or of those engaged in process control or industrial inspection. In consequence, the hypothesis has been advanced that the vigilance decrement occurs principally because subjects are not sufficiently motivated (Nachreiner, 1977; Smith, 1966; see also Chapter 1).

In Chapter 1, motivation theory was discussed both with respect to differences in overall performance and to performance trends over time. It was concluded that although there is quite good support for the theory as far as the overall level of performance is concerned, the evidence for a purely motivational interpretation of the vigilance decrement is equivocal, and other factors must also be implicated. The most important of these are almost certainly task factors and two studies which have been taken to provide evidence for the role of motivation in the explanation of differences between laboratory and "real life" tasks in the extent of the vigilance decrement are now examined from this perspective.

Nachreiner (1977) reported two experiments in each of which eight subjects, divided into two independent groups, performed a laboratory vigilance task. The groups differed in the way in which they were recruited; members of one group (the "experiment" group) were solicited to participate in a routine laboratory experiment, while members of the other (the "test" group) were informed that they would be undergoing a selection test for a desirable student job. In the first experiment an auditory, and in the second a visual, vigilance task was employed. Nachreiner found that, in the auditory vigilance task, subjects in the "experiment" group exhibited a decrement in detection rate (but significant only at the 0·10 level) while subjects in the "test" group did not. In the visual vigilance task there was a reliable interaction for detection rate between time at work and experimental treatments. The detection efficiency of the "experiment" group declined from the first 15-minute period to the second, but improved thereafter, so that performance in the final period of work was superior to that achieved in the first period. The performance of the "test" group improved from the first period to the second but thereafter declined, so that performance in the final period was slightly worse than in the initial period of work. A reliable overall difference in detection rate, in favour of the "test" group, was obtained only with the auditory vigilance task. Nachreiner interpreted the results of these experiments as evidence for a motivational interpretation of the vigilance decrement observed under laboratory conditions, although in view of the failure to obtain a reliable interaction between time periods and treatments in his first experiment, and the nature of the performance trends over time for the two treatment groups in the second, the support for the motivational hypothesis is, perhaps, not as strong as it might be. But even if the motivational hypothesis is accepted, it is clear from Nachreiner's study that task factors, in this case presentation modality, can exert some influence over whether or not a vigilance decrement is obtained.

A similar conclusion may be drawn from the results of a study by Belt

(1971), who compared the performance of the same 40 subjects at a 60-minute visual vigilance task and a 60-minute visual inspection task. Great care was taken to make the tasks and the conditions under which they were performed as similar as possible and signal frequencies (one signal per 200 events) and event presentation rates (over 100 per minute) were closely equated. Belt found that a reliable decrement in detection rate occurred in the vigilance task but not in the inspection task, and that overall detection efficiency was significantly greater for the inspection task than for the vigilance task. False alarm rates declined significantly with time for both tasks, but reliably more false alarms were made in the vigilance task, indicating a lower level of sensitivity. But from Belt's description of his tasks, the vigilance task was a successive discrimination task, requiring the detection of a difference in the length of a visual array consisting of dots of light, while the inspection task was a simultaneous discrimination task, in which subjects were instructed to remove "defective" white plastic balls, designated by the black letters A, D, H or N, from a moving inspection line as it went by. Since the vigilance task was a high event rate successive discrimination task, which would be expected to yield a sensitivity decrement (see Chapter 5), while the inspection task was a high event rate simultaneous discrimination task, a differential decrement could be attributable to differences in task type rather than to differences in motivational level engendered by the two task situations. It may be concluded, therefore, that it has not yet been satisfactorily demonstrated that motivational differences can account for differential performance trends over time that may be obtained when comparing laboratory and "real life" monitoring tasks.

As noted earlier, subjects in laboratory experiments on vigilance are likely to be less well acquainted with the task they are performing than are operators in real world monitoring situations, and it is possible that as a result of practice at and increased experience with a monitoring task the performance decrement disappears. However, as will be seen in more detail in the following section, a decrement in performance is just as likely to be found in the performance of experienced lookouts and radar operators as in the performance of less experienced subjects (N.H. Mackworth, 1950; O'Hanlon et al., 1977) and the administration of repeated sessions, which permits the task to be fully learned, does not seem to eradicate the vigilance decrement.

It has also been argued that there are a number of crucial differences between laboratory vigilance tasks and real world monitoring situations which make generalizations from laboratory findings to operational settings extremely hazardous. Such differences include task duration and work-rest scheduling, the frequency of target occurrence, target discriminability, the number of target attributes to be monitored and the complexity of the response to be executed. These factors are now briefly considered in turn.

As we have noted in previous chapters, the range of task durations employed in laboratory experiments on vigilance is considerable, ranging from a few minutes to several hours. If a vigilance decrement occurs, and such decrements have been observed in laboratory tasks of both short and long duration, it begins during the first few minutes of task performance, although it tends to commence somewhat later in subjects expecting a short vigil than in subjects expecting a long one (see Jerison, 1958, 1959b, 1963). However, in laboratory tasks, the work session is continuous and uninterrupted and usually lasts for at least 30 minutes, whereas in real world monitoring tasks the actual period of work requiring sustained attention is likely to be relatively short (Craig, 1980). Craig cited a survey of inspection procedures in 151 firms in the United Kingdom, conducted by Megaw (1977), which showed that in 39% of the firms surveyed inspectors were expected to work at visual examining for one hour or less without taking a rest break or performing some other task. Similarly Hermann (1977) pointed out that, for various reasons, ship lookouts often spent only 32 minutes in each hour actually observing the sea area assigned to them, and Nachreiner (1977), in an analysis of several different operational monitoring tasks, including bottle and coin inspection and air traffic control, reported that no instance of an uninterrupted observation period lasting for as long as one hour could be found and that observation periods in excess of 20 minutes occurred very infrequently. The periods of continuous attention demanded by laboratory vigilance tasks thus tend to be rather greater than those found in real world monitoring situations.

It has been suggested that the frequencies with which signals occur in laboratory vigilance tasks are generally much higher than those found in operational situations (see, for example, Elliott, 1960; Kibler, 1965). The range of signal to total event ratios in laboratory situations probably varies between two and 20 signals per 100 events. But, as Craig (1980) pointed out, a similar range of signal to total event ratios can be observed in real world monitoring situations, especially industrial inspection, varying from one signal per 100 events for the inspection of rubber seals (Astley and Fox, 1975) to 49 signals per 100 events in knitwear inspection (Mills and Sinclair, 1976). There do not, therefore, appear to be very marked differences between laboratory and industrial monitoring tasks with respect to signal frequency. The same conclusion can be drawn with respect to signal discriminability, since, in both laboratory and industrial tasks, the discriminability of signals, indexed by d' values, can range from the "prohibitively difficult", as in some glassware inspection tasks, to the "exceedingly easy" as in some electronics inspection tasks (Craig, 1980). But in some operational monitoring tasks, particularly those found in military systems, signal events are less likely to be of weak intensity or of brief duration, as they tend to be in laboratory tasks. Indeed, as noted in Chapter 2, such events are frequently not "directly sensed" at all but are "inferred" from a variety of information sources representing the current operational status of the system being monitored (Kibler, 1965; Swets, 1976).

In laboratory tasks the probability of target occurrence is fixed, both in relation to time and to the occurrence of non-target events, while in operational tasks it tends not to be; this can render the assessment of performance trends over time extremely difficult. In laboratory tasks, too, the signal to be detected normally varies along only one dimension, for example, brightness or loudness, so that the observer has to detect the occasional target event which is brighter or louder than the background of non-signal events in which it is embedded. In many real world monitoring tasks, however, particularly industrial inspection, defective articles may differ from non-defective articles along several different dimensions some of which may be more important than others (Craig and Colquhoun, 1977). However, in laboratory studies of inspection tasks in which more than one kind of "fault" had to be detected, Craig and Colquhoun obtained reliable decrements in efficiency with time at work.

In operational monitoring tasks, the operator is more likely to be required to keep watch over several potential signal sources, rather than the single display typically employed in laboratory vigilance tasks, although, as noted in earlier chapters, performance decrements may occur both in multi- and single-source monitoring situations. In laboratory tasks, too, reporting that a signal has been detected is a simple matter, which generally involves no more than a single motor response. In many real world monitoring tasks, however, the determination of the appropriate response to a defective item or a critical target is again much more complex, and often the particular response required depends upon a prior classification of the nature of the defects present in a particular article or the precise attributes of a particular target.

Finally, the environments in which laboratory and real world monitoring tasks are performed are unlikely to be exactly the same. Perhaps the principal difference is that subjects in laboratory vigilance tasks usually work in social isolation, a condition which does not obtain in most real world monitoring situations. However, it is unlikely that social isolation can be regarded as a major determinant of the vigilance decrement in the laboratory, since decrements also occur when subjects are group tested (see, for example, Bergum and Klein, 1962). Yet in industrial inspection tasks it appears that social factors may sometimes influence the reporting of defect rates (McKenzie, 1958).

There are clearly a number of differences between laboratory and real world monitoring situations, although some of them are probably of little importance in determining the vigilance decrement. But the nature and extent of these differences may suggest at first that one should have little confidence in the generalization of laboratory vigilance findings to problems in the field. However, three arguments to the contrary should be considered. First, as described below, the evidence indicates that non-trivial performance decrements do occur in many real occupations. Furthermore, decrements are just as likely to appear or not appear for unpractised volunteers, trained volunteers, or actual operators performing laboratory, simulated, or operational vigilance tasks. Second, the view of the decrement put forward in critiques of laboratory vigilance research is almost entirely based upon changes over time in the "traditional" measures of vigilance performance. Thus a reliable decrement is acknowledged if detection rate or detection speed declines. Yet, as we have emphasized in previous chapters, this view of the vigilance decrement is incomplete, since the decrement in detection rate can be attributed to one of two types of change, one where both the detection and false alarm rates decline without any decrement in overall efficiency (sensitivity), and one where there is a reliable sensitivity decrement. But since false alarm rates are seldom reported, it is not clear from a number of studies of vigilance in the field whether or not a reliable decrement in efficiency has taken place. However, even if only detection rate and response speed are considered, it is clear that a vigilance decrement can occur in operational settings (see below). Third, there is strong evidence to indicate that, irrespective of time-decrements in performance, the level of efficiency in some industrial and military jobs requiring sustained performance is below standard, and often this may pose serious quality-control or safety problems. We turn now to a discussion of this evidence.

Vigilance in operational settings

As mentioned previously, performance decrements may not be observed in industry because the existing work-rest schedules are sufficient to prevent them. Nevertheless, the level of efficiency may be low, and this may have serious repercussions if unrecognized. The most relevant example in this regard is industrial inspection, where for years it was thought that quality control was limited only by the sampling process and not by the fallibility of the human inspector; if there was a faulty product present in the sample, the belief was that it would be immediately detected. Although the problem of inspector errors was recognized several years ago (Wyatt and Langdon, 1932; Tiffin and Rogers, 1941), many quality-control sampling plans in industry are still designed as if defects will always be detected (for a review, see Dorris and Foote, 1979).

Over the last two decades, however, evidence has been mounting that human inspectors commit both omission and commission errors; this evidence has been gathered from both simulated and actual shop-floor studies, and much of it is summarized in the proceedings of a recent conference on human reliability in quality control (Drury and Fox, 1975b). Parenthetically, we may note that this evidence also shows that inspectors make many more omission than commission errors, which is a common finding in vigilance tasks. Thus, more defective products are passed to the consumer than good products falsely rejected for scrapping or reprocessing.

The performance levels achieved by human inspectors of real or simulated items vary considerably from study to study. At one extreme, Astley and Fox (1975) found that inspectors had a detection rate of over 90% for the inspection of flaws in rubber seals. In one of the earlier studies on inspector accuracy, Jacobson (1952) reported detection rates of over 80% for the inspection of soldering defects. At the other extreme of the range, Harris (1968) reported defect detection rates as low as 20% for electronic equipment. Both Astley and Fox (1975) and Chapman and Sinclair (1975) reported near-chance detection rates in their studies (51% for rubber seals and around 60% for chicken carcasses, respectively). A decrement in detection rate over time was also reported in both these studies. In their book on quality control, Harris and Chaney (1969) indicate that detection rates of around 50% are not unusual for experienced electronic inspectors. Clearly, then, the efficiency of the industrial inspector is far from perfect; the overall level of performance is low, and, in some cases, there may be a decrement in detection rate over the inspection period.

The level of efficiency may also be low in radar and sonar monitoring tasks. For classified reasons, data on actual radar and sonar errors in military operations are not generally available. However, there is a limited amount of evidence from non-military applications and simulation studies which clearly indicates that performance is sub-optimal. In most of these studies a vigilance decrement also occurred, and it is to this aspect of performance that we now turn.

Vigilance decrements in laboratory, simulated, and operational tasks
Table 9.1 summarizes the results of a number of studies of vigilance that have employed laboratory, simulated, or real tasks with unpractised volunteers, practised volunteers, or actual operators. The list is not meant to be comprehensive. However, the use of this restricted sample is sufficient to illustrate two important points:

(1) Trained, practised volunteer subjects, as well as experienced operators, are just as likely to show a performance decrement as naive, unpractised, or untrained volunteers.

(2) In any task situation demanding sustained attention, there may or may not be a vigilance decrement (a decline in the detection rate or detection speed over time), regardless of whether the task is artificial, a simulation of a real task, or an actual "operational" task.

With regard to the first point, the evidence suggests that practice alone

Table 9.1. A classification of laboratory and field studies of vigilance according to the experience of the subjects tested, the type of task performed, and the presence or absence of a performance decrement over the vigil (decrement in detection rate or detection speed).

Subjects tested	Performance decrement	Laboratory	Task performed Simulated	Operational
Unpractised volunteers	Yes	Davies et al. (1973)	Craig and Colquhoun (1977)	Riemersma et al. (1977)
	Yes	Jerison and Pickett (1964)	Tickner et al. (1972)	Schmidtke (1966)
	Yes	Williges (1973)	Thackray et al. (1977)	
	No	Annett and Paterson (1967)	Belt (1971)	
	No	Griew and Davies (1962)		
Practised volunteers	Yes	Adams et al. (1962)	Colquhoun (1967)	Schmidtke (1966)
	Yes	Binford and Loeb (1966)	Colquhoun (1977)	
	Yes	Murrell (1975)	Tickner et al. (1972)	
	No	Baker (1962b)	Alluisi et al. (1977)	Brown (1967)
	No	Carpenter (1946)		
Experienced operators	Yes	Mackworth (1950)	Caille et al. (1965)	Fox (1975)
	Yes		Tickner et al. (1972)	Kano (1971)
	Yes		O'Hanlon et al. (1976)	Schmidtke (1966)
	No		Beatty and O'Hanlon (1979)	Dobbins et al. (1963)
	No		Veniar (see Smith and Lucaccini, 1969)	

is insufficient to abolish the vigilance decrement. Poulton (1973a), in a detailed review of the effect of "fatigue" on inspection work, provides several instances of studies employing repeated sessions, in which reliable within-session decrements in detection rate, or increments in detection latency have been found following extensive practice (for example, Adams et al., 1962, 1963; Binford and Loeb, 1966; Wiener, 1968) although in many of these studies the decrement was less marked in later sessions. Some of these studies are referred to in Table 9.1. In one of the studies cited by Poulton (Binford and Loeb, 1966), a decline in perceptual sensitivity (d') was still found in the last of nine sessions, but no decrement in detection rate was obtained. This reiterates the importance of the second of the three points made earlier regarding the assessment of performance decrement in the laboratory and the field.

Practice sometimes improves the overall level of detection efficiency in laboratory vigilance tasks (Binford and Loeb, 1966; Colquhoun and Edwards, 1970), closely simulated sonar tasks (Colquhoun, 1975), and industrial inspection jobs (Thomas, 1962; Wiener, 1975), but although it may attenuate the decrement, it does not abolish it. Poulton (1973a) suggests two reasons for the reduction in the severity of the decrement: first, operator expectancies of the probability of a target become more realistic, and second, the task becomes more familiar and less challenging. Performance may in consequence become more variable with practice, as Carpenter (1946) found in an early study. But, in general, it seems reasonable to conclude that the vigilance decrement cannot be attributed solely to insufficient experience or lack of practice on the part of the subjects involved. Furthermore, as was discussed in Chapter 1, motivation alone does not provide an explanation of the vigilance decrement, and thus the presumed difference in motivation between laboratory subjects and actual industrial or military personnel cannot be invoked to explain differences in their performance. As Table 9.1 shows, experienced radar operators or product inspectors do sometimes show a decrement in operational settings.

Performance decrements have been reported in four main field situations: radar/sonar monitoring and surveillance, industrial inspection, process control, and vehicle operation. We shall discuss each of these areas in turn.

Radar/sonar monitoring and surveillance

Following N.H. Mackworth's (1944, 1948, 1950) laboratory studies with radar operators, decrements in radar and sonar detection performance have been reported in both simulated and operational settings. Wallis and Samuel (1961, p. 71) reported that when naval officers and ratings "had to scan their radar displays continuously for 3 hours, as well as listen for occasional audible pulses, they became progressively less efficient after the first hour". Baker (1962a, p. 153) cited an anonymous 1944 study of operational radar monitoring performance as concluding that "if all watches had been half an hour's duration, there would have been a gain of nearly 50% (in the detection of surfaced submarines)", the majority of the detections of aircraft and submarines being made early in the watchkeeping period. On the other hand, a study of a closely simulated radar system conducted with trained radar operators revealed no decrements during a series of continuous 270-minute vigils spread over 5 consecutive days (Veniar, 1953; cited by Smith and Lucaccini, 1969). In like manner, some studies of simulated sonar tasks have found reliable vigilance decrements (Colquhoun, 1967, 1977; Solandt and Partridge, 1946) while others have not (Baker and Harabedian, 1962b).

A convincing demonstration of the existence of significant and potentially serious decrements in an actual operational setting was reported in a study by Schmidtke (1966, 1976). Naval cadets and experienced radar operators were tested on a navigation and collision avoidance system in which radar contacts had to be monitored for the presence of ships which were on an apparent collision course. Operators stood watch alone or in pairs in repeated four-hour sessions. Both groups of subjects became increasingly sluggish in detecting critical target paths as the watch proceeded. Performance declined to such a low level in the last two hours of work that some subjects failed to detect collision paths sufficiently quickly for preventative action to be taken.

The Schmidtke (1966) study is important for showing that potentially dangerous decrements in detection speed can take place in a realistic environment. Similar increments in detection latency in simulated surveillance at sea were reported by Caille et al. (1965) and by O'Hanlon et al. (1977) for professional air-traffic controllers performing a three-hour simulated radar task containing actual air traffic as the background events. Another example of a vigilance decrement found in a simulated surveillance situation was reported by Tickner and Poulton (1973). This study tested the vigilance of trained observers required to monitor up to 16 closed-circuit television (CCTV) screens for critical incidents. The task was modelled after the job of prison guards who monitor CCTV screens displaying scenes recorded from cameras located at various points in and around a prison. A significant decrement in the detection of certain critical incidents was found over a two-hour watchkeeping period.

Industrial inspection

In general, then, the evidence suggests that performance decrements can occur in such jobs as air-traffic control, surveillance, navigation and radar watching, and other defence-related situations. As mentioned previously, industrial inspection tasks have also been held to involve a vigilance component (Baker, 1964), but evidence for performance decrements in such tasks is limited. The positive findings of Chapman and Sinclair (1975) and Astley and Fox (1975) have been mentioned, but Schoonard et al. (1973) failed to obtain a decrement. Although Wyatt and Langdon (1932) reported finding performance decrements, this aspect of performance has rarely been reported in subsequent studies of industrial inspection. In laboratory studies, the evidence is mixed, and evidence both for (Badalamente and Ayoub, 1969; Craig and Colquhoun, 1977) and against (Belt, 1971) the existence of a decrement can be found.

Thus the question of whether vigilance decrements occur in inspection jobs is unresolved, but it would be incorrect to suppose that they never occur. Existing management practices in the West, such as work-rest scheduling, rotation between inspections and other job-related activities, self-paced work, and so on, may also account for the lack of reported decrements in efficiency. There is a large body of research carried out in Japan, however, in which performance decrements have been noted in various industrial inspection and assembly line jobs (Kano, 1971; Saito, 1972; Saito et al., 1972b; Saito and Tanaka, 1977). The significance of this research is that the performance decrements noted were found almost exclusively under conditions which deviated only slightly from those encountered by the operators in their daily work routine.

Process control

As man—machine systems have become more complex, the human operator has undergone a transition from being a continuous active controller to being a monitor and a supervisor (Sheridan and Ferrell, 1974). In process control, these functions override others in their importance, and the operator is required only to monitor some process which is "automatically" controlled, to execute decisions regarding any change in control parameters, and to detect malfunctions or emergency conditions in the process or in the automatic control system. As monitoring and supervisory functions became more important, failures of vigilance in process control operators may constitute an increasingly serious problem.

The existence of such problems in current systems is not well studied, although vigilance failures have been suspected in safety surveys and accident analyses of chemical and nuclear plants (Lees, 1973; Tye, 1979). Performance data for process controllers working over a period are limited, however. Lees and Sayers (1976) in a study of the behaviour of process operators under simulated emergency conditions, found that the probability of failure to respond with a specified period was about 0·001 and that response speed did not vary with time over a normal eight-hour shift. In a second study carried out in an actual industrial setting, similar results were obtained. The task here was to monitor a small research nuclear reactor and respond to a combined audio-visual alarm signal as quickly as possible.

Signal rates were either 0·35 or 1·5 per hour. Again a failure probability of 0·001 and no vigilance decrement were found.

The detection of continous process failures which occur at random times is another area of application where problems of vigilance are suspected, but again there is little reliable evidence (Curry and Gai, 1976). One laboratory study in which subjects had to detect step changes in the order of control dynamics which they either actively controlled or monitored found that detection speed was slower in the monitoring condition, but no decrement over time was observed in either condition (Wickens and Kessel, 1979).

Vehicle operation

Vehicle operation combines the functions of the active controller and the "passive" monitor, and thus a real life task such as driving will incorporate a vigilance component. Many studies have reported finding significant decrements in performance during prolonged driving; the measures used have included physiological and secondary task measures of vigilance (O'Hanlon and Kelley, 1977) and "spare mental capacity" (Brown, 1967). Decrements in performance have been noted in long term driving, especially at night, in both automobile and truck operation (Boadle, 1976; Mackie and O'Hanlon, 1977; Riemersma *et al.*, 1977). Riemersma *et al.* (1977), for example, reported that performance on a secondary task (detecting changes in the colour of a light) deteriorated over a $3\frac{1}{2}$ hour drive.

The evidence thus indicates that vigilance does decline during long-term driving. It should be noted, however, that very little evidence on the ability of drivers to detect rare but realistic events (such as pedestrians on the road, or a warning signal) is available. Furthermore, most of the reported decrements have been for performance measures (for example, lane drift frequency) that could be influenced by fatigue effects on perceptual motor performance rather than on vigilance *per se*.

In general, then, a survey of the research literature indicates that the vigilance decrement can be observed in many operational settings. It is also true that in some cases, no decrement as such may occur. Yet in this case the overall level of efficiency may be less than optimal, as is sometimes the case in industrial inspection. In other cases, the level of vigilance may be so low that the operator's ability to react to some emergency is seriously impaired. We now consider various methods and procedures which may alleviate the vigilance decrement and improve the overall level of efficiency in operational settings.

The regulation and control of vigilance

The measures that can be adopted to enhance or maintain system efficiency in man–machine systems consist of either "fitting the job to the operator" or "fitting the operator to the job". Accomplishing the former will usually require some sort of task or work design, while selection and training procedures will be involved in satisfying the latter requirement. In addition, physiological methods of regulation can also be considered.

Task and work design

The numerous psychophysical factors that affect vigilance performance, such as signal intensity and signal duration, suggest a number of recommendations for the enhancement of vigilance in the field. Temporal uncertainty, and, to a lesser extent, spatial uncertainty are also characteristic of vigilance tasks. Insofar as these and other sources of uncertainty can be reduced, the likelihood of a vigilance problem will be reduced. We shall not discuss these factors in detail, as comprehensive summaries of the effects of signal and task factors on vigilance performance are available (for example, Davies and Tune, 1970; Loeb and Alluisi, 1977). The reader may also be referred to Meister's (1976) survey of factors influencing operator performance in man-machine systems, in which the effects of task factors on vigilance performance in operations such as air-traffic control and air-defence are evaluated and summarized. Here we will consider only one important task factor and focus primarily on pacing and work-rest scheduling.

In many instances the vigilance decrement occurs without a reduction in perceptual sensitivity but there is change over time in the operator's standards of reporting a target or in some related aspect of his response strategy. Training operators to adopt optimal modes of response may thus be useful in decreasing the extent of the decrement (Colquhoun and Baddeley, 1967; Williges, 1976; see also Chapter 4). When there is a decrement in sensitivity, however, training methods are unlikely to be helpful (see Green and Swets, 1974), and solutions based on task or work re-design will have to be considered. Task modifications may also be called for if operator efficiency does not decline but is at a sub-standard level.

In Chapter 5 we noted that the stimulus event rate is the most important of the many task factors affecting vigilance performance. Jerison (1977), in commenting upon the applied significance of this finding (Jerison and Pickett, 1964), questioned whether practical examples existed in which a task was redesigned to allow for the adverse effects of high stimulus event rates. One such example was reported by Saito (1972), who carried out a shop-floor study of industrial inspectors working in a bottling plant. Saito found that inspection efficiency was markedly improved by reducing the inspection rate of bottles (event rate) from 300 to less than 200 bottles per minute. A physiological measure of fine eye movements was used as an aid in determining the optimum rate at which to pace the worker. In a further study in which performance was assessed during a five-hour period, significant decrements were observed after only a short time at work when the event rate was high (Saito *et al.*, 1972a). Jerison and Pickett's (1964) finding thus appears to be relevant both in the field as well as in the laboratory, and the optimization of the event rate would thus seem to be a general principle for improving vigilance performance. The implication for the design of displays is that input information rates should not exceed the capabilities of the operator. The optimum rate will of course vary for different applications. In reviewing studies of operators who have to keep track of sequential events presented on visual displays, Monty (1973) has concluded that performance tends to deteriorate if input rates higher than 60 events per minute are used. However, the benefits of lowering (or optimizing) the event rate may be outweighed by the slowing of the work rate which is likely to result. In industrial inspection, for example, allowing inspectors more time to inspect individual items may increase labour and operating costs significantly (Chapman and Sinclair, 1975; Drury, 1978), and management will be faced with the problem of balancing these costs against the improvement in inspector accuracy gained.

In occupations in which the work rate is not closely dependent on display or interface requirements, allowing the operator to work at his own pace may result in some improvement of performance. It is generally believed that an operator will be more efficient and will be less likely to show a performance decrement if he is self-paced rather than machine-paced. Unfortunately, the relevant research findings both in vigilance (Broadbent, 1953b; Wilkinson, 1961a; see also Chapter 1) and inspection (Williges and Streeter, 1971; Fox, 1977) have not consistently supported the view that self-pacing is more efficient than machine-paced work. However, in the absence of firm evidence that self-pacing has an *adverse* effect on efficiency, allowing self-paced work may still be recommended as it reportedly increases job satisfaction and reduces operator complaints of fatigue and boredom (McFarling and Heimstra, 1975; Grandjean, 1979).

Work–rest scheduling is another aspect of work design that should be considered in analysing problems of vigilance in the field. Breaking up a period of continuous monitoring or inspection with periods of rest or other activity can have beneficial effects. Breaks from sustained activity as short as five minutes seem to be capable of preventing vigilance decrements. N.H. Mackworth (1950) was the first to recommend that the break should occur during the first 30 minutes of work which is generally held to be the period during which most of the decrement takes place. This recommendation can still be made today, and indeed may be implicitly followed in industry, which may be one reason why performance decrements are rarely reported. Interrupting periods of continuous work with periods of other job-related activity can also enhance efficiency. Wallis and Samuel (1961), for example, found an improvement in radar performance if the vigil was interrupted by ten-minute periods spent on navigation. Similar benefits have been noted by Fox (1977) in a study of coin inspection. It should be noted, however, that the level of performance may still be low, so that the manipulation of work-rest schedules, while having the effect of eliminating the decrement, may keep performance at a steady though sub-optimal level. Many industrial inspectors, especially in the garment and shoe industries, are often engaged in "secondary" tasks such as filling out reports, carrying out minor repairs, or sorting defective items; these activities may serve to arrest any performance decrement, but possibly at the cost of reduced overall efficiency and throughput.

Environmental aspects of work design should also be considered as a potential means of controlling vigilance problems in the field. Laboratory vigilance tasks are typically performed in isolation and under relatively monotonous conditions. While some military applications may require such conditions, most real jobs will not. But this does not mean vigilance problems will disappear in the absence of these conditions. What is the optimal environment for vigilance? Pickett (1978) has suggested that a "coffee shop" atmosphere, one that provides some stimulation but does not distract, may be superior to the typical "quiet library" conditions under which laboratory tasks are performed. Experiments with varied auditory stimulation also support the idea that an interesting and varied environment is conducive to good performance, particularly if the task being performed is repetitive or monotonous (Davies and Shackleton, 1975; Davies et al., in press). As noted in Chapter 7, varying musical schedules can also serve to reduce the extent of the vigilance decrement and Fox and Embrey (1972) reported on the beneficial effects of music on efficiency in industrial inspection. Finally, if these environmental factors cannot be manipulated, a *moderate* amount of stress, in the form of mild heat or low-frequency vibration, can sometimes improve vigilance performance (Poulton, 1973a, 1977a). Some further guidelines to the design of the physical environment are outlined by Poulton (1970), who describes the effects of factors such as noise, cold, and vibration on human performance.

Training

There is a large body of research on the effects of training which indicates that methods such as target specification, target cueing and knowledge of results can have a beneficial effect on vigilance performance (Davies and Tune, 1970; Wiener, 1975; Warm, 1977). Unfortunately, it is not fully understood whether effects on perceptual efficiency are obtained, or whether only standards of reporting (response criteria) are affected. Furthermore, the informative and motivational aspects of training are sometimes confounded. Finally, it is difficult to predict from the research literature which training method will be the most effective for a particular application.

Training procedures for new operators at present have therefore to be developed on an *ad hoc* basis until more is known of the specific effects of training on performance. There is little doubt, however, that trained operators will perform better than naive ones, and that the effects of this training can transfer to subsequent operations (Attwood and Wiener, 1969; Wiener, 1975).

The standard that a human operator adopts for reporting the presence of some target has an effect not only on the relative frequency of omission and commission errors that are made, but also on performance trends over time, as discussed extensively in Chapters 3 and 4. Thus training procedures may be useful in reducing vigilance decrements that are associated with changes in response criteria. Annett and Paterson (1967) tested this possibility by training subjects to adopt either a low or a high criterion in responding to auditory signals. Subjects were tested on a 30-minute auditory vigilance task. The results were somewhat disappointing in that both groups of subjects showed no decrement in performance over time. However, the two groups did maintain the performance differences consistent with the criterion level they had been trained to adopt. Colquhoun and Baddeley (1964) were the first to point out the importance of training subjects to adopt appropriate criterion levels in vigilance situations. They showed that a vigilance decrement may often occur merely because the subject is trained with an inappropriately high signal rate (usually because it is quicker to do so than to use a low signal rate). As a result, the subject makes a number of false alarms in the main task (where the signal rate is much lower); the initial inappropriately high expectancy for signals then declines with time, leading to a fall in the detection rate (see also Williges, 1976). Baddeley (1978) quotes an example of this effect for an actual training situation, where because of the limited time available, training was compressed into a short period of time, leading to subsequent poor performance. The implication for human factors personnel is that the effects of "crammed" training should be taken into account in developing training methods for tasks with a low probability of occurrence of critical targets.

Training operators to adopt different standards of reporting has been studied extensively in industrial inspection, with generally significant results (Harris, 1968, 1969; Drury and Addison, 1973; Embrey, 1975; Swets, 1977). The objective here is not to reduce the probability of a decrement but to optimize the relative frequency of omission and commission errors and their associated costs. Such training procedures will not affect the overall level of efficiency, and thus may be relevant only if the operator uses extreme criteria for reporting (for example, if he never rejects an item, even though later analysis shows that the probability of faulty items is not negligible). The same applies to attempts to provide knowledge of results on "artificial signals" which are deliberately introduced to increase the apparent signal rate and thus to change the operator's response criterion. If the quality of production of an item is very high (if, that is, there are very few faulty items), the probability of detection will also tend to be low, and thus there may be a temptation to insert extra faulty items in an attempt to increase the signal rate and thus the detection rate. However, as already noted, the frequency of both correct and false detections will rise, with no improvement in overall efficiency, and, in terms of throughput, there may well be no significant improvement.

Response criteria can also be manipulated by allowing operators to report with different levels of confidence. As noted in Chapter 4, there is some evidence to indicate that the decrement can be reduced if target reports of both low and high confidence are considered (Broadbent and Gregory, 1963b; Broadbent, 1971). Thus encouraging the operator to respond positively even when doubtful may reduce the extent of the decrement. In inspection tasks, where there may be a problem only with the overall level of performance, this recommendation will have to be weighed against the increased costs of rejecting good production items. In a comprehensive study of sonar monitoring, Rizy (1972) was able to show that allowing multiple levels of reporting had some beneficial effects on performance. Rizy suggested that if the sonar monitor is part of a larger command/ control communication/man-machine system, reports of varying confidence could be "filtered" at the command level for appropriate courses of action, thus eliminating the potentially adverse consequences of allowing doubtful but incorrect reports.

Training with knowledge of results has been successful in elevating vigilance performance, and the evidence also suggests that there is successful transfer of training to later sessions (Wiener, 1963a; Attwood and Wiener, 1969; Warm, 1977). Delayed knowledge of results can usually be given in industrial situations. Drury and Addison (1973) initiated a shop-floor programme of providing feedback to glass inspectors over a limited period and noted a significant improvement in efficiency. Similar effects were noted by Chapman and Sinclair (1975) for inspectors in the food industry. As Drury and Addison (1973) cautioned, however, the effects could merely reflect the influence of supervision on motivation (that is, the "Hawthorne effect").

Selection

Individuals vary widely in the frequency and type of errors they make on vigilance tasks. As noted in Chapter 6, there are also marked individual differences in the extent of the vigilance decrement. Since individual differences can often be a source of variance as great as or greater than that due to task or environmental factors, a reliable procedure for selecting vigilant individuals would be of considerable value in the control of vigilance in the field. Unfortunately, as noted in Chapter 6, no single measure or group of measures that could be used in practice is at present available. Wiener (1975) came to a similar conclusion in reviewing possible selection devices for industrial inspectors, and it seems unlikely that a global test could be developed that could predict an operator's ability to sustain attention in different real world applications.

As noted in Chapter 6, a number of studies have investigated the possibility that more intelligent persons may make better monitors, with generally negative results. IQ tests are thus unlikely to be of help in selecting vigilant operators; none the less, there are indications that such tests may be undergoing a re-evaluation. "Human error" in detecting vital system signs has been suggested as one of the major causes of the accident at the Three Mile Island nuclear reactor, and in an apparent response to this incident, the Tennessee Valley Authority is reportedly embarking on an ambitious selection and training programme entailing the use of IQ tests to select nuclear operators capable of conceptualizing solutions to problems "based on a fundamental understanding of possible contingencies" (News and Comment, *Science*, 1979).

McGrath (1963b) examined intelligence and other psychometric measures in relation to vigilance performance. He was unable to find any reliable predictors of performance, and concluded that individual differences are highly task specific. This would seem to render futile efforts to devise selection tests for vigilant operators. However, as was discussed in Chapter 6, it now seems clear that individual differences are not completely task specific, but are specific to tasks which share certain information processing demands in common (Parasuraman, 1976b; Parasuraman and Davies, 1977; see also Levine *et al.*, 1973). This accords well with the suggestion that information processing measures may be at least as useful as traditional psychometric measures in the assessment of individual differences in cognitive functioning (Hunt *et al.*, 1975).

The implication is that a selection test may only predict performance for groups of tasks which share processing demands (for example, successive or simultaneous discrimination requirements) with the task on which the test was validated. On the other hand, it may be possible to develop a battery of tests, each of which predicts individual differences on different classes of task, to yield a composite test. This would undoubtedly entail a massive research effort, and the possible returns may not justify such an undertaking. The conclusion that individual differences are task type specific does not therefore lend itself to immediate practical application. Moreover, efficiency in the field seems to be much more variable than in the laboratory, and individual differences do not seem to be consistent even when the same task is performed again, as Mills and Sinclair (1976) found for the inspection of clothing. Thus it is reasonable to conclude that, of the two main procedures for "fitting the operator to the job", selection is not a viable approach at present, and training methods are more likely to be successful.

Physiological regulation

The effects of operant control of EEG activity on the maintenance of vigilance were reviewed in Chapter 8. Although some impressive initial results have been obtained, it appears that biofeedback training procedures may only be effective for a limited period of time, since there appears to be little transfer of training (Beatty and O'Hanlon, 1979). Furthermore, these methods may be ineffective if there are disruptions of the normal pattern of work-rest and sleep-waking schedules. When operant control of the EEG is successful, it appears to be effective because it reduces the amount of performance decrement obtained over a 2–3 hour monitoring period. If there is no decrement, however, or if performance is otherwise optimal biofeedback is unlikely to elevate performance beyond the normal level.

Physiological signs of lowered alertness could be used as warning devices in certain occupational environments, much in the same way as physical sensors are used for detecting extremes of heat, humidity, and radiation. Loss of vigilance may be an important safety problem in jobs where the operator has to monitor some display or control process for a prolonged period of time. To counter the potentially hazardous consequences of operator failure, alerting devices may sometimes be introduced into the job. These devices may consist of "synthetic" targets (for which knowledge of performance can be given), or "secondary" tasks imposed on the primary task. The reaction time devices for train drivers used in many railway systems are examples of secondary tasks (Buck, 1968; Cox, 1973).

Since many of these devices cannot be transferred from one job to another (say from vehicle operation to air traffic control), many attempts have been made to devise physiological "alertness indicators". The earliest such attempt used neck EMG activity as the index (Travis and Kennedy, 1947), but this proved to be impractical, and in more recent investigations heart rate variability and EEG measures (Lecret and Pottier, 1971; O'Hanlon, 1971; Carriero, 1977) have been studied. Physiological evaluation of mental workload may aid in the design of displays and alerting devices (Wierwille and Williges, 1978). Two of the most useful measures are event-related potentials in the EEG, and pupillometry (Beatty, 1976; Isreal *et al.*, 1980; Lawrence, 1979). EEG findings indicating that missed signals are preceded by periods of lowered electrocortical activation (see Chapter 8) also have implications for the design of alerting devices. However, a recent finding that train drivers can successfully operate a secondary task vigilance monitoring device even when their EEG record indicates the presence of stage 1 sleep (Fruhstorfer *et al.*, 1977) suggests that many existing devices are poorly designed. Carriero (1977) has argued that physiological measures may enable the construction of a new type of alertness indicator; in his view, it should be possible to obtain physiological profiles corresponding to optimum performance under operational conditions, which could then be used as a "template" to test ongoing physiological activity during actual working conditions for deviations from optimal levels. While such a system could be developed, given current telemetric and computer technology, its acceptability to the operator (who will have to "wear" sensors, electrodes and a transmitter) is open to question.

Conclusions

Despite the differences between laboratory and "real life" monitoring tasks outlined earlier in this chapter, there does appear to be substantial evidence of a "vigilance problem" in operational and industrial situations, either because of the occurrence of a vigilance decrement, or, more commonly and perhaps more importantly, because the average level of detection efficiency is sub-optimal. Nevertheless, there remains a need, as Craig (1980) has indicated, for studies which examine the consistency of operators in detecting different types of signal and the same signal at different times. The most significant advance, both in the theoretical analysis of vigilance per-formance and in its practical application, is likely to be achieved by a broadening of the scope of laboratory research, so that tasks with a complex response requirement, in which observation is not necessarily continuous and uninterrupted, and in which different types of multi-dimensional signals are presented with varying probabilities of occurrence during the work period, may be more extensively investigated in situations approximating more closely to the operational environment.

References

Abrahamson, I.G. and Levitt, H. (1969). Statistical analysis of data from experiments in human signal detection. *Journal of Mathematical Psychology*, **6**, 391–417.

Adams, A.H. (1973). Time of day effects on short-term memory. *Royal Aircraft Establishment, Farnborough, Tech. Memo.*, No. HFG 122.

Adams, J., Brown, T., Colquhoun, P., Hamilton, P., Osborn, J., Thomas, I. and Worsley, D. (1972). Nychthemeral rhythms and air trooping: Some preliminary results from "Exercise Medex". In W.P. Colquhoun (Ed.), *Aspects of Human Efficiency—Diurnal Rhythm and Loss of Sleep*. London: English Universities Press.

Adams, J.A. (1956). Vigilance in the detection of low-intensity visual stimuli. *Journal of Experimental Psychology*, **52**, 204–208.

Adams, J.A. (1963). Experimental studies of human vigilance. *U.S. Air Force Tech. Docum. Rep.*, No. FSD-TDR 63–320.

Adams, J.A. and Boulter, L.R. (1960). Monitoring of complex visual displays: I. Effects of response complexity and intersignal interval for vigilant behaviour when visual load is moderate. *U.S. Air Force CCCD Tech. Note*, No. 60–63.

Adams, J.A. and Humes, J.M. (1963). Monitoring of complex visual displays: IV. Training for vigilance. *Human Factors*, **5**, 147–153.

Adams, J.A., Stenson, H.H. and Humes, J.M. (1961). Monitoring of complex visual displays: II. Effects of visual load and response complexity on human vigilance. *Human Factors*, **3**, 213–221.

Adams, J.A., Humes, J.M. and Stenson, H.H. (1962). Monitoring of complex visual displays: III. Effects of repeated sessions on human vigilance. *Human Factors*, **4**, 149–158.

Adams, J.A., Humes, J.M. and Sieveking, M.A. (1963). Monitoring of complex visual displays: V. Effects of repeated sessions and heavy visual load on human vigilance. *Human Factors*, **5**, 385–389.

Aiken, G. and Lau, A.W. (1966). Memory for the pitch of a tone. *Perception and Psychophysics*, **1**, 232–233.

Alexander, D.A. (1973). Attention dysfunction in senile dementia. *Psychological Reports*, **32**, 229–230.

Altham, P.M.E. (1973). A non-parametric measure of signal discriminability. *British Journal of Mathematical and Statistical Psychology*, **26**, 1–12.

Alluisi, E.A. (1967). Methodology in the use of synthetic tasks to assess complex performance. *Human Factors*, **9**, 375–384.

Alluisi, E.A., Coates, G.D. and Morgan, B.B. (1977). Effects of temporal stressors on vigilance and information processing. In R.R. Mackie (Ed.), *Vigilance: Theory, Operational Performance and Physiological Correlates*. New York: Plenum.

Anderson, R.P., Halcomb, C.G. and Doyle, R.B. (1973). The measurement of attentional deficits. *Exceptional Children*, **39**, 534–539.

Anderson, R.P., Halcomb, C.G., Gordon, W. and Oxolins, D.A. (1974). Measurement of attention distractability in LD children. *Academic Therapy*, **9**, 261–266.

Anderson, K. and Hockey, G.R.J. (1977). Effects of cigarette smoking on incidental memory. *Psychopharmacology*, **52**, 223–226.

Annett, J. and Paterson, L. (1967). Training for auditory detection. In A.F. Sanders (Ed.), *Attention and Performance*. Amsterdam: North Holland.

Antonelli, D.C. and Karas, G.G. (1967). Performance on a vigilance task under conditions of true and false knowledge of results. *Perceptual and Motor Skills*, **25**, 129–138.

Antrobus, J.S., Coleman, R. and Singer, J.L. (1967). Signal-detection performance by subjects differing in predisposition to day-dreaming. *Journal of Consulting Psychology*, **31**, 487–491.

Armington, J.C. and Mitnick, L.L. (1959). Electroencephalogram and sleep deprivation. *Journal of Applied Physiology*, **14**, 247–250.

Astley, R.W. and Fox, J.G. (1975). The analysis of an inspection task in the rubber industry. In C.G. Drury and J.G. Fox (Eds), *Human Reliability in Quality Control*. London: Taylor & Francis.

Attwood, D.A. and Wiener, E.L. (1969). Automated instruction for vigilance training. *Journal of Applied Psychology*, **53**, 218–233.

Audley, R.J. (1973). Some observations on choice reaction time: tutorial survey. In S. Kornblum (Ed.), *Attention and Performance IV*. New York and London: Academic Press.

Audley, R.J. and Pike, A.R. (1965). Some alternative stochastic models of choice. *British Journal of Mathematical and Statistical Psychology*, **18**, 207–225.

Axelrod, S. (1963). Cognitive tasks in several modalities. In R.H. Williams, C. Tibbitts and W. Donahue (Eds), *Processes of Aging, Vol. 1*. New York: Atherton.

Badalamente, R.V. and Ayoub, M.M. (1969). A behavioral analysis of an assembly line inspection task. *Human Factors*, **11**, 339–352.

Baddeley, A.D. (1978). Personal communication.

Baddeley, A.D. and Colquhoun, W.P. (1969). Signal probability and vigilance: A reappraisal of the 'signal rate' effect. *British Journal of Psychology*, **60**, 165–178.

Baddeley, A.D., Hatter, J.E., Scott, D. and Snashall, A. (1970). Memory and time of day. *Quarterly Journal of Experimental Psychology*, **22**, 606–609.

Baeke and, F. and Hoy, P. (1970). Vigilance before and after sleep. *Perceptual and Motor Skills*, **31**, 583–586.

Bakan, P. (1955). Discrimination decrement as a function of time in a prolonged vigil. *Journal of Experimental Psychology*, **50**, 387–390.

Bakan, P. (1959). Extroversion-introversion and improvement in an auditory vigilance task. *British Journal of Psychology*, **50**, 325–332.

Bakan, P. (1960). Effect of meprobamate on auditory vigilance. *Perceptual and Motor Skills*, **12**, 26.

Bakan, P. and Manley, R. (1963). Effect of visual deprivation on auditory vigilance. *British Journal of Psychology*, **54**, 115–119.

Bakan, P., Belton, J.A. and Toth, J.C. (1963). Extroversion-introversion and decrement in an auditory vigilance task. In D.N. Buckner and J.J. McGrath (Eds), *Vigilance: A Symposium*. New York: McGraw-Hill.

Baker, C.H. (1958). Attention to visual displays during a vigilance task. I. Biassing attention. *British Journal of Psychology*, **49**, 279–288.

Baker, C.H. (1959a). Attention to visual displays during a vigilance task. II. Maintaining the level of vigilance. *British Journal of Psychology*, **50**, 30–36.

Baker, C.H. (1959b). Three minor studies of vigilance. *Defence Research Board Laboratory (Canada) Rep.*, No. 234–2.

Baker, C.H. (1959c). Towards a theory of vigilance. *Canadian Journal of Psychology*, **13**, 35–42.

Baker, C.H. (1960). Observing behavior in a vigilance task. *Science*, **132**, 674–675.

Baker, C.H. (1962a). *Man and Radar Displays*. New York: Macmillan.

Baker, C.H. (1962b). On temporal extrapolation. *Canadian Journal of Psychology*, **16**, 37–41.

Baker, C.H. (1962c). Probability of signal detection in a vigilance task. *Science*, **136**, 46–47.

Baker, C.H. (1963a). Signal duration as a factor in vigilance tasks. *Science*, **141**, 1296–1297.

Baker, C.H. (1963b). Consistency of performance in two visual vigilance tasks. In D.N. Buckner and J.J. McGrath (Eds), *Vigilance: A Symposium*. New York: McGraw-Hill.

Baker, C.H. (1963c). Further toward a theory of vigilance. In D.N. Buckner and J.J. McGrath (Eds), *Vigilance: A Symposium*. New York: McGraw-Hill.

Baker, C.H. (1964). Industrial inspection considered as a vigilance task. *Paper presented at the 15th International Congress of Applied Psychology, Ljubljana, Yugoslavia*.

Baker, C.H. and Harabedian, A. (1962a). Performance in an auditory vigilance task while simultaneously tracking a visual target. *Human Factors Research Inc. (Los Angeles) Rep.*, No. 740–742.

Baker, C.H. and Harabedian, A. (1962b). A study of target detection by sonar operators. *Human Factors Research Inc. (Los Angeles) Rep.*, No. 206–216.

Baker, R.A. and Ware, J.R. (1966). The relationship between vigilance and monotonous work. *Ergonomics*, **9**, 109–114.

Baker, R.A., Ware, J.R. and Sipowicz, R.R. (1962a). Vigilance: a comparison in auditory, visual and combined audio-visual tasks. *Canadian Journal of Psychology*, **16**, 192–198.

Baker, R.A., Ware, J.R. and Sipowicz, R.R. (1962b). Signal detection by multiple monitors. *Psychological Record*, **12**, 133–137.

Baker, R.A., Ware, J.R. and Sipowicz, R.R. (1962c). Sustained vigilance: I. Signal detection during a 24-hour continuous watch. *Psychological Record*, **12**, 245–250.

Barmack, J.E. (1937). Boredom and other factors in the physiology of mental effort: an exploratory study. *Archives of Psychology*, **218**, 5–81.

Barmack, J.E. (1939). Studies on the psychophysiology of boredom. I: The effect of 15 mg. of benzedrine sulphate and 60 mg. of ephedrine hydrochloride on blood pressure, report of boredom and other factors. *Journal of Experimental Psychology*, **25**, 494–505.

Beard, R.R. and Grandstaff, N. (1970). Carbon monoxide and cerebral function. *Annals of the New York Academy of Sciences*, **174**, 385–395.

Beard, R.R. and Grandstaff, N. (1975). Carbon monoxide and human functions. In B. Weiss and V.G. Laties (Eds), *Behavioral Toxicology*. New York: Plenum.

Beatty, J. (1971). Effects of initial alpha wave abundance and operant training procedures on occipital alpha and beta wave activity. *Psychonomic Science*, **23**, 197–199.

Beatty, J. (1977a). Learned regulation of alpha and theta frequency activity in the human electroencephalogram. In G.E. Schwarz and J. Beatty (Eds), *Biofeedback:*

Theory and Research. New York: Academic Press.

Beatty, J. (1977b). Activation and attention in the human brain. In M.C. Wittrock, J. Beatty, J.E. Bogen, M.S. Gazzaniga, H.J. Jerison, S.D. Krashen, R.D. Nebes and T.J. Teyler (Eds), *The Human Brain.* Englewood Cliffs, N.J.: Prentice-Hall.

Beatty, J. (1978). A pupillometric index of operator workload. *Paper presented at ARPA Biocybernetics Conference, Chicago.*

Beatty, J. (In preparation). Phasic not tonic pupillary responses reflect detection performance in an auditory vigilance task.

Beatty, J. and Kahneman, D. (1966). Pupillary changes in two memory tasks. *Psychonomic Science,* **5,** 371–372.

Beatty, J. and O'Hanlon, J. (1979). Operant control of posterior theta rhythms and vigilance performance: Repeated treatments and transfer of training. In N. Birbaumer and H.D. Kimmel (Eds), *Biofeedback and Self-Regulation.* Hillsdale, N.J.: Erlbaum.

Beatty, J. and Wagoner, B.L. (1975). Pupillometric assessment of signal analysis and decision processes in acoustic signal direction. Unpublished manuscript, Human Neurophysiology Laboratory, University of California at Los Angeles.

Beatty, J. and Wagoner, B.L. (1978). Pupillometric signs of brain activation vary with level of cognitive processing. *Science,* **199,** 1216–1218.

Beatty, J. and Wilson C. (1977). Activation and sustained attention: A pupillometric study of an auditory vigilance task. *Tech. Rep., No. 12, Human Neurophysiology Laboratory.* University of California, Los Angeles.

Beatty, J., Ahern, S.K. and Katz, R. (1977). Sleep deprivation and the vigilance of anesthesiologists during simulated surgery. In R.R. Mackie (Ed.), *Vigilance: Theory, Operational Performance and Physiological Correlates.* New York: Plenum.

Beatty, J., Greenberg, A., Diebler, W.P. and O'Hanlon, J.F. (1974). Operant control of occipital theta rhythm affects performance in a radar monitoring task. *Science,* **183,** 871–873.

Belt, J.A. (1971). *The Applicability of Vigilance Laboratory Research to a Simulated Industrial Inspection Task.* Unpublished Ph.D. thesis, Texas Tech. University.

Benignus, V.A., Otto, D.A. and Knelson, J.H. (1975). Effect of low frequency random noises on performance of a numeric monitoring task. *Perceptual and Motor Skills,* **40,** 231–239.

Benignus, V.A., Otto, D.A., Prah, J.D. and Benignus, G. (1977). Lack of effects of carbon monoxide on human vigilance. *Perceptual and Motor Skills,* **45,** 1007–1014.

Benedetti, L.H. and Loeb, M. (1972). A comparison of auditory monitoring performance in blind subjects with that of sighted subjects in light and dark. *Perception and Psychophysics,* **11,** 10–16.

Benor, D. and Shvartz, E. (1971). Effect of body cooling on vigilance in hot environments. *Aerospace Medicine,* **42,** 727–730.

Berger, C. and Mahneke, A. (1954). Fatigue in two simple visual tasks. *American Journal of Psychology,* **67,** 509–512.

Bergstrom, B., Gillsberg, M. and Arnberg, P. (1973). Effects of sleep loss and stress on radar watching. *Journal of Applied Psychology,* **58,** 158–162.

Bergum, B.O. (1966). A taxonomic analysis of continuous performance. *Perceptual and Motor Skills,* **23,** 47–54.

Bergum, B.O. and Klein, I.C. (1962). A survey and analysis of vigilance research. *U.S. Army Air Defense and Human Research Unit, Research Rep., No. 8. Fort Bliss, Texas.*

Bergum, B.O. and Lehr, D.J. (1962a). Vigilance performance as a function of paired monitoring. *Journal of Applied Psychology*, **46**, 341–343.

Bergum, B.O. and Lehr, D.J. (1962b). Vigilance performance as a function of interpolated rest. *Journal of Applied Psychology*, **46**, 425–427.

Bergum, B.O. and Lehr, D.J. (1963a). End spurt in vigilance. *Journal of Experimental Psychology*, **66**, 383–385.

Bergum, B.O. and Lehr, D.J. (1963b). Vigilance performance as a function of task and environmental variables. *U.S. Army Air Defense Human Research Unit Research Rep.*, No. 11. Fort Bliss, Texas.

Bergum, B.O. and Lehr, D.J. (1963c). Effects of authoritarianism on vigilance performance. *Journal of Applied Psychology*, **47**, 75–77.

Bergum, B.O. and Lehr, D.J. (1964). Monetary incentives and vigilance. *Journal of Experimental Psychology*, **67**, 197–198.

Berlyne, D.E. (1960). *Conflict, Arousal and Curiosity*. New York: McGraw-Hill.

Berlyne, D.E. and Lewis, J.L. (1963). Effects of heightened arousal on human exploratory behavior. *Canadian Journal of Psychology*, **17**, 398–411.

Betts, G.H. (1909). *The Distribution and Functions of Mental Imagery*. Columbia, N.Y.: Teachers College.

Bevan, W. and Turner, E.O. (1965). Vigilance performance with a qualitative shift in verbal reinforcers. *Journal of Experimental Psychology*, **70**, 83–86.

Bicknell, A. (1970). *Aging, Arousal and Vigilance*. Unpublished Ph.D. thesis, Texas Tech. University.

Bills, A.G. (1931). Blocking: a new principle in mental fatigue. *American Journal of Psychology*, **43**, 230–245.

Binford, J.R. and Loeb, M. (1966). Changes within and over repeated sessions in criterion and effective sensitivity in an auditory vigilance task. *Journal of Experimental Psychology*, **72**, 339–345.

Bjerner, B. (1949). Alpha depression and lowered pulse rate during delayed reactions in a serial reaction test. *Acta Physiologica Scandinavica*, **19**, Supplement No. 65.

Black, A.H. (1971). The direct control of neural processes by reward and punishment. *Biofeedback and Self-Control*, **1**, 213–232.

Blackwell, P.J. and Belt, J.A. (1971). Effect of differential levels of ambient noise on vigilance performance. *Perceptual and Motor Skills*, **32**, 734.

Blair, W.C. (1958). Measurement of observing responses in human monitoring. *Science*, **128**, 255–256.

Blake, H. and Gerard, R. (1937). Brain potentials during sleep. *American Journal of Physiology*, **119**, 697–703.

Blake, M.J.F. (1965). Physiological and temperamental correlates of performance at different times of day. *Ergonomics*, **8**, 375–376 (Abstract).

Blake, M.J.F. (1967a). Time of day effects in a range of tasks. *Psychonomic Science*, **4**, 349–350.

Blake, M.J.F. (1967b). Relationships between circadian rhythm of body temperature and introversion-extroversion. *Nature*, **215**, 896–897.

Blake, M.J.F. (1971). Temperament and time of day. In W.P. Colquhoun (Ed.), *Biological Rhythms and Human Performance*. London and New York: Academic Press.

Boadle, J. (1976). Vigilance and simulated night driving. *Ergonomics*, **19**, 217–225.

Boggs, D.H. and Simon, J.R. (1968). Differential effect of noise on tasks of varying complexity. *Journal of Applied Psychology*, **52**, 148–153.

Bonnet, M.H. (1980). Sleep, performance and mood after the energy-expenditure equivalent of 40 hours of sleep deprivation. *Psychophysiology*, **17**, 56–63.

Bonnet, M.H. and Webb, W.B. (1978). The effect of repetition of relevant and irrelevant tasks over day and night work periods. *Ergonomics*, **21**, 999–1005.

Boring, E.G. (1957). *History of Experimental Psychology* (2nd edition). New York: Appleton-Century-Crofts.

Botwinick, J. (1966). Cautiousness in advanced age. *Journal of Gerontology*, **21**, 347–353.

Botwinick, J. (1967). *Cognitive Processes in Maturity and Old Age*. New York: Springer.

Botwinick, J. (1969). Disinclination to venture response versus cautiousness in responding: Age differences. *Journal of Genetic Psychology*, **115**, 55–62.

Botwinick, J., Brinley, J.F. and Robbin, J.S. (1958). The interaction effects of perceptual difficulty and stimulus exposure time on age differences in speed and accuracy of response. *Gerontologia*, **2**, 1–10.

Boulter, L.R. and Adams, J.A. (1963). Vigilance decrement, the expectancy hypothesis and intersignal interval. *Canadian Journal of Psychology*, **17**, 201–209.

Bowen, H.M. (1956). *On the Appreciation of Serial Displays*. Unpublished Ph.D. thesis, University of Cambridge.

Broadbent, D.E. (1950). The twenty dials test under quiet conditions. *Medical Research Council Applied Psychology Unit Rep.*, No. 130/50.

Broadbent, D.E. (1951). The twenty dials and twenty lights tests under noise conditions. *Medical Research Council Applied Psychology Unit Rep.*, No. 160/51.

Broadbent, D.E. (1953a). Noise, paced performance and vigilance tasks. *British Journal of Psychology*, **44**, 295–303.

Broadbent, D.E. (1953b). Classical conditioning and human watchkeeping. *Psychological Review*, **60**, 331–339.

Broadbent, D.E. (1954). Some effects of noise on visual performance. *Quarterly Journal of Experimental Psychology*, **6**, 1–15.

Broadbent, D.E. (1957a). A mechanical model for human attention and immediate memory. *Psychological Review*, **64**, 205–215.

Broadbent, D.E. (1957b). Effects of noise on behavior. In C.M. Harris (Ed.), *Handbook of Noise Control*. New York: McGraw-Hill.

Broadbent, D.E. (1958). *Perception and Communication*. London: Pergamon Press.

Broadbent, D.E. (1961). Human arousal and efficiency in performing vigilance tasks. *Discovery*, **22**, 314–320.

Broadbent, D.E. (1963a). Possibilities and difficulties in the concept of arousal. In D.N. Buckner and J.J. McGrath (Eds), *Vigilance: A Symposium*. New York: McGraw-Hill.

Broadbent, D.E. (1963b). Differences and interactions between stresses. *Quarterly Journal of Experimental Psychology*, **15**, 205–211.

Broadbent, D.E. (1963c). Some recent research from the Applied Psychology Research Unit. In D.N. Buckner and J.J. McGrath (Eds), *Vigilance: A Symposium*. New York: McGraw-Hill.

Broadbent, D.E. (1965). A reformulation of the Yerkes-Dodson Law. *British Journal of Mathematical and Statistical Psychology*, **18**, 145–147.

Broadbent, D.E. (1970). Noise and work performance. In W. Taylor (Ed.), *Proceedings of the Symposium on the Psychological Effects of Noise*. London: Research Panel of the Society of Occupational Medicine.

Broadbent, D.E. (1971). *Decision and Stress*. London and New York: Academic Press.

Broadbent, D.E. (1973). *In Defence of Empirical Psychology*. London: Methuen.

Broadbent, D.E. (1975). Personal communication.

Broadbent, D.E. (1978). The current state of noise research: Reply to Poulton.

Psychological Bulletin, **85**, 1052–1067.

Broadbent, D.E. (1979). Human performance in noise. In C.M. Harris (Ed.), *Handbook of Noise Control* (2nd edition) New York: McGraw-Hill.

Broadbent, D.E. and Gregory, M. (1963a). Division of attention and the decision theory of signal detection. *Proceedings of the Royal Society*, Series B **13**, 158, 221–231.

Broadbent, D.E. and Gregory, M. (1963b). Vigilance considered as a statistical decision. *British Journal of Psychology*, **54**, 309–323.

Broadbent, D.E. and Gregory, M. (1965). Effects of noise and of signal rate upon vigilance analysed by means of decision theory. *Human Factors*, **7**, 155–162.

Broadbent, D.E. and Gregory, M. (1967). Perception of emotionally toned words. *Nature*, **215**, 581–584.

Broadbent, D.E. and Little, E.A.J. (1960). Effects of noise reduction in a work situation. *Occupational Psychology*, **34**, 133–140.

Broca, P. (1865). Sur le siège de la faculté du langage articulé. *Bulletin de la Société d'Anthropologie*, **6**, 337–393.

Bromley, D.B. (1974). *The Psychology of Human Ageing*. (2nd edition). Harmondsworth: Penguin.

Brown, I.D. (1967). Measurement of control skills, vigilance and performance of a subsidiary task during 12 hours of car driving. *Ergonomics*, **10**, 665–673.

Bruel, P.V. (1976). Determination of noise levels. In G. Rossi and M. Vigone (Eds), *Man and Noise*. Turin: Minerva Medica.

Buck, L. (1966). Reaction time as a measure of perceptual vigilance. *Psychological Bulletin*, **65**, 291–308.

Buck, L. (1968). Experiments on railway vigilance devices. *Ergonomics*, **11**, 557–564.

Buckner, D.N. (1963). An individual-difference approach to explaining vigilance performance. In D.N. Buckner and J.J. McGrath (Eds), *Vigilance: A Symposium*. New York: McGraw-Hill.

Buckner, D.N. and McGrath, J.J. (Eds) (1963a). *Vigilance: A Symposium*. New York: McGraw-Hill.

Buckner, D.N. and McGrath, J.J. (1963b). A comparison of performance on single and dual sensory mode vigilance tasks. In D.N. Buckner and J.J. McGrath (Eds), *Vigilance: A Symposium*. New York: McGraw-Hill.

Buckner, D.N., Harabedian, A. and McGrath, J.J. (1960). A study of individual differences in vigilance performance. *Human Factors Research Inc. (Los Angeles)*, Tech. Rep., No. 2.

Buckner, D.N., Harabedian, A. and McGrath, J.J. (1966). Individual differences in vigilance performance. *Journal of Engineering Psychology*, **5**, 69–85.

Bull, R.H. and Gale, M.A. (1973). The reliability of and interrelationships between various measures of electrodermal activity. *Journal of Experimental Research in Personality*, **6**, 300–306.

Burdick, J.A. (1966). Autonomic lability and neuroticism. *Journal of Psychosomatic Research*, **9**, 339–342.

Byrne, D.G. (1976). Vigilance and arousal in depressive states. *British Journal of Social and Clinical Psychology*, **15**, 267–274.

Cahoon, R.L. (1970a). Vigilance performance under hypoxia. *Journal of Applied Psychology*, **54**, 479–483.

Cahoon, R.L. (1970b). Vigilance performance under hypoxia: II. Effects of work-rest schedule. *Perceptual and Motor Skills*, **31**, 619–626.

Cahoon, R.L. (1973). Auditory vigilance under hypoxia. *Journal of Applied Psychology*, **57**, 350–352.

Caille, E.J., Peyronne, J.C., Legros, J.G., Rossi, A.M. and Drovard, P. (1965). *Psychophysiological study of the radar watch.* (Rep. 07/65). Toulon, France: Centre d'Etudes et de Recherche de Psychologie Appliqué.

Callaway, E. (1975). *Brain Electrical Potentials and Individual Psychological Differences.* New York: Grune and Stratton.

Callaway, E. and Dembo, D. (1958). Narrowed attention: a psychological phenomenon that accompanies a certain physiological change. *Journal of Neurology and Psychiatry,* **79,** 74–90.

Canestrari, R.E. (1962). The effects of aging on vigilance performance. *Paper Presented to a Meeting of the Gerontological Society, Miami, Florida.*

Carr, G.D. (1969). *Introversion-Extraversion and Vigilance Performance.* Unpublished Ph.D. thesis. Tufts University.

Carriero, N. (1977). Physiological correlates of performance in a long duration repetitive task. In R.R. Mackie (Ed.), *Vigilance: Theory, Operational Performance and Physiological Correlates.* New York: Plenum.

Carpenter, A. (1946). Does performance on the clock test improve with practice? *Medical Research Council Applied Psychology Unit Rep.,* No. 41/46.

Carterette, E.C., Friedman, M.P. and Cosmides, R. (1965). Reaction-time distributions in the detection of weak signals in noise. *Journal of the Acoustical Society of America,* **38,** 531–542.

Chapanis, A. (1967). The relevance of laboratory studies to practical situations. *Ergonomics,* **10,** 557–577.

Chapman, D.E. and Sinclair, M.A. (1975). Ergonomics in inspection tasks in the food industry. In C.G. Drury and J.G. Fox (Eds), *Human Reliability in Quality Control.* London: Taylor & Francis.

Chiles, W.D., Cleveland, J.M. and Fox, R.E. (1960). A study of the effects of ionized air on behavior. *WADD Tech. Rep.,* No. 60–59. Wright Patterson Air Force Base, Ohio.

Chiles, W.D., Fox, R.E., Rush, J.H. and Stilson, D.V. (1962). Effects of ionised air on decision making and vigilance performance. *U.S. Air Force Tech. Docum. Rep.,* No. 62–51.

Chinn, R. McC. and Alluisi, E.A. (1964). Effects of knowledge-of-results information on three measures of vigilance performance. *Perceptual and Motor Skills,* **18,** 901–912.

Christensen, C.L., Gliner, J.A., Horvath, S.M. and Wagner, J.A. (1977). Effects of three kinds of hypoxias on vigilance performance. *Aviation Space and Environmental Medicine,* **48,** 491–496.

Claridge, G.S. (1960). The excitation-inhibition balance in neurotics. In H.J. Eysenck (Ed.), *Experiments in Personality, Vol. 2.* London: Routledge and Kegan Paul.

Clark, W.C. and Mehl, L. (1971). Signal detection theory procedures are not equivalent when thermal stimuli are judged. *Journal of Experimental Psychology,* **97,** 148–153.

Coburn, R.F. (Ed.) (1970). Biological effects of carbon monoxide. *Annals of the New York Academy of Sciences,* **174,** 1–430.

Cohen, A. (1973). Industrial noise and medical absence and accident record data on exposed workers. In *Proceedings of the International Congress on Noise as a Public Health Problem, Dubrovnik, Yugoslavia.* Washington, D.C.: U.S. Environmental Protection Agency. 550/9–73–008.

Cohen, G. (1977). *The Psychology of Cognition.* London and New York: Academic Press.

Cohen, H.H., Conrad, D.W., O'Brien, J.F. and Pearson, R.G. (1973). *Noise effects, arousal and information processing: task difficulty and performance.* Unpublished report, Department of Psychology and Industrial Engineering, North Carolina State University.

Cohen, S. (1978). Environmental load and the allocation of attention. In A. Baum, J.E. Singer and S. Valins (Eds), *Advances in Environmental Psychology*, Vol. 1. Hillsdale, New Jersey: Erlbaum.

Cohen, S. (1980). Aftereffects of stress on human performance and social behavior: A review of research and theory. *Psychological Bulletin*, **88**, 82–108.

Cohen, S. and Scapacan, S. (1978). The aftereffects of stress: An attentional interpretation. *Environmental Psychology and Nonverbal Behavior*, **3**, 43–57.

Coles, M.G.H. and Gale, A. (1971). Physiological reactivity as a predictor of performance in a vigilance task. *Psychophysiology*, **8**, 594–599.

Coles, M.G.H., Gale, M.A. and Kline, P. (1971). Personality and habituation of the orienting reaction: Tonic and response measures of electrodermal activity. *Psychophysiology*, **8**, 54–63.

Colquhoun, W.P. (1959). The effect of a short rest pause on inspection efficiency. *Ergonomics*, **2**, 367–372.

Colquhoun, W.P. (1960). Temperament, inspection efficiency and time of day. *Ergonomics*, **3**, 377–378.

Colquhoun, W.P. (1961). The effect of unwanted signals on performance in a vigilance task. *Ergonomics*, **4**, 41–52.

Colquhoun, W.P. (1962a). Effects of a small dose of alcohol and certain other factors on the performance of a vigilance task. *Bulletin du C.E.R.P.*, **11**, 27–44 (in French, English summary).

Colquhoun, W.P. (1962b). Effects of hyoscine and meclozine on vigilance and short-term memory. *British Journal of Industrial Medicine*, **19**, 287–296.

Colquhoun, W.P. (1966a). The effects of unwanted signals on performance in a vigilance task: A reply to Jerison. *Ergonomics*, **9**, 417–419.

Colquhoun, W.P. (1966b). Training for vigilance: a comparison of different techniques. *Human Factors*, **8**, 7–12.

Colquhoun, W.P. (1967). Sonar target detection as a decision process. *Journal of Applied Psychology*, **51**, 187–190.

Colquhoun, W.P. (1969). Effects of raised ambient temperature and event rate on vigilance performance. *Aerospace Medicine*, **40**, 413–417.

Colquhoun, W.P. (1971). Circadian variations in mental efficiency. In W.P. Colquhoun (Ed.), *Biological Rhythms and Human Performance*. London and New York: Academic Press.

Colquhoun, W.P. (1975). Evaluation of auditory, visual, and dual-mode displays for prolonged sonar monitoring in repeated sessions. *Human Factors*, **17**, 425–437.

Colquhoun, W.P. (1977). Simultaneous monitoring of a number of sonar outputs. In R.R. Mackie (Ed.), *Vigilance: Theory, Operational Performance and Physiological Correlates*. New York: Plenum Press.

Colquhoun, W.P. and Baddeley, A.D. (1964). Role of pretest expectancy in vigilance decrement. *Journal of Experimental Psychology*, **68**, 156–160.

Colquhoun, W.P. and Baddeley, A.D. (1967). Influence of signal probability during pretraining on vigilance decrement. *Journal of Experimental Psychology*, **73**, 153–155.

Colquhoun, W.P. and Edwards, R.S. (1970). Practice effects on a visual vigilance task with and without search. *Human Factors*, **12**, 537–546.

Colquhoun, W.P. and Goldman, R.F. (1972). Vigilance under induced hyperthermia. *Ergonomics*, **15**, 621–632.

Colquhoun, W.P., Blake, M.J.F. and Edwards, R.S. (1968a). Experimental studies of shift work, I: A comparison of 'rotating' and 'established' 4-hour shift systems. *Ergonomics*, **11**, 437–453.

Colquhoun, W.P., Blake, M.J.F. and Edwards, R.S. (1968b). Experimental studies of shift work, II: Stabilized 8-hour shift systems. *Ergonomics*, **11**, 527–556.

Conrad, D.W. (1973). The effects of intermittent noise on human serial decoding performance and physiological response. *Ergonomics*, **16**, 739–747.

Corah, N.L. and Stern, J.A. (1963). Stability and adaptation of some measures of electrodermal activity in children. *Journal of Experimental Psychology*, **65**, 80–85.

Corballis, M.C. (1975). Access to memory: An analysis of recognition times. In P.M.A. Rabbitt and S. Dornic (Eds), *Attention and Performance, V*. London and New York: Academic Press.

Corcoran, D.W.J. (1962). Noise and loss of sleep. *Quarterly Journal of Experimental Psychology*, **14**, 178–182.

Corcoran, D.W.J. (1963). Doubling the rate of signal presentation in a vigilance task during sleep deprivation. *Journal of Applied Psychology*, **47**, 412–415.

Corcoran, D.W.J. (1965). Personality and the inverted-U relation. *British Journal of Psychology*, **56**, 267–273.

Corcoran, D.W.J. (1972). Studies of individual differences at the Applied Psychology Unit. In J.A. Gray and V. Neblitzin (Eds), *Biological Bases of Individual Behaviour*. London and New York: Academic Press.

Corcoran, D.W.J., Mullin, J., Rainey, M.T. and Frith, G. (1977). The effects of raised signal and noise amplitude during the course of vigilance tasks. In R.R. Mackie (Ed.), *Vigilance: Theory, Operational Performance and Physiological Correlates*. New York: Plenum.

Coules, J. and Avery, D.L. (1966). Human performance and basal skin conductance in a vigilance-type task with and without knowledge of results. *Perceptual and Motor Skills*, **23**, 1295–1302.

Cox, J.J. (1973). Train control, stress, and vigilance. *Proceedings of the 10th Annual Conference of the Ergonomics Society of Australia and New Zealand*, 16.1–16.22.

Craig, A. (1976). Signal recognition and the probability-matching decision rule. *Perception and Psychophysics*, **20**, 157–162.

Craig, A. (1977). Broadbent and Gregory revisited: vigilance and statistical decision. *Human Factors*, **19**, 25–36.

Craig, A. (1978). Is the vigilance decrement simply a response adjustment towards probability matching? *Human Factors*, **20**, 441–446.

Craig, A. (1979a). Personal communication.

Craig, A. (1979b). Discrimination, temperature and time of day. *Human Factors*, **21**, 61–68.

Craig, A. (1980). *Human engineering: The control of vigilance*. Personal communication.

Craig, A. and Colquhoun, W.P. (1975). Vigilance: A review. In C.G. Drury and J.G. Fox (Eds), *Human Reliability in Quality Control*. London: Taylor and Francis.

Craig, A. and Colquhoun, W.P. (1977). Vigilance effects in complex inspection. In R.R. Mackie (Ed.), *Vigilance: Theory, Operational Performance and Physiological Correlates*. New York: Plenum.

Craig, A., Colquhoun, W.P. and Corcoran, D.W.J. (1976). Combining evidence presented simultaneously to the eye and the ear: A comparison of some predictive models. *Perception and Psychophysics*, **19**, 473–484.

Craik, F.I.M. (1966). The effects of ageing on the detection of faint auditory signals. *Paper presented at the 7th International Congress of Gerontology, Vienna, Austria*.

Craik, F.I.M. (1969). Applications of signal detection theory to studies of aging. In A.T. Welford and J.E. Birren (Eds), *Decision Making and Age*. Basel: Karger.

Craik, K.J.W. and Mackworth, N.H. (1943). Unpublished report to R.A.F. Coastal Command cited in N.H. Mackworth (1950), *Researches on the Measurement of Human Performance*. *Medical Research Council Special Rep.*, No. 268. London: HMSO.

Crider, A. and Augenbraun, C.B. (1975). Auditory vigilance correlates of electrodermal response habituation speed. *Psychophysiology*, **12**, 36–40.

Crider, A. and Lunn, R. (1971). Electrodermal lability as a personality dimension. *Journal of Experimental Research in Personality*, **5**, 145–150.

Curry, R.E. and Gai E.G. (1976). Detection of random process failures by human monitors. In T.B. Sheridan and G. Johannsen (Eds), *Monitoring Behavior and Supervisory Control*. New York: Plenum.

Daniel, R.S. (1967). Alpha and theta EEG in vigilance. *Perceptual and Motor Skills*, **25**, 697–703.

Dannhaus, D.M., Hopson, J.A. and Halcomb, C.G. (1976). Effect of instructional set on end spurt phenomenon. *Perceptual and Motor Skills*, **43**, 786.

Dardano, J.F. (1962). Relationships of intermittent noise, intersignal interval and skin conductance to vigilance behavior. *Journal of Applied Psychology*, **46**, 106–114.

Dardano, J.F. (1969). Observing behavior of mental patients under a fixed interval schedule. *Psychological Reports*, **24**, 635–653.

Davenport, W.G. (1968). Auditory vigilance: The effects of costs and values on signals. *Australian Journal of Psychology*, **20**, 213–218.

Davenport, W.G. (1969). Vibrotactile vigilance: effects of costs and values of signals. *Perception and Psychophysics*, **5**, 25–29.

Davenport, W.G. (1972). Vigilance and arousal: Effects of different types of background stimulation. *Journal of Psychology*, **82**, 339–346.

Davenport, W.G. (1974). Arousal theory and vigilance: Schedules for background stimulation. *Journal of General Psychology*, **91**, 51–59.

Davies, A.D.M. and Davies, D.R. (1975). The effects of noise and time of day upon age differences in performance at two checking tasks. *Ergonomics*, **18**, 321–336.

Davies, D.R. (1961). Vigilance and arousal. *Ergonomics*, **4**, 283 (Abstract).

Davies, D.R. (1962). *An experimental study of some aspects of auditory vigilance performance*. Unpublished Ph.D. thesis, University of Bristol.

Davies, D.R. (1968a). Physiological and psychological effects of exposure to high intensity noise. *Applied Acoustics*, **1**, 215–233.

Davies, D.R. (1968b). Age differences in paced inspection tasks. In G.A. Talland (Ed.), *Human Aging and Behavior*. New York and London: Academic Press.

Davies, D.R. (1972). Music and task behaviour. *Bulletin of the British Psychological Society*, **26**, 54–55 (Abstract).

Davies, D.R. (1976). Noise and the autonomic nervous system. In G. Rossi and M. Vigone (Eds), *Man and Noise*. Turin: Minerva Medica.

Davies, D.R. and Griew, S. (1963). A further note on the effect of aging on auditory vigilance performance: the effect of low signal frequency. *Journal of Gerontology*, **18**, 370–371.

Davies, D.R. and Hockey, G.R.J. (1966). The effects of noise and doubling the signal frequency on individual differences in visual vigilance performance. *British Journal of Psychology*, **57**, 381–389.

Davies, D.R. and Horne, J.A. (1975). Human sleep: Measurement, characteristics and individual differences. In A.D. Clift (Ed.), *Sleep Disturbance and Hypnotic*

Drug Dependence. Amsterdam: Excerpta Medica.

Davies, D.R. and Jones, D.M. (1975). The effects of noise and incentives upon attention in short-term memory. *British Journal of Psychology*, **66**, 61–68.

Davies, D.R. and Jones, D.M. (in press). Hearing and Noise. In W.T. Singleton (Ed.), *The Body at Work*. Cambridge: Cambridge University Press.

Davies, D.R. and Krkovic, A. (1965). Skin conductance, alpha-activity, and vigilance. *American Journal of Psychology*, **78**, 304–306.

Davies, D.R. and Parasuraman, R. (1976). Vigilanz, Antwortlatenzen, und Kortikale evozierte Potentiale. *Probleme und Ergebnisse der Psychologie*, **59**, 95–99.

Davies, D.R. and Parasuraman, R. (1977). Cortical evoked potentials and vigilance: A decision theory analysis. In R.R. Mackie (Ed.), *Vigilance: Theory, Operational Performance, and Physiological Correlates*. New York: Plenum.

Davies, D.R. and Shackleton, V.J. (1975). *Psychology and Work*. London: Methuen.

Davies, D.R. and Treacher, A.C.C. (1966). An experimental study of impulsivity and autonomic lability in older and younger subjects. *Paper presented at the 7th International Congress of Gerontology, Vienna, Austria*.

Davies, D.R. and Tune, G.S. (1970). *Human Vigilance Performance*. London: Staples.

Davies, D.R., Hockey, G.R.J. and Taylor, A. (1969). Varied auditory stimulation, temperament differences and vigilance performance. *British Journal of Psychology*, **60**, 453–457.

Davies, D.R., Shackleton, V.J. and Lang, L. (1972). The effects of complexity and uncertainty on performance at a problem-solving task. *Psychonomic Science*, **27**, 193–194.

Davies, D.R., Lang, L. and Shackleton, V.J. (1973). The effects of music and task difficulty on performance at a visual vigilance task. *British Journal of Psychology*, **64**, 383–389.

Davies, D.R., Shackleton, V.J. and Parasuraman, R. (in press). Monotony and boredom. In G.R.J. Hockey (Ed.), *Stress and Fatigue*. Chichester: Wiley.

Deaton, M., Tobias, J.S. and Wilkinson, R.T. (1971). The effects of sleep deprivation on signal detection parameters. *Quarterly Journal of Experimental Psychology*, **23**, 449–451.

Deese, J. (1955). Some problems in the theory of vigilance. *Psychological Review*, **62**, 359–368.

Dember, W.P. and Warm, J.S. (1979). *The Psychology of Perception*. New York: Holt, Rinehart and Winston.

Dimond, S.J. (1976). Depletion of attentional capacity after total commissurotomy in man. *Brain*, **99**, 347–356.

Dimond, S.J. (1977). Vigilance and split-brain research. In R.R. Mackie (Ed.), *Vigilance: Theory, Operational Performance, and Physiological Correlates*. New York: Plenum.

Dimond, S.J. (1979). Tactual and auditory vigilance in split-brain man. *Journal of Neurology, Neurosurgery, and Psychiatry*, **42**, 70–74.

Dimond, S.J. and Beaumont, J.G. (1971). Hemisphere function and vigilance. *Quarterly Journal of Experimental Psychology*, **23**, 443–448.

Dimond, S.J. and Beaumont, J.G. (1973). Differences in the vigilance performance of right and left hemispheres. *Cortex*, **9**, 259–265.

Dobbins, D.A., Tiedemann, J.G. and Skordahl, D.M. (1963). Vigilance under highway driving conditions. *Perceptual and Motor Skills*, **16**, 38.

Docter, R.F. and Friedman, L.F. (1966). Thirty-day stability of spontaneous galvanic skin responses in man. *Psychophysiology*, **2**, 311–315.

Docter, R.F., Naitoh, P. and Smith, J.C. (1966). Electroencephalographic changes and vigilance behavior during experimentally induced intoxication with alcoholic subjects. *Psychosomatic Medicine*, **28**, 605–615.

Donchin, E. (1969). Data analysis techniques in average evoked potential research. In E. Donchin and D.B. Lindsley (Eds), *Average Evoked Potentials: Methods, Results and Evaluations*. Washington, D.C.: U.S. Government Printing Office.

Donchin, E. (1975). Brain electrical correlates of pattern recognition. In G.F. Inbar (Ed.), *Signal Analysis and Pattern Recognition in Biomedical Engineering*. New York: Wiley.

Donchin, E. and Lindsley, D.B. (1966). Averaged evoked potentials and reaction times to visual stimuli. *Electroencephalography and Clinical Neurophysiology*, **20**, 217–223.

Donchin, E. and Heffley, E. (1975). Minicomputers in the signal averaging laboratory. *American Psychologist*, **30**, 299–312.

Donchin, E., Tueting, P., Ritter, W., Kutas, M. and Heffley, E. (1975). On the independence of the CNV and P300 components of the human averaged evoked potential. *Electroencephalography and Clinical Neurophysiology*, **38**, 449–461.

Donchin, E., Kutas, M. and McCarthy, G. (1977). Electrocortical indices of hemispheric utilization. In S.R. Harnad (Ed.), *Lateralization in the Nervous System*. New York and London: Academic Press.

Donchin, E., Ritter, W. and McCallum, W.C. (1978). Cognitive psychophysiology: The endogenous components of the ERP. In E. Callaway and S.H. Koslow (Eds), *Event-Related Brain Potentials in Man*. New York and London: Academic Press.

Dorfman, D.D. and Alf, E. (1968). Maximum likelihood estimation of parameters of signal detection theory—a direct solution. *Psychometrika*, **33**, 117–124.

Dornic, S. (1967). Expectancy of signals and the memory trace. *Studia Psychologica*, **9**, 87–91.

Dorris, A.L. and Foote, B.L. (1978). Inspector errors and statistical quality control. *AIIE Transactions*, **10**, 184–192.

Douglas, V.I. (1972). Stop, look and listen: The problems of sustained attention and impulse control in hyperactive and normal children. *Canadian Journal of Behavioral Science*, **4**, 259–282.

Doyle, R.B., Anderson, R.P. and Halcomb, C.G. (1976). Attention deficits and the effects of visual distraction. *Journal of Learning Disabilities*, **9**, 48–54.

Drucker, E.H., Cannon, L.D. and Ware, J.R. (1969). The effects of sleep deprivation on performance over a 48-hour period. *Human Resources Research Office Tech. Rep.*, No. 69–8.

Drury, C.G. (1978). Integrating human factors models into statistical quality control. *Human Factors*, **20**, 561–572.

Drury, C.G. and Addison, J.C. (1973). An industrial study of the effects of feedback and fault devising on inspection performance. *Ergonomics*, **16**, 159–169.

Drury, C.G. and Fox, J.G. (1975a). Models of inspector performance: conclusions. In C.G. Drury and J.G. Fox (Eds), *Human Reliability in Quality Control*. London: Taylor and Francis.

Drury, C.G. and Fox, J.G. (Eds) (1975b). *Human Reliability in Quality Control*. London: Taylor and Francis.

Dudley, R.C. (1966). *Sex differences in an auditory vigilance task under conditions of visual deprivation*. Unpublished B.A. thesis, University of Leicester.

Duffy, E. (1932). The relationship between muscular tension and quality of performance. *American Journal of Psychology*, **44**, 535–546.

Duffy, E. (1951). The concept of energy mobilization. *Psychological Review*, **58**, 30–40.

Duffy, E. (1957). The psychological significance of the concept of "arousal" or "activation". *Psychological Review*, **64**, 265–275.

Duffy, E. (1962). *Activation and Behavior*. New York: Wiley.

Duffy, E. (1972). Activation. In N.S. Greenfield and R.A. Sternbach (Eds), *Handbook of Psychophysiology*. New York: Holt, Rinehart and Winston.

Dusoir, A.E. (1974). Thomas and Legge's matching hypothesis for detection and recognition tasks: two tests. *Perception and Psychophysics*, **16**, 466–470.

Dusoir, A.E. (1975). Treatments of bias in detection and recognition models— review. *Perception and Psychophysics*, **17**, 167–178.

Dykman, R.A., Ackerman, P.T., Clements, S.D. and Peters, J.E. (1971). Specific learning disabilities: an attentional deficit syndrome. In H.R. Mykebust (Ed.), *Progress in Learning Disabilities, Vol. II*. New York: Grune and Stratton.

Dykman, R.A., Ackerman, P.T., Galbrecht, C.R. and Reese, W.G. (1963). Physiological reactivity to different stressors and methods of evaluation. *Psychosomatic Medicine*, **25**, 37–59.

Eason, R.G., Beardshall, A. and Jaffee, S. (1965). Performance and physiological indicants of activation in a vigilance situation. *Perceptual and Motor Skills*, **20**, 3–13.

Easterbrook, J.A. (1959). The effect of emotion on cue utilization and the organization of behavior. *Psychological Review*, **66**, 183–201.

Egan, J.P. (1975). *Signal Detection Theory and ROC Analysis*. New York and London: Academic Press.

Egan, J.P. and Clarke, F.R. (1966). Psychophysics and signal detection. In J.B. Sidowski (Ed.), *Experimental Methods and Instrumentation in Psychology*. New York: McGraw-Hill.

Egan, J.P., Greenberg, G.Z. and Schulman, A.J. (1961). Operating characteristics, signal detectability and the method of free response. *Journal of the Acoustical Society of America*, **33**, 993–1007.

Eisdorfer, C. (1963). The effects of increasing exposure interval on verbal (rote) learning in the aged: Studies II and III. *Excerpta Medica (International Congress Series)*, **57**, 139–140.

Eisdorfer, C. (1965). Verbal learning and response time in the aged. *Journal of Genetic Psychology*, **107**, 15–22.

Eisdorfer, C., Axelrod, S. and Wilkie, F.L. (1963). Stimulus exposure time as a factor in serial learning in an aged sample. *Journal of Abnormal and Social Psychology*, **67**, 594–600.

Elliott, E. (1957). Auditory vigilance tasks. *Advancement of Science*, **13**, 393–399.

Elliott, E. (1960). Perception and alertness. *Ergonomics*, **3**, 357–399.

Embrey, D.E. (1975). Training the inspector's sensitivity and response strategy. In C.G. Drury and J.G. Fox (Eds), *Human Reliability in Quality Control*. London: Taylor and Francis.

Emmerich, D.S. (1968). ROCs obtained with two signal intensities presented in random order, and a comparison between Yes–No and rating ROCs. *Perception and Psychophysics*, **3**, 35–40.

Emmerich, D.S., Gray, J.L., Watson, C.S. and Tanis, D.C. (1972). Response latency, confidence and ROCs in auditory signal detection. *Perception and Psychophysics*, **11**, 65–72.

Ehrlich, P.R. and Ehrlich, A.H. (1970). *Population, Resources and Environment*. San Francisco: Freeman.

Erwin, C.W., Wiener, E.L., Hartwell, J.W., Truscott, T.R. and Linnoila, M.I. (1975). Alcohol effect on vigilance performance. *Paper presented to Automobile Engineering Meeting, Society of Automotive Engineers, Detroit.*

Evans, F.J. (1967). Field dependence and the Maudsley Personality Inventory. *Perceptual and Motor Skills*, **24**, 526.

Eysenck, H.J. (1957). *The Dynamics of Anxiety and Hysteria.* New York: Praeger.

Eysenck, H.J. (1967). *The Biological Basis of Personality.* Springfield, Ill.: Thomas.

Eysenck, M.W. (1977). *Human Memory.* Oxford: Pergamon.

Eysenck, M.W. and Folkard, S. (1980). Personality, time of day and caffeine: Some theoretical and conceptual problems in Revelle *et al. Journal of Experimental Psychology: General*, **109**, 32–41.

Farley, F. and Farley, S.V. (1967). Extraversion and stimulus-seeking motivation. *Journal of Consulting Psychology*, **31**, 215–216.

Faulkner, T.W. (1962). Variability of performance in a vigilance task. *Journal of Applied Psychology*, **46**, 325–328.

Finkelman, J.M. and Glass, D.C. (1970). Reappraisal of the relationship between noise and human performance by means of a subsidiary task measure. *Journal of Applied Psychology*, **54**, 211–213.

Fleishman, E.A. (1967). Performance assessment based on an empirically derived task taxonomy. *Human Factors*, **9**, 349–366.

Fleishman, E.A. (1972). On the relation between abilities, learning and human performance. *American Psychologist*, **27**, 1017–1032.

Fleishman. E.A. (1975a). Toward a taxonomy of human performance. *American Psychologist*, **30**, 1127–1149.

Fleishman, E. (1975b). Taxonomic problems in human performance research. In W.T. Singleton and P. Spurgeon (Eds), *Measurement of Human Resources.* London: Taylor and Francis.

Folkard, S. and Monk, T.H. (1979a). Time of day and processing strategy in free recall. *Quarterly Journal of Experimental Psychology*, **31**, 461–475.

Folkard, S. and Monk, T.H. (1979b). Shiftwork and performance. *Human Factors*, **21**, 483–492.

Folkard, S., Knauth, P., Monk, T.H. and Rutenfranz, J. (1976). The effect of memory load on the circadian variation in performance efficiency under a rapidly rotating shift system. *Ergonomics*, **19**, 479–488.

Folkard, S., Monk, T.H., Bradbury, R. and Rosenthal, J. (1977). Time of day effects in school children's immediate and delayed recall of meaningful material. *British Journal of Psychology*, **68**, 45–50.

Folkard, S., Monk, T.H. and Lobban, M.C. (1979). Towards a predictive test of adjustment to shift work. *Ergonomics*, **22**, 79–91.

Forster, P.M. and Grierson, A.T. (1978). Noise and attentional selectivity: A reproducible phenomenon? *British Journal of Psychology*, **69**, 489–498.

Fox, J.G. (1975). Vigilance and arousal: a key to maintaining inspectors' performance. In C.G. Drury and J.G. Fox (Eds), *Human Reliability in Quality Control.* London: Taylor and Francis.

Fox, J.G. (1977). Quality control of coins. In J.S. Weiner and H.G. Maule (Eds), *Case Studies in Ergonomics Practice. Vol. 1: Human Factors in Work Design and Production.* London: Taylor and Francis.

Fox, J.G. and Embrey, D.E. (1972). Music: an aid to productivity. *Applied Ergonomics*, **3**, 202–205.

Frankenhaeuser, M., Myrsten, A.L. Post, B. and Johanson, G. (1970). Behavioral and physiological effects of cigarette smoking in a monotonous situation. *Department of Psychology, University of Stockholm, Rep.*, No. 301.

Fraser, D.C. (1953). The relation of an environmental variable to performance in a prolonged visual task. *Medical Research Council, Applied Psychology Unit, Rep.*, No. 108/50.

Fraser, D.C. (1957). *Vigilance and Fatigue*. Unpublished Ph.D. thesis, University of Edinburgh.

Freeman, G.L. (1938). The optimal muscular tensions for various performances. *American Journal of Psychology*, **51**, 146–151.

Freeman, G.L. (1940). The relationship between performance level and bodily activity level. *Journal of Experimental Psychology*, **26**, 602–608.

Freeman, P.R. (1973). *Tables of d′ and β*. Cambridge: Cambridge University Press.

Fruhstorfer, H. and Bergstrom, R.M. (1969). Human vigilance and auditory evoked potentials. *Electroencephalography and Clinical Neurophysiology*, **27**, 346–365.

Fruhstorfer, H., Langanke, P., Meinzer, K., Peter, J.H. and Pfaff, U. (1977). Neurophysiological vigilance indicators and operational analysis of a train vigilance device: A laboratory and field study. In R.R. Mackie (Ed.), *Vigilance: Theory, Operational Performance, and Physiological Correlates*. New York: Plenum.

Fuller, R.G.C. and Forrest, D.W. (1973). Behavioural aspects of cigarette smoking in relation to arousal level. *Psychological Reports*, **33**, 115–121.

Galbrecht, C.R., Dykman, R.A., Reese, W.G. and Suzuki, T. (1965). Intrasession adaptation and intrasession extinction of the components of the orienting response. *Journal of Experimental Psychology*, **70**, 585–597.

Gale, A. (1969). "Stimulus hunger": Individual differences in operant strategy in a button-pressing task. *Behaviour Research and Therapy*, **7**, 265–274.

Gale, A. (1973). The psychophysiology of individual differences: Studies of extraversion and the EEG. In P. Kline (Ed.), *New Approaches to Psychological Measurement*. Chichester: Wiley.

Gale, A. (1977). Some EEG correlates of sustained attention. In R.R. Mackie (Ed.), *Vigilance: Theory, Operational Performance, and Physiological Correlates*. New York: Plenum.

Gale, A. and Lynn, R. (1972). A developmental study of attention. *British Journal of Educational Psychology*, **42**, 260–266.

Gale, A., Coles, M.G.H. and Blaydon, J. (1969). Extroversion-introversion and the EEG. *British Journal of Psychology*, **60**, 209–223.

Gale, A., Haslum, M. and Penfold, V. (1971). EEG correlates of cumulative expectancy in a vigilance type task. *Quarterly Journal of Experimental Psychology*, **23**, 245–254.

Gale, A., Harpham, B. and Lucas, B. (1972a). Time of day and the EEG: Some negative results. *Psychonomic Science*, **28**, 269–271.

Gale, A., Morris, P.E., Lucas, B. and Richardson, A. (1972b). Types of imagery and imagery types: An EEG study. *British Journal of Psychology*, **63**, 523–531.

Gale, A., Haslum, M. and Lucas, B. (1972c). Arousal value of the stimulus and EEG abundance in an auditory visual task. *British Journal of Psychology*, **63**, 515–522.

Gale, A., Bull, R., Penfold, V., Coles, M. and Barraclough, R. (1972d). Extroversion, time of day, vigilance performance and physiological arousal: Failure to replicate traditional findings. *Psychonomic Science*, **29**, 1–5.

Gale, A., Davies, R. and Smallbone, A. (1977). EEG correlates of signal rate, time in task, and individual differences in reaction time during a five-stage sustained attention task. *Ergonomics*, **20**, 363–376.

Gange, J.J., Geen, R.G. and Harkins, S.G. (1979). Autonomic differences between extraverts and introverts during vigilance. *Psychophysiology*, **16**, 392–397.

Garvey, W.D., Gulledge, I. and Henson, J.B. (1958). Effect of length of observing time on visual threshold for detecting a faint satellite. *Science*, **127**, 1243–1244.

Gesheider, G.A., Wright, J.H. and Evans, M.B. (1968). Reaction time in the detection of vibrotactile signals. *Journal of Experimental Psychology*, **77**, 501–504.

Gettys, C.F. (1964). The alerted effective threshold in an auditory vigilance task. *Journal of Auditory Research*, **4**, 23–38.

Gevins, A.S., Zeitlein, G.H., Doyle, J.E., Yingling, C.D., Schaffer, R.E., Calloway, E. and Yeager, C.L. (1979). Electroencephalogram correlates of higher cortical functions. *Science*, **203**, 665–668.

Glass, D.C. and Singer, J.E. (1972). *Urban Stress: A Study of the Effects of Noise and other Social Stressors*. New York and London: Academic Press.

Goldwater, B.C. (1972). Psychological significance of pupillary movements. *Psychological Bulletin*, **77**, 340–355.

Grandjean, E. (1979). Fatigue in industry. *British Journal of Industrial Medicine*, **36**, 175–186.

Gray, J.A. (1964). *Pavlov's Typology*. Oxford: Pergamon.

Green, D.M. (1964). General prediction relating Yes–No and forced-choice results. *Journal of the Acoustical Society of America*, **36**, 1042.

Green, D.M. and Swets, J.A. (1966). *Signal Detection Theory and Psychophysics*. New York: Wiley.

Green, D.M. and Swets, J.A. (1974). *Signal Detection Theory and Psychophysics* (Reprint). Huntington, N.Y.: Krieger.

Gregory, R. (1959). Increase in "neurological noise" as a factor in aging. *Proceedings of the Fourth International Congress on Gerontology*, **1**, 314–324.

Grether, W. (1971). Effects on human performance of combined environmental stresses. *U.S. Air Force, Wright Patterson Air Force Base, Dayton, Ohio: Aerospace Medical Research Laboratory Tech. Rep.*, No. 68–70.

Grey, D.R. and Morgan, B.J.T. (1972). Some aspects of ROC curve-fitting: normal and logistic models. *Journals of Mathematical Psychology*, **9**, 128–139.

Grier, J.B. (1971). Non-parametric indexes for sensitivity and bias: computing formulas. *Psychological Bulletin*, **79**, 424–429.

Griew, S. and Davies D.R. (1962). The effect of aging on auditory vigilance performance. *Journal of Gerontology*, **17**, 88–90

Griew, S., Davies, D.R. and Treacher, A. (1963). Heart rate during auditory vigilance performance. *Nature*, **200**, 1026.

Groll, E. (1966). Central nervous system and peripheral activation variables during vigilance performance. *Zeitschrift für Experimentelle und Angewandte Psychologie*, **13**, 248–264. (In German, English summary.)

Groll-Knapp, E., Haider, M., Hoeller, H., Jenkner, H. and Stidl, H.G. (1978). Neuro- and psychophysiological effects of moderate carbon monoxide exposure. In D.A. Otto (Ed.), *Multidisciplinary Perspectives in Event-related Brain Potential Research*. Washington, D.C.: U.S. Environmental Protection Agency.

Groves, P.M. and Thompson, R.F. (1970). Habituation: A dual process theory. *Psychological Review*, **77**, 419–450.

Gruber, A. (1964). Sensory alternation and performance in a vigilance task. *Human Factors*, **6**, 3–12.

Grunzke, M.E., Kirk, R.E. and Fischer, S.C. (1974). Effects of visual and auditory knowledge of results and reward on vigilance performance. *Perceptual and Motor Skills*, **38**, 831–836.

Gulevich, G., Dement, W.C. and Johnson, L.C. (1966). Psychiatric and EEG observations on a case of prolonged (264 hours) wakefulness. *Archives of General Psychiatry*, **15**, 29–35.

Gulian, E. (1970). Effects of noise on arousal in auditory vigilance. *Acta Psychologica*, **33**, 381–393.

Guralnick, M.J. (1972). Observing responses and decision processes in vigilance. *Journal of Experimental Psychology*, **93**, 239–244.

Guralnick, M.J. (1973). Effects of event rate and signal difficulty on observing responses and detection measures. *Journal of Experimental Psychology*, **99**, 261–265.

Guralnick, M.J. and Harvey, K.G. (1970). Response requirement and performance in a visual vigilance task. *Psychonomic Science*, **20**, 215–217.

Gunn, W.J. and Loeb, M. (1967). Correlation of performance in detecting visual and auditory signals. *American Journal of Psychology*, **80**, 236–242.

Haagen-Smit, A.J. (1966). Carbon monoxide levels in city driving. *Archives of Environmental Health*, **12**, 548.

Haider, M., Spong, P. and Lindsley, D.B. (1964). Attention, vigilance and cortical evoked potentials in humans. *Science*, **145**, 180–182.

Hakerem, G. and Sutton, S. (1966). Pupillary response at visual threshold. *Nature*, **212**, 485–486.

Halcomb, C.G. and Blackwell, P.J. (1969). Motivation and the human monitor. I: The effect of contingent credit. *Perceptual and Motor Skills*, **28**, 623–629.

Halcomb, C.G. and Kirk, R.E. (1965a). Organismic variables as predictors of vigilance behaviour. *Perceptual and Motor Skills*, **21**, 547–552.

Halcomb, C.G. and Kirk, R.E. (1965b). Effects of air ionisation upon the performance of a visual task. *Journal of Engineering Psychology*, **4**, 120–126.

Halcomb, C.G., McFarland, B.P. and Waag, W.L. (1970). Motivation and the human monitor. II: Source of instructions. *Perceptual and Motor Skills*, **31**, 145–146.

Hamilton, P. (1969). Selective attention in multisource monitoring tasks. *Journal of Experimental Psychology*, **82**, 34–37.

Hamilton, P., Hockey, G.R.J. and Rejman, M. (1977). The place of the concept of activation in human information processing theory: An integrative approach. In S. Dornic (Ed.), *Attention and Performance, VI*. Hillsdale, New Jersey: Erlbaum.

Hamilton, P., Wilkinson, R.T. and Edwards, R.S. (1972). A study of four days' partial sleep deprivation. In W.P. Colquhoun (Ed.), *Aspects of Human Efficiency*. London: English Universities Press.

Hammerton, M. and Altham, P.M.E. (1971). A non-parametric alternative to d'. *Nature*, **234**, 487–488.

Hardesty, D., Trumbo, D. and Bevan, W. (1963). Influence of knowledge of results on performance in a monitoring task. *Perceptual and Motor Skills*, **16**, 629–634.

Harding, G.F.A. (1974). The visual evoked response. *Advances in Ophthalmology*, **28**, 2–28.

Harkins, S.G. and Geen, R.G. (1975). Discriminability and criterion differences between extraverts and introverts during vigilance. *Journal of Research in Personality*, **9**, 335–340.

Harkins, S.W. (1974). *Aspects of the psychobiology of attention: Visual evoked potentials and performance in a task demanding sustained attention*. Unpublished Ph.D. thesis, University of North Carolina at Chapel Hill.

Harkins, S.W. and Chapman, C.R. (1976). Detection and decision factors in pain perception in young and elderly men. *Pain*, **2**, 253–264.

Harkins, S.W., Nowlin, J.B., Ramm, D. and Schroeder, S. (1974). Effects of age, sex and time-on-watch on a brief continuous performance task. In E. Palmore (Ed.), *Normal Aging Vol. 2*. Durham, North Carolina: Duke University Press.

Harris, D.H. (1968). Effect of defect rate on inspection accuracy. *Journal of Applied Psychology*, **52**, 377–379.

Harris, D.H. (1969). The nature of industrial inspection. *Human Factors*, **11**, 139–148.

Harris, D.H. and Chaney, F.B. (1969). *Human Factors in Quality Assurance*. New York: Wiley.

Hartley, L.R. (1973a). Effect of prior noise or prior performance on serial reaction. *Journal of Experimental Psychology*, **101**, 255–261.

Hartley, L.R. (1973b). Cigarette smoking and stimulus selection. *British Journal of Psychology*, **64**, 593–599.

Hartley, L.R. (1974). A comparison of continuous and distributed sleep schedules. *Quarterly Journal of Experimental Psychology*, **26**, 8–14.

Hartley, L.R. (1981). Noise, attentional selectivity, serial reactions and the need for experimental power. *British Journal of Psychology*, **72**, 101–107.

Hartley, L.R. and Carpenter, A. (1974). Comparison of performance with headphone and free-field noise. *Journal of Experimental Psychology*, **103**, 377–380.

Hartley, L.R. and Williams, T. (1977). Steady state noise and music and vigilance. *Ergonomics*, **20**, 277–285.

Hartley, L.R., Olsson, R. and Ingleby, J.D. (1973). Visual assistance in an auditory detection task. Cited by Poulton (1973a).

Haslum, M.J. and Gale, A. (1973). Inter-modal and intra-subject consistency of EEG abundance gradients in a vigilance task. *Biological Psychology*, **1**, 139–150.

Hastrup, J.L. (1979). Effects of electrodermal lability and introversion on vigilance decrement. *Psychophysiology*, **16**, 302–310.

Hastrup, J.L. and Katkin, E.S. (1976). Electrodermal lability: An attempt to measure its psychological correlates. *Psychophysiology*, **13**, 296–301.

Hatfield, J.L. and Loeb, M. (1968). Sense mode and coupling in a vigilance task. *Perception and Psychophysics*, **4**, 29–36.

Hatfield, J.L. and Soderquist, D.R. (1970). Coupling effects and performance in vigilance tasks. *Human Factors*, **12**, 351–359.

Hauty, G.T. and Payne, R.B. (1955). Mitigation of work decrement. *Journal of Experimental Psychology*, **49**, 60–67.

Hauty, G.T., Payne, R.B. and Bauer, R.O. (1957). Effects of normal air and dextro-amphetamine upon work decrement induced by oxygen impoverishment and fatigue. *Journal of Pharmacology*, **119**, 385–389.

Hawkes, G.R. and Loeb, M. (1961). Vigilance for cutaneous and auditory signals. *Journal of Auditory Research*, **4**, 272–284.

Hawkins, L.H. and Baker, T. (1978). Air ions and human performance. *Ergonomics*, **21**, 273–278.

Hebb, D.O. (1955). Drives and the C.N.S. (Conceptual nervous system). *Psychological Review*, **62**, 243–253.

Hebb, D.O. (1958). *A Textbook of Psychology*. Philadelphia: Saunders.

Helper, M.M. (1957). The effects of noise on work output and physiological activation. *U.S. Army Medical Research Laboratory Rep.*, No. 270.

Henkin, R.I. (1970). The neuroendocrine control of perception. In *Perception and its Disorders*. Research publication ARNMD, 48, 54–107.

Hermann, R. (1977). Two studies for optimising operating bridges and their application in inland- and sea-navigation. In D. Anderson, H. Instance and J. Spencer (Eds), *Human Factors in the Design and Operation of Ships.* London: Taylor and Francis.

Hess, E.H. (1972). Pupillometrics. In N.S. Greenfield and R.A. Sternbach (Eds), *Handbook of Psychophysiology.* New York: Holt, Rinehart and Winston.

Hess, E.H. and Polt, J.M. (1964). Pupil size in relation to mental activity during simple problem-solving. *Science,* **143,** 1190–1192.

Hicks, L.H. and Birren, J.E. (1970). Aging, brain damage, and psychomotor slowing. *Psychological Bulletin,* **74,** 377–396.

Hickey, A.E. and Blair, W.C. (1958). Man as a monitor. *Human Factors,* **1,** 8–15.

Hill, A.B. (1975). Extraversion and variety-seeking in a monotonous task. *British Journal of Psychology,* **66,** 9–13.

Hillyard, S. and Picton, T.W. (1978). Event-related brain potentials and selective information processing in man. In J.E. Desmedt (Ed.), *Progress in Clinical Neurophysiology: Vol. 6: Cognitive Components in Event-related Cerebral Potentials.* Basel: Karger.

Hillyard, S., Hink, R.F., Schwent, V.L. and Picton, T.W. (1973). Electrical signs of selective attention in the human brain. *Science,* **182,** 177–180.

Hillyard, S., Squires, K.C., Bauer, J.W. and Lindsay, P.H. (1971). Evoked potential correlates of auditory signal detection. *Science,* **172,** 1357–1360.

Hink, R.F., Van Voorhis, S.T. and Hillyard, S.A. (1977). The division of attention and the human auditory potential. *Neuropsychologia,* **15,** 597–605.

Hink, R.F., Fenton, W.H., Tinklenberg, J.R., Pfefferbaum, A. and Kopell, B.S. (1978). Vigilance and human attention under conditions of methylphenidate and secobarbital intoxication: An assessment using brain potentials. *Psychophysiology,* **15,** 116–125.

Hockey, G.R.J. (1970a). Effect of loud noise on attentional selectivity. *Quarterly Journal of Experimental Psychology,* **22,** 28–36.

Hockey, G.R.J. (1970b). Signal probability and spatial location as possible bases of increased selectivity in noise. *Quarterly Journal of Experimental Psychology,* **22,** 37–42.

Hockey, G.R.J. (1970c). Changes in attention allocation in a multi-component task under loss of sleep. *British Journal of Psychology,* **61,** 473–480.

Hockey, G.R.J. (1973). Changes in information selection patterns in multisource monitoring as a function of induced arousal shifts. *Journal of Experimental Psychology,* **101,** 35–42.

Hockey, G.R.J. (1978). Attentional selectivity and the problems of replication: A reply to Forster and Grierson. *British Journal of Psychology,* **69,** 499–504.

Hockey, G.R.J. and Colquhoun, W.P. (1972). Diurnal variation in human performance: A review. In W.P. Colquhoun (Ed.), *Aspects of Human Efficiency: Diurnal Rhythm and Loss of Sleep.* London: English Universities Press.

Hockey, G.R.J. and Hamilton, P. (1970). Arousal and information selection in short-term memory. *Nature,* **226,** 866–867.

Hockey, G.R.J., Davies, S. and Gray, M.M. (1972). Forgetting as a function of sleep at different times of day. *Quarterly Journal of Experimental Psychology,* **24,** 386–393.

Hodos, W. (1970). Nonparametric index of response bias for use in detection and recognition experiments. *Psychological Bulletin,* **74,** 351–354.

Hogan, M.J. (1966). Influence of motivation on reactive inhibition in extraversion-introversion. *Perceptual and Motor Skills,* **22,** 187–192.

Holland, J.G. (1957). Technique for behavioral analysis of human observing. *Science*, **125**, 348–350.

Holland, J.G. (1958). Human vigilance. *Science*, **128**, 61–67.

Hord, D., Wilson, C.E., Townsend, R. and Johnson, L.C. (1975). Theta suppression effects on complex visual sonar operation. *Paper presented at the Fifth Annual ARPA Self-Regulation Symposium, Grand Teton, Wyoming*.

Horne, J.A. (1978). A review of the biological effects of total sleep deprivation in man. *Biological Psychology*, **7**, 55–102.

Horne, J.A. and Ostberg, O. (1976). A self-assessment questionnaire to determine morningness—eveningness in human circadian rhythms. *International Journal of Chronobiology*, **4**, 97–110.

Horne, J.A. and Ostberg, O. (1977). Individual differences in human circadian rhythms. *Biological Psychology*, **5**, 179–190.

Horne, J.A., Brass, C.G. and Pettitt, A.N. (1980). Circadian performance differences between morning and evening types. *Ergonomics*, **23**, 29–36.

Horvath, M., Frantick, E., Kopriva, K. and Meissner, J. (1975). EEG theta activity increase coinciding with performance decrement in a monotonous task. *Activitas Nervosa Superior*, **18**, 207–210.

Horvath, S.M., Dahms, T.E. and O'Hanlon, J.F. (1971). Carbon monoxide and human vigilance: a deleterious effect of present urban concentrations. *Archives of Environmental Health*, **23**, 343–349.

Howell, W.C., Johnston, W.A. and Goldstein, I.L. (1966). Complex monitoring and its relation to the classical problems of vigilance. *Organizational Behaviour and Human Performance*, **1**, 129–150.

Howland, D. (1958). An investigation of the performance of the human monitor. *U.S. Air Force, Wright Air Development Center Tech. Rep.*, No. 57–431.

Hunt, E., Lunneborg, C. and Lewis, J. (1975). What does it mean to be high verbal? *Cognitive Psychology*, **7**, 194–227.

Ingham, J.G. (1970). Individual differences in signal detection. *Acta Psychologica*, **34**, 39–50.

Ingleby, J.D. (1968). *Decision-making processes in human perception and memory*. Unpublished Ph.D. thesis, University of Cambridge.

Isreal, J.B., Wickens, C.D., Chesney, G.L. and Donchin, E. (1980). The event-related brain potential as an index of display-monitoring workload. *Human Factors*, **22**, 211–214.

Iversen, S.D. and Iversen, L.L. (1975). *Behavioral Pharmacology*. Oxford: Oxford University Press.

Jacobson, H.J. (1952). A study of inspector accuracy. *Industrial Quality Control*, **9**, 16–25.

James, W. (1890). *Principles of Psychology*. New York: Holt.

Jasper, H.H. (1958). The ten twenty electrode system of the International Federation. *Electroencephalography and Clinical Neurophysiology*, **10**, 371–375.

Jenkins, H.M. (1958). The effects of signal rate on performance in visual monitoring. *American Journal of Psychology*, **71**, 647–651.

Jerison, H.J. (1958). Experiments on vigilance: IV. Duration of vigil and the decrement function. *U.S. Air Force, Wright Air Development Center Tech. Rep.*, No. 58–369.

Jerison, H.J. (1959a). Effects of noise on human performance. *Journal of Applied Psychology*, **43**, 96–101.

Jerison, H.J. (1959b). Experiments on vigilance: V. The empirical model for human vigilance. *U.S. Air Force, Wright Air Development Center, Tech. Rep.*, No. 58–526.

Jerison, H.J. (1963). On the decrement function in human vigilance. In D.N. Buckner and J.J. McGrath (Eds), *Vigilance: A Symposium*. New York: McGraw-Hill.

Jerison, H.J. (1965). Human and animal vigilance. *Perceptual and Motor Skills*, **21**, 580–582.

Jerison, H.J. (1966). Remarks on Colquhoun's "The effect of 'unwanted' signals on performance in a vigilance task". *Ergonomics*, **9**, 413–416.

Jerison, H.J. (1967). Signal detection theory in the analysis of human vigilance. *Human Factors*, **9**, 285–288.

Jerison, H.J. (1970a). Vigilance: A paradigm and some physiological speculations. *Acta Psychologica*, **33**, 367–380.

Jerison, H.J. (1970b). Vigilance, discrimination and attention. In D.I. Mostofsky (Ed.), *Attention: Contemporary Theory and Analysis*. New York: Appleton-Century Crofts.

Jerison, H.J. (1977). Vigilance: Biology, psychology, theory and practice. In R.R. Mackie (Ed.), *Vigilance: Theory, Operational Performance and Physiological Correlates*. New York: Plenum.

Jerison, H.J. and Pickett, R.M. (1964). Vigilance: The importance of the elicited observing rate. *Science*, **143**, 970–971.

Jerison, H.J. and Wallis, R.A. (1957a). Experiments on vigilance: II. One-clock and three-clock monitoring. *U.S. Air Force, Wright Air Development Center, Tech. Rep.*, No. 57–206.

Jerison, H.J. and Wallis, R.A. (1957b). Experiments on vigilance: III. Performance on a simple vigilance task in noise and quiet. *U.S. Air Force, Wright Air Development Center Tech. Rep.*, No. 57–318.

Jerison, H.J. and Wing, S. (1957). Effects of noise and fatigue on a complex visual task. *U.S. Air Force, Wright Air Development Center, Tech. Rep.*, No. 57–14.

Jerison, H.J. and Wing, S. (1961). Human vigilance and operant behavior. *Science*, **133**, 880–881.

Jerison, H.J., Pickett, R.M. and Stenson, H.H. (1965). The elicited observing rate, and decision processes in vigilance. *Human Factors*, **7**, 107–128.

Johnson, E., Smith, S. and Myers, T.I. (1968). Vigilance throughout seven days of sensory deprivation. *Psychonomic Science*, **11**, 293–294.

Johnson, E.H. and Payne, M.C. (1966). Vigilance: Effects of frequency of knowledge of results. *Journal of Applied Psychology*, **50**, 33–34.

Johnson, L.C. (1963). Some attributes of spontaneous electrodermal activity. *Journal of Comparative and Physiological Psychology*, **56**, 415–422.

Johnson, L.C., Slye, E.S. and Dement, W.C. (1965). Electroencephalographic and autonomic activity during and after prolonged sleep deprivation. *Psychosomatic Medicine*, **27**, 415–423.

Johnston, W.A., Howell, W.C. and Williges, R.C. (1969). The components of complex monitoring. *Organizational Behaviour and Human Performance*, **4**, 112–124.

Jones, D.M. (1974). *Time of day and human performance*. Unpublished Ph.D. thesis,

University of Wales.

Jones, D.M., Davies, D.R., Hogan, K.M., Patrick, J. and Cumberbatch, W.G. (1978). Short-term memory during the working day. In M.M. Gruneberg, P.E. Morris and R.N. Sykes (Eds), *Practical Aspects of Memory*. London and New York: Academic Press.

Jones, D.M., Smith, A.P. and Broadbent, D.E. (1979). Effects of moderate intensity noise on the Bakan vigilance task. *Journal of Applied Psychology*, **64**, 627–634.

Jung, R. and Hassler, R. (1960). The extrapyramidal motor system. In J. Field, H.W. Magoun and V.E. Hall (Eds), *Handbook of Physiology, Section 1: Neurophysiology. Vol. III*. Washington, D.C.: American Physiological Society.

Kahneman, D. (1973). *Attention and Effort*. Englewood Cliffs, New Jersey: Prentice-Hall.

Kahneman, D. and Beatty, J. (1966). Pupil diameter and load on memory. *Science*, **154**, 1583–1585.

Kahneman, D. and Beatty, J. (1967). Pupillary responses in a pitch-discrimination task. *Perception and Psychophysics*, **2**, 101–105.

Kano, H. (1971). Psychological aspects of inspection tasks. *Journal of Science of Labour*, **47**, 173–197. (In Japanese.)

Kappauf, W.E. and Payne, M.C. (1959). Performance decrement at an observer paced task. *American Journal of Psychology*, **72**, 443–446.

Kappauf, W.E. and Powe, W.E. (1959). Performance decrement at an audio-visual checking task. *Journal of Experimental Psychology*, **57**, 49–56.

Karlin, L. (1970). Cognition, preparation and sensory-evoked potentials. *Psychological Bulletin*, **73**, 122–136.

Katkin, E.S. and McCubbin, R.J.C. (1969). Habituation of the orienting response as a function of individual differences in anxiety and autonomic lability. *Journal of Abnormal Psychology*, **74**, 54–60.

Keister, M.E. and McLaughlin, R.J. (1972). Vigilance performance related to introversion-extraversion and caffeine. *Journal of Experimental Research in Personality*, **6**, 5–11.

Kennedy, R.S. (1971). Comparison of performance on visual and auditory vigilance tasks. *Human Factors*, **13**, 93–98.

Kennedy, R.S. (1977). The relationship between vigilance and eye movements induced by vestibular stimulation. In R.R. Mackie (Ed.), *Vigilance: Theory, Operational Performance and Physiological Correlates*. New York: Plenum.

Kerr, W.A. (1943). Where they work: Workplace performance of 228 electrical workers in terms of music. *Journal of Applied Psychology*, **27**, 438–442.

Kerr, W.A. (1945). Experiments on the effects of music on factory production. *Applied Psychology Monographs*, No. 5.

Kerr, W.A. (1950). Accident proneness of factory departments. *Journal of Applied Psychology*, **34**, 167–175.

Kibler, A.W. (1965). The relevance of vigilance research to aerospace monitoring tasks. *Human Factors*, **7**, 93–99.

Kibler, A.W. (1968). The relationship between stimulus-oriented changes in heart rate and detection efficiency in a vigilance task. *U.S. Air Force Wright-Patterson Air Force Base, Dayton, Ohio, Aerospace Medical Research Laboratory Tech. Rep.*, No. AMRL–TR–67–233.

Kinchla, R. and Smyzer, F. (1967). A diffusion model of perceptual memory. *Perception and Psychophysics*, **2**, 219–229.

Kirchner, G.L. and Knopf, I.J. (1974). Vigilance performance of second grade children as related to sex and achievement. *Child Development*, **45,** 490–495.

Kirkpatrick, F.H. (1943). Music in industry. *Journal of Applied Psychology*, **27,** 268–274.

Kishida, K. (1973). Temporal change of subsidiary behavior in monotonous work. *Journal of Human Ergology*, **2,** 75–89.

Klein, K.E., Herrman, R., Kuklinski, P. and Wegmann, H.M. (1977). Circadian performance rhythms: Experimental studies in air operations. In R.R. Mackie (Ed.), *Vigilance: Theory, Operational Performance and Physiological Correlates*. New York: Plenum.

Kleitman, N. (1939). *Sleep and Wakefulness* (first edition). Chicago: Chicago University Press.

Kleitman, N. (1963). *Sleep and Wakefulness* (second edition). Chicago: Chicago University Press.

Knopf, I.J. and Mabel, R.M. (1975). Vigilance performance in second graders as a function of interstimulus intervals, socioeconomic levels and reading. *Merrill-Palmer Quarterly of Behavior and Development*, **21,** 195–203.

Koepke, J.E. and Pribram, K.H. (1966). Habituation of GSR as a function of stimulus duration and spontaneous activity. *Journal of Comparative and Physiological Psychology*, **61,** 442–448.

Kopell, S. (1976). Latency function hypothesis and Pike's multiple observations model for latencies in signal-detection. *Psychological Review*, **83,** 308–309.

Koriat. A., Averill, J.R. and Mahlmstrom, E.J. (1973). Individual differences in habituation—some methodological and conceptual issues. *Journal of Research in Personality*, **7,** 88–101.

Kornfeld, C.M. and Beatty, J. (1977). EEG spectra during a long-term compensatory tracking task. *Bulletin of the Psychonomic Society*, **10,** 46–48.

Krulewitz, J.E. and Warm, J.S. (1977). Event rate context in vigilance: Relation to signal probability and expectancy. *Bulletin of the Psychonomic Society*, **10,** 429–432.

Krulewitz, J.E., Warm, J.S. and Wohl, T.H. (1975). Effects of shifts in the rate of repetitive stimulation on sustained attention. *Perception and Psychophysics*, **18,** 245–249.

Krupski, A., Raskin, D.C. and Bakan, P. (1971). Physiological and personality correlates of commission errors in an auditory vigilance task. *Psychophysiology*, **8,** 304–311.

Kryter, K.D. (1970). *The Effects of Noise on Man*. London and New York: Academic Press.

Kupietz, S.S. (1976). Attentiveness in behaviorally deviant and non deviant children. I. Auditory vigilance performance. *Perceptual and Motor Skills*, **43,** 1095–1101.

Lacey, J.I. and Lacey, B.C. (1958). The relationship of resting autonomic activity to motor impulsivity. *Research Publications of the Association for Nervous and Mental Disease*, **36,** 144–209.

Lader, M.H. and Wing, L. (1966). *Physiological Measures, Sedative Drugs and Morbid Anxiety*. Oxford: Oxford University Press.

Laming, D.R.J. (1968). *Information Theory of Choice-reaction Times*. London and New York: Academic Press.

Laming, D.R.J. (1973). *Mathematical Psychology*. London and New York: Academic Press.

Laties, V.G. and Merigan, W.H. (1979). Behavioral effects of carbon monoxide on animals and man. *Annual Review of Pharmacology and Toxicology*, **19,** 357–392.

Lawrence, G.H. (1979). Brain waves and the enhancement of pilot performance. In

B.O. Hartman and R.E. McKenzie (Eds), *Survey of Methods to Assess Workload.* Neuilly-sur-Seine: Nato AGARD Report No. 246.

Lawrence, G.H. and Johnson, L.C. (1977). Biofeedback and performance. In G.E. Schwartz and J. Beatty (Eds), *Biofeedback: Theory and Research.* New York and London: Academic Press.

Layton, B.C. (1975). Perceptual noise and aging. *Psychological Bulletin,* **82,** 875–883.

Lecret, F. and Pottier, M. (1971). Vigilance as a safety indicator in car driving. *Le Travail Humain,* **34,** 51–68. (In French, English summary.)

Lees, F.P. (1973). Quantification of man-machine system reliability in process control. *IEEE Transactions on Reliability,* **R22,** 124–131.

Lees, F.P. and Sayers, B. (1976). The behaviour of process operators under emergency conditions. In T.B. Sheridan and G. Johannsen (Eds), *Monitoring Behavior and Supervisory Control.* New York: Plenum.

Leonard, J.A. (1959). Five-choice serial reaction apparatus. *Medical Research Council Applied Psychology Unit Rep.,* No. 326/59.

Levine, J.M. (1966). The effects of values and costs on the detection and identification of signals in auditory vigilance. *Human Factors,* **8,** 525–537.

Levine, J.M., Romashko, T. and Fleishman, E.A. (1971). *Development of a taxonomy of human performance: Evaluation of an abilities classification system for integrating and generating research findings.* Report No. TR-12. American Institutes for Research, Washington, D.C.

Levine, J.M., Romashko, T. and Fleishman, E.A. (1973). Evaluation of an abilities classification system for integrating and generalizing human performance research findings: An application to vigilance tasks. *Journal of Applied Psychology,* **58,** 149–157.

Lewis, J., Baddeley, A.D., Bonham, K.G. and Lovett, D. (1970). Traffic pollution and mental efficiency. *Nature,* **225,** 95–96.

Lindsley, D.B. (Ed.) (1944). Radar operator "fatigue": the effects of length and repetition of operating periods on efficiency of performance. *Office of Scientific Research and Development Rep.,* No. 33334.

Lindsley, D.B. (1951). Emotion. In S.S. Stevens (Ed.), *Handbook of Experimental Psychology.* New York: Wiley.

Lindsley, D.B. (1952). Psychological phenomena and the electroencephalogram. *Electroencephalography and Clinical Neurophysiology,* **4,** 443–456.

Lindsley, D.B. (1960). Attention, consciousness, sleep and wakefulness. In J. Field, H.W. Magoun and V.E. Hall (Eds), *Handbook of Physiology, Section 1: Neurophysiology. Vol. III.* Washington, D.C.: American Physiological Society.

Lindsley, D.B. and Wicke, J.D. (1974). The electroencephalogram: Autonomous electrical activity in man and animals. In R.F. Thompson and M.M. Patterson (Eds), *Biolectrical Recording Techniques, Part B: Electroencephalography and Human Brain Potentials.* New York and London: Academic Press.

Link, S.W. and Heath, R.A. (1975). Sequential theory of psychological discrimination. *Psychometrika,* **40,** 77–105.

Lisper, H.O., Kjellberg, A. and Melin, A. (1972). Effects of signal intensity on increase of reaction time in an auditory monitoring task. *Perceptual and Motor Skills,* **34,** 439–444.

Loeb, M. and Alluisi, E.A. (1977). An update of findings regarding vigilance and a reconsideration of underlying mechanisms. In R.R. Mackie (Ed.), *Vigilance: Theory, Operational Performance and Physiological Correlates.* New York: Plenum.

Loeb, M. and Binford, J.R. (1963). Some factors affecting the effective auditory intensive difference limen. *Journal of the Acoustical Society of America,* **35,** 884–891.

Loeb, M. and Binford, J.R. (1964). Vigilance for auditory intensity changes as a function of preliminary feedback and confidence level. *Human Factors*, **7**, 445–458.

Loeb, M. and Binford, J.R. (1968). Variation in performance on auditory and visual monitoring tasks as a function of signal and stimulus frequencies. *Perception and Psychophysics*, **4**, 361–366.

Loeb, M. and Binford, J.R. (1971). Modality, difficulty and coupling in vigilance behaviour. *American Journal of Psychology*, **84**, 529–541.

Loeb, M. and Hawkes, G.R. (1962). Detection of differences in duration of acoustic and electrical cutaneous signals in a vigilance task. *Journal of Psychology*, **54**, 101–111.

Loeb, M. and Jones, P.D. (1978). Noise exposure, monitoring and tracking performance as a function of signal bias and task priority. *Ergonomics*, **21**, 265–272.

Loeb, M. and Schmidt, E.A. (1963). A comparison of the effects of different kinds of information in maintaining efficiency on an auditory monitoring task. *Ergonomics*, **6**, 75–82.

Loeb, M., Hawkes, G.R., Evans, W.O. and Alluisi, E.A. (1965). The influence of d-amphetamine, benactyzine, and chlorpromazine on performance in an auditory vigilance task. *Psychonomic Science*, **3**, 29–30.

Loveless, N.E. (1976). Distribution of response to non-signal stimuli. In W.C. McCallum and J.R. Knott (Eds). *The Responsive Brain*. Bristol: John Wright.

Loveless, N.E., Brebner, J. and Hamilton, P. (1970). Bisensory presentation of information. *Psychological Bulletin*, **73**, 161–199.

Lowenstein, O. (1920). Experimentelle Beiträge zur Lehre von den Katatonischen Pupillenveranderungen. *Monatsschrift für Psychiatrie und Neurologie*, **47**, 194–215.

Lucaccini, L.F. (1968). *Vigilance and irrelevant stimulation: A test of the arousal hypothesis*. Unpublished Ph.D. thesis, University of California at Los Angeles.

Lucaccini, L.F., Freedy, A. and Lyman, J. (1968). Motivational factors in vigilance: effects of instructions on performance in a complex vigilance task. *Perceptual and Motor Skills*, **26**, 783–786.

Luce, R.D. (1963). A threshold theory for simple detection experiments. *Psychological Review*, **70**, 61–79.

Luce, R.D. and Green, D.M. (1974). Detection, discrimination and recognition. In: E.C. Carterette and M.P. Friedman (Eds), *Handbook of Perception, Vol. 2*. New York and London: Academic Press.

Luce, T.S. (1964). Vigilance as a function of stimulus variety and response complexity. *Human Factors*, **6**, 101–110.

McCallum, W.C. (1976). Brain slow potential changes and motor response in a vigilance situation. In: W.C. McCallum and J.R. Knott (Eds), *The Responsive Brain*. Bristol: John Wright.

McCormack, P.D. (1958). Performance in a vigilance task as a function of interstimulus interval and interpolated rest. *Canadian Journal of Psychology*, **12**, 242–246.

McCormack, P.D. (1959). Performance in a vigilance task with and without knowledge of results. *Canadian Journal of Psychology*, **13**, 68–71.

McCormack, P.D. (1960). Performance in a vigilance task as a function of length of inter-stimulus interval. *Canadian Journal of Psychology*, **14**, 265–268.

McCormack, P.D. (1962). A two-factor theory of vigilance. *British Journal of Psychology*, **53**, 357–363.

McCormack, P.D. (1967). A two-factor theory of vigilance in the light of recent studies. In: A.F. Sanders (Ed.), *Attention and Performance: I*. Amsterdam: North Holland.

McCormack, P.D. and McElheran, W.G. (1963). Follow-up of effects on reaction time with partial knowledge of results. *Perceptual and Motor Skills*, **17**, 565–566.

McCormack, P.D. and Prysiazniuk, A.W. (1961). Reaction time and regularity of inter-stimulus interval. *Perceptual and Motor Skills*, **13**, 15–18.

McCormack, P.D., Binding, F.R.S. and Chylinski, J. (1962). Effects on reaction-time of knowledge of results of performance. *Perceptual and Motor Skills*, **14**, 367–372.

McCormack, P.D., Binding, F.R.S. and McElheran, W.G. (1963). Effects on reaction time of partial knowledge of results of performance. *Perceptual and Motor Skills*, **17**, 279–281.

McDonald, R.D. and Burns, S.B. (1964). Visual vigilance and brain damage: An empirical study. *Journal of Neurology, Neurosurgery and Psychiatry*, **27**, 206–209.

McFarland, R.A., Holway, A.N. and Hurvich, L.M. (1942). *Studies of Visual Fatigue*. Harvard Graduate School of Business Administration Report.

McFarling, L.H. and Heimstra, N.W. (1975). Pacing, product complexity and task perception in simulated inspection. *Human Factors*, **17**, 361–367.

McGehee, W. and Gardiner, J.E. (1949). Music in a complex industrial job. *Personnel Psychology*, **2**, 405–417.

McGrath, J.J. (1960). The effect of irrelevant environmental stimulation on vigilance performance. *Human Factor Problems in Anti Submarine Warfare, Tech. Rep.*, No. 6. Los Angeles: Human Factors Research Inc.

McGrath, J.J. (1963a). Some problems of definition and criteria in the study of vigilance performance. In: D.N. Buckner and J.J. McGrath (Eds), *Vigilance: A Symposium*. New York: McGraw-Hill.

McGrath, J.J. (1963b). Cross-validation of some correlates of vigilance performance. In D.N. Buckner and J.J. McGrath (Eds), *Vigilance: A Symposium*. New York: McGraw-Hill.

McGrath, J.J. (1963c). Irrelevant stimulation and vigilance performance. In D.N. Buckner and J.J. McGrath (Eds), *Vigilance: A Symposium*. New York: McGraw-Hill.

McGrath, J.J. and O'Hanlon, J. (1967). Temporal orientation and vigilance performance. In A.F. Sanders (Ed.), *Attention and Performance: I*. Amsterdam: North Holland.

McGrath, J.J., Harabedian, A. and Buckner, D.N. (1960). *Review and Critique of the Literature on Vigilance Performance. Tech. Rep.*, No. 1. Los Angeles: Human Factors Research Inc.

McKenzie, R.M. (1958). On the accuracy of inspectors. *Ergonomics*, **1**, 258–272.

McNicol, D. (1972). *A Primer of Signal Detection Theory*. London: Allen and Unwin.

MacDonald, R.R. (1976). The effect of sequential dependancies on some signal detection parameters. *Quarterly Journal of Experimental Psychology*, **28**, 643–652.

MacFarland, B.P. and Halcomb, C.G. (1970). Expectancy and stimulus generalization in vigilance. *Perceptual and Motor Skills*, **30**, 147–151.

Mackie, R.R. (1977). Introduction, In R.R. Mackie (Ed.), *Vigilance: Theory, Operational Performance and Physiological Correlates*. New York: Plenum.

Mackie, R.R. and O'Hanlon, J.F. (1977). A study of the combined effects of extended driving and heat stress on driver arousal and performance. In R.R. Mackie (Ed.), *Vigilance: Theory, Operational Performance and Physiological Correlates*. New York: Plenum.

Mackworth, J.F. (1964a). The effect of true and false knowledge of results on the detectability of signals in a vigilance task. *Canadian Journal of Psychology*, **18**, 106–117.

Mackworth, J.F. (1964b). Performance decrement in vigilance, threshold and high speed perceptual-motor tasks. *Canadian Journal of Psychology*, **18**, 209–224.

Mackworth, J.F. (1965a). Deterioration of signal detectability during a vigilance task as a function of background event rate. *Psychonomic Science*, **3**, 421–422.

Mackworth, J.F. (1965b). Decision interval and signal detectability during a vigilance task. *Canadian Journal of Psychology*, **19**, 111–117.

Mackworth, J.F. (1965c). Effect of amphetamine on the detectability of signals in a vigilance task. *Canadian Journal of Psychology*, **19**, 104–110.

Mackworth, J.F. (1968a). Effect of signal rate on performance in two kinds of vigilance task. *Human Factors*, **10**, 11–17.

Mackworth, J.F. (1968b). Vigilance, arousal and habituation. *Psychological Review*, **75**, 308–322.

Mackworth, J.F. (1969). *Vigilance and Habituation: A Neuropsychological Approach.* Harmondsworth: Penguin.

Mackworth, J.F. (1970). *Vigilance and Attention: A Signal Detection Approach.* Harmondsworth: Penguin.

Mackworth, J.F. and Taylor, M.M. (1963). The d' measure of signal detectability in vigilance-like situations. *Canadian Journal of Psychology*, **17**, 302–325.

Mackworth, N.H. (1944). Notes on the Clock Test—A new approach to the study of prolonged perception to find the optimum length of watch for radar operators. *Air Ministry F.P.R.C. Report*, No. 586.

Mackworth, N.H. (1948). The breakdown of vigilance during prolonged visual search. *Quarterly Journal of Experimental Psychology*, **1**, 6–21.

Mackworth, N.H. (1950). Researches on the measurement of human performance. *Medical Research Council Special Report*, No. 268. London: H.M.S.O.

Mackworth, N.H. (1957). Some factors affecting vigilance. *Advancement of Science*, **53**, 389–393.

Mackworth, N.H., Kaplan, I.T. and Metlay, W. (1964). Eye movements during vigilance. *Perceptual and Motor Skills*, **18**, 397–402.

Magoun, H.W. (1958). *The Waking Brain.* Springfield, Ill.: Thomas.

Malmo, R.B. (1959). Activation: A neuropsychological dimension. *Psychological Review*, **66**, 367–386.

Malmo, R.B. and Shagass, C.G. (1949). Physiological studies of reaction to stress in anxiety states and early schizophrenia. *Psychosomatic Medicine*, **11**, 9–24.

Mangan, G.L. and O'Gorman, J.G. (1969). Initial amplitude and rate of habituation of orienting reaction in relation to extraversion and neuroticism. *Journal of Experimental Research in Personality*, **3**, 275–282.

Markowitz, J. and Swets, J.A. (1967). Factors affecting the slope of empirical ROC curves: comparison of binary and rating responses. *Perception and Psychophysics*, **2**, 91–100.

Marsh, G.R. and Thompson, L.W. (1977). Psychophysiology of aging. In: J.E. Birren and K.W. Schaie (Eds), *Handbook of the Psychology of Aging.* New York: Van Nostrand.

Martz, R.L. and Harris, J.D. (1961). Signal presentation rate and auditory vigilance. *Journal of the Acoustical Society of America*, **33**, 855.

Mast, T.M. and Heimstra, N.W. (1964). Effects of fatigue on vigilance performance. *Journal of Engineering Psychology*, **3**, 73–79.

Masterton, J.P. (1965). Patterns of sleep. In O.G. Edholm and A.L. Bacharach (Eds), *Physiology of Human Survival.* London and New York: Academic Press.

Megaw, E.D. (1977). The analysis of visual search strategies to improve industrial inspection. *Progress Report to the U.K. Science Research Council*, Contract No. B/RG/7380.

Meister, D. (1976). *Behavioral Foundations of System Development.* New York: Wiley.

Metzger, K.R., Warm, J.S. and Senter, R.J. (1974). Effects of background event rate and artificial signals on vigilance performance. *Perceptual and Motor Skills*, **38**,

1175–1181.

Miller, E. (1972). *Clinical Neuropsychology*. Harmondsworth: Penguin Books.

Mills, R. and Sinclair, M.A. (1976). Aspects of inspection in a knitwear company. *Applied Ergonomics*, **7**, 97–107.

Milner, A.D., Walker, V.J. and Beech, H.R. (1967). Obsessional behavior and decision-making—a signal detection approach. Unpublished paper cited by Craik (1966).

Milosevic, S. (1969). Signal detection as a function of the response criterion *Le Travail Humain*, **32**, 81–86. (In French, English summary.)

Milosevic, S. (1974). Effect of time and space uncertainty on a vigilance task. *Perception and Psychophysics*, **15**, 331–334.

Milosevic, S. (1975). Changes in detection measures and skin resistance during an auditory visual task. *Ergonomics*, **18**, 1–18.

Mirsky, A.F. and Cardon, P.V. (1962). A comparison of the behavioural and physiological changes accompanying sleep deprivation and chloropromazine administration in man. *EEG and Clinical Neurophysiology*, **14**, 1–10.

Mirsky, A.F. and Rosvold, H.E. (1960). The use of psychoactive drugs as a neuro-psychological tool in studies of attention in man. In: J.G. Miller and L. Uhr (Eds), *Drugs and Behavior*. New York: Wiley.

Mirsky, A.F., Primac, D.W., Ajmone-Marsan, C., Rosvold, H.E. and Stevens, J.R. (1960). A comparison of the psychological test performance of patients with focal and non-focal epilepsy. *Experimental Neurology*, **2**, 75–89.

Montague, W.E. and Webber, C.E. (1965). Effects of knowledge of results and differential monetary reward on six uninterrupted hours of monitoring. *Human Factors*, **7**, 173–180.

Montague, W.E., Webber, C.E. and Adams, J.A. (1965). The effects of signal and response complexity on 18 hours of visual monitoring. *Human Factors*, **7**, 163–172.

Monty, R.A. (1962). Effects of post-detection response complexity on subsequent monitoring behaviour. *Human Factors*, **4**, 201–207.

Monty, R.A. (1973). Keeping track of sequential events: Implications for the design of displays. *Ergonomics*, **16**, 443–454.

Moore, S.F. and Gross, S.J. (1973). Influence of critical signal regularity, stimulus event matrix and cognitive style on vigilance performance. *Journal of Experimental Psychology*, **99**, 137–139.

Moray, N. (1969). *Attention: Selective Processes in Vision and Hearing*. London: Hutchinson.

Morgan, B.B. and Alluisi, E.A. (1972). Synthetic work: Methodology for assessment of human performance. *Perceptual and Motor Skills*, **35**, 835–845.

Morgan, B.B., Brown, B.R. and Alluisi, E.A. (1970). Effects of 48 hours of continuous work and sleep loss on sustained performance. *University of Louisville Performance Research Laboratory Rep.*, No. ITR–70–16.

Morgan, B.B., Brown, B.R. and Alluisi, E.A. (1974). Effects on sustained performance of 48 hours of continuous work and sleep loss. *Human Factors*, **16**, 406–414.

Morgan, B.B. and Coates, G.D. (1975). *Enhancement of performance during sustained operations through the use of EEG and heart rate autoregulation* (Annual Progress Report under Contract No. 0014–70–C–0350 submitted to San Diego State University Foundation). Norfolk, Va.: Old Dominion University.

Morris, P.E. and Gale, A. (1974). A correlational study of variables related to imagery. *Perceptual and Motor Skills*, **38**, 659–665.

Moscovitch, M. (1976). Representation of language in right hemisphere of right-handed people. *Brain and Language*, **3**, 47–71.

Moskowitz, H. and Depry, D. (1968). Differential effects of alcohol on auditory vigilance and divided attention. *Quarterly Journal of Studies on Alcohol*, **29**, 54–63.

Mullin, J. and Corcoran, D.W.J. (1977). Interaction of task amplitude with circadian variation in auditory vigilance performance. *Ergonomics*, **20**, 193–200.

Murray, E.J., Williams, H.L. and Lubin, A. (1958). Body temperature and psychological ratings during sleep deprivation. *Journal of Experimental Psychology*, **56**, 204–210.

Murrell, G.A. (1975). A reappraisal of artificial signals as an aid to a visual monitoring task. *Ergonomics*, **18**, 693–700.

Myers, T.I., Murphy, D.B., Smith, S. and Coffard, S.J. (1966). Experimental studies of sensory deprivation and social isolation. *Human Resources Research Office Tech. Rep.*, No. 66–8. Alexandria, Va.

Naatanen, R. and Michie, P.T. (1979). Early selective attention effects on the evoked potential: A critical review and reinterpretation. *Biological Psychology*, **8**, 81–136.

Nachmias, J. (1968). Effects of presentation probability and number of response alternatives on simple visual detection. *Perception and Psychophysics*, **3**, 151–155.

Nachreiner, F. (1977). Experiments on the validity of vigilance experiments. In R.R. Mackie (Ed.), *Vigilance: Theory, Operational Performance and Physiological Correlates*. New York: Plenum.

Naitoh, P. (1975). Sleep deprivation in humans. In P.H. Venables and M.J. Christie (Eds), *Research in Psychophysiology*. Chichester: Wiley.

Naitoh, P., Kales, A., Kollar, E.J., Smith, J.C. and Jacobson, A. (1969). Electroencephalographic activity after prolonged sleep loss. *Electroencephalography and Clinical Neurophysiology*, **27**, 2–11.

Neal, G.L. (1967). Some effects of differential pretask instructions on auditory vigilance performance. *Paper presented at the South-Western Psychological Association Meeting, Houston, Texas.*

Neal, G.L. and Pearson, R.G. (1966). Comparative effects of age, sex and drugs upon two tasks of auditory vigilance. *Perceptual and Motor Skills*, **23**, 967–974.

Newman, R.I., Hunt, D.L. and Rhodes, F. (1966). Effects of music on employee attitude and productivity in a skateboard factory. *Journal of Applied Psychology*, **50**, 493–496.

News and Comment, Science (1979). I.Q. Tests for reactor operators. *Science*, **204**, 1285.

Noland, E.C. and Schuldt, W.J. (1971). Sustained attention and reading retardation. *Journal of Experimental Education*, **40**, 73–76.

Norman, D.A. and Bobrow, D.G. (1975). On data-limited and resource-limited processes. *Cognitive Psychology*, **7**, 44–64.

Norman, D.A. and Wickelgren, W.A. (1969). Strength theory of decision rules and latency in retrieval from short-term memory. *Journal of Mathematical Psychology*, **6**, 192–208.

O'Hanlon, J. (1964). Adrenaline, noradrenaline and performance in a visual vigilance task. *Human Factors Research Inc. (Los Angeles) Rep.*, No. 750–755.

O'Hanlon, J.F. (1965). Adrenaline and noradrenaline: Relation to performance in a visual vigilance task. *Science*, **150**, 507–509.

O'Hanlon, J.F. (1970). Vigilance, the plasma catecholamines, and related biochemical and physiological variables. *Human Factors Research Inc. Tech. Rep.*, No 787–2. Goleta, California.

O'Hanlon, J.F. (1971). Heart rate variability: A new index of driver alertness/fatigue. *Human Factors Research Inc. Tech. Rep.*, No. 1712–1. Goleta,

O'Hanlon, J.F. (1975). Preliminary studies of the effects of carbon monoxide on vigilance in man. In B. Weiss and V.G. Laties (Eds), *Behavioral Toxicology*. New York: Plenum.

O'Hanlon, J.F. and Beatty, J. (1976). Catecholamine correlates of radar monitoring performance. *Biological Psychology*, **4**, 293–304.

O'Hanlon, J.F. and Beatty, J. (1977). Concurrence of electroencephalographic and performance changes during a simulated radar watch and some implications for the arousal theory of vigilance. In R.R. Mackie (Ed.), *Vigilance: Theory, Operational Performance and Physiological Correlates*. New York: Plenum.

O'Hanlon, J.F. and Horvath, S.M. (1973a). Neuroendocrine, cardio-respiratory and performance reactions of hypoxic men during a monitoring task. *Aerospace Medicine*, **44**, 129–134.

O'Hanlon, J.F. and Horvath, S.M. (1973b). Interrelationships among performance, circulating concentrations of adrenaline, noradrenaline and the free fatty acids in men performing a monitoring task. *Psychophysiology*, **10**, 251–259.

O'Hanlon, J.F. and Kelly, G.R. (1977). Comparison of performance and physiological changes between drivers who perform well and poorly during prolonged vehicular operation. In R.R. Mackie (Ed.), *Vigilance: Theory, Operational Performance and Physiological Correlates*. New York: Plenum.

O'Hanlon, J.F., Schmidt, A. and Baker, C.H. (1964). A study to determine the effect of placebos upon performance in a vigilance task. *Human Factors Research Inc. (Los Angeles) Rep.*, No. 750–753.

O'Hanlon, J.F., Royal, J.W. and Beatty, J. (1977). Theta regulation and radar vigilance performance. In J. Beatty and H. Legewie (Eds), *Biofeedback and Behavior*. New York: Plenum.

O'Neill, D.M. (1966). Music to enhance the work environment. *Management of Personnel Quarterly*, **5**, 17–23.

Orris, J.B. (1969). Visual monitoring performance in 3 subgroups of male delinquents. *Journal of Abnormal Psychology*, **74**, 227–229.

Osborn, W.C., Sheldon, R.W. and Baker, R.A. (1963). Vigilance performance under conditions of redundant and non-redundant presentation. *Journal of Applied Psychology*, **47**, 130–134.

Oswald, I. (1962). *Sleeping and Waking*. Amsterdam: Elsevier.

Parasuraman, R. (1975). Response bias and physiological reactivity. *Journal of Psychology*, **91**, 309–313.

Parasuraman, R. (1976a). *Task classification and decision Processes in monitoring behaviour*. Unpublished Ph.D. Thesis, University of Aston in Birmingham.

Parasuraman, R. (1976b). Consistency of individual differences in human vigilance performance: An abilities classification analysis. *Journal of Applied Psychology*, **61**, 486–492.

Parasuraman, R. (1978). Auditory evoked potentials and divided attention. *Psychophysiology*, **15**, 460–465.

Parasuraman, R. (1979). Memory load and event rate control sensitivity decrements in sustained attention. *Science*, **205**, 924–927.

Parasuraman, R. and Beatty, J. (1979). Event-related potentials in detection and recognition. *Paper presented at the Annual Meeting of the Society for Psychophysiological Research, Cincinnati, Ohio*.

Parasuraman, R. and Davies, D.R. (1975). Response and evoked potential latencies associated with commission errors in visual monitoring. *Perception and Psychophysics*, **17**, 465–468.

Parasuraman, R. and Davies, D.R. (1976). Decision theory analysis of response latencies in vigilance. *Journal of Experimental Psychology: Human Perception and Performance*, **2**, 578–590.

Parasuraman, R. and Davies, D.R. (1977). A taxonomic analysis of vigilance performance. In R.R. Mackie (Ed.), *Vigilance: Theory, Operational Performance and Physiological Correlates*. New York: Plenum.

Parks, T.E. (1966). Signal-detectability theory of recognition memory performance. *Psychological Review*, **73**, 44–58.

Paul, D.D. and Sutton, S. (1972). Evoked potential correlates of response criterion in auditory signal detection. *Science*, **177**, 362–364.

Patrick, G.T.W. and Gilbert, J.A. (1896). On the effects of loss of sleep. *Psychological Review*, **3**, 469–483.

Pavlov, I. (1927). *Conditioned Reflexes* (translated by G.V. Anrep). London: Oxford University Press.

Payne, R.B. and Hauty, G.T. (1954). The effect of experimentally induced attitudes upon task proficiency. *Journal of Experimental Psychology*, **47**, 267–273.

Pearson, R.G. (1968). Alcohol-hypoxia effects on operator tracking, monitoring and reaction. *Aerospace Medicine*, **39**, 303–307.

Peck, A.W., Adams, R., Bye, C. and Wilkinson, R.T. (1976). Residual effects of hypnotic drugs: Evidence for individual differences in vigilance. *Psychopharmacology*, **47**, 213–216.

Pepler, R.D. (1953). The effect of climatic factors on the performance of skilled tasks by young European men living in the tropics: A task of prolonged visual vigilance. *Medical Research Council, Applied Psychology Unit Rep.*, No. 156–53.

Perkoff, G.T., Eik-nes, K., Nugent, C.A., Fred, H.L., Nimmer, R.A., Rush, L., Samuels, N.T. and Tyler, F.H. (1959). Studies of the diurnal variation of plasma 17-hydroxycortico steroids in man. *Journal of Clinical Endocrinology and Metabolism*, **19**, 432–443.

Peterson, W.W., Birdsall, T.G. and Fox, W.C. (1954). The theory of signal detectability. *Transactions of the IRE Professional Group on Information Theory, PGIT–4*, 171–212.

Pickett, R.M. (1978). Personal communication.

Pigache, R.M. (1976). Comparison of scoring methods for tests of attention, including an error index for use with schizophrenic patients. *Perceptual and Motor Skills*, **42**, 243–253.

Pike, R. (1973). Response latency models for signal detection. *Psychological Review*, **80**, 53–68.

Pollack, I. and Norman, D.A. (1964). A nonparametric analysis of recognition experiments. *Psychonomic Science*, **1**, 125–126.

Poock, G. and Wiener, E.L. (1966). Music and other auditory backgrounds during visual monitoring. *Journal of Industrial Engineering*, **17**, 318–323.

Poock, G.K., Tuck, G.A. and Tinsley, J.H. (1969). Physiological correlates of visual monitoring. *Perceptual and Motor Skills*, **29**, 334.

Pope, L.T. and McKechnie, D.F. (1963). Correlation between visual and auditory vigilance performance. *U.S. Air Force, Aerospace Medical Research Laboratory Tech. Rep.*, No. TR–63–57.

Posner, M. (1975). Psychobiology of attention. In M. Gazzaniga and C. Blakemore (Eds), *Handbook of Psychobiology*. New York and London: Academic Press.

Poulton, E.C. (1960). The optimal perceptual load in a paced auditory inspection task. *British Journal of Psychology*, **51**, 127–139.

Poulton, E.C. (1965). On increasing the sensitivity of measures of performance. *Ergonomics*, **8**, 69–76.

Poulton, E.C. (1970). *Environment and Human Efficiency*. Springfield, Ill.: Thomas.

Poulton, E.C. (1973a). The effects of fatigue upon inspection work. *Applied Ergonomics*, **4**, 73–83.

Poulton, E.C. (1973b). Unwanted range effects from using within-subject experimental designs. *Psychological Bulletin*, **80**, 113–121.

Poulton, E.C. (1976). Continuous noise interferes with work by masking auditory feedback and inner speech. *Applied Ergonomics*, **7**, 79–84.

Poulton, E.C. (1977a). Arousing stresses increase vigilance. In R.R. Mackie (Ed.), *Vigilance: Theory, Operational Performance and Physiological Correlates*. New York: Plenum.

Poulton, E.C. (1977b). Continuous noise masks auditory feedback and inner speech. *Psychological Bulletin*, **84**, 977–1001.

Poulton, E.C. (1978). A new look at the effects of noise: a rejoinder. *Psychological Bulletin*, **85**, 1068–1075.

Poulton, E.C. and Edwards, R.S. (1974a). Interactions and range effects in experiments on pairs of stresses: mild heat and low-frequency noise. *Journal of Experimental Psychology*, **102**, 621–626.

Poulton, E.C. and Edwards, R.S. (1974b). Interactions, range effects and comparisons between tasks in experiments measuring performance with pairs of stresses: mild heat and 1 mg. of L-hyoscine hydrobromide. *Aerospace Medicine*, **45**, 735–741.

Poulton, E.C. and Freeman, P.R. (1966). Unwanted asymmetrical transfer effects with balanced experimental designs. *Psychological Bulletin*, **66**, 1–8.

Poulton, E.C. and Kerslake, D. McK. (1965). Initial stimulating effect of warmth upon perceptual efficiency. *Aerospace Medicine*, **36**, 29–32.

Poulton, E.C., Edwards, R.S. and Colquhoun, W.P. (1974). The interaction of the loss of a night's sleep with mild heat: Task variables. *Ergonomics*, **17**, 59–73.

Poulton, E.C., Hitchings, N.B. and Brooke, R.B. (1965). Effect of cold and rain on the vigilance of lookouts. *Ergonomics*, **8**, 163–168.

Price, R.L. and Smith, D.B.D. (1974). The P3(00) wave of the average evoked potential: A bibliography. *Physiological Psychology*, **2**, 387–391.

Primac, D.W., Mirsky, A.F. and Rosvold, H.E. (1957). Effects of centrally acting drugs on two tests of brain damage. *Archives of Neurology and Psychiatry*, **77**, 328–332.

Purohit, A.K. (1972). Personality types and signal detection. *Indian Journal of Psychology*, **47**, 161–165.

Putz, V.R. (1975). The effects of different modes of supervision on vigilance behaviour. *British Journal of Psychology*, **66**, 157–160.

Putz, V.R. (1979). Effects of carbon-monoxide on dual-task performance. *Human Factors*, **21**, 13–24.

Rees, J.N. and Botwinick, J. (1971). Detection and decision factors in auditory behavior of the elderly. *Journal of Gerontology*, **26**, 133–136.

Revelle, W., Humphreys, M.S., Simon, L. and Gilliland, K. (1980). The interactive effect of personality, time of day, and caffeine: A test of the arousal model. *Journal of Experimental Psychology: General*, **109**, 1–31.

Riemersma, J.B.J., Sanders, A.F., Wildervanck, C. and Gaillard, A.W. (1977). Performance decrement during prolonged night driving. In R.R. Mackie (Ed.), *Vigilance: Theory, Operational Performance, and Physiological Correlates*. New York: Plenum.

Ritter, W. and Vaughan, M.G. (1969). Averaged evoked responses in vigilance and discrimination: A reassessment. *Science*, **164**, 326–328.

Ritter, W., Vaughan, M.G. and Costa, L.O. (1968). Orienting and habituation to auditory stimuli: A study of short term changes in average evoked responses. *Electroencephalography and Clinical Neurophysiology*, **25**, 550–556.

Rizy, E.F. (1972). Effect of decision parameters on a detection/localization paradigm quantifying sonar operator performance. *Office of Naval Research Engineering Psychology Program Rep.*, No. R–1156.

Rodin, R.A., Luby, E.D. and Gottlieb, J.S. (1962). The electroencephalogram during prolonged experimental sleep deprivation. *Electroencephalography and Clinical Neurophysiology*, **14**, 544–551.

Rohrbaugh, J.W., Donchin, E. and Eriksen, C.W. (1974). Decision making and the P300 component of the cortical evoked response. *Perception and Psychophysics*, **15**, 368–374.

Rohrbaugh, J.W., Syndulko, K. and Lindsley, D.B. (1978). Electrocortical negative waves following unpaired stimuli. I: Effects of task variables. *Electroencephalography and Clinical Neurophysiology*, **45**, 551–567.

Rosvold, H.E., Mirsky, A.F., Sarason, I., Bransome, E.D. and Beck, L.N. (1956). A continuous performance test of brain damage. *Journal of Consulting Psychology*, **20**, 343–350.

Roth, W.T. and Kopell, B.S. (1969). The auditory evoked response to repeated stimuli during a vigilance task. *Psychophysiology*, **6**, 301–309.

Saito, M. (1972). A study on bottle inspection speed—determination of appropriate work speed by means of electro-nystagmography. *Journal of Science of Labour*, **48**, 395–400. (In Japanese.)

Saito, M. and Tanaka, T. (1977). Visual bottle inspection performance in highly paced belt-conveyor systems. *Journal of Human Ergology*, **6**, 127–137.

Saito, H., Endo, Y., Kishida, K. and Saito, M. (1972a). Studies on monotonous work (III): On the optimum conveyor line speed in empty bottle inspection. *Journal of Science of Labour*, **48**, 239–259. (In Japanese, English summary.)

Saito, H., Kishida, K., Endo, Z. and Saito, M. (1972b). Studies on bottle inspection tasks. *Journal of Science of Labour*, **48**, 475–525. (In Japanese, English summary.)

Sakitt, B. (1973). Indices of discriminability. *Nature*, **241**, 133–134.

Sayers, B., Beagley, H.A. and Henshall, W.R. (1974). The mechanisms of auditory evoked responses. *Nature*, **247**, 481–483.

Schmidtke, H. (1966). *Leistungsbeeinflussende Faktoren im Radar-Beobachtungstdienst*. Köln: Opladen.

Schmidtke, H. (1976). Vigilance. In E. Simonson and P.C. Weiser (Eds), *Psychological Aspects and Physiological Correlates of Work and Fatigue*. Springfield, Ill.: Thomas.

Schoonard, J.W., Gould, J.D. and Miller, L.A. (1973). Studies of visual inspection. *Ergonomics*, **16**, 365–379.

Schroeder. S.R. and Holland, J.G. (1968). Operant control of eye movement during human vigilance. *Science*, **161**, 292–293.

Schulman, A.I. and Greenberg, G.Z. (1970). Operating characteristics and a priori probability of the signal. *Perception and Psychophysics*, **8**, 317–320.

Schulman, A.I. and Mitchell, R.R. (1966). Operating characteristics from Yes–No and forced-choice procedures. *Journal of the Acoustical Society of America*, **40**, 473–477.

Searleman, A. (1977). A review of right hemisphere linguistic capabilities. *Psychological Bulletin*, **84**, 503–528.

Sharpless, S. and Jasper, H.H. (1956). Habituation of the arousal reaction. *Brain*, **79**, 655–680.

Sheehan, J.J. and Drury, C.C. (1971). The analysis of industrial inspection. *Applied Ergonomics*, **2**, 74–78.

Sheridan, T.B. and Ferrell, W.R. (1974). *Man-Machine Systems: Information, Control and Decision Models of Human Performance*. Cambridge, Mass.: MIT Press.

Shoenberger, R.W. (1967). Effects of vibration on complex psychomotor performance. *Aerospace Medicine*, **38**, 1264–1269.

Siddle, D.A.T. (1972). Vigilance decrement and speed of habituation of the G.S.R.

component of the orienting response. *British Journal of Psychology*, **63**, 191–194.

Siddle, D.A.T. and Smith, D.G. (1974). Effects of monotonous stimulation on cortical alertness in fast and slow habituation groups. *Journal of Research in Personality*, **8**, 324–334.

Silverman, I. (1963). Age and the tendency to withhold response. *Journal of Gerontology*, **17**, 362–365.

Simpson, A.J. (1967). *Signal Detection and Vigilance*. Unpublished Ph.D. thesis, University of Reading.

Simpson, A.J. and Fitter, M.J. (1973). What is the best measure of detectability? *Psychological Bulletin*, **80**, 481–488.

Sipos, I. (1970). Vigilance performance in verbal signals. *Studia Psychologica*, **12**, 29–33.

Sipowicz, R.R. and Baker, R.A. (1961). Effects of intelligence on vigilance: A replication. *Perceptual and Motor Skills*, **13**, 398.

Sipowicz, R.R., Ware, J. and Baker, R.A. (1962). The effects of reward and knowledge of results on the performance of a simple vigilance task. *Journal of Experimental Psychology*, **64**, 58–61.

Smith, H.C. (1947). Music in relation to employee attitudes, piece-work production and industrial accidents. *Applied Psychology Monographs*, No. 14. Stanford, California: Stanford University Press.

Smith, L.A. and Barany, J.W. (1970). An elementary model of human performance on paced visual inspection tasks. *AIEE Transactions*, **2**, 298–308.

Smith, P.T. (1968). Cost, discriminability and response bias. *British Journal of Mathematical and Statistical Psychology*, **21**, 35–60.

Smith, R.L. (1966). *Monotony and Motivation: A Theory of Vigilance*. Los Angeles, California: Dunlop and Associates, Inc.

Smith, R.L. and Lucaccini, L.F. (1969). Vigilance research: Its relevance to industrial problems. *Human Factors*, **11**, 149–156.

Smith, R.L. Lucaccini, L.F. and Epstein, M.H. (1967). The effects of monetary rewards and punishments on vigilance performance. *Journal of Applied Psychology*, **51**, 411–416.

Smith, S., Myers, T.I. and Murphy, D.B. (1967). Vigilance during sensory deprivation. *Perceptual and Motor Skills*, **24**, 971–976.

Solandt, D.Y. and Partridge, D.M. (1946). Research on auditory problems presented by naval operations. *Journal of the Canadian Medical Service*, **3**, 323–329.

Sostek, A.J. (1976). *Vigilance performance as a function of autonomic lability and differential payoffs*. Unpublished Ph.D. thesis, State University of New York at Buffalo.

Sostek, A.J. (1978). Effects of electrodermal lability and payoff instructions on vigilance performance. *Psychophysiology*, **15**, 561–568.

Squires, K.C., Squires, N.K. and Hillyard, S.A. (1975a). Vertex evoked potentials in a rating-scale detection task: Relation to signal probability. *Behavioural Biology*, **13**, 21–34.

Squires, K.C., Squires, N.K. and Hillyard, S.A. (1975b). Decision-related cortical evoked potentials during an auditory signal detection task with cued observation intervals. *Journal of Experimental Psychology: Human Perception and Performance*, **1**, 268–279.

Stern, R.M. (1966). Performance and physiological arousal during two vigilance tasks varying in signal presentation rate. *Perceptual and Motor Skills*, **23**, 691–700.

Stroh, C.M. (1971). *Vigilance: The Problem of Sustained Attention*. Oxford: Pergamon.

Suedfeld, P. (1969). Changes in intellectual performance and in susceptibility to influence. In J.P. Zubek (Ed.), *Sensory Deprivation: Fifteen Years of Research.* New York: Appleton-Century-Crofts.

Suedfeld, P. (1975). Benefits of boredom—sensory deprivation reconsidered. *American Scientist*, **63**, 60–69.

Surwillo, W.W. (1966). The relation of autonomic activity to age differences in vigilance. *Journal of Gerontology*, **21**, 257–260.

Surwillo, W.W. and Quilter, R.E. (1964). Vigilance, age and response time. *American Journal of Psychology*, **77**, 614–620.

Surwillo, W.W. and Quilter, R.E. (1965). The relationship of spontaneous skin potential responses to vigilance and to age. *Psychophysiology*, **1**, 272–276.

Sutton, S., Braren, M., Zubin, J. and John, E.R. (1965). Evoked potential correlates of stimulus uncertainty. *Science*, **150**, 1187–1188.

Sutton, S., Tueting, P., Zubin, J. and John, E.R. (1967). Information delivery and the sensory evoked potential. *Science*, **155**, 1436–1439.

Sverko, B. (1968). Intermodel correlations in vigilance performance. In *Proceedings of the 16th International Congress of Applied Psychology.* Amsterdam: Swets and Zeitlinger.

Swets, J.A. (1959). Indices of detectability obtained with various psychophysical procedures. *Journal of the Acoustical Society of America*, **31**, 511–513.

Swets, J.A. (1973). The relative operating characteristic in psychology. *Science*, **182**, 990–1000.

Swets, J.A. (1976). *Human Monitoring Behavior in a Command/Control/Communication System.* Cambridge, Mass.: Bolt Beranek and Newman Inc., Tech. Rep., (ARPA Contract No. MDA903–76C–0207).

Swets, J.A. (1977). Signal detection theory applied to vigilance. In R.R. Mackie (Ed.), *Vigilance: Theory, Operational Performance and Physiological Correlates.* New York: Plenum.

Swets, J.A. and Kristofferson, A.B. (1970). Attention. *Annual Review of Psychology*, **21**, 339–366.

Sykes, D.H., Douglas, V.I. and Morgenstern, G. (1973). Sustained attention in hyperactive children. *Journal of Child Psychology and Child Psychiatry*, **14**, 213–221.

Talland, G.A. (1966). Visual signal detection as a function of age, input rate and signal frequency. *Journal of Psychology*, **63**, 105–115.

Talland, G.A. and Quarton, G. (1966). The effects of drugs and familiarity on performance in continual search. *Journal of Nervous and Mental Diseases*, **143**, 266–274.

Tanner, T.A., Haller, R.W. and Atkinson, R.C. (1967). Signal recognition as influenced by presentation schedules. *Perception and Psychophysics*, **2**, 349–358.

Tanner, W.P. and Swets, J.A. (1954). A decision-making theory of visual detection. *Psychological Review*, **61**, 401–409.

Tarrière, C. (1964). Comparison of objective and subjective data pertaining to vigilance tests. *Le Travail Humain*, **27**, 1–36. (In French, English summary.)

Tarrière, C. and Wisner, A. (1962). Effects of administration of meaningful and meaningless noise during a vigilance task. *Le Travail Humain*, **25**, 1–28. (In French, English summary.)

Tarrière, C., Hartemann, F. and Niarfeix, M. (1966). Influence of cigarette smoking upon the course of performance in a watchkeeping task. *Le Travail Humain*, **29**, 1–21. (In French, English summary.)

Taub, J.M. and Berger, R.J. (1969). Extended sleep and performance: The Rip van

Winkle effect. *Psychonomic Science*, **16**, 204–205.

Taub, J.M. and Berger, R.J. (1973). Performance and mood following variations in the length and timing of sleep. *Psychophysiology*, **10**, 559–570.

Taub, J.M. and Berger, R.J. (1974). Acute shifts in the sleep-wakefulness cycle—Effects on performance and mood. *Psychosomatic Medicine*, **36**, 164–173.

Taub, J.M. and Berger, R.J. (1976). The effects of changing the phase and duration of sleep. *Journal of Experimental Psychology: Human Perception and Performance*, **2**, 30–41.

Taub, H.A. and Osborne, H. (1968). Effects of signal and stimulus rates on vigilance performance. *Journal of Applied Psychology*, **52**, 133–138.

Taylor, M.M. (1965). Detectability measures in vigilance: Comment on a paper by Wiener, Poock and Steele. *Perceptual and Motor Skills*, **20**, 1217–1221.

Taylor, M.M. (1967). Detectability theory and the interpretation of vigilance data. In A.F. Sanders (Ed.), *Attention and Performance, I*. Amsterdam: North Holland.

Teichner W.H. (1974). The detection of a simple visual signal as a function of time on watch. *Human Factors*, **16**, 339–353.

Thackray, R.I., Jones, K.N. and Touchstone, R.M. (1973). Self-estimates of distractibility as related to performance decrement on a monotonous task requiring sustained attention. *Ergonomics*, **16**, 141–152.

Thackray, R.I., Jones, K.N. and Touchstone, R.M. (1974). Personality and physiological correlates of performance decrement on a monotonous task requiring sustained attention. *British Journal of Psychology*, **65**, 351–358.

Thackray, R.I., Bailey, J.P. and Touchstone, R.M. (1977). Physiological, subjective, and performance correlates of reported boredom and monotony while performing a simulated radar control task. In R.R. Mackie (Ed.), *Vigilance: Theory, Operational Performance and Physiological Correlates*. New York: Plenum.

Theologus, G.C. and Fleishman, E.A. (1971). *Development of a taxonomy of human performance: Validation study for classifying human tasks*. American Institute for Research TR–10, Washington, D.C.

Thomas, E.A.C. (1973). On a class of additive learning models: error correcting and probability matching. *Journal of Mathematical Psychology*, **10**, 241–264.

Thomas, E.A.C. (1975). Criterion adjustment and probability matching. *Perception and Psychophysics*, **18**, 158–162.

Thomas, E.A.C. and Legge, D. (1970). Probability matching as a basis for detection and recognition decisions. *Psychological Review*, **77**, 65–72.

Thomas, E.A.C. and Myers, J.L. (1972). Implications of latency data for threshold and nonthreshold models of signal detection. *Journal of Mathematical Psychology*, **9**, 263–285.

Thomas, L.F. (1962). Perceptual organization in industrial inspectors. *Ergonomics*, **5**, 429–434.

Thompson, L.W. and Marsh, G.R. (1974). Psychophysiological studies of aging. In C. Eisdorfer and M.P. Lawton (Eds), *The Psychology of Adult Development and Aging*. Washington, D.C.: American Psychological Association.

Thompson, L.W., Opton, E.M. and Cohen, L.D. (1963). Effects of age, presentation speed, and sensory modality, on performance of a 'vigilance' task. *Journal of Gerontology*, **18**, 366–369.

Thompson, R.F. and Spencer, W.A. (1966). Habituation: A model phenomenon for the study of neuronal substrates of behaviour. *Psychological Review*, **73**, 16–43.

Thorndike, E.L. (1907). *The Elements of Psychology* (2nd edition). New York: Seiler.

Thornton, C.L., Barrett, G.V. and Davis, J.A. (1968). Field dependence and target identification. *Human Factors*, **10**, 493–496.

Thorsheim, H.I. (1967). EEG and vigilance behaviour. *Psychonomic Science*, **8,** 499–500.

Tickner, A.H. and Poulton, E.C. (1973). Monitoring up to 16 synthetic television pictures showing a great deal of movement. *Ergonomics*, **16,** 381–401.

Tickner, A.H., Poulton, E.C., Copeman, A.K. and Simmonds, D.C.V. (1972). Monitoring 16 television screens showing little movement. *Ergonomics*, **15,** 279–291.

Tiffin, J. and Rogers, H.B. (1941). The selection and training of inspectors. *Personnel*, **18,** 14–31.

Toh, K-Y. (1978). *Time of day, task type and vigilance performance.* Unpublished M.Sc. thesis, University of Aston in Birmingham.

Tolin, P. and Fisher, P.G. (1974). Sex differences and effects of irrelevant auditory stimulation on performance of a visual task. *Perceptual and Motor Skills*, **39,** 1255–1262.

Tong, J.E., Knott, V.J., McGraw, D.J. and Leigh, G. (1974). Smoking and human experimental psychology. *Bulletin of the British Psychological Society*, **27,** 533–538.

Tong, J.E., Leigh, G., Campbell, J. and Smith, D. (1974). Tobacco smoking, personality and sex factors in auditory vigilance performance. *British Journal of Psychology*, **68,** 365–370.

Travis, R.C. and Kennedy, J.L. (1947). Prediction and automatic control of alertness, I. Control of lookout alertness. *Journal of Comparative and Physiological Psychology*, **40,** 457–461.

Tueting, P. (1978). Event-related potentials, cognitive events and information processing. In D.A. Otto (Ed.), *Multi-disciplinary Perspectives in Event-related Brain Potential Research.* Washington, D.C.: U.S. Environmental Protection Agency.

Tune, G.S. (1964). Psychological effects of hypoxia: review of certain literature from the period 1950–1963. *Perceptual and Motor Skills*, **19,** 551–562.

Tune, G.S. (1966a). Errors of commission as a function of age and temperament in a type of vigilance task. *Quarterly Journal of Experimental Psychology*, **18,** 358–361.

Tune, G.S. (1966b). Age differences in errors of commission. *British Journal of Psychology*, **57,** 391–392.

Tune, G.S. (1968). The human sleep debt. *Science Journal*, **4** (12), 67–71.

Tune, G.S. (1969). The influence of age and temperament on the adult human sleep-wakefulness pattern. *British Journal of Psychology*, **60,** 431–442.

Tye, L.S. (1979). *Looking but not seeing: The federal nuclear power plant inspection program.* Cambridge, Mass.: Union of Concerned Scientists.

Tyler, D.M. and Halcomb, C.G. (1974). Monitoring performance with a time shared encoding task. *Perceptual and Motor Skills*, **38,** 383–386.

Tyler, D.M., Waag, W. and Halcomb, C.G. (1972). Monitoring performance across sense modes: An individual differences approach. *Human Factors*, **14,** 539–549.

Uhrbrock, R.S. (1961). Music on the job: Its influence on worker morale and production. *Personnel Psychology*, **14,** 9–38.

Veniar, S. (1953). The effect of continuous operation on the AEW function of air control officers in the airborne CIC. *Special Devices Center, SDC Tech. Rep.*, No. 279–3–12.

Verschoor, A.M. and van Wieringen, P.C. (1970). Vigilance performance and skin conductance. *Acta Psychologica*, **33,** 394–401.

Vickers, D., Leary, J. and Barnes, P. (1977). Adaptation to decreasing signal probability. In R.R. Mackie (Ed.), *Vigilance: Theory, Operational Performance and Physiological Correlates.* New York: Plenum.

Waag, W.L., Halcomb, C.G. and Tyler, D.M. (1973). Sex differences in monitoring performance. *Journal of Applied Psychology*, **58**, 272–274.

Waag, W.L., Tyler, D.M. and Halcomb, C.G. (1973). Experimenter effects in monitoring performance. *Bulletin of the Psychonomic Society*, **1**, 387–388.

Wallach, M.A. and Kogan, N. (1961). Aspects of judgment and decision making: Interrelationships and changes with age. *Behavioral Science*, **6**, 23–36.

Wallis, D. and Samuel, J.A. (1961). Some experimental studies of radar operating. *Ergonomics*, **4**, 155–168.

Walter, W.G., Cooper, R., Aldridge, V.J., McCallum, W.C. and Winter, A.L. (1964). Contingent negative variation: An electrical sign of sensorimotor association and expectancy in the human brain. *Nature*, **203**, 380–384.

Ware, J.R. (1961). Effects of intelligence on signal detection in visual and auditory monitoring. *Perceptual and Motor Skills*, **13**, 99–102.

Ware, J.R. and Baker, R.A. (1964). Effects of method of presentation, modes and response category knowledge of results on detection performance in a vigilance task. *Journal of Engineering Psychology*, **3**, 111–116.

Ware, J.R., Sipowicz, R.R. and Baker, R.A. (1961). Auditory vigilance in repeated sessions. *Perceptual and Motor Skills*, **13**, 127–129.

Ware, J.R., Baker, R.A. and Sipowicz, R.R. (1962). Performance of mental deficients on a simple vigilance task. *American Journal of Mental Deficiency*, **66**, 647–650.

Ware, J.R., Kowal, B. and Baker, R.A. (1964). The role of experimenter attitude and contingent reinforcement in a display. *Human Factors*, **6**, 111–115.

Warm, J.S. (1977). Psychological processes in sustained attention. In R.R. Mackie (Ed.), *Vigilance: Theory, Operational Performance and Physiological Correlates*. New York: Plenum.

Warm, J.S., Foulke, E. and Loeb, M. (1966). The influence of stimulus modality and duration on changes in temporal judgments over trials. *American Journal of Psychology*, **79**, 628–631.

Warm, J.S., Loeb, M., and Alluisi, E.A. (1970). Variations in watchkeeping performance as a function of the rate and duration of visual signals. *Perception and Psychophysics*, **7**, 97–99.

Warm, J.S., Kanfer, F.H., Kuwada, S. and Clark, J.L. (1972). Motivation in vigilance: Effects of self-evaluation and experimenter controlled feedback. *Journal of Experimental Psychology*, **92**, 123–127.

Warm, J.S., Reichmann, W., Grasha, A.F. and Siebel, B. (1973). Motivation in vigilance: A test of the goal-setting hypothesis of the effectiveness of knowledge of results. *Bulletin of the Psychonomic Society*, **1**, 291–292.

Warm, J.S., Epps, B.D. and Ferguson, R.P. (1974). Effects of knowledge of results and signal regularity on vigilance performance. *Bulletin of the Psychonomic Society*, **4**, 272–274.

Warm, J.S., Fishbein, H.D., Howe, S. and Kendell, L. (1976a). Effects of event rate and cognitive-complexity of critical signals on sustained attention. *Bulletin of the Psychonomic Society*, **8**, 257.

Warm, J.S., Schumsky, D.A. and Hawley, D.K. (1976b). Ear asymmetry and the temporal uncertainty of signals in sustained attention. *Bulletin of the Psychonomic Society*, **7**, 413–416.

Warm, J.S., Wait, R.G. and Loeb, M. (1976c). Head restraint enhances visual monitoring performance. *Perception and Psychophysics*, **20**, 299–304.

Watson, C.S. and Nichols, T.L. (1976). Detectability of auditory signals presented without defined observation intervals. *Journal of the Acoustical Society of America*, **59**, 655–667.

Webb, W.B. and Agnew, H.W. (1974). The effects of a chronic limitation of sleep length. *Psychophysiology*, **11**, 265–274.

Weerts, T.C. and Lang, P.J. (1973). The effects of eye fixation and stimulus and response location on the contingent negative variation. *Biological Psychology*, **1**, 1–19.

Weidenfeller, E.W., Baker, R.A. and Ware, J.R. (1962). Effect of knowledge of results (true and false) on vigilance performance. *Perceptual and Motor Skills*, **14**, 211–215.

Weiss, B. and Laties, V.G. (1962). Enhancement of human performance by caffeine and the amphetamines. *Pharmacological Reviews*, **14**, 1–36.

Weitzel, C. and Dobson, R. (1974). Sensitivity to visual Gaussian noise patterns as determined by binary and rating procedures. *Perceptual and Motor Skills*, **38**, 147–154.

Welford, A.T. (1962). Arousal, channel capacity and decision. *Nature*, **194**, 365–366.

Welford, A.T. (1978). Mental work-load as a function of demand, capacity, strategy and skill. *Ergonomics*, **21**, 151–168.

Wertheimer, M. (1955). The variability of auditory and visual absolute thresholds in time. *Journal of General Psychology*, **52**, 111–147.

Weston, H.C. and Adams, S. (1935). The performance of weavers under varying conditions of noise. *Industrial Health Research Board Rep.*, No. 70. London: H.M.S.O.

Whittenburg, J.A., Ross, S. and Andrews, T.G. (1956). Sustained perceptual efficiency as measured by the Mackworth "Clock" test. *Perceptual and Motor Skills*, **6**, 109–116.

Wickens, C.D. and Kessel, C. (1979). The effects of participatory mode and task workload on the detection of dynamic system failures. *IEEE Transactions on Systems, Man, and Cybernetics*, SMC–9, 24–34.

Wiener, E.L. (1963a). Knowledge of results and signal rate in monitoring: a transfer of training approach. *Journal of Applied Psychology*, **47**, 214–222.

Wiener, E.L. (1963b). Note on the probability of detection of a signal by multiple monitors. *Psychological Record*, **13**, 79–81.

Wiener, E.L. (1964). Multiple channel monitoring. *Ergonomics*, **7**, 453–460.

Wiener, E.L. (1967). Transfer of training from one monitoring task to another. *Ergonomics*, **10**, 649–658.

Wiener, E.L. (1968). Training for vigilance: Repeated sessions with knowledge of results. *Ergonomics*, **11**, 547–556.

Wiener, E.L. (1969). Money and the monitor. *Perceptual and Motor Skills*, **29**, 627–634.

Wiener, E.L. (1973). Adaptive measurement of vigilance decrement. *Ergonomics*, **16**, 353–363.

Wiener, E.L. (1974). An adaptive vigilance task with knowledge of results. *Human Factors*, **16**, 333–338.

Wiener, E.L. (1975). Individual and group differences in inspection. In C.G. Drury and J.G. Fox (Eds), *Human Reliability in Quality Control*. London: Taylor and Francis.

Wierwille, W.W. and Williges, R.C. (1978). *Survey and Analysis of Operator Workload Assessment Techniques*. Blacksburg, Va.: Systemetrics, Tech. Rep., No. S–78–101.

Wilkinson, R.T. (1958). The effects of sleep loss on performance. *Medical Research Council Applied Psychology Unit Research Rep.*, No. 323/58.

Wilkinson, R.T. (1960). The effect of lack of sleep on visual watchkeeping. *Quarterly Journal of Experimental Psychology*, **12**, 36–40.

Wilkinson, R.T. (1961a). Comparison of paced, unpaced, irregular and continuous displays in watchkeeping. *Ergonomics*, **4**, 259–267.

Wilkinson, R.T. (1961b). Interaction of lack of sleep with knowledge of results, repeated testing and individual differences. *Journal of Experimental Psychology*, **62**, 263–271.

Wilkinson, R.T. (1963a). Interaction of noise with knowledge of results and sleep deprivation. *Journal of Experimental Psychology*, **66**, 332–337.

Wilkinson, R.T. (1963b). After-effect of sleep deprivation. *Journal of Experimental Psychology*, **66**, 439–442.

Wilkinson, R.T. (1964a). Artificial "signals" as an aid to an inspection task. *Ergonomics*, **7**, 63–72.

Wilkinson, R.T. (1964b). Effects of up to 60 hours sleep deprivation on different types of work. *Ergonomics*, **7**, 175–186.

Wilkinson, R.T. (1965). Sleep deprivation. In O.G. Edholm and A.L. Bacharach (Eds), *The Physiology of Human Survival*. London and New York: Academic Press.

Wilkinson, R.T. (1968). Sleep deprivation: Performance tests for partial and selective sleep deprivation. In L. Abt and B.F. Reiss (Eds), *Progress in Clinical Psychology, Vol. 7*. New York: Grune and Stratton.

Wilkinson, R.T. (1969). Some factors influencing the effect of environmental stresses upon performance. *Psychological Bulletin*, **72**, 260–272.

Wilkinson, R.T. (1972). Sleep deprivation: Eight questions. In W.P. Colquhoun (Ed.), *Aspects of Human Efficiency: Diurnal Rhythm and Loss of Sleep*. London: English Universities Press.

Wilkinson, R.T. (1976). Relationship between CNV, its resolution and the evoked response. In W.C. McCallum and J.R. Knott (Eds), *The Responsive Brain*. Bristol: John Wright.

Wilkinson, R.T. and Colquhoun, W.P. (1968). Interaction of alcohol with incentive and with sleep deprivation. *Journal of Experimental Psychology*, **76**, 623–629.

Wilkinson, R.T. and Gray, R. (1974). Effects of duration of vertical vibration beyond the proposed ISO "fatigue decreased proficiency" time on the performance of various tasks. *Paper Presented at the AGARD Conference on Vibration and Combined Stresses in Advanced Systems, Oslo*.

Wilkinson, R.T. and Haines, E. (1970). Evoked response correlates of expectancy during vigilance. *Acta Psychologica*, **33**, 402–413.

Wilkinson, R.T. and Seales, D.M. (1978). EEG event-related potentials and signal detection. *Biological Psychology*, **7**, 13–28.

Wilkinson, R.T., Fox, R.H., Goldsmith, R., Hampton, I.F.G. and Lewis, H.E. (1964). Psychological and physiological responses to raised body temperature. *Journal of Applied Physiology*, **19**, 287–291.

Wilkinson, R.T., Edwards, R.S. and Haines, E. (1966). Performance following a night of reduced sleep. *Psychonomic Science*, **4**, 471–472.

Wilkinson, R.T., Morlock, H.C. and Williams, H.L. (1966). Evoked cortical response during vigilance. *Psychonomic Science*, **4**, 221–222.

Williams, M. (1970). *Brain Damage and the Mind*. Harmondsworth: Penguin.

Williams, H.L., Lubin, A. and Goodnow, J.J. (1959). Impaired performance with acute sleep loss. *Psychological Monographs*, **73**, No. 14, Whole No. 484.

Williams, H.L., Granda, A.L., Jones, R.C., Lubin, A. and Armington, J.C. (1962). EEG frequency and finger pulse volume as predictors of reaction time during sleep loss. *Electroencephalography and Clinical Neurophysiology*, **14**, 64–70.

Williams, H.L., Tepas, D.I. and Morlock, H.C. (1962). Evoked responses to clicks and electroencephalographic stages of sleep in man. *Science*, **183**, 685–686.

Williams, H.L., Kearney, O.F. and Lubin, A. (1965). Signal uncertainty and sleep loss. *Journal of Experimental Psychology*, **69**, 401–407.

Williges, R.C. (1969). Within session criterion changes compared to an ideal observer criterion in a visual monitoring task. *Journal of Experimental Psychology*, **81**, 61–66.

Williges, R.C. (1971). The role of payoffs and signal ratios on criterion changes during a monitoring task. *Human Factors*, **13**, 261–267.

Williges, R.C. (1973). Manipulating the response criterion in visual monitoring. *Human Factors*, **15**, 179–185.

Williges, R.C. (1976). The vigilance increment: An ideal observer hypothesis. *Paper Presented at the NATO Symposium on Monitoring Behaviour and Supervisory Control, Berchtesgaden, West Germany.*

Williges, R.C. and North, R.A. (1972). Knowledge of results and decision making performance in visual monitoring. *Organizational Behavior and Human Performance*, **8**, 44–57.

Williges, R.C. and Streeter, H. (1971). Display characteristics in inspection tasks. *Journal of Applied Psychology*, **55**, 123–125.

Winneke, G., Fodor, G. and Schlipkoter, H. (1978). Carbon monoxide, trichloroethylene and alcohol: Reliability and validity of neurobehavioral effects. In D.A. Otto (Ed.), *Multidisciplinary Perspectives in Event-related Brain Potential Research.* Washington, D.C.: U.S. Environmental Protection Agency.

Witkin, H.A., Dyk, R.B., Faterson, H.F., Goodenough, D.R. and Karp, S.A. (1962). *Psychological Differentiation: Studies of Development.* New York: Wiley.

Wittenborn, J.R. (1943). Factorial equations for tests of attention. *Psychometrika*, **8**, 19–35.

Wohlwill, J.F., Nasar, J.L., Dejoy, D.M. and Foruzani, H.H. (1976). Behavioral effects of a noisy environment: Task involvement versus passive exposure. *Journal of Applied Psychology*, **61**, 67–74.

Wokoun, W. (1963). Vigilance with background music. *Human Engineering Laboratory Rep.*, No. TH–16–63. Aberdeen Proving Ground, Maryland.

Wokoun, W. (1968). Effect of music on work performance. *Human Engineering Laboratory Rep.*, No. TM–1–68. Aberdeen Proving Ground, Maryland.

Wokoun, W. (1969). Music for working. *Science Journal*, **5A** (5), 54–59.

Woodhead, M.M. (1964). Searching a visual display in intermittent noise. *Journal of Sound and Vibration*, **1**, 157–161.

Woodhead, M.M. (1966). An effect of noise on the distribution of attention. *Journal of Applied Psychology*, **50**, 296–299.

Wyatt, S. (1950). Autobiography. *Occupational Psychology*, **24**, 65–74.

Wyatt, S. and Fraser, J.A. (1929). The effect of monotony in work. *Industrial Fatigue Research Board Rep.*, No. 56. London: H.M.S.O.

Wyatt, S. and Langdon, J.N. (1932). Inspection processes in industry. *Industrial Health Research Board Rep.*, No. 63. London: H.M.S.O.

Wyatt, S. and Langdon, J.N. (1937). Fatigue and boredom in repetitive work. *Industrial Health Research Board Rep.*, No. 77. London: H.M.S.O.

York, C.M. (1962). Behavioral efficiency in a monitoring task as a function of signal rate and observer age. *Perceptual and Motor Skills*, **15**, 404.

Yoss, R.E., Moyer, N.J. and Hollenhorst, R.W. (1970). Pupil size and spontaneous pupillary waves associated with alertness, drowsiness and sleep. *Neurology*, **201**, 545–554.

Zubek, J.P. and MacNeill, M. (1966). Effects of immobilisation: behavioural and

EEG changes. *Canadian Journal of Psychology*, **20**, 316–336.

Zubek, J.P., Pushkar, D., Sansom, W. and Gowing, J. (1961). Perceptual changes after prolonged sensory isolation (darkness and silence). *Canadian Journal of Psychology*, **15**, 83–100.

Zuckerman, M., Kolin, E.A., Price, L. and Zoob, I. (1964). Development of a sensation-seeking scale. *Journal of Consulting Psychology*, **28**, 477–482.

Zuercher, J.D. (1965). The effects of extraneous stimulation on vigilance. *Human Factors*, **7**, 101–105.

Zunzanyika, X.K. and Drury, C.G. (1975). Effects of information on industrial inspection performance. In C.G. Drury and J.G. Fox (Eds), *Human Reliability in Quality Control*. London: Taylor and Francis.

Zwislocki, J., Maire, F., Feldman, A.S. and Rubin, H. (1958). On the effect of practice and motivation on the threshold of audibility. *Journal of the Acoustical Society of America*, **30**, 254–262.

Author Index

Subject Index